MEL BAY PRESENTS

JAZZ
and the Classical Guitar
THEORY AND APPLICATION

by Ken Hatfield

CD CONTENTS

1 2 3 4 5 6 7 8 9 0

Visit us on the Web at www.melbay.com — E-mail us at email@melbay.com

Table of Contents

Part I

Part II

Preface

In the December 2001 installment of Nat Hentoff's monthly *JazzTimes* column "Final Chorus," he states, "In jazz, whether singing or playing, the basics are: swing (implicit or as pulsing as a heartbeat); feeling (which can't be taught as such because it comes out of your life and how deeply you understand who you are as you keep changing); and your own unmistakable sound, which comes out of the preceding elements."

That is as good a place to start as I've found. The path each artist takes is ultimately one of self-exploration. The results are manifested in an artist's works. For the jazz artist, this requires the ability to dig deep and spontaneously express what is found. Acquiring the skills necessary to perform at this level of artistry demands years of hard work. Most jazz musicians begin by studying and emulating the work of the masters who have preceded them. This presents a unique challenge to the classical guitarist interested in playing jazz, because few of the major figures in jazz history have been guitarists, and fewer still have favored the nylon string guitar over the steel string. I believe this was primarily due to the volume constraints that are part of our instrument's natural charm. In the very early days of jazz, when the chordal instrument of choice was not the piano but often either tenor banjo or steel string guitar, the classical guitar would certainly have been used had it been a louder instrument.

In any event, prior to amplification, the primary role of all guitarists in jazz was that of rhythm guitarist, not soloist, because without amplification a guitar solo is unlikely to be heard over a drummer playing with sticks and brass instruments playing without mutes. Though some may view the rhythm guitarist's gig as unglamorous, its importance should not be underestimated. Those guitarists who fail to develop the skills required to play rhythm guitar do so to their own detriment. The great Freddie Green, whose entire career was focused on rhythm guitar, was said to be the glue that held the rhythm section together in what was often called the "swingingest band in the land" (Count Basie's Band). Rhythm guitarists such as Freddie Green, Carl Kress, and Alan Reuss added much to the swing feel of the rhythm sections in jazz. But it was the soloists that shaped the linear vocabulary of jazz. And the soloists were predominantly horn players.

It is very important for the serious jazz student to check out other instrumentalists' phrasing approaches. As I've developed my approach (from its rudimentary stages through its ongoing evolution), I have studied and continue to check out the work of many great jazz artists who didn't play my chosen instrument, such as pianists Wynton Kelly, Bobby Timmons, Bill Evans, and Herbie Hancock, saxophone players Lester Young, Coleman Hawkins, Charlie Parker, and John Coltrane, and trumpet players Louis Armstrong, Dizzy Gillespie, Clifford Brown, and Miles Davis.

This study of other instrumentalists is particularly important for understanding the "swing feel" of the rhythms of jazz and the intricacies of the phrasing of its lines. Phrasing techniques which are idiomatic to wind instruments, especially saxophones and trumpets, are so prevalent throughout the linear vocabulary of jazz that the metaphor for playing that jazz musicians often employ is "blowing" (not exactly the first verb that comes to mind when one thinks of the mechanics of playing the guitar). And many of these phrasing techniques cannot always be clearly represented by traditional methods of notation. So hearing how horn players phrase the music is a crucial component in the process of understanding how it is supposed to sound when you play it. This is essential for instruments like the guitar, piano, or vibes, which can't sustain a pitch for long or easily reshape it after a note has been sounded, like wind instruments can. Non-wind instruments have to find ways of duplicating (where possible) and mimicking or approximating (where necessary) the phrasing techniques of horn players in order to master the intricacies of jazz phrasing.

Despite the obstacles, some guitarists have found ways to develop unquestionably individual voices and contribute brilliantly imaginative music to the jazz canon. Notable examples are Charlie Christian, Wes Montgomery, Joe

Pass, and, in the all acoustic (drummer-less) format with the Quintet of the Hot Club of France, Django Reinhardt. There have even been a handful of guitarists whose love of the nylon string guitar encouraged them to champion its use in jazz despite its additional obstacles. The late Charlie Byrd, along with Bill Harris and Eddie Duran, were early prime jazz exponents of our beloved instrument, even before it could be amplified. And great contemporary artists like Gene Bertoncini and Ralph Towner are demonstrating what a versatile and expressive jazz instrument the classical guitar is in the right hands.

Jazz is a music where innovations that resonate with the truth will be accepted regardless of instrument. But merely being different is insufficient grounds for acceptance into the jazz community. The classical guitar has much to offer that is unique. But any aspiring classical guitarists who wish to play jazz must master both the instrument and the intricacies of the jazz vocabulary before they can make the kind of contributions that will influence not only other classical guitarists, but other instrumentalists as well. And only when this begins to occur will the classical guitar be championed by major figures in whatever becomes the future of jazz.

With the advent of better microphones and piezo pickups, which sense the vibration of the strings directly (so they work with nylon strings), along with amplifiers designed for classical guitars, and great luthiers such as John Buscarino, Thomas Humphrey, and Greg Smallman expanding the classical guitar's possibilities by building instruments that are more responsive and accommodate the way jazz players want to play a guitar, we could be at the dawn of a new era when those who love both jazz and the classical guitar will be encouraged to expand upon what pioneers like Charlie Byrd, Baden Powell, and Laurindo Almeida had the courage, vision, and talent to begin half a century ago.

I hope this book can make a contribution by encouraging classical players to become more familiar with the musical vocabulary of jazz and by encouraging jazz guitarists to explore the beautiful sonorities and limitless expressive potential of the classical guitar.

Introduction

Jazz is a music that is in a constant state of evolution. It is a music capable of accommodating a great deal of individual expression and innovation. Historically, most of the innovation has come from the players rather than the composers, because it is predominantly a player's art form. Unlike classical music, which is largely composed in advance of performance, jazz is spontaneously created by the players themselves through a process of improvisation. There is a great deal of harmonic and melodic sophistication in both jazz and classical music. In addition, jazz demands that the player be able to deal with a high level of rhythmic sophistication. Both musics require great virtuosity, and the best musicians of each tradition spend lifetimes developing and fine-tuning their artistry.

Improvisation is essentially spontaneous composition. For most of jazz's history this improvisation has occurred within very specific contexts that are exemplified by the songs and song forms upon which the musicians improvise. From a classical perspective these song forms are analogous to the strophic form of some of Schubert's Lieder, where the form and harmonic content repeat chorus after chorus while the lyrics change stanza after stanza as the story unfolds.

Thematic development is a highly desirable aesthetic ideal in both classical and jazz music, but in jazz, thematic development during improvisation doesn't generate the harmonic accompaniment, because jazz musicians traditionally are improvising on the form and harmonic content of the songs that they perform. Jazz musicians call this blowing (improvising) on the changes (harmonic structure accompanying the melody). Great jazz artists such as Sonny Rollins, Jim Hall, and Paul Desmond employ abundant thematic development in their improvisations, but they shape their ideas to conform to the chord changes of the songs they are blowing on. Unlike the development sections of much of Beethoven's music, where the thematic material gives rise to the entire work, including the harmonic content, jazz musicians use the harmonic content and form of the songs they play to generate their improvisations. This kind of improvising is not totally without restrictions or guidelines; it is not freeform. For example, if the song you are improvising upon has an A A B A form, you cannot indiscriminately go to the bridge (B) whenever you choose. You must follow the song form.[1]

Now there are other approaches in jazz, exemplified by the music of Ornette Coleman or Cecil Taylor, but dealing with their music at this stage is like dealing with the Second Viennese School (Schoenberg, Berg, and Webern) when you've yet to address Haydn or Mozart. In any event, the so-called *avant garde* is not the focus of this book. This book's scope will be limited to jazz which has a tonal orientation and is rooted in the traditions embodied in the music of artists such as Duke Ellington, Charlie Parker, Bill Evans, Wes Montgomery, and Thelonious Monk. This music swings hard and gets to the point while being harmonically, melodically, and rhythmically adventurous. It is not in the tradition of so-called free jazz.

Having said that, it is important to state that one of the primary goals of this book is to demonstrate that all twelve notes of the chromatic scale do indeed work on any chord in any situation at any time. **All notes are available to those who can hear how to use them!** Acquiring command of all twelve notes of the chromatic scale in any situation gives the player incredible freedom, the freedom to express yourself within the context of the song you are playing, limited only by your own imagination.

---

[1] There are of course times when a solo may end after a chorus of the A A B A form is completed and then return to the melody at letter B, for the out head, thereby altering the song form momentarily, but this is an exception done for the purpose of contrast, or to be concise.

Most of the first section of this book is designed to guide the student toward complete command of all notes in any situation. The second section of the book is designed to demonstrate the artful use of this approach within the context of compositions representing three musical genres that have served as wellsprings of renewal throughout jazz's deep and illustrious history: blues, rhythm changes, and standards.

* * * * *

In order to deal with the myriad of chord changes a jazz musician routinely encounters, it is important to be able to hear your way through the chord changes of any song on which you wish to improvise. There are many ways to go about this, but ultimately you have to *recognize* (the changes), *react* (to them), and *execute* (your musical response to those changes) virtually instantaneously in order to function as an improvising musician on a jazz bandstand. The first step is to recognize the chord changes. This is really an aural process, but to address it we have to use theoretical explanations of the harmonic function of chords within various contexts. Please remember that theory always follows practice; theory does not generate practice. Whether it is Johann Fux's *Gradus ad Parnassum* using Palestrina as the model for the teacher who explains species counterpoint, Arnold Schoenberg's *Theory of Harmony*, or John Mehegan's books on harmonic analysis of jazz chord progressions, the music created by musicians predates and motivates the theoretical attempts to explain it. Theoretical explanations are only a tool intended to guide the student in acquiring his or her own understanding of various aspects of the creative process.

I am not a theoretician. I am a composer-musician, and my explanations come from years of experience, study, and practice. My explanations are not the only way to interpret these musical phenomena, but they are the ones that I've found to work best as theoretical representations of what is actually experientially acquired knowledge. Imagine trying to describe the color lavender or Vermeer's *View of Delft* when you know that words pale before the experience of seeing. Well, that's what theoretical explanations of music are like. They invariably fall short of the experience of listening. So use my theoretical explanations only as the guide they are intended to be, and listen (especially when in doubt) to the music—both mine and that of the great artists who are frequently mentioned throughout this book.

Chapter 1:
Major Tonalities and Their Scales and Chords

All music is comprised (to varying degrees) of three elements: rhythm, melody, and harmony. Music that has a tonal orientation, such as most of the repertoire of jazz, manifests this orientation through melody and harmony. This does not in any way minimize the importance of rhythm. But rhythm alone cannot establish a tonality or key, while a melody or a couple of chords can. So in studying the harmonic content of jazz, which is the most prominent manifestation of the relationships within its tonal orientation, we have to deal with chords and scales. There is much debate in jazz about which gives rise to which: do chords come from scales, or vice versa? We know historically that the individual pitch (note) gave rise to the scale through its overtone series. When the overtones of an individual pitch are arranged in linear fashion, the result is an arrangement of notes that is called a scale (example 1).[2]

Example 1

Pythagorean System

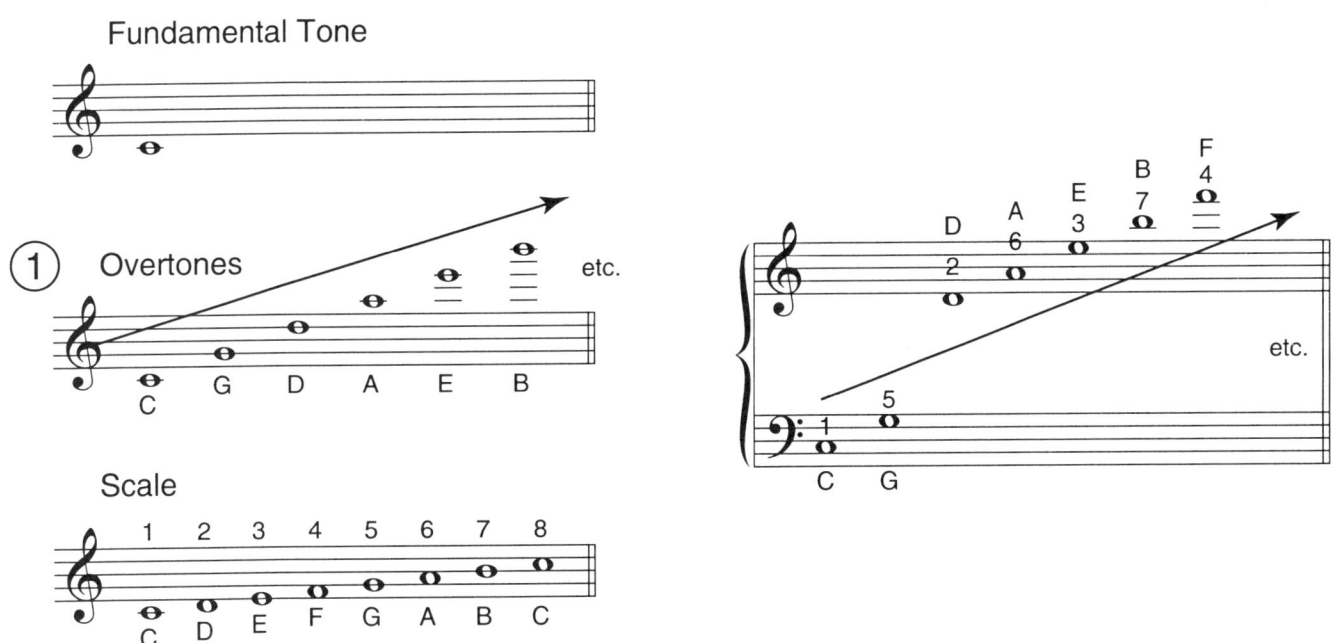

---

[2] Example 1, model 1, represents the Pythagorean system, which derives the scale tones by building a structure in ascending 5ths above the fundamental tone. Example 1, model 2, actually shows the fundamental tone and the first 15 overtones of the note "C♮."

In theory, if extended far enough, all of the pitches of the chromatic scale can be found in the overtones of any pitch. But the distances between these notes are irregular, and very few of us would recognize the intervals created when using the remotest overtones. For example, the 4th overtone of C♮ (5th note of example 1, model 2) is E♮ (the 3rd note of a C Major scale). A note with the same name an octave higher would also be the 14th overtone of F♮ (based on a transposition of example 1, model 2, up a 4th, that used F♮ as the fundamental tone. Numbering F♮ as one, we would find E♮ the 14th overtone represented as the 15th note). This E♮ would be the 7th note of an F Major scale. However, these two E♮s (i.e., the 4th overtone of C♮, and the 14th overtone of F♮) would be out of tune with each other, despite their identical alphabetical names. These problems (and many others) were rectified by the tempered tuning system developed by Andreas Werkmeister in the late 1600s. This system was favored by Dieterich Buxtehude and championed by J.S. Bach, whose preludes and fugues in *The Well-Tempered Clavier*, volumes I and II, demonstrate the workability and rich potential of this equal tempered tuning system. This system is the basis for the current method of tuning our instruments. While it may seem remote, its development is much closer to us than the mathematical system of ratios devised by Pythagoras in the 6th century B.C., which is still the model for the layout of the fingerboards of all stringed instruments, including our guitars.

(2) Fundamental tone & first 15 overtones:

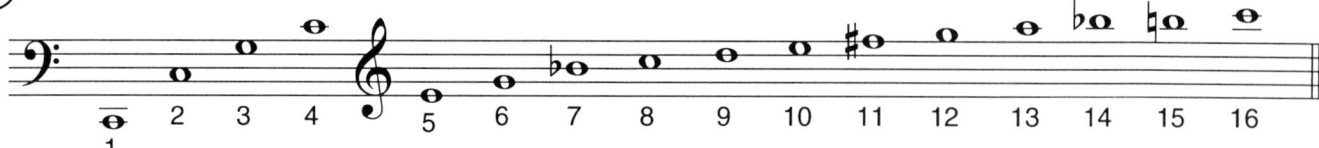

Corresponding scale degrees:

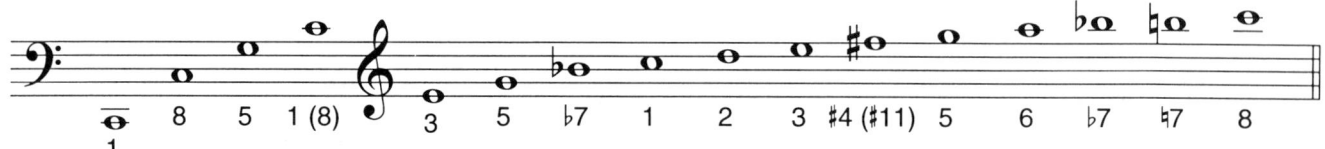

Linear arrangement: = C Major scale

When we build structures in ascending thirds upon the notes of this scale and use only notes contained within that scale, the results are the diatonic triads and chords of western harmony.[3] And western harmony is the basis of the harmonic structures of jazz, much as West African rhythmic concepts are the basis for the rhythmic structures of jazz. Debating which came first or which should be prominently emphasized—the chord or the scale—is like debating which came first—the chicken or the egg. In jazz, as indeed in most music, we must deal with both chords and scales, just as we must deal with rhythm, melody, and harmony!

Since jazz inherited a vocabulary of scales and chords from Western European musical traditions, and those traditions use a (fundamental) tone as the originator of the scale, which in turn yields chords, we shall adhere to this schematic and base our method of presentation upon it.

There are two prime tonalities in western harmony: the Major and the minor. There are many subspecies and a great deal of shared material between these two types of tonalities, but these two are the progenitors of our present harmonic system.

Determining harmonic function (something all jazz musicians do whether consciously or otherwise) requires context. There are no easy rules that explain any note's or any chord's use in all situations, just as there are no simple hard and fast rules for the use of the letter "u" or the sound it represents everywhere it occurs in the English language. Since any chord may (and in fact does) occur in several keys and many pieces of music, we can only understand a chord's harmonic function within the context in which it occurs. Major and minor are the most basic contexts for defining tonality and have been around since the dawn of our music. So they will be our prime categories for organizing the harmonic phenomena we will analyze. We will start by examining Major and then proceed to minor.

---

[3] By western harmony I mean the harmonic traditions and conventions that evolved in Western Europe (from Italy west to England).

Because the fundamental tone gave birth to the scale through its overtones, we will examine the scale first (in this case the C Major scale; example 2).

Example 2 – C Major Scale

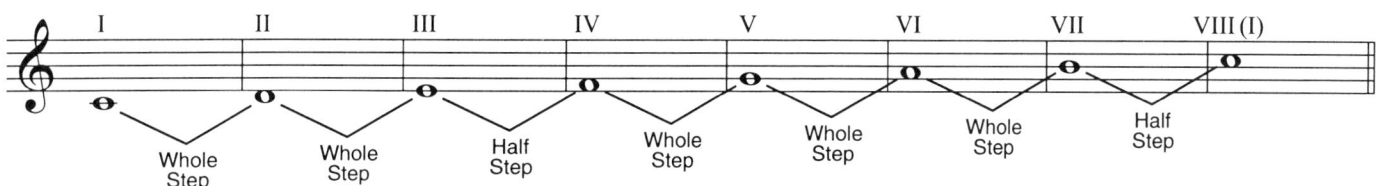

The intervallic structure of all Major scales is identical regardless of key, as follows: whole step, whole step, half step, whole step, whole step, whole step, half step.

Definitions of Symbols

The following symbols occur throughout this book and are used to identify qualities such as Major and minor. They are applied to chords, scales, intervals, and tonalities.

Δ = Major

– = minor

O = diminished

P = Perfect (as in perfect fifth)

+ = Augmented

Now let's add a note to each note of our Major scale. These added notes will be placed above the notes of our scale. The distance above will be the interval of a third. But not just any third—we must use only the notes of the scale we started with. In other words, these thirds will be diatonically constructed. And each will have a different quality, which is determined by the distance between the two notes of each 3rd. Some will be Major, and others will be minor (example 3).

Example 3 – C Major Scale: Diatonic Thirds

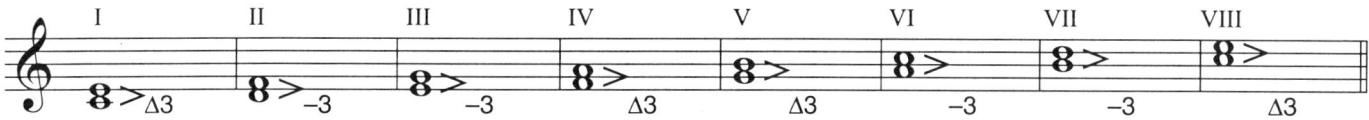

When we add another 3rd diatonically above each of the 3[rd]s we just constructed, we get diatonic triads (example 4). This added note is called the 5th because it is a 5th above the root, as well as a 3rd above the 3rd. These triads are the basis for our chords, and their relationships are the basis for our harmony.

Just like the diatonic 3rds we previously constructed, these triads will have differing qualities, or character, depending upon their differing intervallic structures. I, IV and V are Δ (Major), while II, III, and VI are – (minor), and VII is O (diminished).

Example 4 – C Major Scale: Diatonic Triads

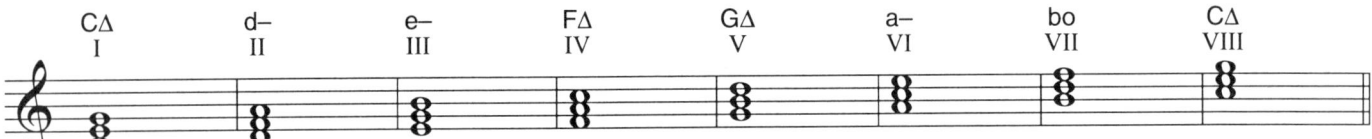

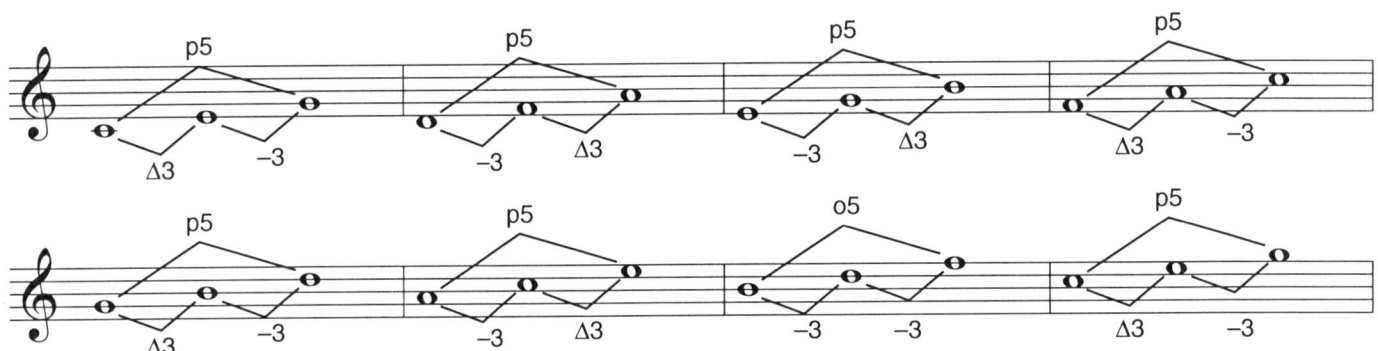

Δ   The intervallic structure of all Major triads is identical regardless of key as follows: a root, plus a note which is a Major 3rd above that root (referred to as the 3rd), plus a note a minor 3rd above the 3rd (of the triad) which is also a Perfect 5th above the root (and is referred to as the 5th).

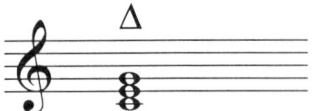

–   The intervallic structure of all minor triads is identical regardless of key as follows: a root, plus a note a minor 3rd above that root (referred to as the 3rd), plus a note a Major 3rd above the 3rd (of the triad) which is also a Perfect 5th above the root (and is referred to as the 5th).

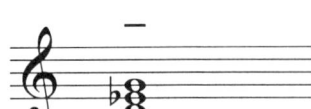

O   The intervallic structure of all diminished triads is identical regardless of key as follows: a root, plus a note a minor 3rd above the root, plus a note a minor 3rd above the 3rd (of the triad) which is also a diminished 5th above the root (and is referred to as the diminished 5th or the flat 5th).

+   The intervallic structure of all augmented triads is identical regardless of key as follows: a root plus a note a Major 3rd above the root, plus a note a Major 3rd above the 3rd (of the triad), which is also an Augmented 5th above the root (that is referred to as the +5th or ♯5th). The unique intervallic structure of these augmented triads excludes them from diatonic inclusion within a Major tonality. We will first encounter them diatonically in the minor tonalities.

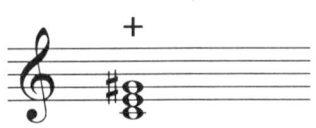

Major Tonality: Diatonic Chords

When we add another note a diatonic 3rd above the 5th of each triad we previously constructed, we get diatonic 7th chords built on each scale degree. They are called 7th chords because this (added) note is a 7th above the root. Just like our diatonic triads, these chords will have different qualities that are the result of their differing intervallic structures (example 5). These qualities are reflected in their names, and, as with diatonic triads, they can be represented by either a chord symbol or a Roman numeral. For example, FΔ7 (the chord symbol) in the key of C Major could also be represented as IVΔ7 (the Roman numeral). The former (chord symbol) representation is sufficient to construct the chord with no additional information. But the latter (Roman numeral) representation requires the additional contextual information of the key that this chord is IVΔ7 in. To be able to construct this chord correctly we must know what key it belongs to, because all Major keys have a IVΔ7 chord.

Example 5 – Diatonic 7th Chords: Key of C

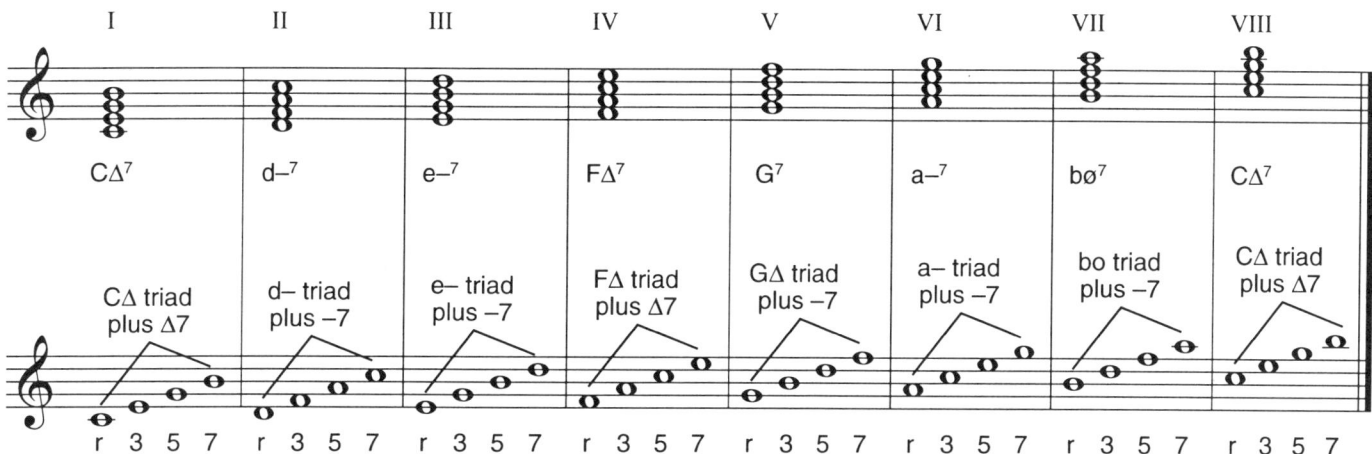

Δ7th   The intervallic structure of all Major 7th (Δ7th) chords is identical regardless of key, as follows: a Major (Δ) triad plus a note that is an interval of a Major 7th above the root. This note is also a Major 3rd above the 5th of the triad, and is referred to as the 7th of the chord. Δ7th chords occur diatonically on the Ist and IVth degrees of the Major scale.

7th   The intervallic structure of all dominant 7th (7th) chords (the chord built on the Vth degree of the scale) is identical regardless of key, as follows: a Major (Δ) triad plus a note which is an interval of a minor 7th above the root. This note is also a minor 3rd above the 5th of the triad and is referred to as the 7th (sometimes the ♭7th).

−7th   The intervallic structure of all minor 7th (−7th) chords is identical regardless of key, as follows: a minor triad, plus a note which is an interval of a minor 7th above the root. This note is also a minor 3rd above the 5th of the triad and is referred to as the 7th. −7th chords occur diatonically on the IInd, IIIrd, and VIth degrees of the Major scale.

Ø7th   The intervallic structure of all half diminished 7th (Ø7th) chords is identical regardless of key, as follows: a diminished triad, plus a note which is an interval of a minor 7th above the root of the triad. This note is also a Major 3rd above the diminished 5th of the triad and is referred to as the 7th (often the ♭7th). Ø7th chords occur diatonically on the VIIth degree of the Major scale.

The following diatonic arpeggio exercises are intended to familiarize the student with the seven diatonic triads and 7th chords in root position ascending and descending through two octaves in one position (the VIIth position). The first exercise triads are in triplets (3 notes per beat), while the second exercise rhythmically displaces each 3 note triad unit over a 16th note division of each $\frac{2}{4}$ bar. The third exercise is in 8th notes and is comprised of 8th note arpeggios of each diatonic 7th chord, ascending the IΔ7 (R, 3, 5, 7), then descending the II–7 (7, 5, 3, 1) and moving on to each successive chord.

Exercises 1 through 3:

Arpeggio exercises for diatonic triads and 7th chords in the key of C Major

Exercise 1

Exercise 2

Exercise 3

The fingerings used in exercise 1 apply to exercises 2 and 3. In exercise 3 the additional notes (the 7th of each chord) are accompanied by the necessary fingerings available in the VIIth position. There are of course many other possible fingerings and positions for these exercises. I recommend that the student explore them on his or her own.

To recap:

The structure of the diatonic triads and chords built in ascending 3[rds]s (from the root up), which are represented by Roman numerals (i.e., IΔ7, II–7, etc.), are identical in all Major keys as follows: the first degree yields a Δ triad and a Δ7[th] chord referred to as the I chord; the 2nd degree yields a – triad and a –7th chord referred to as the II chord; the 3rd degree yields a – triad and a –7th chord referred to as the III chord; the 4th degree yields a Δ triad and a Δ7[th] chord referred to as the IV chord; the 5th degree yields a Δ triad and a dominant 7th chord referred to as the V chord; the 6th degree yields a – triad and a –7th chord referred to as the VI chord; and the 7th degree yields a O triad and a Ø7 chord (half diminished, also called a –7th ♭5 chord) which is referred to as the VII chord.

Modes of the Major Tonalities

When improvising on a chord or chord progression, all twelve notes of the chromatic scale are available. However, some are easier to deal with than others. I break the twelve notes of the chromatic scale down into four basic categories, which we will discuss in detail later. But for now we want to examine the chord-scale relationships between the seven modes and their corresponding seven diatonic chords, which naturally occur in Major tonalities. The prime reason for focusing on these chord-scale relationships first is that each mode contains seven of the twelve notes of the chromatic scale. So acquiring facility with these modes carries us seven-twelfths of the way toward using all twelve notes for chords that diatonically occur in Major tonalities.

A chord's harmonic function will determine which scale or mode will best outline its tonality. This is determined by the context in which it occurs and the manner of its use.

Only context will clarify function!

The process of using context to define the harmonic function of a chord is often called "harmonic analysis." In effect, the application of this process in jazz determines chord-scale relationships in a song, which helps an improviser choose the proper tools, for example, the scale or mode that works best to define a particular chord's function and its relationship to the tonality in which it occurs. Since we began with diatonic triads and chords, we will now examine and listen to the modes that apply to each of them.

Each Major scale has 7 modes, one corresponding to each of the 7 degrees of the Major scale and transversing an octave above its starting pitch. In turn, each mode corresponds to the chord built on its degree.

The chords we previously built on each degree of the Major scale have unique intervallic structures that distinguish them from one another (e.g., IΔ7 differs from II–7). The modes built on each degree of the Major scale also have unique intervallic structures that distinguish them from one another (e.g., Ionian differs from Dorian). And just like each of the 7 diatonic chords which has an individual intervallic structure that remains uniform regardless of key (e.g., all Δ7[th] chords = root, Δ3, p5, and Δ7), so too each of the modes has a unique intervallic structure that remains uniform regardless of key (e.g., all Phrygian modes = 1, ♭2, ♭3, 4, 5, ♭6, ♭7, and 8). In addition, the pattern which emerges when viewing the 7 diatonic chords of a Major tonality as a unit remains uniform regardless of key (i.e., IΔ7, II–7, III–7, IVΔ7, V7, VI–7, VIIØ7) and mirrors the pattern that emerges when viewing the 7 modes of the Major scale as a unit, which also remains uniform regardless of key as follows: I = Ionian, II = Dorian, III = Phrygian, IV = Lydian, V = Mixolydian, VI = Aeolian, VII = Locrian.

These principles apply to all modes and scales as well as chords and are illustrated in examples 6 and 7.

Example 6 – Diatonic Modes: Key of C

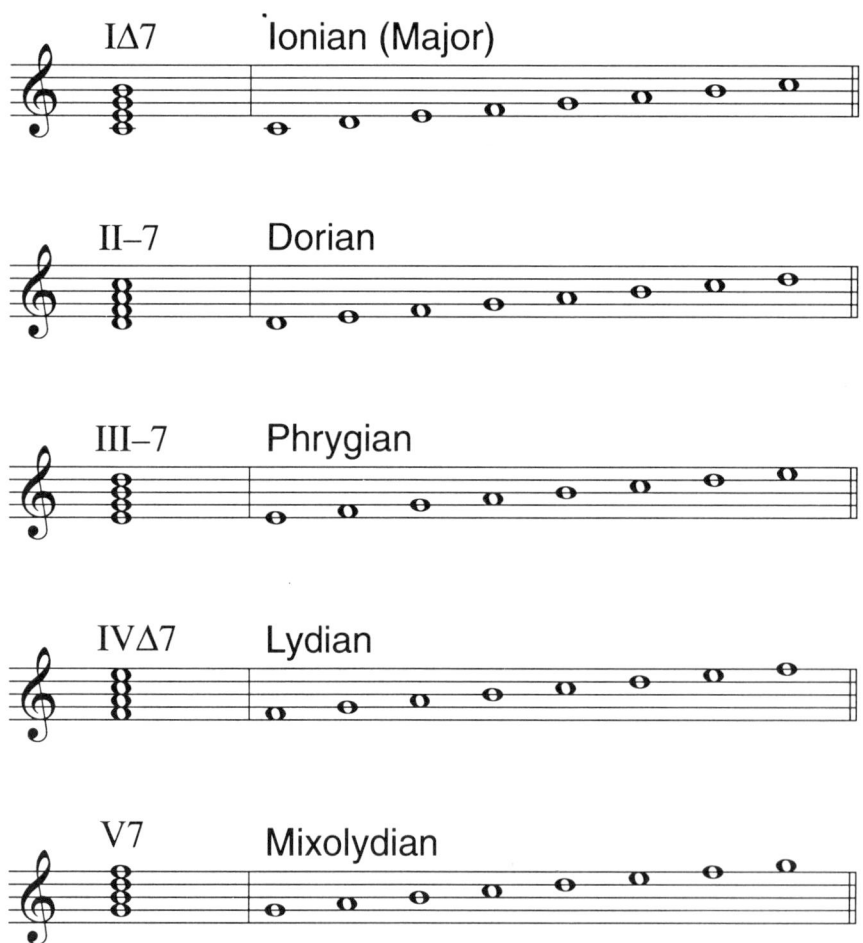

VI–7
Aeolian
VIIø7
Locrian

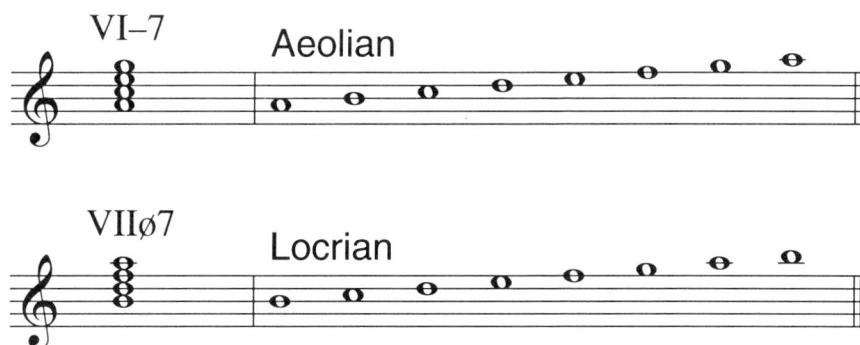

Example 7 – Intervallic Modal Structure

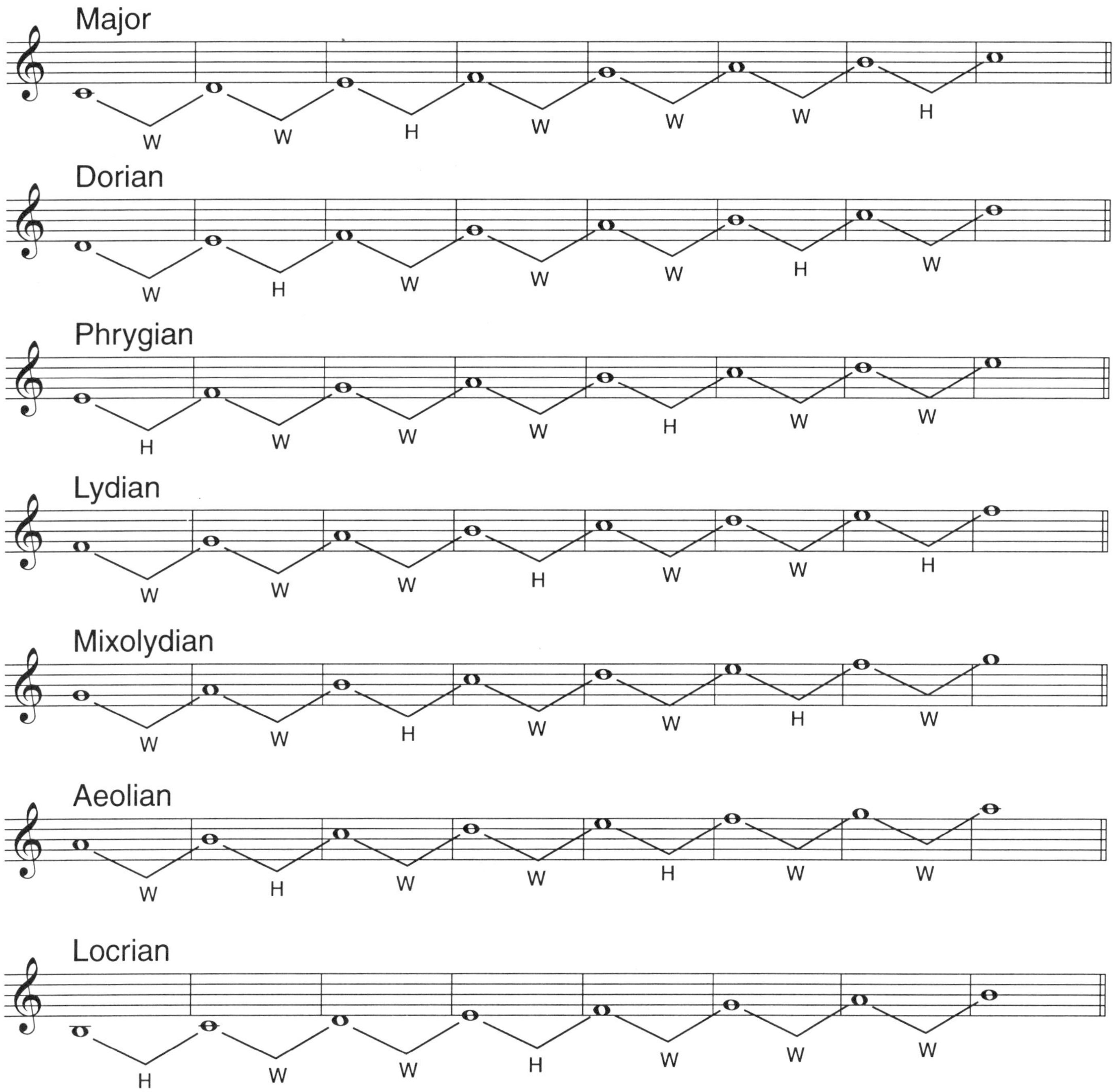

Major
W W H W W W H
Dorian
W H W W W H W
Phrygian
H W W W H W W
Lydian
W W W H W W H
Mixolydian
W W H W W H W
Aeolian
W H W W H W W
Locrian
H W W H W W W

The following exercise (exercise 4) addresses the diatonic 7th chords built on each degree of the Major scale and their corresponding modes. First a chord is played (in a guitar-friendly voicing). This is followed by an arpeggio of the chord. Then the mode that corresponds to the chord built on each scale degree is played, followed by the same chord we began with in a different voicing. The fingerings and positions accompanying each chord-scale group of this exercise are but one possible option. As with all the exercises in this book, I encourage the serious student to explore other options in addition to the other eleven keys.

Please remember to hear each chord tone's relationship to the other notes of its corresponding mode. Don't just mindlessly run up and down the various modes out of context.

I've always found it very helpful to sing (using solfège syllables) each mode as I play the corresponding chord. I suggest you give this a try. The solfège syllables would be: do, re, mi, fa, sol, la, ti, and do (for Ionian-Major). Just start on the appropriate syllable for each mode: Dorian = re, mi, fa, sol, la, ti do, re; Phrygian = mi, fa, sol, la, ti, do, re, mi, etc.

Exercise 4

17

In the intervallic comparison of the modes that follows, I have used the Major scale (Ionian mode) as the basis for comparison. Therefore, since Major is represented as: 1, 2, 3, 4, 5, 6, 7, 8, Dorian is represented as: 1, 2, ♭3, 4, 5, 6, ♭7, 8, etc. (example 8).

Example 8

Intervallic comparison of modes

Exercise 5 gives each chord, arpeggio, and corresponding mode as it is presented in the intervallic comparison. So the root of each chord and the starting note of each mode is C. They are all in the same area of the fingerboard (2nd and 3rd positions). But you should explore other areas (for example, 7th and 8th positions).

Exercise 5

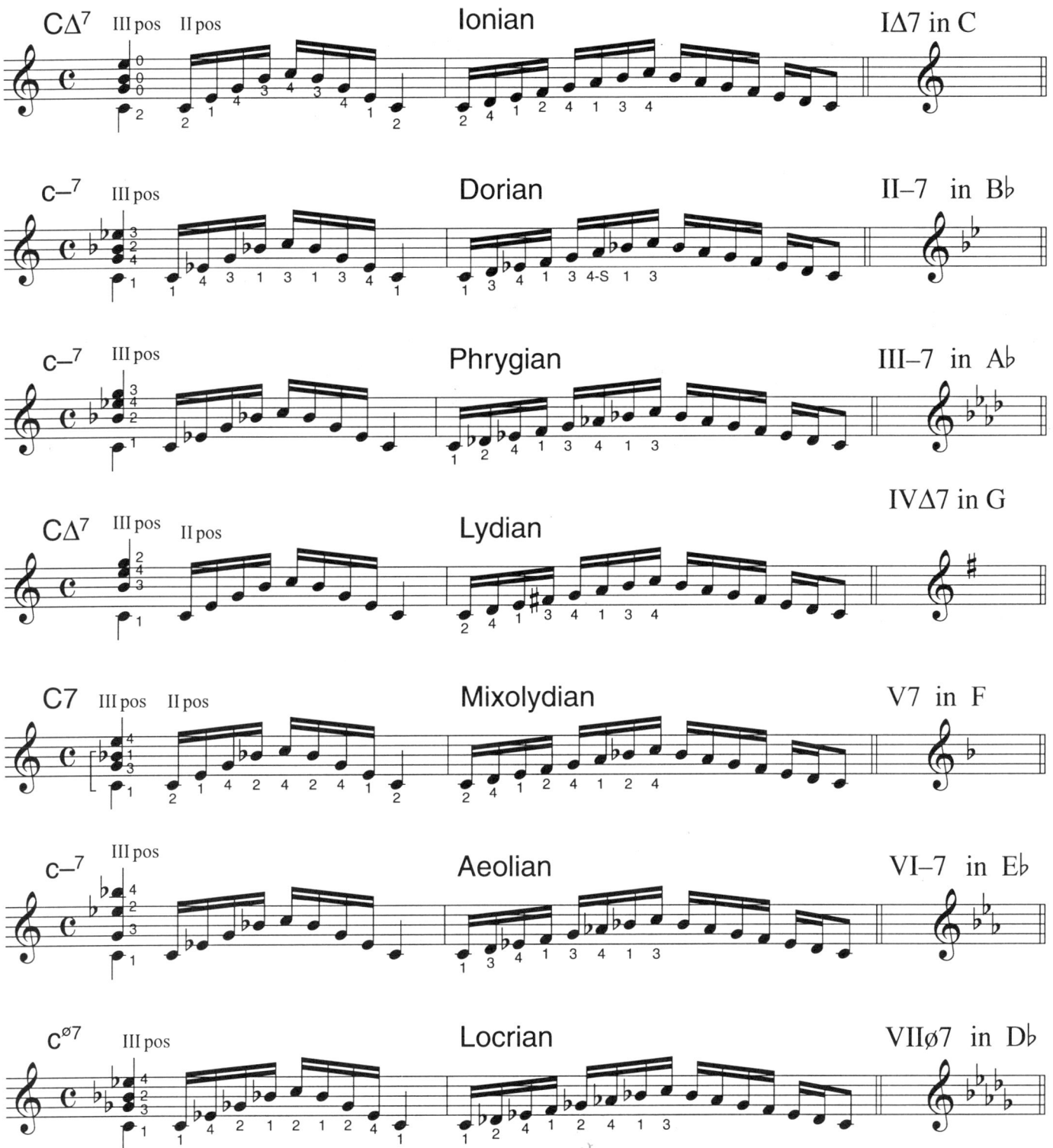

It is important to be able to hear these differences clearly, because, among other things, when improvising one must recognize the chord change happening at the moment, react to it, and execute one's musical idea (which is your reaction!).

For example, when hearing an a–7th chord, one must both recognize that it is a minor 7th chord and determine its harmonic function. This is not easy for those unfamiliar with distinguishing between identical chords that have subtle differences in their respective harmonic functions. As a case in point, consider how identical a–7 chords could function as II–7 in the key of G Major (requiring an a Dorian mode), or as III–7 in F Major (requiring an a Phrygian mode), or as VI–7 in C Major (requiring an a Aeolian mode).[4]

Once this recognition has taken place, the player reacts by forming a musical idea, which must then be performed (executed). All this may have occurred in the space of two beats (or less) as the chord changes of a tune pass by.

For those students with some experience in jazz musical improvisation, you already know this. For those with little or no such experience, it may be helpful to compare this process with that of learning and using a new language. If you only speak English and are learning Italian, you may know what you want to say in English and have to consciously translate your thoughts into Italian before you speak. This cumbersome process is analogous to hearing a set of chord changes, recognizing it, analyzing the harmonic function of its chords, locating the appropriate tools, and then formulating and executing your reaction. But the more you do it, the more seamless the process becomes. Eventually it's like speaking in a language you know; the conception and expression occur simultaneously. You actually think in the new language, in this case, the language of music, and the vernacular of jazz.

Since diatonic 7th chords constructed on the degrees of a Major scale yield a pattern that is common to all twelve keys, and each Major key contains two Δ7[th], three -7th, one dominant 7th, and one ø7[th] chord, there is going to be some duplication. A close examination of the cycle of 5[th]s (also referred to as the circle of 5[th]s; example 9) and the various diatonic 7th chords constructed on seven degrees of each of its twelve keys (example 10) reveals just how much duplication there is.

---

[4] I often hear a chord's harmonic function first, then find the key in order to reveal the chord's root, and thereby determine which II–, III–, or VI– it actually is.

Example 9

Cycle of Fifths (5ths)

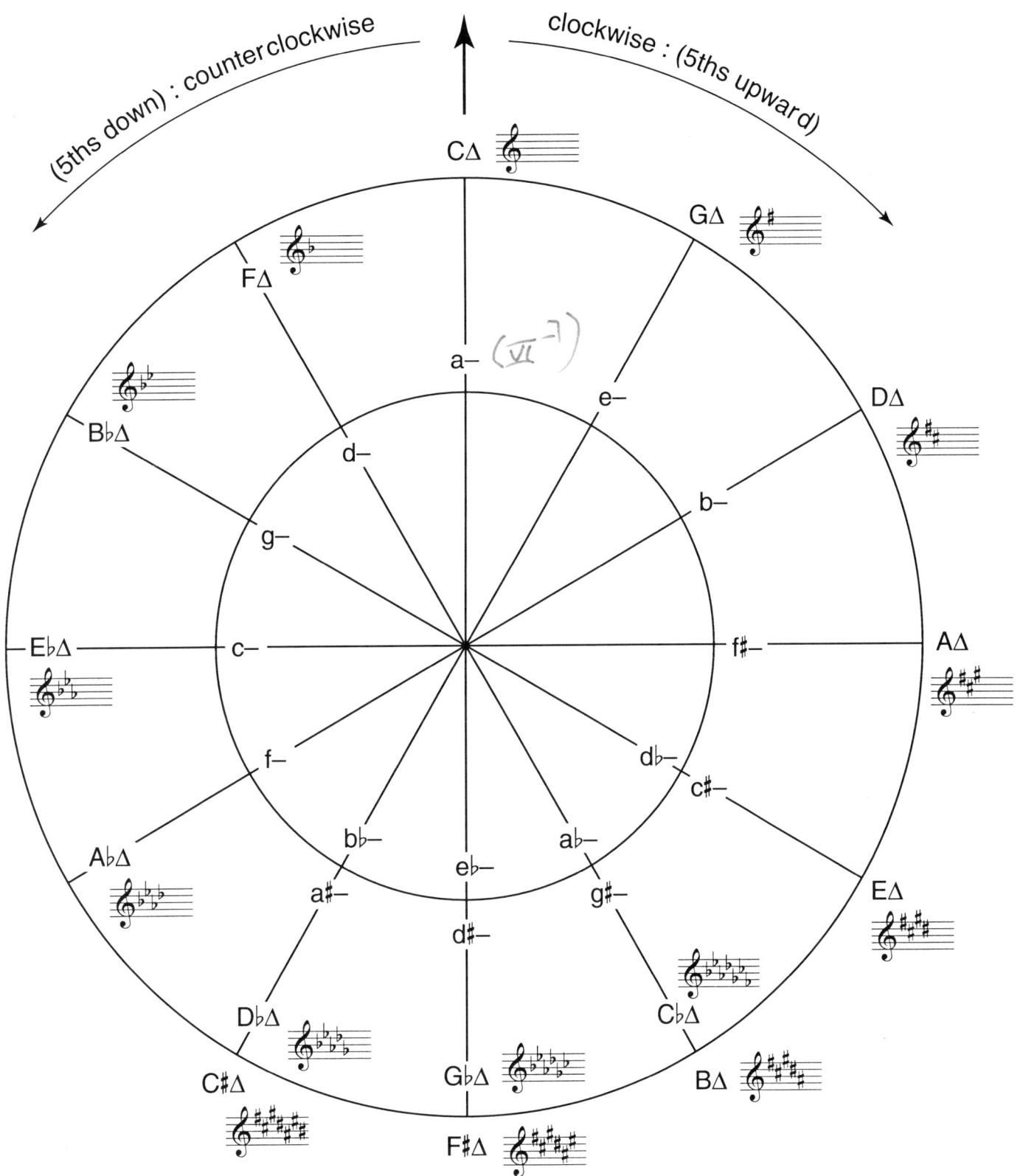

Example 10

Diatonic 7th Chords : 12 Major Keys

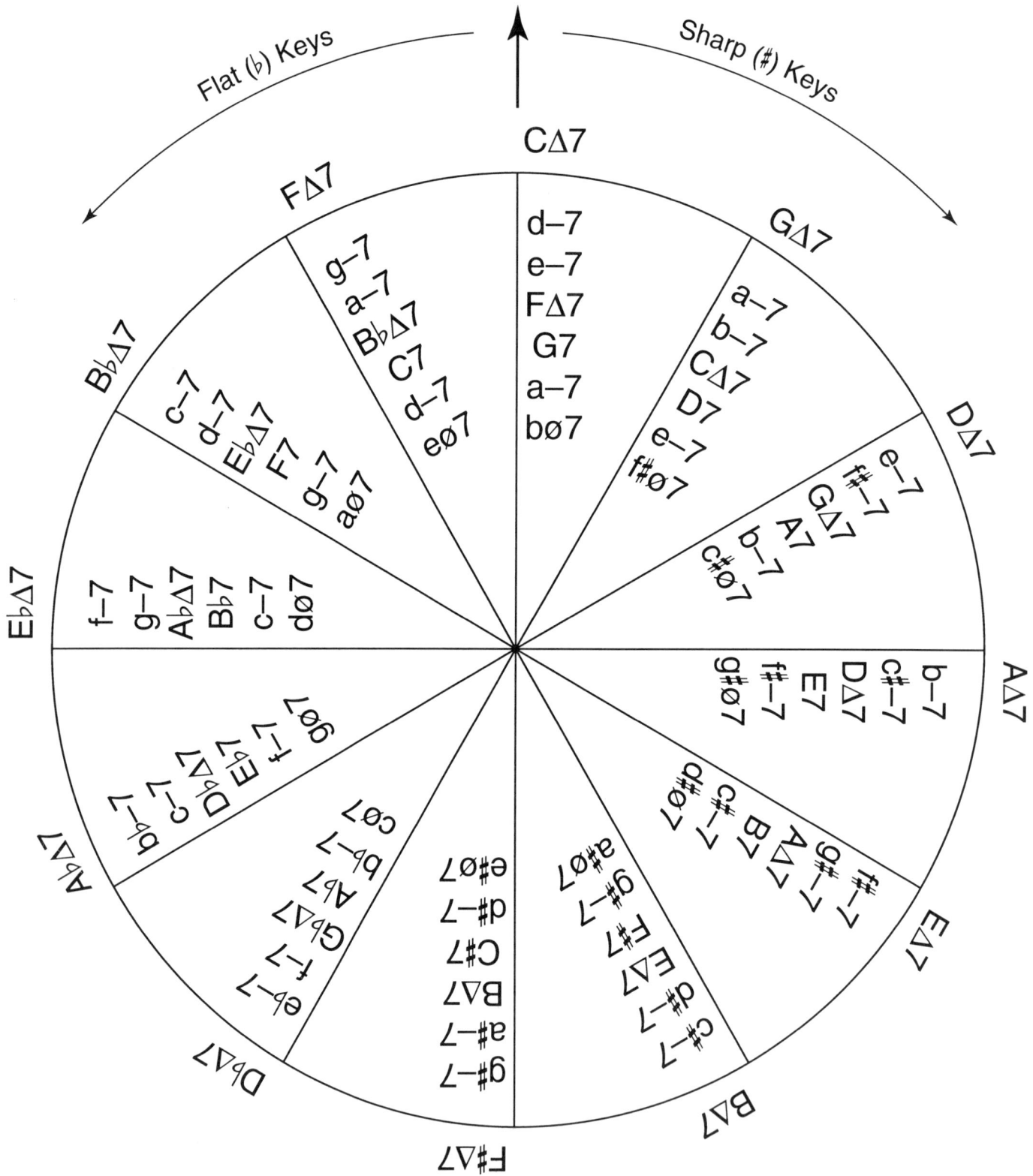

Consider this: each Major scale contains two Major 7th chords (IΔ7 and IVΔ7) and three minor 7th chords (II–7, III–7, and VI–7), plus one dominant 7th chord (V7), and one half-diminished 7th chord (VIIØ7).

When we compare chords found in the key of C with those found in two adjacent keys from the circle of 5ths, i.e., C to G (one clockwise step around the circle of 5ths from C), and C to F (one counterclockwise step around the circle of 5ths from C), we begin to see just how much duplication there is. I've already mentioned the three different a–7th chords (see above), so let's look at a few others. FΔ7 is IVΔ7 in C and IΔ7 in F, d–7 is II–7 in C and VI–7 in F, e–7 is III–7 in C and VI–7 in G (example 11).

Example 11

I	II	III	IV	V	VI	VII	I or VIII
CΔ7	d–7	e–7	FΔ7	G7	a–7	b⌀7	CΔ7
GΔ7	a–7	b–7	CΔ7	D7	e–7	f♯⌀7	GΔ7
FΔ7	g–7	a–7	B♭Δ7	C7	d–7	e⌀7	FΔ7

So how do we determine a chord's harmonic function? The answer is <u>context</u>. How do we interpret the clues which context provides? Listen for and examine the <u>differences</u>! For example, we all know that what distinguishes CΔ from c– is the 3rd of each chord (*E♮* for CΔ and *E♭* for c–). So let's find out what makes a IΔ7 (say CΔ7) in the key of C differ from a IVΔ7 (again CΔ7) in the key of G. Since both chords are identical, let's check out their respective modes: C Major (Ionian) and C Lydian. There is a difference: the 4th degree in C Major is *F♮*, and in C Lydian it's *F♯* (example 12).

Example 12

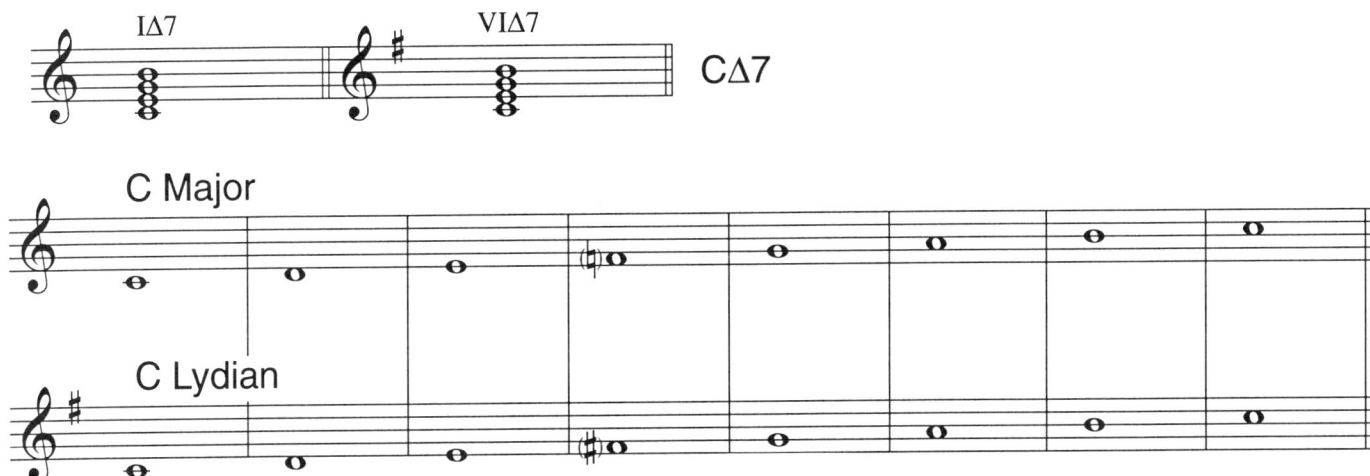

23

Let's look closer at the three a–7th chords mentioned earlier: a–7 functioning as II–7 in G, a–7 functioning as III–7 in F, and a–7 functioning as VI–7 in C. Again, since the chord tones of each a–7 chord are identical, let's examine their respective modes and compare the differences. a Dorian (for II–7) has a Major 6th degree, while a Aeolian (VI–7) has a ♭6th degree, and a Phrygian (III–7) has a ♭2nd degree, and a ♭6th degree. And just like the ♭3rd degrees that one would expect for modes that correspond to –7th chords, all the remaining degrees are common among the three modes. So the differences in their respective modes are indicators of the chords' differing harmonic functions (example 13)! When such differences are encountered in either a melody or an adjacent chord, they tell you what mode to use. For example, a CΔ chord followed or preceded by a DΔ chord would indicate C Lydian, because the DΔ chord contains the ♯4 indicator note (F♯ as in C Lydian), or a d–7 chord followed by a G7 chord would indicate d Dorian, because the G7 chord contains the B♮ indicator note (Δ6 in d Dorian). There is also the obvious possibility of a chord itself containing one of these indicator notes as an available tension, for example, CΔ7♯11 (♯11 is an available tension which is ♯4 up an octave and indicates C Lydian). More about this later.

Example 13

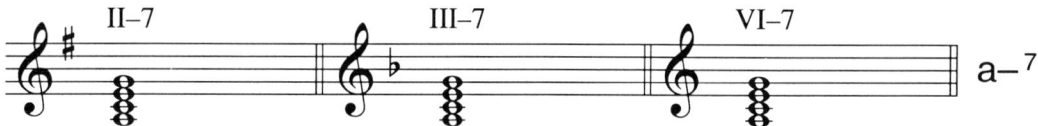

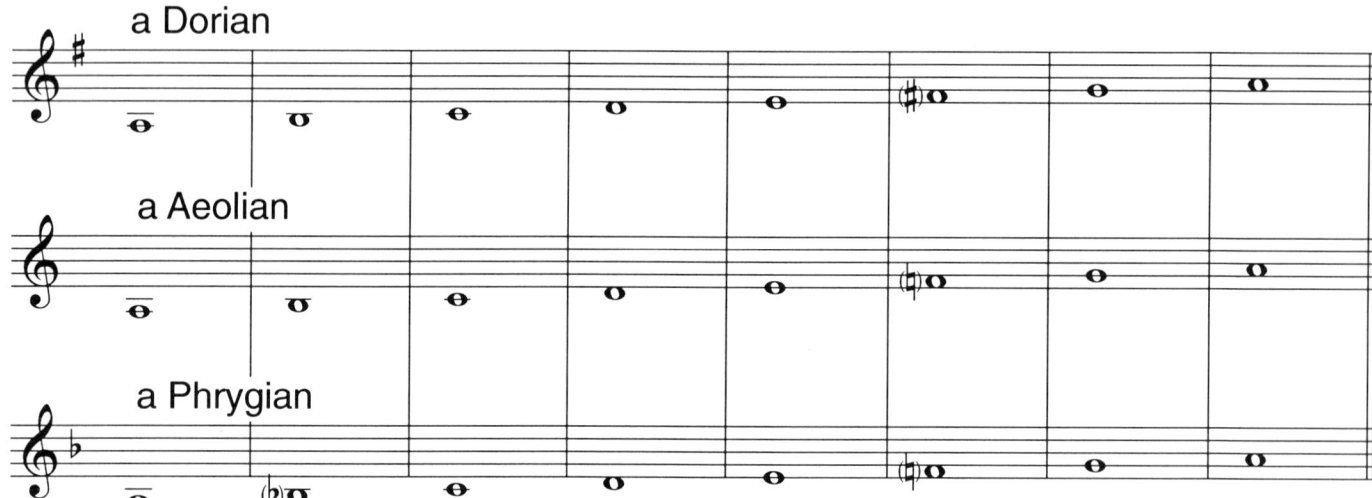

When we add the V7 chord, which uses the Mixolydian mode, and the VIIØ7 chord, which uses the Locrian mode, we have all the possibilities for diatonic 7th chords constructed from a Major tonality covered. Since V7 and VIIØ7 occur only once in each Major key, when you encounter these chords in a Major tonality, their function is easier to determine than –7th and Δ7th chords.

There are other options of course, but we will get to those later.

First, let's work on hearing the consonant chord tones' relationship to the dissonant passing tones, which together make up the seven notes of each mode (the 8th note being the octave of the 1st). In exercise 6 we use the 1st inversion of the diatonic triads from the key of C in closed position.[5] This is the one we will start with, because it leaves the Major scale intact in the top voice. So when we move that voice to the neighboring tones above and below, we can hear the consonant-dissonant relationship more clearly. The notes beamed down are the chord tones that complete the triad.

Looking at the 1st triad: C, E, and G are chord tones (beamed down), and C, B, D, C comprise the melody that illustrates the consonant-dissonant relationship (C being the consonant note, B and D being the upper and lower diatonic neighbors which are passing tones and are dissonant). We then move to the triad built on each successive degree of the scale, applying the same approach, and reverse it coming down the scale.

In exercise 7 we will then go to the 2nd inversion and follow the same procedure. And in exercise 8 we do the same for root position triads. Exercise 9 demonstrates each passing tone in relation to the top voice of each inversion of each triad (in 1st and 2nd inversions) and root position for each triad and 7th chord.

---

[5] For those unfamiliar with inversions or open and closed positions, let me point out that each triad contains three notes, and explain that in closed position that means the notes are arranged so that the smallest possible interval exists between each note. Since these triads are built in 3rds, that means in root position closed all notes have a 3rd between them. To create the 1st inversion, take the bottom note (the root) and raise it an octave, leaving the 3rd on the bottom. The 2nd inversion is created by taking the bottom note of the 1st inversion (the 3rd) and raising it an octave, leaving the 5th in the bottom. To recap: root position has the root in the bottom, 1st inversion has the 3rd in the bottom, and 2nd inversion has the 5th in the bottom. To create an open position voicing, raise a voice to establish a spread between the outer voices (i.e., top and bottom notes) that exceeds an octave. This can be done by raising the 2nd voice an octave, creating a 10th between the top and bottom voices in root position open, and 1st inversion open, and creating a spread of an 11th between the outer voices in the 2nd inversion open.

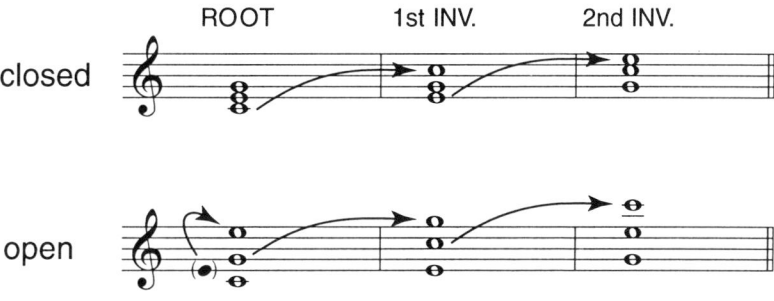

The examples I've given are in the key of C. However, it is imperative that the serious student acquires facility in all twelve keys. So please take the time to write the examples and play all the exercises in the remaining eleven keys.

Exercise 6

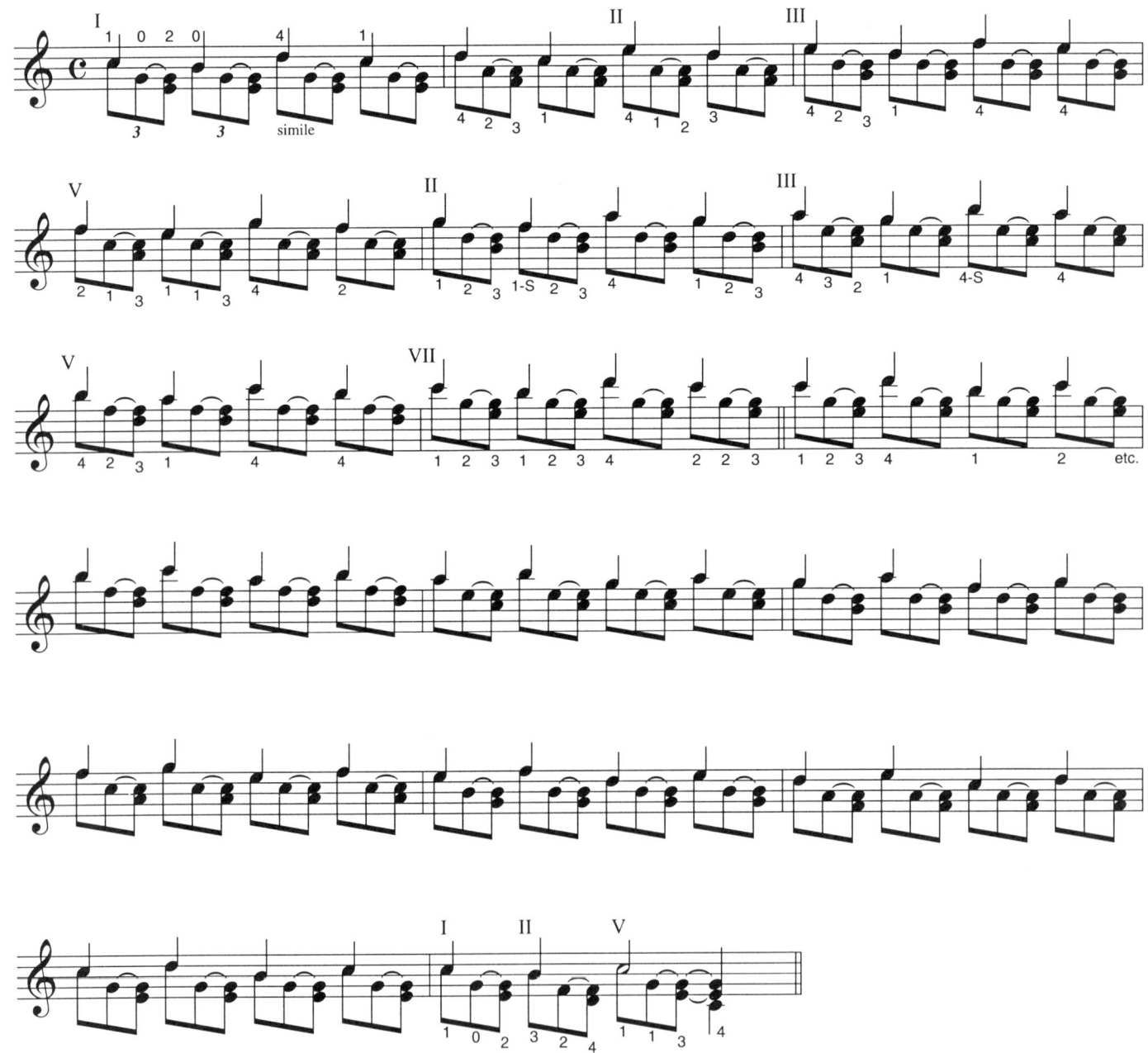

Exercise 7

Exercise 8

Exercise 9

Explanation, Demonstration, and Justification of the Use of Each Note of the Chromatic Scale for Any Chord Found in a Major Tonality

Art Tatum and Charlie Parker were among the first jazz musicians to hear and employ all twelve notes of the chromatic scale in any musical situation over any chord at any time. While it is certainly true that the increasing chromaticism found in the works of 19th century European classical composers such as Chopin, Brahms, and Wagner predates the work of the aforementioned jazz artists and ultimately led to Schoenberg's twelve-tone system, the music of these classical composers was not improvised; it was through-composed, and in Schoenberg's case, his late compositional works were no longer rooted in any sense of tonality or key. Even though many jazz musicians probably heard and may have been influenced by these classical composers' works, jazz musicians during the bebop era (and much of what followed it), such as Charlie Parker, were improvising on the chord changes (harmonic sequences) which accompanied the melodies of the popular songs of their day, not creating serial compositions or constructing tone rows.

I mentioned earlier that I break down the possible uses of each note of the chromatic scale, on any chord at any time, into four categories. They are: (1) **chord tones**, (2) **available tensions**, (3) **passing tones**, and (4) **approach tones**.

Chord tones are a primary melodic tool employed in both composition and improvisation. As the name implies, these are notes contained in the actual chord over which one is improvising at a specific moment during a harmonic sequence from a song, or a chord accompanying a melody at a particular place in a composition.

Melodies that are constructed exclusively from chord tones are generally pretty bland, but, as with all art, the ingenuity of the musician improvising or composing can work wonders with any tool. To increase interest in melodic lines, chord tones are often approached by notes above or below them, creating a sense of tension and release traditionally explained in terms such as dissonance (tension) resolving to consonance (release). This process is one way of giving shape to a melodic line resulting in more interesting and appealing musical ideas. Two ways of approaching chord tones are by neighboring scale tones (passing tones) and by (chromatic) approach tones.

If you randomly compare notes from the chromatic scale to any chord, you will find that some notes work unconditionally, while others need to be handled with care. The notes that work unconditionally are consonant and may be considered points of rest or release. You can play these anywhere at any time and may end an idea on them. They are generally **chord tones** (example 14).

Example 14

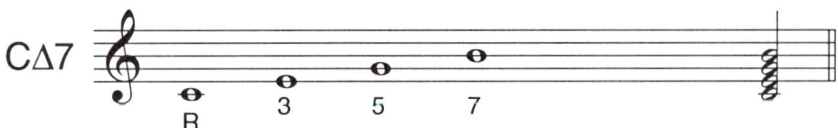

Another type of note that can be a point of rest is called an **available tension**. Available tensions are notes that come from the upper structure of a chord. They are the notes above the root, 3rd, and 5th of the triad, such as the 7th, 9th, 11th, and 13th of a chord (example 15).

Example 15 – Upper Structure

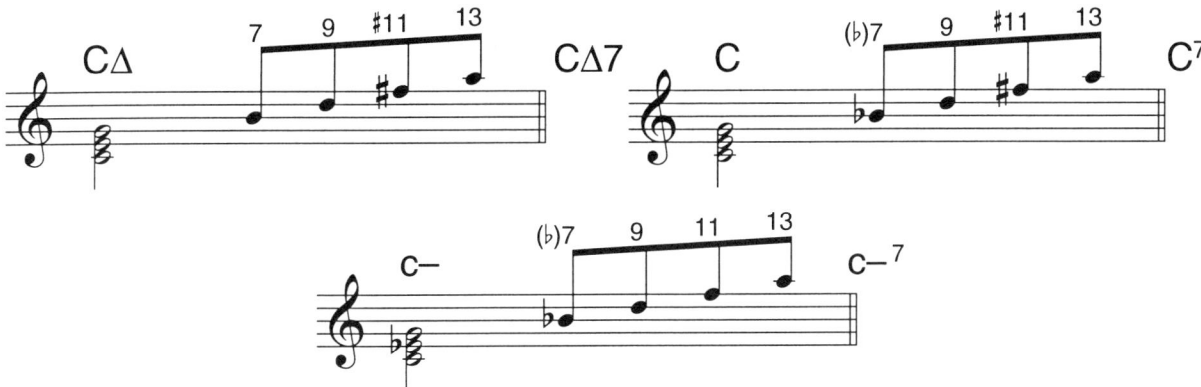

These tensions would traditionally have been considered dissonances in need of resolution, but some jazz musicians, as well as some modern classical composers, heard the potential for unusual resolutions that credibly ended on these available tensions (example 16).

Example 16 – Available Tensions

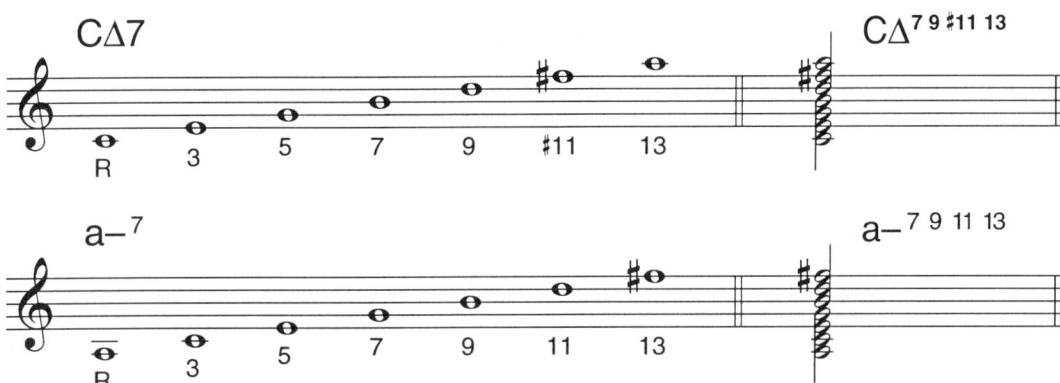

Occasionally these available tensions may have a dual function. For example, a *D♯* over a C∆7 chord could function as 9 if rested on (available tension), or as 2 if passing between *C* and *E* (passing tone).

This brings us to the next category of notes: **passing tones**. As the name implies, these notes pass between notes which are consonant and which precede and/or follow them. These passing tones usually have a dissonant quality and occur in scale-wise phrases alternating with consonant notes (most likely chord tones). For example, in a melody comprised of the pitches *C*, *D*, and *E*, over a C∆ chord, the *D* would be a passing tone (*C* and *E* being chord tones; example 17). But a similar melody over a G7 chord would produce *C* as a passing tone, and *D* as the 5th of the G7 chord.

Example 17

In fact, for any diatonic chord built in thirds, every note from the scale that would best outline its tonality would be either a chord tone or a passing tone (they generally alternate). For example, a CΔ7th chord in the key of G Major would have the function of the IVΔ7 chord requiring a C Lydian scale: *C, d, E, f♯, G, a, B, C*. *C* would be the root of CΔ7, *d* a passing tone (or 9 if sounded up an octave), *E* is the Δ3rd of the CΔ7 chord, *f♯* is a passing tone (or ♯11 if sounded up an octave), *G* would be the 5th of the CΔ7 chord, *a* would be a passing tone (or the 13th if sounded up an octave), *B* would be the Δ7 of the CΔ7 chord, and *C* would again be the root (example 18).

Example 18

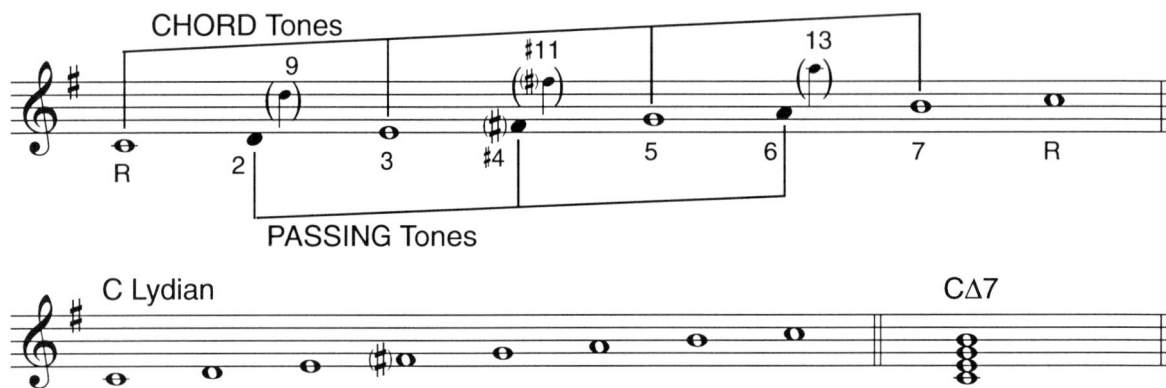

The appropriate use of any mode or chord-scale automatically covers the use of seven of the twelve notes of the chromatic scale, leaving only five unaccounted for. These five notes belong to the last classification of notes from the chromatic scale. This last category of notes involves the use of **approach tones** both above and/or below a targeted note (a chord tone or available tension). For example, if *G♮* were the 5th of the same CΔ7th chord (functioning as IV in the key of G) and the targeted tone in a phrase, it could be approached by *A♮* above and *F♯* below, or even *A♭* above and *F♯* below. Similarly, *E♮* (the 3rd of a CΔ7 chord) could be approached by *F♮* and *D♯*, and *C* (the root) could be approached by *B♮* and *D♭*, while the *B♮* (Δ7) could be approached by *C* and *A♯*. This accounts for the remaining five notes of the chromatic scale (*A♭, F♮, D♯, D♭*, and *A♯*). There are other ways to interpret some of the notes of the chromatic scale, but the principle of consonance/dissonance generally guides them all (example 19).

Example 19

To recap: all twelve notes of the chromatic scale are usable on any chord at any time. Their harmonic functions can be classified in four categories, two of which are consonant, and two of which are dissonant. Some notes are points of rest and are consonant (release). These are (1) **chord tones** and, if handled properly, (2) **available tensions**. Some notes are points of motion and are dissonant (tension) and need to be handled with care. These are (3) **passing tones** and (4) **approach tones**. Passing tones come from the scale that best outlines the tonal function of a specific chord in a particular situation. They are often neighboring tones either above or below a chord tone, and some may also function as available tensions. Approach tones (sometimes called chromatic approach tones) are notes that approach chord tones (and in some cases, if properly handled, available tensions). Approach tones are often outside of the key and dissonant, and they resolve in stepwise fashion. Example 20 shows the breakdown of each of the 12 notes of the chromatic scale and how each relates to a CΔ7 chord functioning as IΔ7 in the key of C Major. The passing tones an octave higher are also the available tensions.[6]

Example 20

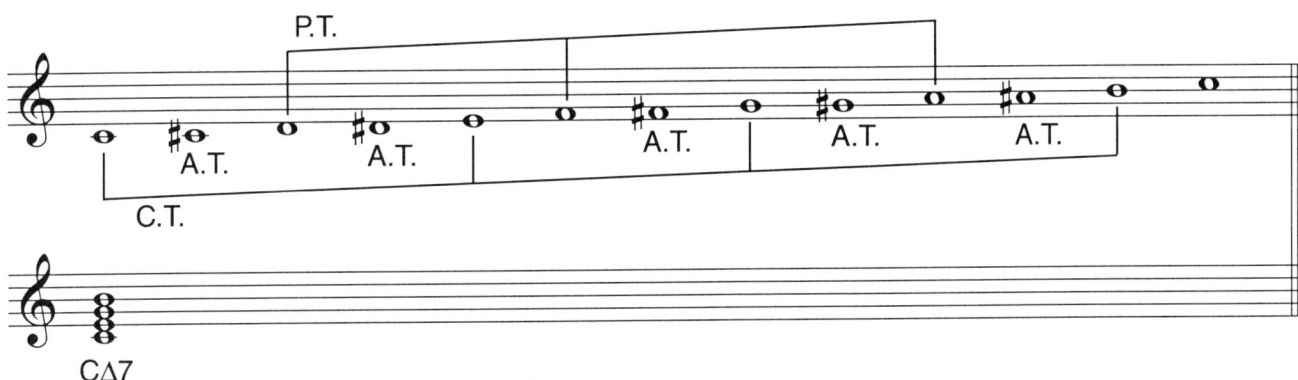

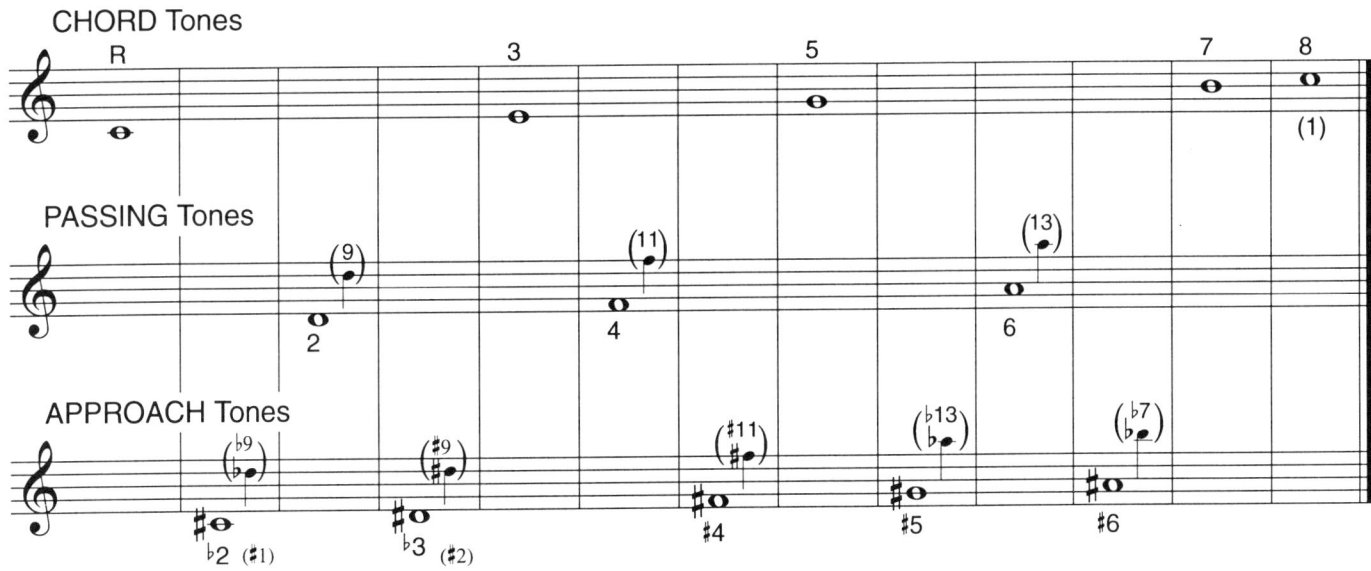

The following exercise (exercise 10) is designed to familiarize the student with the use of both chromatic approach tones and diatonic passing tones in a variety of combinations. These two means are employed to approach targeted chord tones from above and below.

---

[6] Some approach tones an octave higher could function as altered tensions on dominant 7th chords (C7 in this case) with the ♯6 also being the ♭7th of the chord, while the ♯4 could be a ♯11 on either a Δ7th or a dominant 7th chord.

Exercise 10

There are no fingerings or positions indicated in exercise 10 because I want you to discover and explore the many options for yourself. Begin by locating a good place to play the targeted note of each triplet (generally the last note of each triplet). Then visualize the approach notes above and below this targeted note. Choose a fingering that will accommodate playing each three note group on the same string, then move to the next triplet following this procedure. Most of the target notes will be played with either the 2nd or 3rd finger, and the upper approach note(s) will therefore be played by either the 3rd or 4th finger, while the lower approach note(s) will then be played by either the 1st or the 2nd finger. Some of the voicings contain available tensions in the middle of the chords (i.e., FΔ [♯11], G7 [2], and a–7 [9]). These voicings involve the use of open strings (as indicated).

Chapter 2:
Minor Tonalities and Their Diatonic Chords

We have already looked at the different harmonic functions of the three minor triads and their respective minor 7th chords, which occur diatonically in Major tonalities (i.e., II–, III– and VI–). The modal treatment of these chords has often been employed to novel effect by jazz musicians. Classic jazz tunes such as "So What" and "Milestones" by Miles Davis, and "Impressions" by John Coltrane exemplify what was at the time of their creation a new approach to improvisation, intended to free the improviser from the veritable harmonic obstacle course of much of the jazz of the time (late 1950s). A good example of the type of harmonic obstacle course some jazz musicians were striving to free themselves from is John Coltrane's "Giant Steps," whose chord changes are quite difficult to blow on. Some of the music that was in part created as a reaction to the harmonic constraints imposed by such difficult changes had a much less cluttered harmonic structure and is often called modal jazz.

Jazz musicians' creative use of minor 7th chords in modal jazz contributed a new approach, which we will discuss later and contrast with the approaches that predate it. Today there are many jazz musicians who unselectively apply a modal approach to all minor chords, making them minor 7th chords and treating them as if they are all Dorian; or worse, they indiscriminately interchange Dorian, Phrygian, and Aeolian modes with Melodic minor, Harmonic minor, and the Traditional minor (which has an ascending form identical to the Melodic minor and a differing descending form which is identical to the Aeolian mode). The inappropriate use of Dorian, for example, to define the tonic (I–) chord in a minor tonality that is not modal often causes the lines created from such an approach to lack harmonic clarity. While I know there are musicians who like and indeed insist that they are striving to create such ambiguity, I cannot in good conscience advocate this method as a pedagogical approach any more than I could recommend using the principle of androgyny as the best way to teach children growing up on a farm how to determine the sex of a newborn calf.

So we will start by examining the traditional minor tonalities. Later we will compare and contrast them with the modal jazz approaches and offer some suggestions about what works best in different circumstances. But remember that a good toolbox is well equipped, and a master craftsman knows what tool works best for each task. In short, all tools are of use, and ultimately your judgment will have to be your guide.

First let's briefly discuss the evolution of the traditional treatment of minor tonalities. As I have already mentioned, jazz inherited its tonal system of chords and scales from Europe. During the late Middle Ages and the early Renaissance, the music of western Europe had not yet developed a tempered scale (that is, our present chromatic scale in which the octave is divided into 12 equally spaced notes). Instead, the musicians of that time used the seven church modes as their primary tools to create music. The seven church modes parallel our present Ionian, Dorian, Phrygian, Lydian, Mixolydian, Aeolian, and Locrian, all of which were derived from the overtones of a fundamental note. Locrian was rarely if ever used because no one could create credible cadences with its tonic chord (since neither a O triad nor a Ø7 chord sounds like the end of a phrase or composition). As composers such as Ockcghcm, De Lassus, Des Pres, and Palestrina developed the polyphonic music which evolved out of the plainsong and Gregorian chant of church music into what is the basis of our harmony, they found it difficult to create cadences in the minor modes that were as believably final as those they created when using the Major modes. This was particularly problematic with melodies that ascended to their conclusion in the minor modes. And since ascending is a very effective way to build to a climactic ending, these composers had to find a means of ending minor movements of masses and motets without always resorting to the pitches of the Aeolian mode, which only sounded final when descending.

Some of these composers started creating cadences with melodic devices built from the Major tetrachord[7] that concludes a Major scale (for example, sol, la, ti, do; that is, 5, Δ6, Δ7, to 8, which in the key of C would be *g*, *a*, *b*, *c*; example 21). These composers were in effect grafting a Major tetrachord onto a minor tetrachord, creating our present-day Melodic minor scale for ascending lines.

Example 21

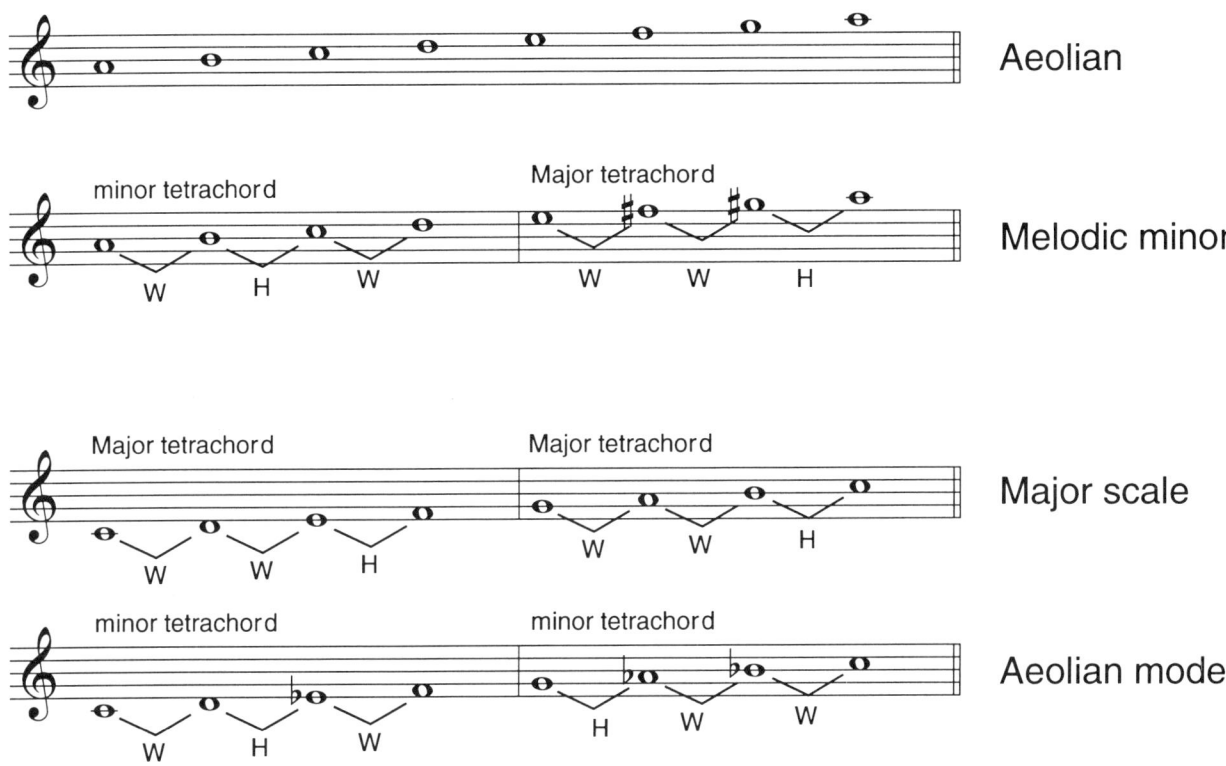

Combining the Melodic minor scale (which ends with a Major tetrachord) for ascending, and the Aeolian mode (which ends with a minor tetrachord) for descending, they created what I am calling the "Traditional minor" scale. This scale not only solved the cadential problems Renaissance composers encountered when working in minor tonalities, but it also greatly enriched the harmonic possibilities for music in general, because when you diatonically construct triads and chords built in 3[rd]s on this scale (Traditional minor), you get a different set for each: one set of chords and triads for the ascending, and one set for the descending (example 22).

Example 22

Traditional minor

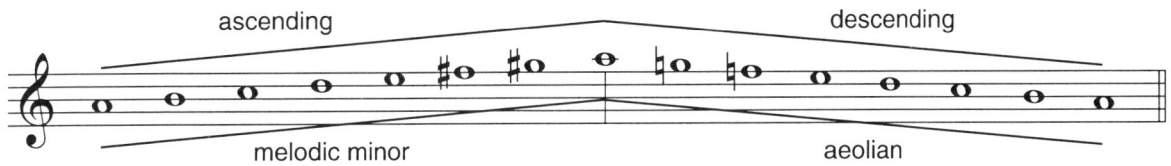

---

[7] In ancient Greek music, a tetrachord was a succession of four notes, usually descending, normally consisting of two consecutive whole tones followed by a half tone, for example, *e*, *d*, *c*, *b*. Nowadays the term refers to any 4-note segment taken intact from a scale, ascending or descending: *c*, *d*, *e*, *f* is an example of a Major tetrachord (that is, whole, whole, half); *c*, *d*, *eb*, *f* is an example of a minor tetrachord (that is, whole, half, whole). There are others such as the Phrygian tetrachord: *c*, *db*, *eb*, *f* (that is, half, whole, whole).

These different chords have harmonic implications depending upon their origin and context, which carry with them obligations that a musician should deal with from knowledge, not ignorance. Whether these obligations are merely a culturally constructed habit as some believe, or they reveal deeper truths about our relationship to the physical universe that can only be manifested by audible vibration (i.e., sound), is a subject to be debated elsewhere. But what is historically clear is that this approach predates the modal jazz approach. I believe that, when properly addressed by the player, the obligations inferred by the harmonic implications of the chords and lines that best exemplify each of the various minor tonalities go a long way toward making one's ideas clearer and aid the audience's comprehension of the music. I suggest that anyone who doubts the veracity of what I'm advocating take a good listen to Cannonball Adderley's remarkable playing. Even within the modally based context of Miles Davis's classic *Kind of Blue* recording (which contains the aforementioned "So What"), Cannonball's playing stands out as an example of precision and clarity at its swingingest, no matter what the tonality is.

If we take a close listen to the intervallic construction of this "Traditional minor" scale, we immediately notice the Δ6th and Δ7th degrees in its ascending form (the Melodic minor) and the ♭6th and ♭7th degrees in its descending form (Aeolian mode).

In Schoenberg's explanation of the rules of harmony, he refers to these scale degrees as "pivot points," and he states: "The two forms [of the Traditional minor scale, i.e., ascending and descending] are not mixed. In upward

38

progression only the raised tones [Δ6 and Δ7] may appear, in downward only the ♮ [♭6 and ♭7] tones."[8] Schoenberg refers to what I'm calling ♭6 and ♭7 as the natural forms of the 6th and 7th degrees of the scale, and he refers to what I'm calling Δ6 and Δ7 as the raised forms, because he is using Aeolian as the basis for comparison, much as I used the Major scale as the basis for intervallic comparison of the seven modes of the Major scale. Since these degrees naturally occur as f♮ and g♮ in *a* Aeolian and must be raised to f♯ and g♯ in order to convert *a* Aeolian to *a* Melodic minor, Schoenberg's terminology makes sense. However, I want to aid the student in acquiring the ability to hear all chords and scales and their functions in all contexts related to jazz. Consequently, I feel that one standard must be the basis for comparison, and what I call the Δ6th and Δ7th of the Melodic minor scale correspond to the 6th and 7th degrees of the Major scale. Since the Major scale has been our standard for comparison thus far, why change that standard now? Given that the Melodic minor scale ends with a Major tetrachord anyway, this approach seems sound to me. And years of experience with jazz music has taught me that the rapid harmonic motion of jazz creates enough difficulties without shifting our standard for audible comparison of scales and chords depending upon the tonality of a portion of a song which may be fleeting. In addition, when reading the chord symbols one routinely encounters in jazz, the symbols are uniformly interpreted regardless of key or harmonic function. Consequently, in jazz when one encounters the chord symbol for an a–6th chord in a chord chart or lead sheet, it is understood that the notes of that chord will be *A, C, E,* and *F♯.* This chord will not contain an *F♮*! Conversely, if the chord were intended to have an *F♮,* it would be called an a–♭6, or even an a–♯5 if the *F♮* were enharmonically named, or functioning as an *E♯.*[9]

So my terminology is based on an intervallic comparison of all scales and all modes using one standard, and the Major scale is that standard. And this terminology corresponds to the accepted nomenclature for chord symbols found in jazz. Hence, Melodic minor contains the Δ6th and Δ7th degrees as they appear in the Major scale, and the Aeolian mode contains a flatted version of these same 6th and 7th degrees in my terminology. Since the student must primarily learn to hear and recognize the differences in all scale and chord construction, the terminology used to explain them is of secondary importance.

Anyway, Schoenberg sums up his discussion of the pivot tones (the two differing forms of the 6th and 7th degrees formed in the ascending and descending forms of the traditional minor scale) with what he calls "the *four laws of the pivot tones . . . of the minor scale.*"[10] (I'll use my terminology to avoid any confusion.) They are:

(1) First pivot tone: Δ7 (g♯ in *a* [Melodic] minor) must move upward to the tonic (*a* in *a* minor), because Δ7 (g♯ in *a* minor) functions as the leading tone. Δ7 (g♯ in *a* minor) must not precede or follow ♭7 or ♭6 (g♮ or f♮ in *a* minor).

(2) Second pivot tone: Δ6 (f♯ in *a* [Melodic] minor) must go to Δ7 (g♯ in *a* minor), for it appears only for the sake of Δ7 (g♯ in *a* minor) and may not precede or follow ♭6 or ♭7 (f♮ and g♮ in *a* minor).

(3) Third pivot tone: ♭7 (g♮ in *a* minor) must go to ♭6 (f♮ in *a* minor), because it belongs to the descending form of the scale (Aeolian). Neither Δ6 nor Δ7 (f♯ nor g♯ in *a* minor) may precede or follow it.

(4) Fourth pivot tone: ♭6 (f♮ in *a* minor) must go to 5 (*e* in *a* minor), because it belongs to the descending form of the scale (Aeolian). Δ6 (f♯ in *a* minor) may not precede or follow it.

These rules are based on the assumption that chords are properly voice led, giving each voice (note of a chord) an independent life. So if any voice sounds one of these pivot tones, that voice must adhere to the rules guiding the proper use of those pivot tones, hence the difficulties and the prohibition of mixing the two forms (ascending and

---

[8] Arnold Schoenberg, *Theory of Harmony,* trans. Roy E. Carter (Berkeley and Los Angeles: University of California Press, 1983), 98.
[9] Of course, these chords may be heard (and in fact may be functioning) as inversions of other chords, i.e., a–6 is an inversion of f♯Ø7, and a–♭6 is an inversion of an FΔ7 chord. But it is common to encounter these chords in jazz represented as a–6 and a–♭6, or a–♯5.
[10] Schoenberg, *Theory of Harmony,* 98.

descending) in one chord or progression. While these restrictions may be a bit too limiting for zealous application in jazz, with its shifting tonal centers, their use as guidelines does in fact clarify the tonal functions of chord progressions and lines constructed in minor tonalities. And I would suggest that students refrain from mixing chords from the two forms of the Traditional minor scale back to back, and pay close attention to the pivot tones, striving to hear where they want to go when using these scales in improvisation, especially in tonalities which are clearly minor. Closely examine (and listen to) the triads and chords constructed on the two different versions of the Traditional minor scale. Play them and listen carefully to them (see example 22).

Just like Major, in minor tonalities you will find chord tones, passing tones, available tensions, and approach tones. I've given you some exercises similar to those we used in Major, in three forms starting with the first inversion, designed to help you to hear the consonant-dissonant relationship of the chord tones to the passing tones and how they differ in the two forms of the triads diatonically constructed on the Traditional minor scale (exercises 11 through 13).

Exercise 11

Exercise 12

Exercise 13

Now let's turn our attention to the Harmonic minor scale. The Harmonic minor scale has the same form ascending and descending. This scale has an awkward place in the history of (classical) harmony because of the problems created by the +2nd interval that occurs between its 6th and 7th degrees (example 23).

Example 23

Harmonic minor

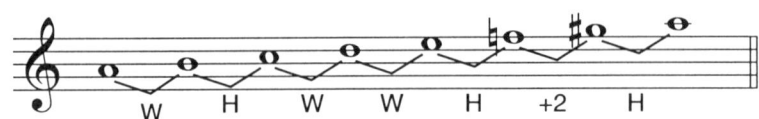

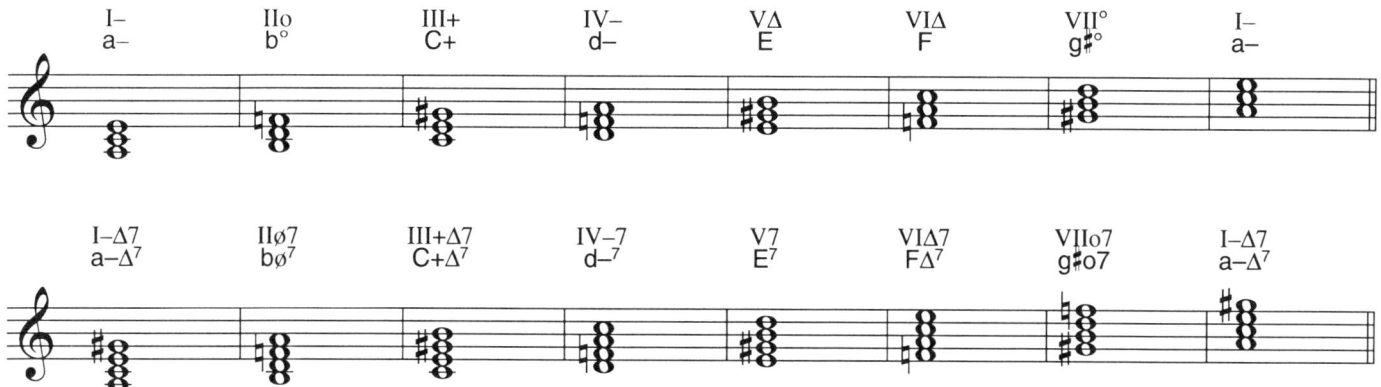

The old guidelines for the preparation and resolution of dissonances in counterpoint required a dissonance to begin (this is the preparation) as a consonance, then as one or more voices moved, one or more of the consonant voices remained the same, creating a dissonant relationship with the voices that moved. This dissonance was supposed to be resolved in stepwise fashion, usually down, but up was also used. As the name implies, stepwise fashion requires either a half step or a whole step move. So the +2nd (which could also be interpreted as a minor 3rd) that occurs between the 6th and 7th degrees of the Harmonic minor scale created a problem that was dealt with by avoiding it or, in extreme cases, prohibiting its use.

The following exercises (14 through 16) mirror those on the Traditional minor (minor exercises 11 through 13), except they are in Harmonic minor. Exercise 16 is an open form of the root position voicings, which lays better on the guitar fingerboard than the root position closed voicings employed in minor exercise 13 and in Major exercise 8. You should pay close attention to the problematic +2nd interval occurring between the b6th and Δ7th degrees, particularly where they occur as either upper or lower neighboring tones, and judge for yourself where these dissonances are useful and where they are just cacophonous. While playing these exercises, listen with an ear toward considering Schoenberg's "four laws of the pivot tones," because this scale (the Harmonic minor) in effect mixes the two forms (ascending Δ7 and descending b6) of the Traditional minor, which he warns against. I think you'll see he is largely correct, but, as always, judge for yourself!

Exercise 14

Exercise 15

Exercise 16

J.S. Bach was among the first to use chords created from this scale, even while avoiding the linear use of the +2nd interval found between its 6th and 7th degrees. Bach rightly heard the potential for additional means of resolution created by the O7th chord that exists diatonically on the 7th degree of this scale, and which itself contains the +2nd, in inversion within its chord tones. In the key of *a* (Harmonic) minor, the VIIO7 chord would be g#O7. The outer voices of this chord in root position closed are *g#* (bottom voice) and *f#* (top voice). This diminished 7th interval is in fact an +2nd interval inverted (example 24).[11]

Example 24

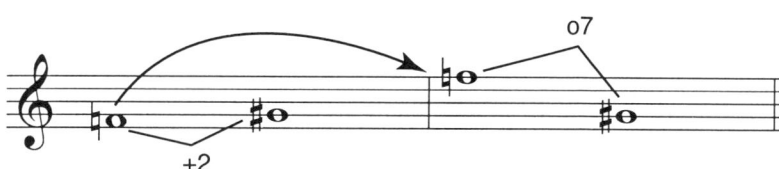

[11] As long as the rules guiding the use of the pivot tones are followed, i.e., *g#* (Δ7) goes up to *a* (tonic of a–), and *f#* (b6) goes down to *e* (5th of a– chord), this chord (g#O7 or any of its inversions) is a clear exception that works well despite the fact that it mixes pivot tones from the two different forms of the Traditional minor scale in one chord voicing and/or progression.

One of the best possible ways to establish a key is to create a V7 to I resolution. When voice leading such a resolution it is advisable to lead the parts so as to take advantage of the contrary motion created when the tritone (+4th or O5th) interval which naturally occurs between the 3rd and 7th of the V7 chord resolves in contrary motion to the root and 3rd of the I chord. (In the key of a minor the V7 chord would be E7, and its 3rd and 7th would be *g♯* and *d♮*, while the I– chord would be a minor whose root is *a*, which the *g♯* resolves up to, and whose 3rd is *c,* to which the *d* resolves down; example 25).

Example 25

The potential for employing contrary motion to resolve the tritone of a chord that would establish a tonality is doubled if a O7th chord is used, because all O7th chords are constructed of consecutive –3rds (an interval which is the same as an +2nd), and a group of three consecutive –3rds also contains two groups of tritones (+4ths). For a *g♯*O7 chord you have *g♯* and *d♮*, plus *b♮* and *f♮*. If you resolve the *b* to *c* and the *f* to *e*, you get another possibility for a resolution employing contrary motion of a different tritone (example 26). So *g♯*O7 going to a– gives you two possible tritones resolving in contrary motion. The first is *g♯* and *d♮* going to *a* and *c*. The second is *b♮* and *f♮* going to *c* and *e*. This means two voices, both *b♮* and *d♮*, are resolving to *c*, potentially creating a situation where a 4 note chord resolves to a 3 note chord. This only seems odd if you fail to observe the motion of the individual voices, something I'm loath to admit guitarists rarely do (example 26).

Example 26

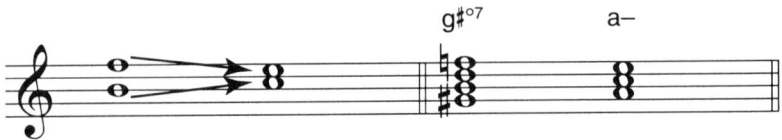

In his *Theory of Harmony* Arnold Schoenberg refers to both O7th chords and + chords as vagrant chords. Because of their potential for multiple resolutions, their function can only be determined by observing (i.e., hearing) where they go. Hence, they are homeless until they light somewhere. We will deal with this in more detail later. However, I think there is a great deal of truth in this idea about vagrant chords. A O7 chord can be heard to function as a V7 chord with its root replaced by the O7th (note) of the O7th chord. This note in the case of a *g♯*O7 chord (substituting for an E7 chord) would be *f♮* and could also be interpreted as *♭9* replacing the tonic (of the E7 chord it is substituting for). Jazz musicians often take advantage of the ambiguities these vagrant chords create, coming up with unorthodox resolutions that take the music to interesting places. For example, pianist Bill Evans frequently employed alternate tritones from a diminished chord over a different root motion (often supplied by the bass player) to resolve a dominant 7th♭9 chord that had no 3rd in it, to a I chord, or, deceptively, to ♭VI. He might take a three note voicing comprised of *b, d,* and *f♮* over an *e♮* (bass note) and resolve it to an a– chord, or resolve it to an a–6 chord (which in turn could be interpreted as the first inversion of an f♯Ø7 chord), or even resolve it to an FΔ7 chord (example 27).

Example 27

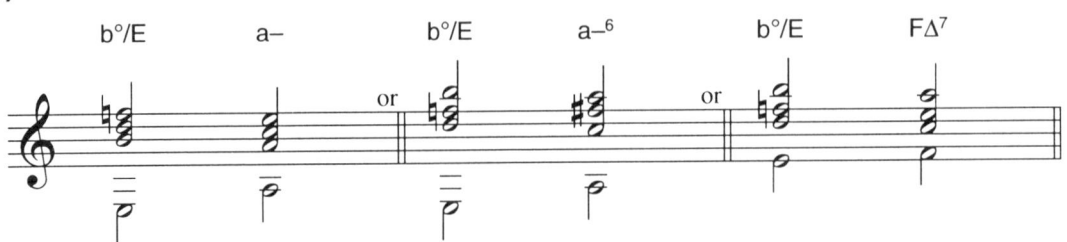

Determining the harmonic functions of the various chords diatonically constructed on each degree of the different minor scales is similar to the process we employed with the chords constructed in the Major tonalities, that is: examining the differences and learning to recognize those differences when encountered in the chord changes of a piece of music.

First let's make an intervallic comparison of the structure of each of the minor scales. As with the intervallic comparison we did of the seven modes of the Major scale, we will use the Major scale as the model for comparison. So, with Major being represented as 1, 2, 3, 4, 5, 6, 7, and 1 (or 8), this means all minor scales will have a ♭3rd, so observe the other differences and learn to hear and recognize them.

The differences among the various minor scales exist primarily on the 6th and 7th degrees, with an additional difference in Phrygian, which occurs on the 2nd degree. So lines and/or chords containing these differences are the distinguishing factors we must pay attention to when identifying harmonic functions within various minor tonalities. They are also devices we need to employ when creating lines and voicings that possess harmonic clarity within the various minor tonalities.

I have not included the Traditional minor scale in the intervallic comparison, because it is constructed from Melodic minor (ascending) and Aeolian (descending), which are both included (example 28).

Example 28 – Intervallic Comparison of Minor Scales

When we continue the process of building diatonically constructed chords by adding a 3rd above the 7th, we get the 9th. And just as with the 3rds, 5ths, and 7ths of all the chords we have previously constructed, the intervallic structure of each scale creates differences among the chords this process yields. In other words, just as some 3rds are Major, and some are minor, and some 7ths are Major, tand some are minor, so, too, some 9ths are ♮, and some are ♭9ths, and in Harmonic minor, one is even ♯9.

47

Diatonically constructing 9th chords built in 3rds on Melodic minor, Aeolian, and Harmonic minor yields many of the sophisticated chords often used in jazz, such as Ø7 9, ♭9th, +Δ79, and −Δ79 chords. These particular chords don't diatonically occur in Major tonalities, while some of the others do, such as −7 9, 7 9, Ø7 ♭9, etc. The harmonic functions of all of these chords and the appropriate chord scales to use with them are determined in much the same way as with the diatonic chords of Major tonalities. So let's take a look at the chords these scales yield and compare them (example 29).

Example 29

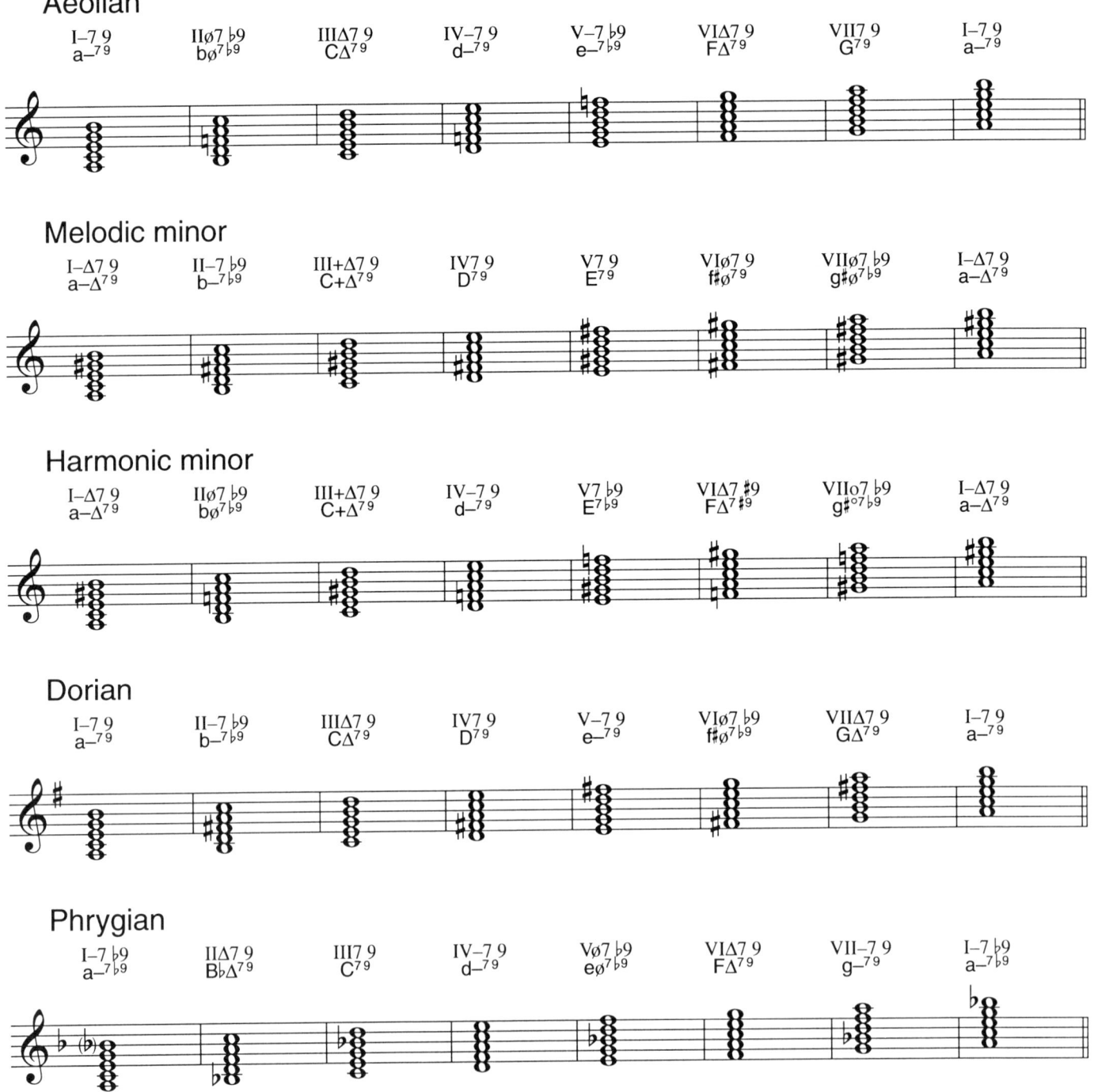

Some of these chords, when extended to the 9th, are impractical, because their diatonically constructed upper structures create 9ths (as well as 11ths and 13ths) that are so dissonant in relationship to their other chord tones that these notes cannot really function as available tensions. In other words, these notes can only function as either diatonic passing tones or as chromatic approach tones. When functioning as chromatic approach tones, they are no more or less available than any other chromatic dissonance. They can rarely be rested on except to create effect, and must be handled with great care!

Chords such as the –7♭9 from the IInd degree of the Melodic minor scale and the Vth degree of the Aeolian are good examples of how impractical some of these chords can be (example 30).

Example 30

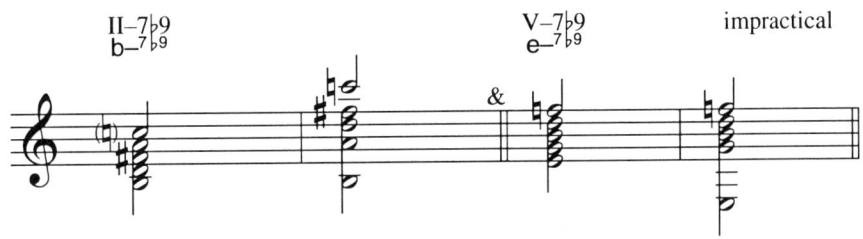

Others, like the Ø7 9 chord constructed on the VIth degree of the Melodic minor scale, and the +Δ7 9 chord constructed on the IIIrd degrees of both the Melodic minor and Harmonic minor scales, are so rich in complex overtones that even though they are very useful, they must be handled properly (example 31).

Example 31

On the other hand, the dominant 7♭9 chord constructed on the Vth degree of the Harmonic minor scale is one of the most commonly occurring and versatile chords in jazz (example 32).

Example 32

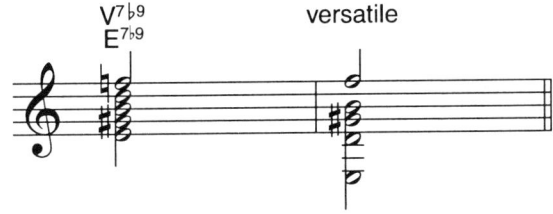

And the –7 9 chords built on the I[st] and IVth degrees of Aeolian, and the IVth degree of the Harmonic minor scale are very common and so indistinguishable from one another and the –7 9 chords which diatonically occur on the IInd and VIth degrees of Major tonalities, that they are easy to use, even though their function can only be determined by the context in which they occur (example 33).

Example 33

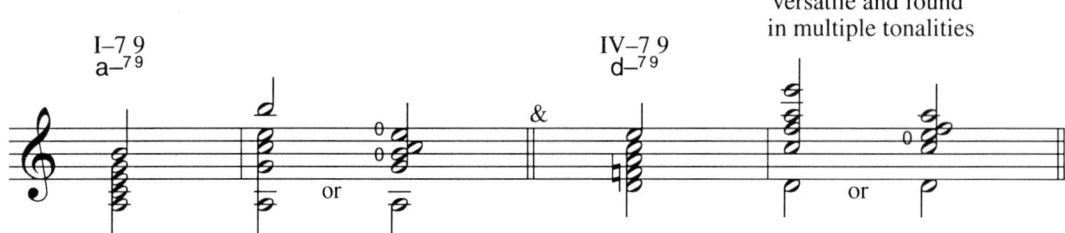

The same is true of the dominant 7 9 chords found on the VIIth degree of Aeolian, and the IVth and V[th] degrees of the Melodic minor scale. These dominant 7th chords with a ♮9th are virtually indistinguishable from the V7♭9 chords diatonically occurring in Major tonalities (or any secondary dominant chord with a ♮9th, which we will address shortly), and, like the chords in example 33, their harmonic function can be ambiguous when they are taken out of context (example 34).

Example 34

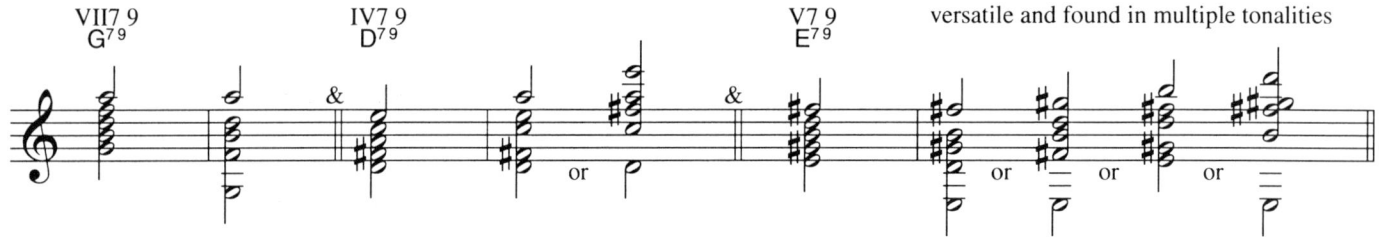

The I–Δ7 9 chords found on the I[st] degree of both the Melodic minor scale and the Harmonic minor scale are quite useful and occur diatonically only in these tonalities (example 35).

Example 35

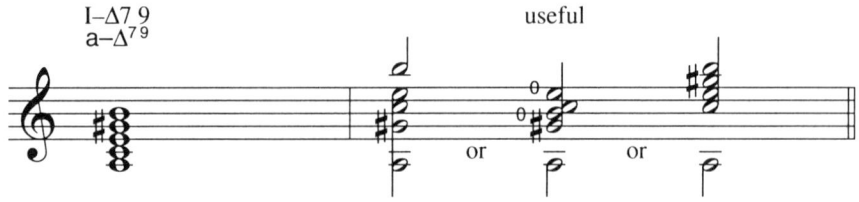

However, the IIØ7 (♭9) found in both the Aeolian and Harmonic minor scales, which is identical to the VIIØ7 (♭9) found diatonically in Major tonalities, is impractical due to its dissonant ♭9th (example 36).

Example 36   # Example 37

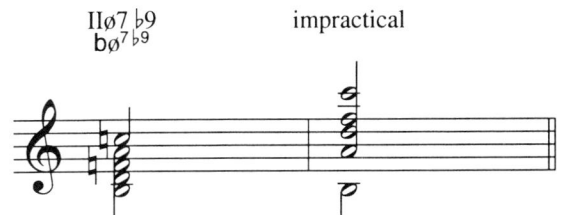

Also impractical but a bit more useful is the diminished 7♭9 chord built on the VIIth degree of the Harmonic minor scale (example 37).

Since many of these chords are unplayable on the guitar in the root position closed voicings in which they appear in the theoretical examples, I am showing them in playable voicings next to the theoretical examples, so you can play them, listen to them, and judge their usefulness for yourself (examples 30 through 37). But as you play the compositions that comprise the second half of this book and play through other jazz compositions, keep your ears open, because many of these chords do occur in the music.

Now let's examine the modes of the various minor tonalities and their chord-scale relationships. We will concentrate on the modes of the Melodic minor and the Harmonic minor, because the modes of Dorian, Phrygian, and Aeolian would in effect be modes of modes, and, as mentioned before (prior to example 28), the Traditional minor is comprised of the Melodic minor scale (which is included here) and the Aeolian mode (which was previously covered). There are, however, some other ways of interpreting non-tonic modal chords from the modes, which we will address in the modal section of this book. The various modes and their corresponding diatonic chords from Melodic minor and Harmonic minor cover many of the sophisticated chord-scale relationships encountered in the music of modern jazz musicians whose approaches are still rooted in a tonal sensibility, such as Herbie Hancock, Wayne Shorter, Joe Zawinul, and Joe Henderson.

In the following exercises (17 and 18), the chords that are not extended to the 9th are the ones whose diatonic upper structures are too dissonant for these chords' 9[th]s to function as available tensions. These 9[th]s appear as quarter notes in parentheses.

The first voicing for each chord is in root position closed, and therefore virtually unplayable on the guitar. The second voicing of each chord is playable on the guitar and is made so in some cases by substituting the 9th for the 5th of the chord. The IV 9 chord (in root position) shows the ♯11 in parentheses, because it is the Lydian indicator note, and it (♯11) and 9 are both included in the 2nd voicing (which is playable on the guitar) to help you hear this tonality more clearly. These voicings are followed by arpeggios of each chord, which in turn are followed by each chord's corresponding chord-scale (mode).

Exercise 17

Melodic minor

Exercise 18

Harmonic minor

Two of the modes of the Melodic minor scale, i.e, the one built on the 4ᵗʰ degree (the Lydian ♭7 scale), and the one built on the 7ᵗʰ degree (the Altered Dominant scale), are in such common usage that they have acquired the names that I have indicated for them.

The same is true of the mode built on the 5ᵗʰ degree of the Harmonic minor scale, which is called the Dominant 7♭9 scale. This scale is often used for a dominant 7ᵗʰ chord resolving to a minor chord, especially if the ♭9 is contained in the melody (in the case of E7 going to a–, this indicator note would be F♮), or is contained in either the V7 (♭9) chord itself, or the chord preceding the V7 chord (for example, IIØ7 [b♭7] or ♭VIΔ7 [FΔ7]). Other modes of these scales (Melodic minor and Harmonic minor) are also quite useful. For example, a Ø7♭9 chord requires the mode built on the 6ᵗʰ degree of the Melodic minor scale. (This is the only place this chord exists diatonically!)

Let's examine the intervallic structures of the modes of these two minor scales and compare their respective differences (example 38). Since we have already subjected Dorian, Aeolian, and Phrygian to this analysis in the Major section of the book and will examine them in more detail in the modal section, we will exclude them for the time being. Remember we are still using the Major scale as our basis for comparison. The abbreviations Mm (for Melodic minor) and Hm (for Harmonic minor) are used. And since only a few of the modes of these scales have acquired names, I'll refer to the others by the number of the scale degree each mode begins on, along with the appropriate abbreviated prefix. For example, the mode built on the 2ⁿᵈ degree of the Harmonic minor scale will be represented as Hm 2.

Example 38

Mm6

1	2	♭3	4	♭5	♭6	♭7	8

Altered dominant

1	♭2	♭3	♭4	♭5	♭6	♭7	8

Harmonic minor

1	2	♭3	4	5	♭6	Δ7	8

Hm2

1	♭2	♭3	4	♭5	Δ6	♭7	8

Hm3

1	2	Δ3	4	#5	Δ6	Δ7	8

Hm4

1	2	♭3	#4	5	Δ6	♭7	8

Dominant 7 ♭9

1	♭2	Δ3	4	5	♭6	♭7	8

Hm6

1	#2	Δ3	#4	5	Δ6	Δ7	8

Hm7

1	♭2	♭3	♭4	♭5	♭6	♭♭7	8

Just like the chords diatonically occurring in Major tonalities, those that occur in minor tonalities relate to the chromatic scale as follows: These chords are themselves composed of **chord tones**, which may be approached by **passing tones** (which come from the chord-scale [mode] that best outlines their tonality). Some of these passing tones may also function as **available tensions**. Both the chord tones and available tensions (if handled properly) may also be approached by chromatic notes outside the key (of the moment), which are called **approach tones**.

This explanation mirrors the one in the Major sections, because all chords relate to the chromatic scale in the same way. Their respective differences lie in their own unique intervallic structure(s) (i.e., their chord tones) and their relationship to a tonality (which is exemplified by the chord scale that best outlines their tonality). And in virtually every case this arrangement (i.e., the chord scale that is unique to each chord in each situation) accounts for seven of the twelve notes of the chromatic scale in any musical circumstance, leaving only five notes unaccounted for.[12] These remaining five notes are never more than a half step away from a chord tone or available tension to which they could resolve in stepwise fashion.

The following seven studies which comprise exercise 19 mirror those at the end of the Major section and are designed to demonstrate a variety of means of approaching targeted chord tones with approach tones and upper or lower neighboring passing notes for chords found in Melodic minor tonalities. I've given no fingerings, because I want you to explore the many possibilities that exist on the fingerboard. Please bear in mind that the fingering(s) you use often determine(s) which phrasing possibilities are available. Try to think of this as you explore the various options. And do so with an ear toward making these phrases speak!

Exercise 19

---

[12] There are some scales, such as the whole tone (which has fewer than seven notes) and the symmetric diminished (which has more than seven notes), whose use would obviously either increase or decrease the number of notes left unaccounted for from the chromatic scale. We will address these scales in the chapter on vagrant chords.

While the particular studies in exercise 19 only deal with diatonic chords found in Melodic minor tonalities, the same approaches may be applied to the diatonic chords found in Harmonic minor tonalities as well. In fact, these methods of using (chromatic) approach tones and passing tones to target chord tones work for all chords.

Fingering guidelines are similar to those used for exercise 10 in the Major chapter, that is: locate the targeted note of each three-note grouping and visualize it in relationship to the tones approaching it. Use this visualization to locate a place on the fingerboard that will accommodate playing each three-note group on the same string, then move on to the next triplet using the targeted note as your guide. Except for the portions of these studies that employ double chromatic approach tones to approach the targeted notes, such as the second half of the I–Δ7 chord study, you'll find that the targeted note is the center of each three-note group, because even though the targeted note is the last note of each triplet, it is generally being approached from both above and below, making its physical location the <u>central</u> note of each triplet on the fingerboard. As always, I encourage the serious student to explore these methods in other tonalities on your own and to apply the result to all twelve keys!

Chapter 3: Modal Jazz

At the beginning of the chapter on minor tonalities, I alluded to the fact that in the late 1950s some jazz musicians had begun to experiment with an approach that focused on looser harmonic structures that were derived from the seven modes of the Major scale. This resulted in a different kind of improvisation, one that involved blowing on scales or modes over simple chord sequences. Previous approaches often involved relatively elaborate chord changes that could actually aid a soloist, in that dealing effectively with the harmonic obstacle course that these chord changes presented could be sufficient to give shape and direction to one's ideas. But the absence of any such harmonic framework required a higher degree of interaction between the soloist(s) and the rhythm section to achieve shape and direction. It is hard now to imagine what a quantum shift this was at the time. Yet Miles Davis's groundbreaking recording *Kind of Blue*, which established the standard for this approach, went unheralded by the critics at the time of its creation (1959). Miles's band for this recording contained two musicians whose approaches dramatically differed from one another, yet each was to profoundly affect the future development of jazz. The first was saxophonist John Coltrane, whose composition "Giant Steps" epitomized the harmonic obstacle course approach at its zenith and was recorded in the same year as *Kind of Blue*. The second was pianist Bill Evans, whose unique approach to harmony was the catalyst for Miles's initial excursions into the modal approach, which *Kind of Blue* exemplified.

This modal jazz approach still exerts a powerful influence on the way many musicians address jazz improvisation even today, because many of the chords found in the shifting tonal centers of more harmonically complex forms of jazz either imply modally-based harmonic structures or can be interpreted as if they do.

The basic modal approach involves the use of a dominant modal cadence. This is simply two chords which, when taken together, are sufficient to establish a modal tonality. All that is required to achieve such a dominant modal cadence is the appropriate modal tonic chord (i.e., one of the seven diatonic chords of the Major scale [IΔ7, II–7, III–7, IVΔ7, V7, VI–7, or VIIØ7]) which corresponds to the mode used, plus an additional diatonic chord from the same tonality which contains the note(s) that would distinguish this mode from any other that could correspond to a chord with the same intervallic structure as the tonic modal chord. For example, a *d* Dorian dominant modal cadence would need the chord that corresponds to this mode, i.e., d–7 (this is the tonic modal chord). And since there are three possible ways of modally interpreting the harmonic function of an isolated minor 7th chord (i.e., either Dorian, Phrygian, or Aeolian), we also need a chord which contains the note(s) that distinguish(es) Dorian from the other two possibilities (Phrygian and Aeolian).

If you remember our intervallic comparison of the modes of a Major tonality (example 8, p. 18), you know this means we need a chord which contains the note that corresponds to the Δ6th degree of this mode, (which would be a B♮ when measuring from the starting note of a d Dorian mode), because d Aeolian contains a B♭ (i.e., ♭6), and d Phrygian contains both a B♭ (♭6) and an E♭ (♭2). So either e–7 or G7 would be a good choice to go with the d–7 to create a dominant modal cadence for d Dorian, because both contain a B♮, and e–7 also contains an E♮ (example 39).

Example 39

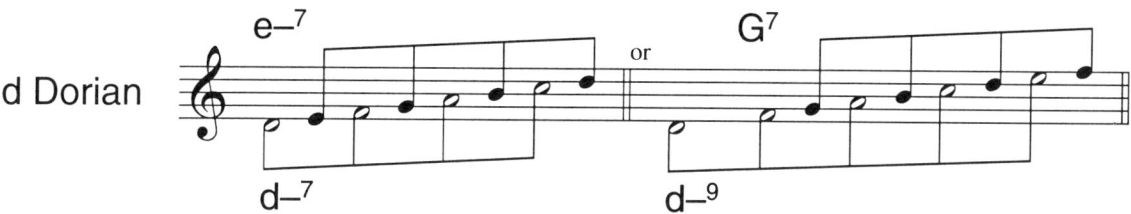

59

You can see from example 39 that d–7 and e–7 taken together cover all seven notes of the d Dorian mode. And while it appears that the absence of any kind of *E* (either ♮ or ♭) from the G7 chord could possibly create some ambiguity, in actuality there are no purely modal tonalities where both *E♭* and *B♮* coexist with the other notes found in the tonic modal chord (d–7).[13]

So d–7 to G7 is sufficient to infer d Dorian, even if it doesn't completely spell it out. And one could always add the *E♮* either as 9 to the d–7 (as I have done) or as 13 to the G7 in order to alleviate any confusion.

Let's examine the opening phrase from the theme of Miles Davis's famous tune "So What" from the aforementioned *Kind of Blue* (example 40).

Example 40

"So What"

© Miles Davis 1959

etc.

You can clearly hear the tonality (d Dorian) from the two chords (e–7 plus 4 and d–7 plus 4) that answer the bass line. This is a textbook example of how a dominant modal cadence immediately establishes a modal tonality.

If you don't already have a recording of Miles Davis's *Kind of Blue*, get it and listen carefully. Check out how much these great musicians make out of two Dorian modes a half step apart on "So What," and how each player's distinctive style stands out while blending into a cohesive unit. Some of you may recall that I previously praised Cannonball Adderley's playing on this recording. Pay close attention to how he masterfully varies his approach. At times he plays modally; at times he plays around the upper structures of the chords. At one point he even uses blues notes (during the e♭ Dorian section of his last chorus). He also uses chromatic approach tones to target available tensions, all the while swinging and telling a very soulful tale!

Now let's check out the dominant modal cadences for each of the seven modes. Actually, the tonality that corresponds to the 1st degree, Ionian (Major), is exemplified by the mother of all dominant cadences, i.e., V7 to IΔ(7), since virtually all cadences strive to achieve what this cadence naturally accomplishes, namely the clear establishment of a specific tonality (example 41).

Example 41 - Dominant Modal Cadences

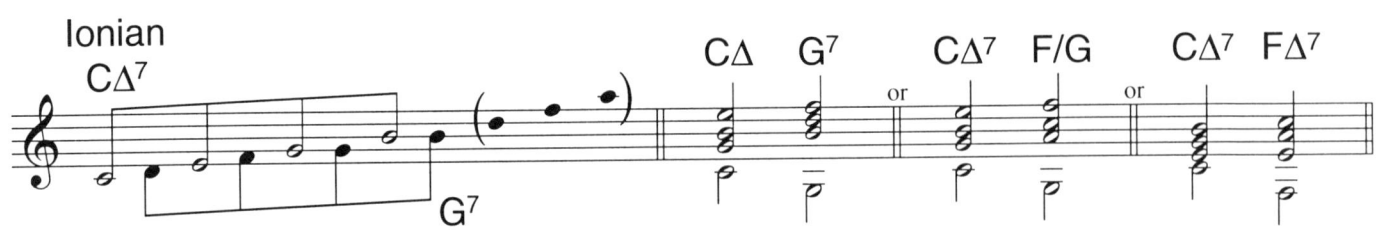

Ionian
CΔ7

G7

CΔ G7   CΔ7 F/G   CΔ7 FΔ7
       or   or

---

[13] There is of course the possibility of Mm2 (melodic minor from the 2nd degree), which contains all of these notes. But this scale doesn't really function modally, as it usually occurs with a II–7 that precedes a secondary dominant chord either containing or inferring ♮9 and ♭13, which resolves to a minor chord of some kind.

The second option (CΔ7 and F/G) as well as the third option (CΔ7 and FΔ7) are contemporary treatments which feel a bit more modal than the traditional IΔ7 and V7.

The Dorian dominant modal cadence is one that contains a minor 7th chord followed or preceded by another minor 7th chord whose root would be one whole step higher than that of the modal tonic chord. In d Dorian d–7 is the modal tonic chord, and e–7 would be the other chord. Another option is a dominant 7th chord whose root would be a perfect 5th below the root of the modal tonic chord. In d Dorian this would be G7. Both chords (either e–7 or G7) contain the prime Dorian indicator note Δ6 (*B♮* in d Dorian; example 42).

Example 42

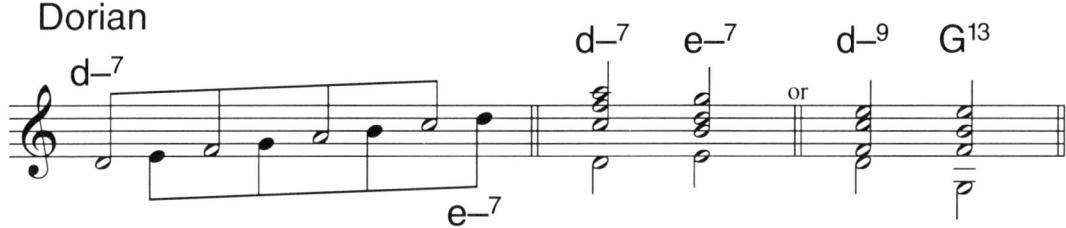

The Phrygian dominant modal cadence is created by using two adjacent diatonic chords a half step apart. The tonic modal chord is a minor 7th chord preceded or followed by a Major 7th chord whose root is a half step above the root of the tonic modal chord. This second chord contains both Phrygian indicator notes ♭2 and ♭6. In e Phrygian these two chords would be e–7, which is the tonic modal chord, and FΔ7 (♭IIΔ7), which when combined with the tonic modal chord clearly establishes the Phrygian tonality. This second chord functions much like a Neapolitan chord in classical harmony (example 43).

Example 43

The Lydian dominant modal cadence uses the tonic modal chord preceded or followed by a diatonic chord that contains the raised 4th degree, which is the Lydian indicator note, such as a Δ chord whose root is one whole step above the root of the tonic modal chord. In F Lydian the tonic modal chord would be FΔ7, and the other chord would be G(7). Often these two chords move over the root of the tonic modal chord, in effect using this note as a pedal (example 44).

Example 44

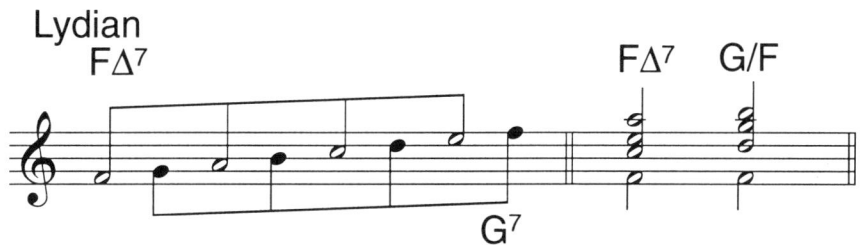

The Mixolydian dominant modal cadence commonly uses two Major triads whose roots are one whole step apart. In G Mixolydian G(7) would be the modal tonic chord, and F would be the other chord. Think of the rhythm guitar part that Phil Upchurch plays on George Benson's classic recording of the Lieber and Stoller R&B chestnut "On Broadway," and you'll recognize this Mixolydian dominant modal cadence (example 45).

Example 45

The Aeolian mode presents a situation similar to the one that Ionian represents, because this mode is often associated with either the relative minor or the tonic minor, and it can be interpreted in several ways. (Remember the descending form of the Traditional minor scale?) Any purely modal treatment must involve not only the tonic modal chord (in a Aeolian this would be an a–7 chord) but also a chord or combination of chords containing the ♭6th degree (f♮ in a Aeolian), such as IV–7 (d–7 in a Aeolian) preceding or following the tonic modal chord: I–7 (a–7 in a Aeolian). It also is common to encounter the ♭VIΔ chord, moving to the ♭VIIΔ chord, which moves to the I– chord as a cadence for Aeolian. In a Aeolian this would be F(Δ7), to G, to a– (example 46). Even though this root motion disregards Schoenberg's laws guiding the use of the pivot tones (because ♭6 goes to ♭7 instead of 5, which it could easily do), it (♭VI) is going to a chord that is an acceptable substitution for V– (i.e., ♭VII), and this modal cadence (which has its origins in ancient folk music) predates Schoenberg, whose guidelines were never intended for purely modal application.

Example 46

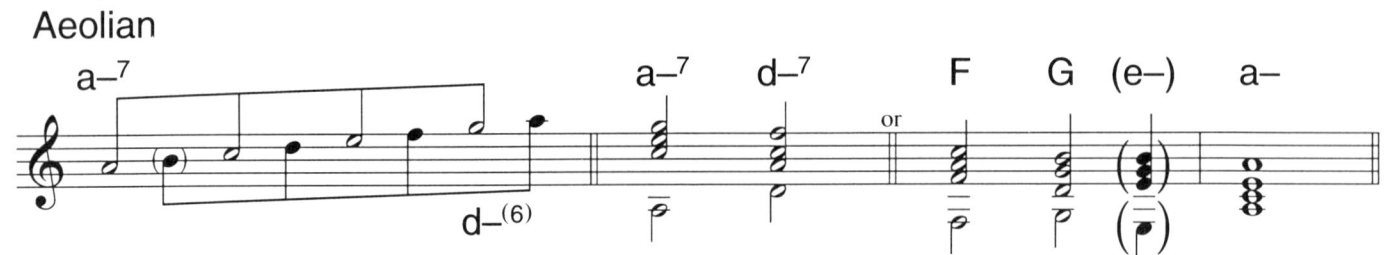

Locrian rarely occurs as a modal tonality on its own.[14] It often occurs in relation to a IIØ7 chord preceding a V7/of VI– in what is essentially a II V I progression in a minor tonality, or as one of a series of II V chord progressions in sequence (example 47).

[14] Joe Henderson's tune "Inner Urge" is a possible exception that employs a Ø7 chord as the first in a series of four chords built on a descending bass line (f♯Ø7, FΔ7♯11, E♭Δ7♯11, and D♭Δ7♯11) for the first part of the song. While not purely modal, the amount of time spent on each chord (four bars) renders its treatment as potentially modal, because if you stay on an f♯Ø7 chord for four bars, it begins to sound like an independent tonality, and likely candidates to define such a tonality would be f♯ Locrian or f♯ Mm6.

Example 47

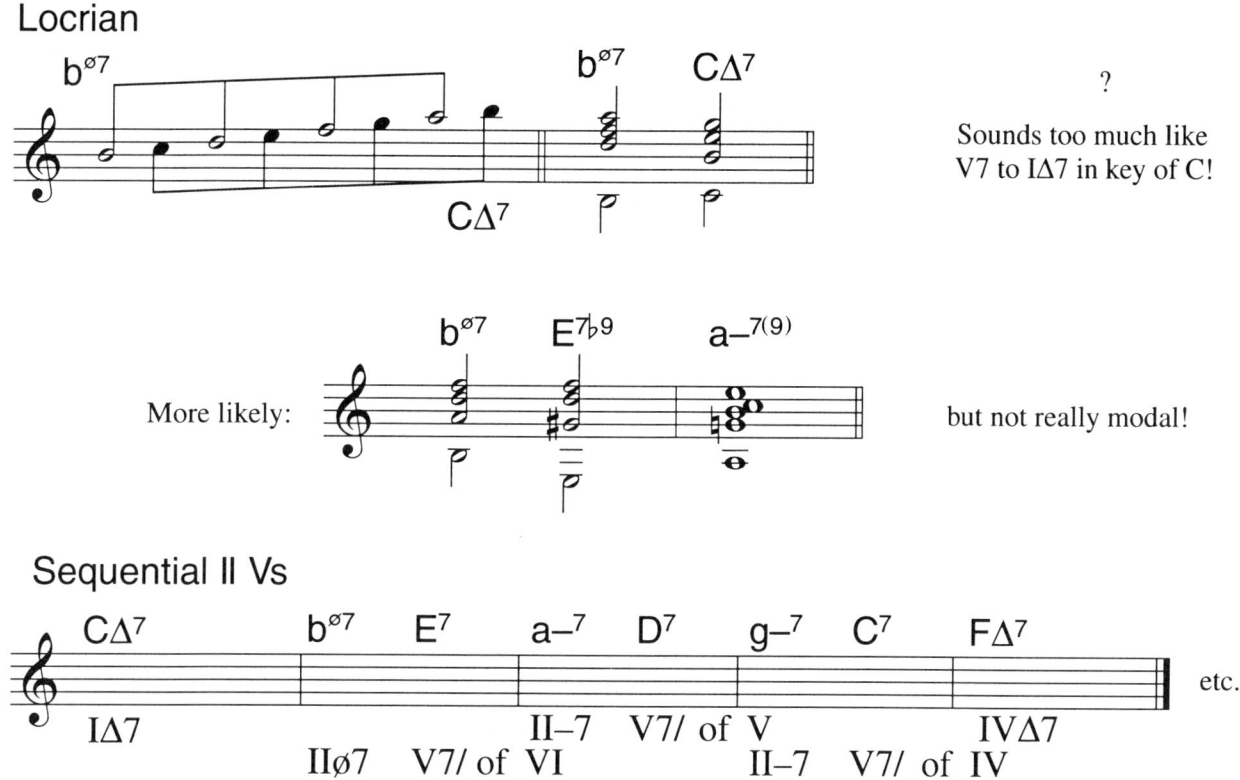

As you can hear, the dominant modal cadence in Locrian is not very convincing, because the augmented 4th interval that exists between the root and ♭5th of its tonic modal chord (B♮ and F♮ for b∅7) mirrors that found between the Δ3rd and ♭7th of the V7 (G7) chord taken from its relative Major key (C Major). This relationship is further reinforced by resolving to the very chord to which this V7 chord would naturally resolve: IΔ7 (i.e., CΔ7). So the modal tonic chord from the Locrian mode is very rarely treated modally. This doesn't mean we don't use the Locrian mode when we encounter ∅7 chords, however. It merely means we don't often find this chord functioning as a tonic modal chord for much the same reason that the Renaissance composers who wrote primarily with the church modes didn't often compose in the Locrian mode, because a ∅7 chord simply doesn't lend itself to sounding like the end of a phrase or a composition!

It is assumed that by now the student can recognize the basic differences between Major and minor, tonalities and chords. So we will make an intervallic comparison of the modes and their respective dominant modal cadences from the perspective of comparing those whose tonic modal chords either have identical intervallic structures (II–7, III–7, and VI–7) or sufficiently similar ones to potentially create some confusion (IΔ7, IVΔ7, and V7). We will do this in order to focus on the notes and chords that distinguish these similar tonalities from one another. As with the previous intervallic comparisons, the Major scale will be our basis, and each mode will begin with C. In addition, the root of each tonic modal chord will also be C.

First we will compare the three modes whose modal tonic chords are built upon Major triads, i.e, I, IV, and V (example 48).

Example 48

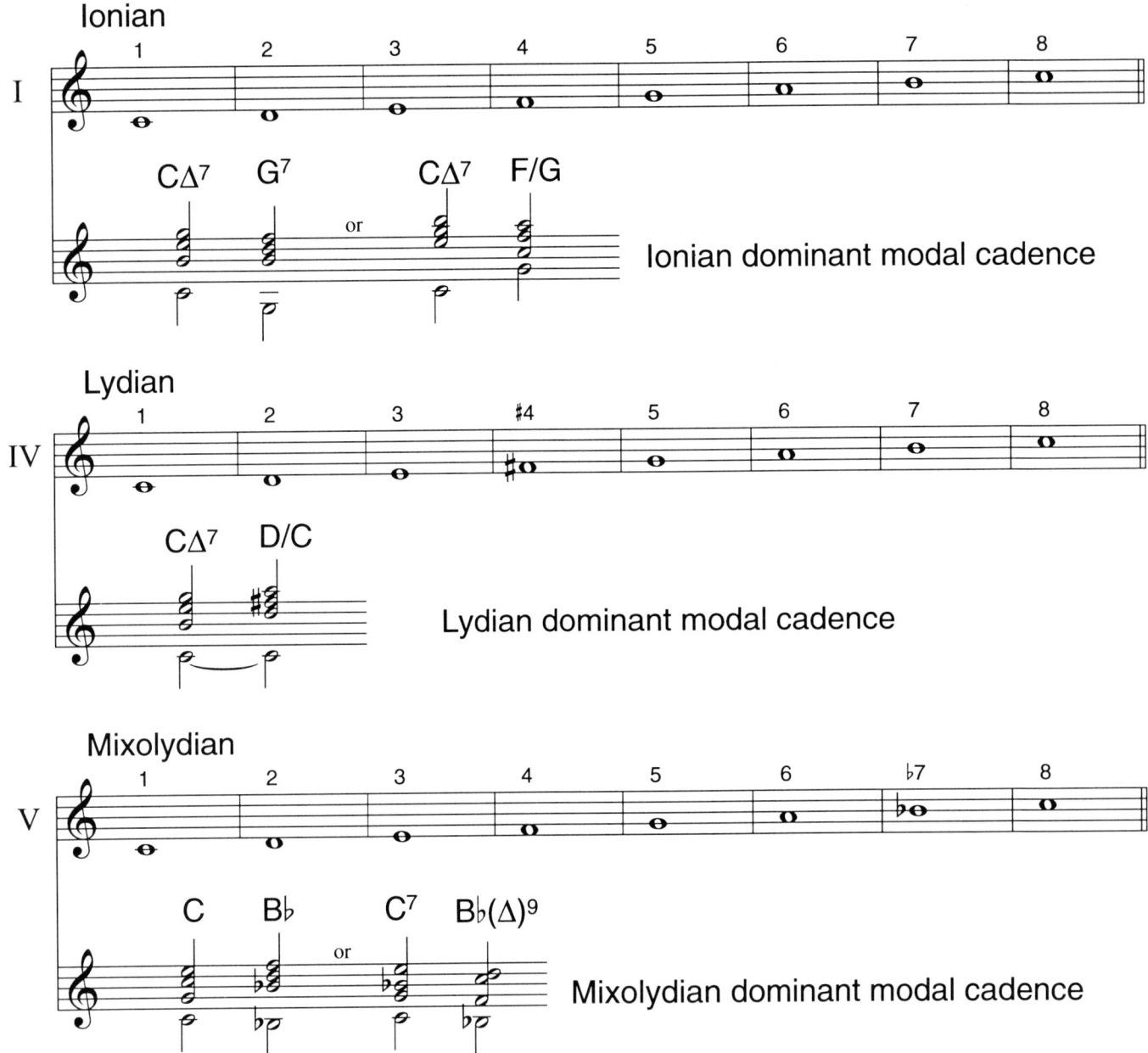

As you can hear (and see), both Ionian and Mixolydian differ from Lydian at the 4th degree, and Mixolydian differs from both Ionian and Lydian at the 7th degree (and consequently Mixolydian and Lydian differ from each other at both the 4th and 7th degrees). So hearing, recognizing, and emphasizing these distinct differences brings clarity to these three tonalities despite their similarities! This is true of both the modes themselves and the chords that comprise their respective dominant modal cadences.

If we examine the chords constructed on each degree of these three modes, we can find additional places where the differences that distinguish these tonalities from one another manifest themselves (example 49).

Example 49

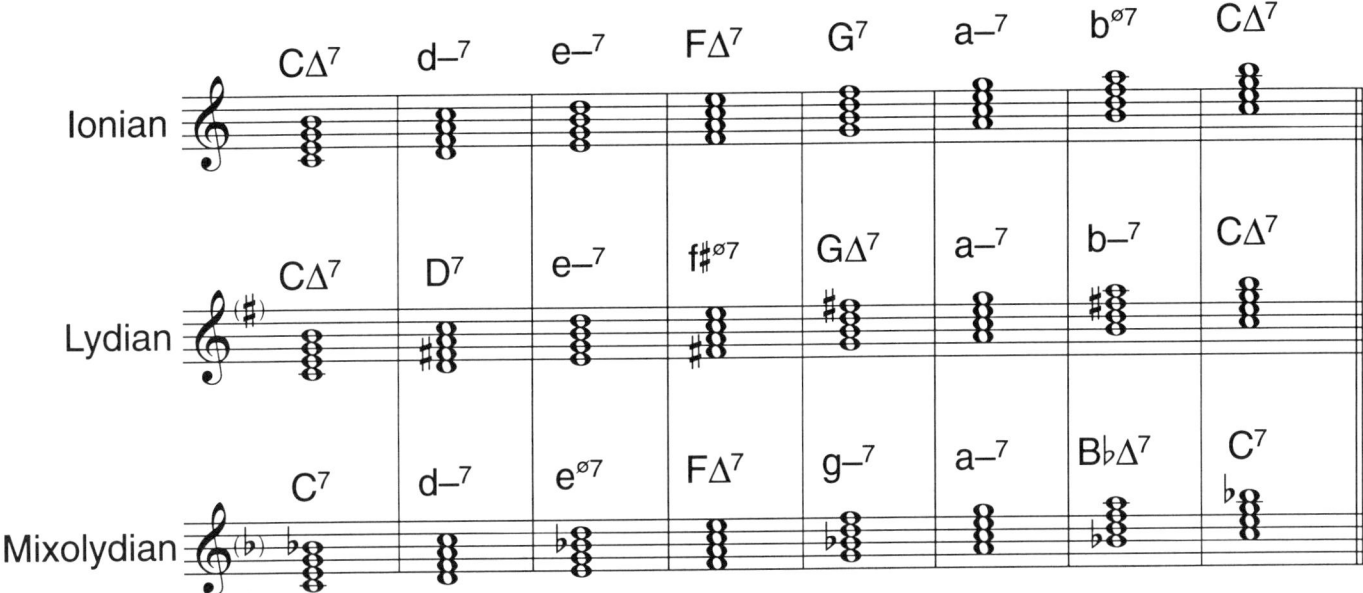

Now let's examine the three modal tonalities whose tonic modal chord each has the identical intervallic structure of a minor 7th chord, namely, II–7, III–7, and VI–7 (example 50).

Example 50

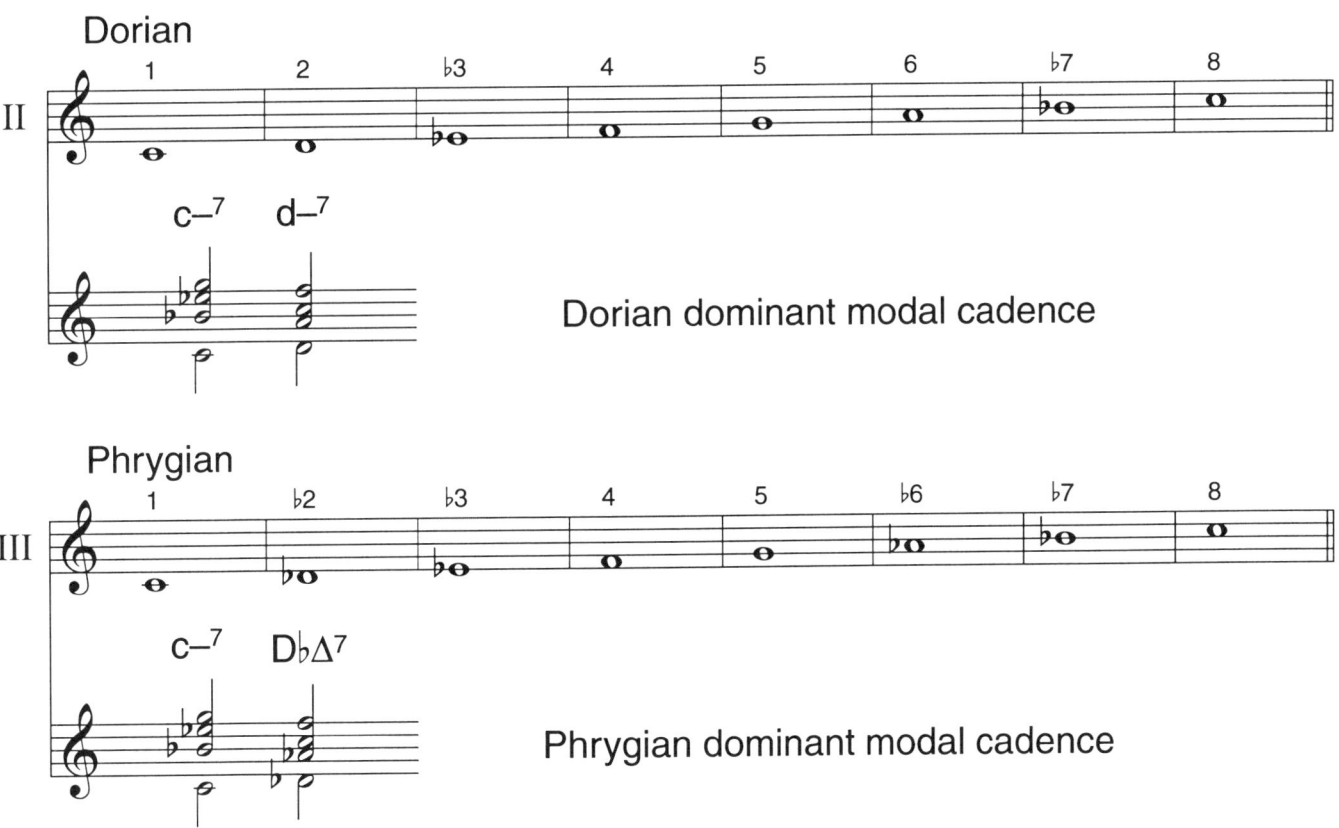

You can clearly hear that Dorian differs from both Phrygian and Aeolian at the 6th degree, and that Phrygian differs from both Dorian and Aeolian at the 2nd degree (and consequently Phrygian differs from Dorian at both the 2nd and 6th degrees). Just as with the three previous modes we compared (Ionian, Lydian, and Mixolydian), hearing, recognizing, and employing the distinct differences which distinguish these modes from one another is the key to using them correctly.

Now let's examine the various chords constructed on each degree of these three modes, i.e., Dorian, Phrygian, and Aeolian (example 51).

Example 51

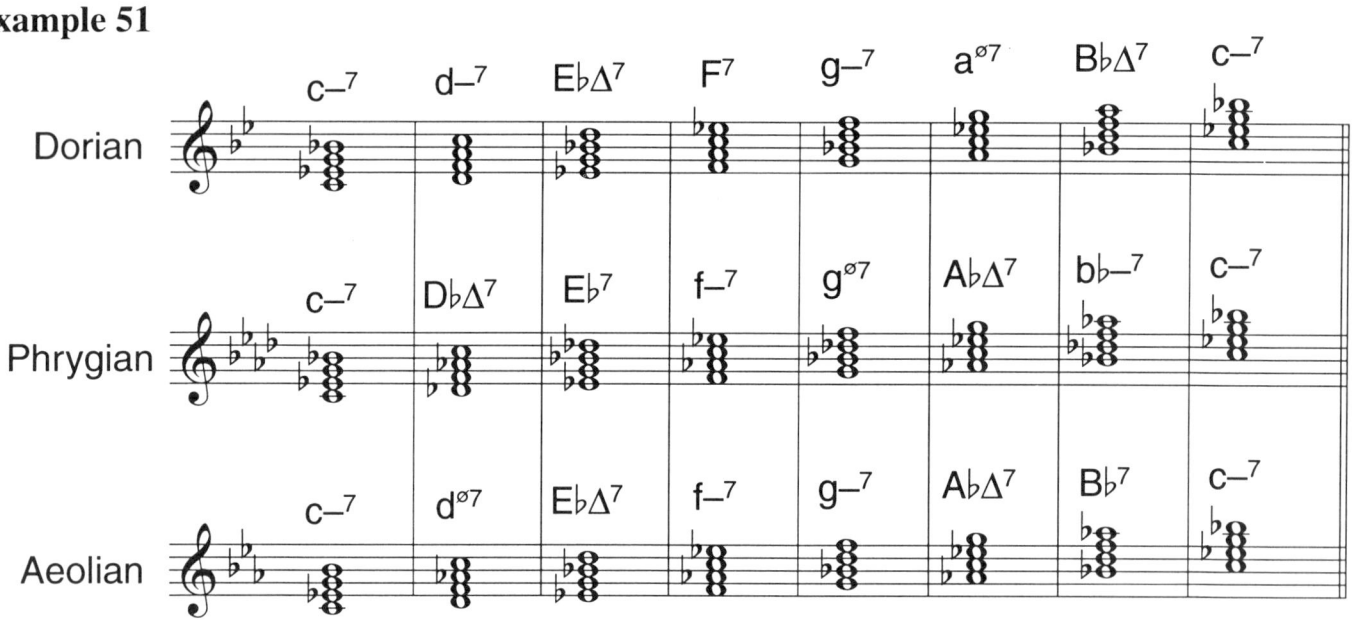

These chords reveal other means of distinguishing these three minor modal tonalities from one another.

Some of you may have noticed the Roman numerals at the left hand margins of examples 48 and 50, which indicate each mode's relationship to its parent Major tonality. And you probably recognized the I IV V relationship between the three Major tonalities in example 48 as that of the three chord relationship of the blues. Well, the same relationship applies to the three minor tonalities found in example 50, since VI is to II and III as I is to IV and V. This is because the basis of our entire musical system is a cyclical numerical structure which correlates the first seven letters of the alphabet with the notes of an Aeolian mode (*a, b, c, d, e, f,* and *g*), meaning that if the modal tonality represented as VI (Aeolian) is considered I, then II (Dorian) becomes IV, and III (Phrygian) becomes V. In other words, if *a*–7 is I, then *d*–7 is IV, and *e*–7 is V. And just like the I IV V relationship in Major, this I IV V relationship in minor is the basis for another kind of blues called a minor blues. This doesn't necessarily imply that these modes have to be used for blues; it merely infers something deeper about the interrelatedness of our harmonic system and the blues-based foundations of jazz, which we will explore in greater detail later.

I have omitted Locrian from the intervallic comparison of the modes and their dominant modal cadences because, as I demonstrated in example 47, its modal tonic chord doesn't really function as a tonic chord of a modal tonality. But I will include Locrian in the exercise vamps which follow, since you do need to acquire facility with this mode, because it is often used for the IIØ7 chord in II V I progressions in minor tonalities, and for IIØ7 chords preceding secondary dominant chords.

In the following exercises (20-26) I have given you chordal vamps comprised of variations on the dominant modal cadences for each mode. You should play the vamps and then improvise with the mode that corresponds to each vamp. You can do this alone, with another guitarist, another instrumentalist, or record these vamps yourself and play with that recording. But the key is to explore the modes you're using all over the fingerboard. For example, limit your exploration of a particular mode to two octaves in one position across six strings, then limit yourself to one string up and down the fingerboard (try each of the six strings [or more if you have them]), then try to play on just two adjacent strings (and try each group of two adjacent strings [i.e., 1 and 2, 2 and 3, 3 and 4, 4 and 5, 5 and 6, etc.]), then try groups of three adjacent strings, then try using each mode through three octaves (in some cases this means you can't go from root to root). Don't always start with the root of the modal tonic chord. Instead, try starting with the 3rd, 5th, or 7th of the tonic modal chord. Learn to hear each tonality's various relationships among the chord tones, passing tones, and available tensions that comprise each mode.

Today many players are so accustomed to playing with practice tapes, CDs, and/or software programs that they are reluctant to play a vamp long enough to get it sufficiently imbedded in their memory banks that they can then improvise over it with only their imaginations to accompany them. Despite the fact that this may seem unnecessarily difficult, in all honesty it is how I learned to improvise. And while it may take some time to get used to this approach, it's well worth the effort, because you won't just be exercising your chops, you'll also be exercising your imagination. And imagination is the cornerstone of musical creativity!

Modal Vamp Exercises

Exercise 20

Exercise 21

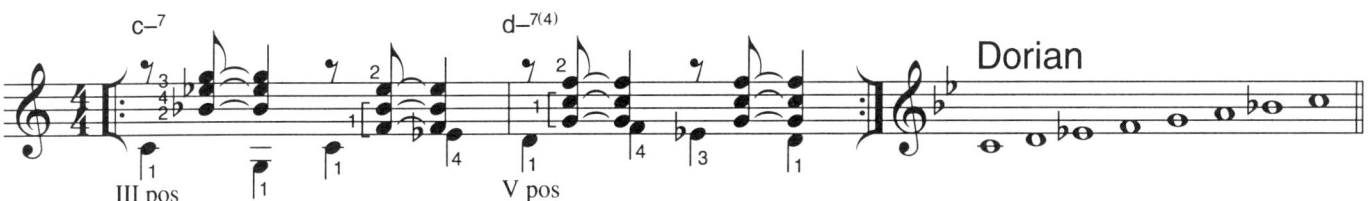

Exercise 22

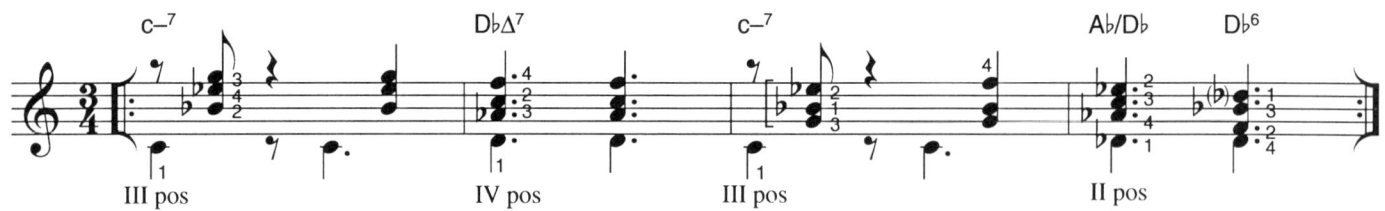

Exercise 23

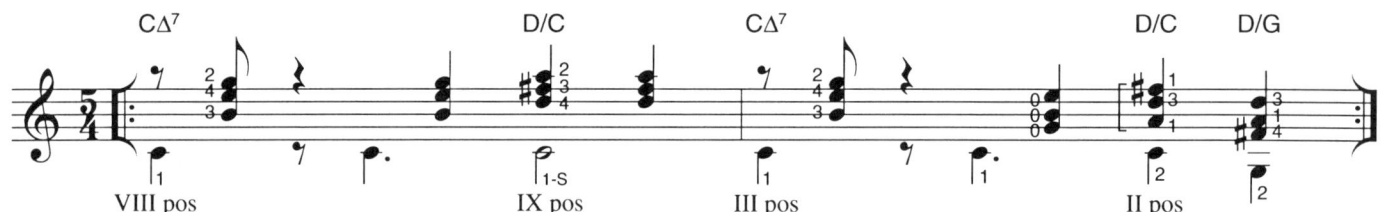

Exercise 24

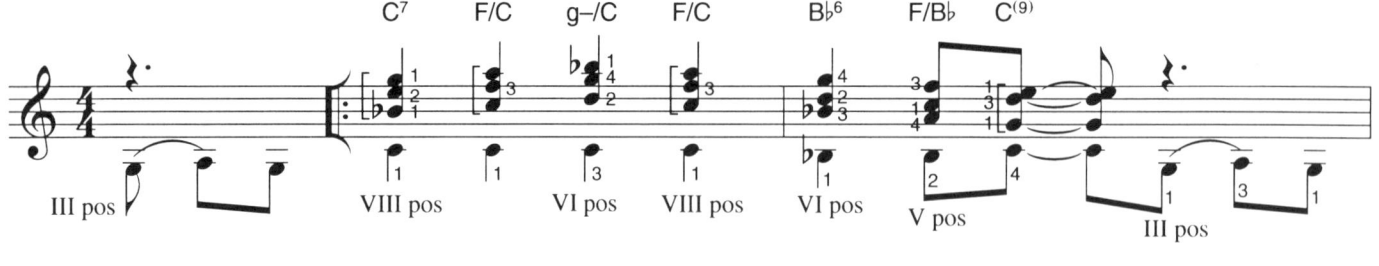

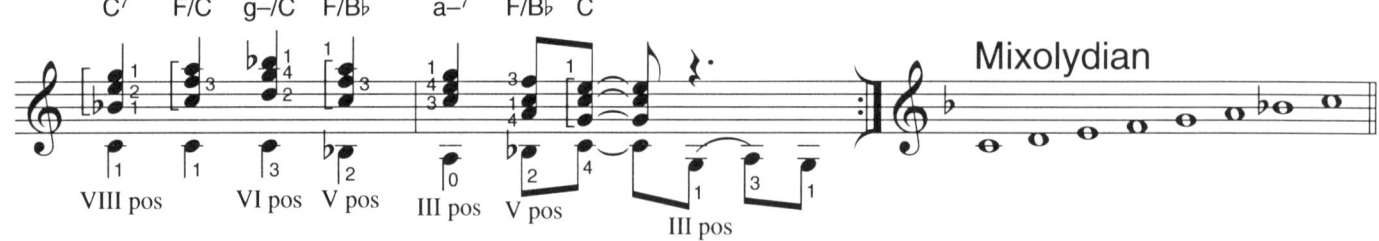

Exercise 25

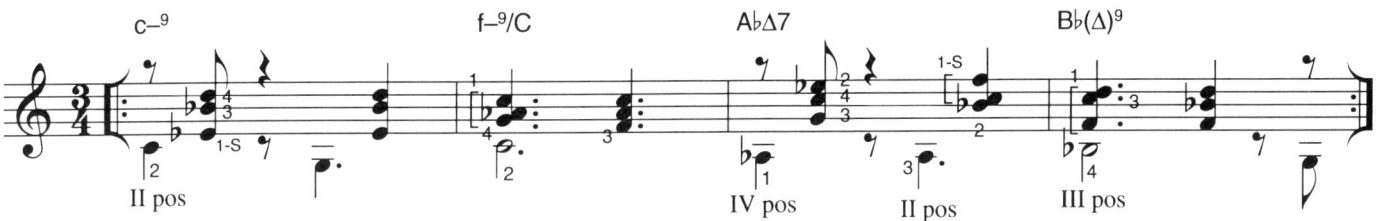

Exercise 26

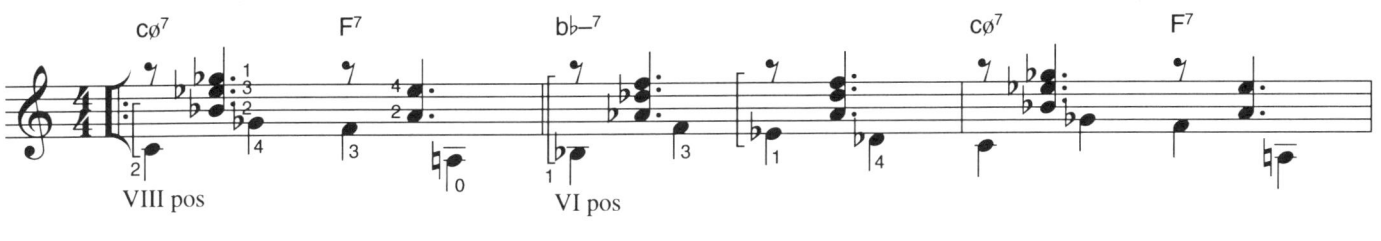

As with all the material in this book, make sure you explore the remaining eleven keys for each mode and its corresponding dominant modal cadence. Also explore each mode by moving around the circle of fifths, both clockwise (i.e., *c* Dorian to *g* Dorian, to *d* Dorian, etc.) and counterclockwise (i.e., *c* Dorian to *f* Dorian, to *bb* Dorian, etc.), and explore each mode moving chromatically as well (i.e., *c* Phrygian to *c#* Phrygian, to *d* Phrygian, etc.). Then explore them in relationship to their relative Major (parent) tonalities (i.e., all the modes of C Major [*C* Ionian, *d* Dorian, *e* Phrygian, *F* Lydian, *G* Mixolydian, *a* Aeolian, and *b* Locrian]), proceeding both ways around the circle of fifths and chromatically. Also try different tempos and experiment with changing the time signatures of each exercise, and try inventing your own modal vamps.

Chapter 4:
Secondary Dominant Chords

Many of the songs that one finds in the jazz repertoire were created by very skilled composers who wrote them for Broadway musicals produced during a period that roughly spans the early 1920s through the early 1960s. In addition to being imaginative and inquisitive, most of these talented composers were musically educated. Their approach is exemplified by the work of composers such as George Gershwin, Jerome Kern, Cole Porter, Harold Arlen, and Richard Rodgers, who were influenced by both classical music and jazz music. And their songs in turn exerted a powerful influence on the jazz musicians who improvised on them, as well as the jazz arrangers and composers who admired them.

Quite a few of the popular tunes from this period have become staples of the jazz repertoire and are called "standards." Of the numerous sophisticated harmonic devices employed in these standards, one of the most prevalent is the secondary dominant chord. A secondary dominant chord is a chord that functions as the dominant (V) of a chord other than the tonic (I). No matter how one explains the evolution of the secondary dominant chord, it is historically clear that its use predates the development of both jazz and the genre of the show tune.

I believe it quite likely that secondary dominant chords evolved out of a process of chromatic alteration of pitches within each of the church modes, like the process that converts an Aeolian mode into a Melodic minor scale by raising its 6th and 7th degrees. This seems credible to me because all of the secondary dominant chords may easily be created by such a procedure. For example, when you simply raise the 7th degree of each of the three minor church modes, among the chords that diatonically occur on the resulting altered modes is a dominant 7th chord on the 5th degree of each mode. These chords are secondary dominant chords, and their respective Roman numeral designations are: V of II, V of III, and V of VI (example 52).

Example 52

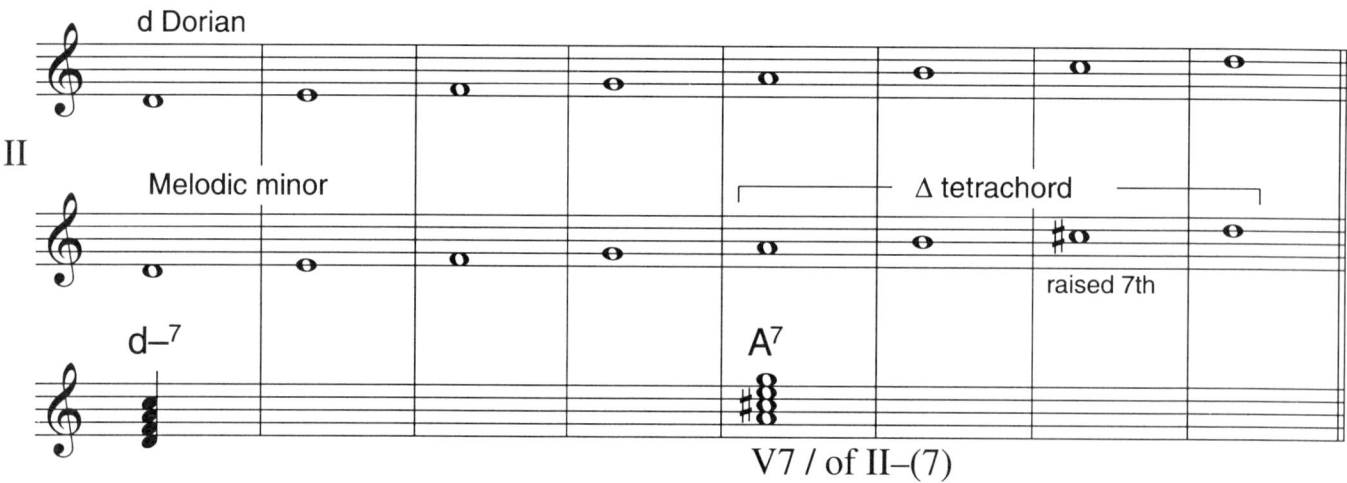

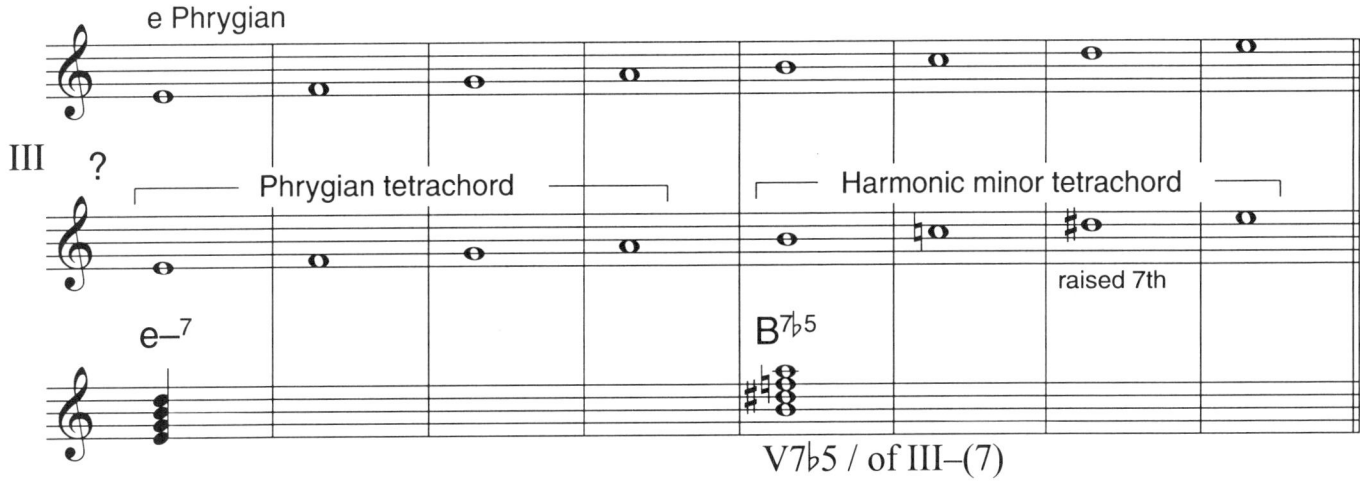

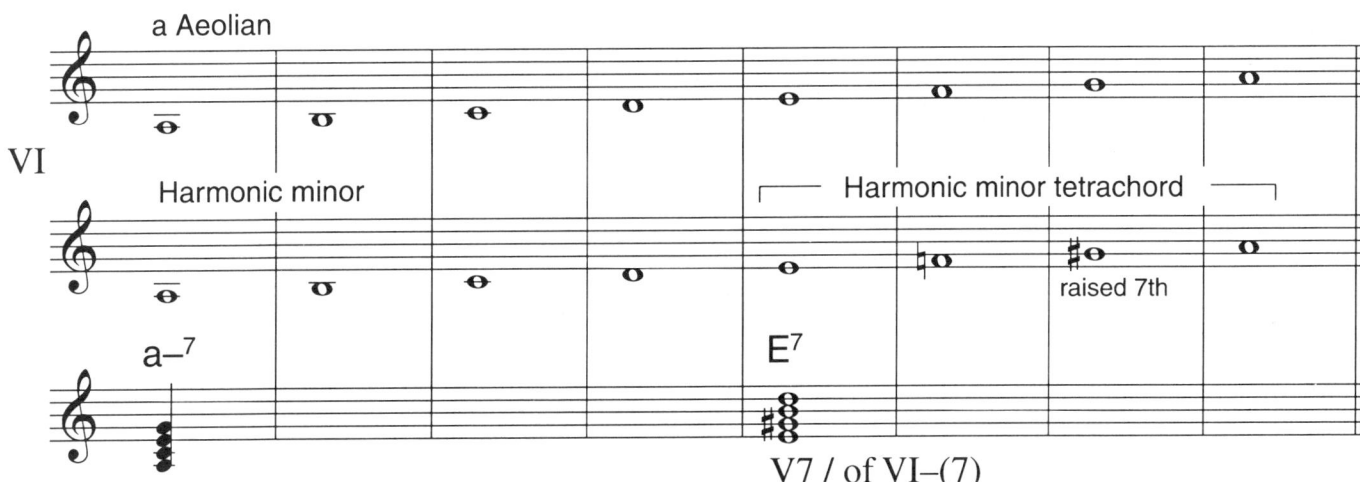

We have already discussed the identical intervallic structures of these three minor modes' modal tonic chords (i.e., II–7, III–7, and VI–7). When you raise the 7th degree of the Dorian and Aeolian modes, the resulting altered church modes are identical to two of the minor scales addressed earlier in the chapter on minor tonalities, namely: Dorian becomes Melodic minor, and Aeolian becomes Harmonic minor, and, as we demonstrated in that chapter, the chords which diatonically occur on the 5th degree of each of these two minor scales are both intervallically identical dominant 7th chords. However, the dominant 7♭5 chord found on the 5th degree of the altered Phrygian mode that this procedure produces is intervallically different from those found on the 5th degrees in the altered Dorian (i.e., Mm) and altered Aeolian (i.e., Hm) modes. Both the altered Phrygian mode and the V7♭5 chord found on its 5th degree rarely occur as I've derived them in example 52 because the unruly dissonances created in a minor tonality containing both ♭2 and Δ7 tend to cancel any relation to the "mode's" tonic.

We will, however, encounter secondary dominant chords both designated and functioning as V of III–. But their intervallic structures will generally be indistinguishable from any other dominant 7th chord (i.e., root, Δ3rd, **P5**, and ♭7), meaning their functions are contextually determined.

Now let's apply a process of chromatic alteration to the three modes whose tonic modal chords are based on a Major triad (Ionian, Lydian, and Mixolydian) and examine the results. Since the model for all secondary dominant chords is the V7 of IΔ relationship naturally occurring in the Major scale, no alteration of the Ionian mode is necessary to create one. Producing a secondary dominant chord for each of the other two modes whose tonic modal chords are based upon a Major triad (i.e., Lydian and Mixolydian) merely requires a half step alteration of one note for each mode. Lydian requires the lowering of the 4th by one half step, while for Mixolydian, raising the 7th by one half step will suffice. You may have realized that the resulting "altered" modes are now both Major scales (i.e., intervallically identical Ionian modes; example 53).

Example 53

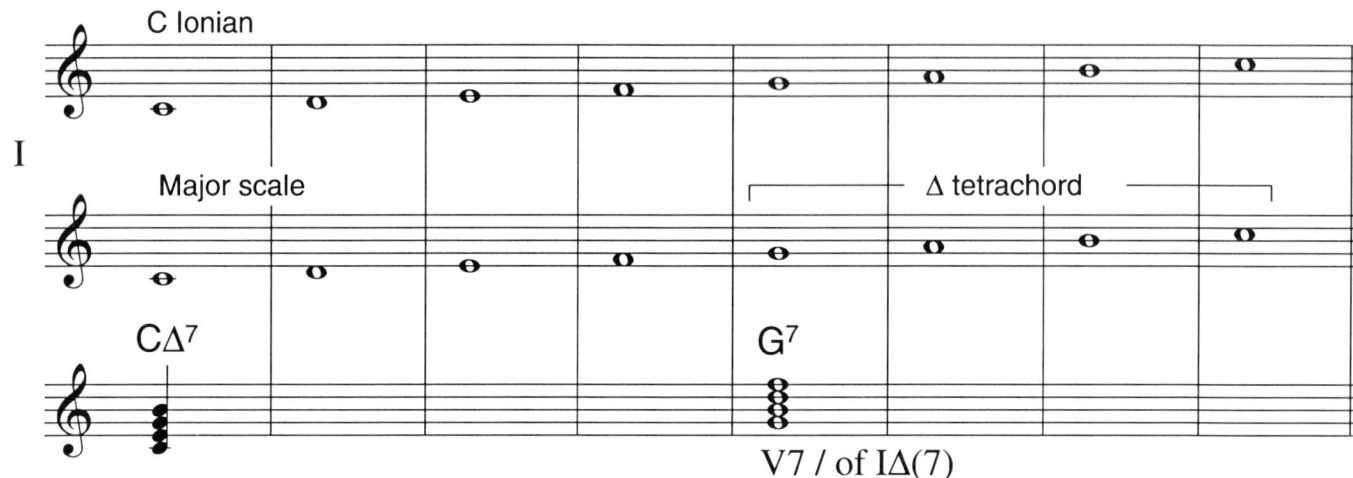

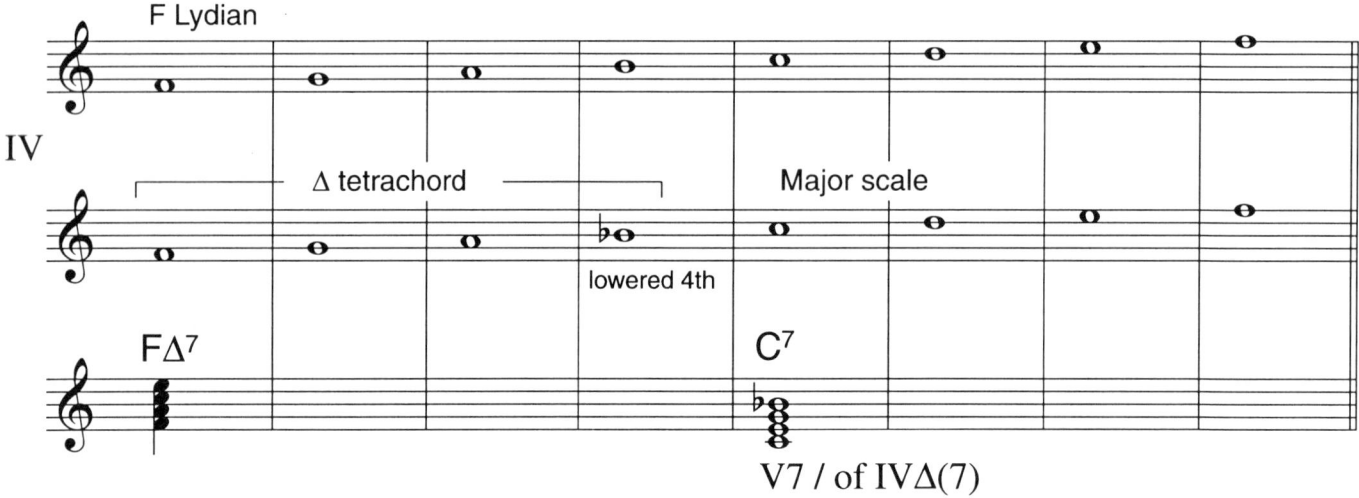

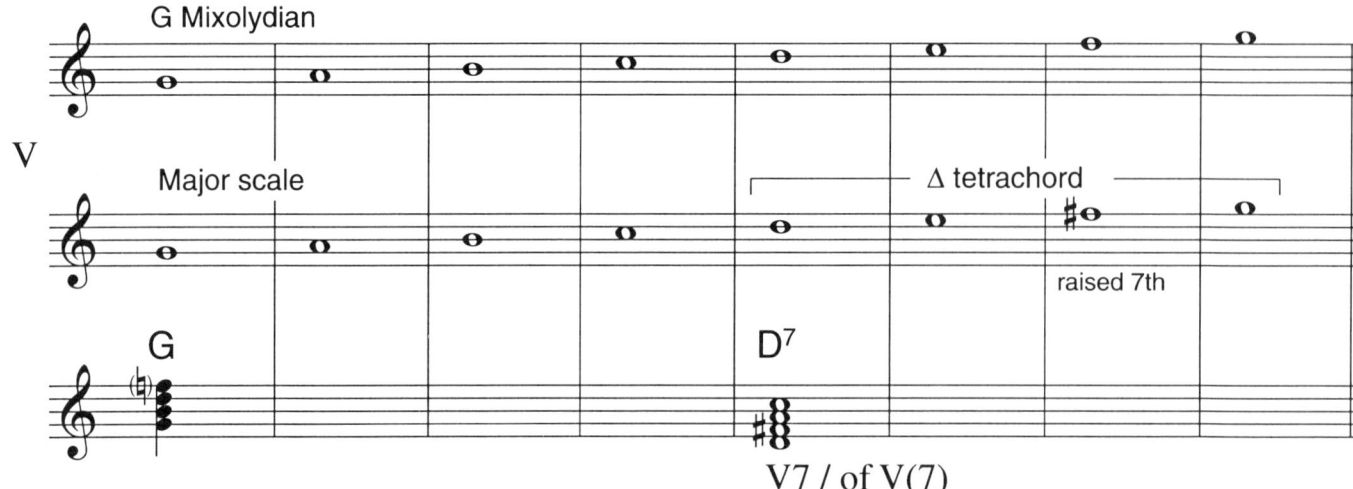

Another option for deriving secondary dominant chords by altering the church modes involves lowering the 7th degree of a Lydian mode. The resulting scale is the same Lydian ♭7 scale that occurs on the 4th degree of the Melodic minor (see chapter on minor tonalities). We can also create a Lydian ♭7 scale by raising the 4th degree of a Mixolydian mode.

This Lydian ♭7 scale, and the Altered Dominant scale which can be derived by lowering the 4th degree of the Locrian mode, are more likely candidates for V7♭5 of III– than the altered Phrygian that I questioned in example 52 (examples 54 and 55).

Example 54

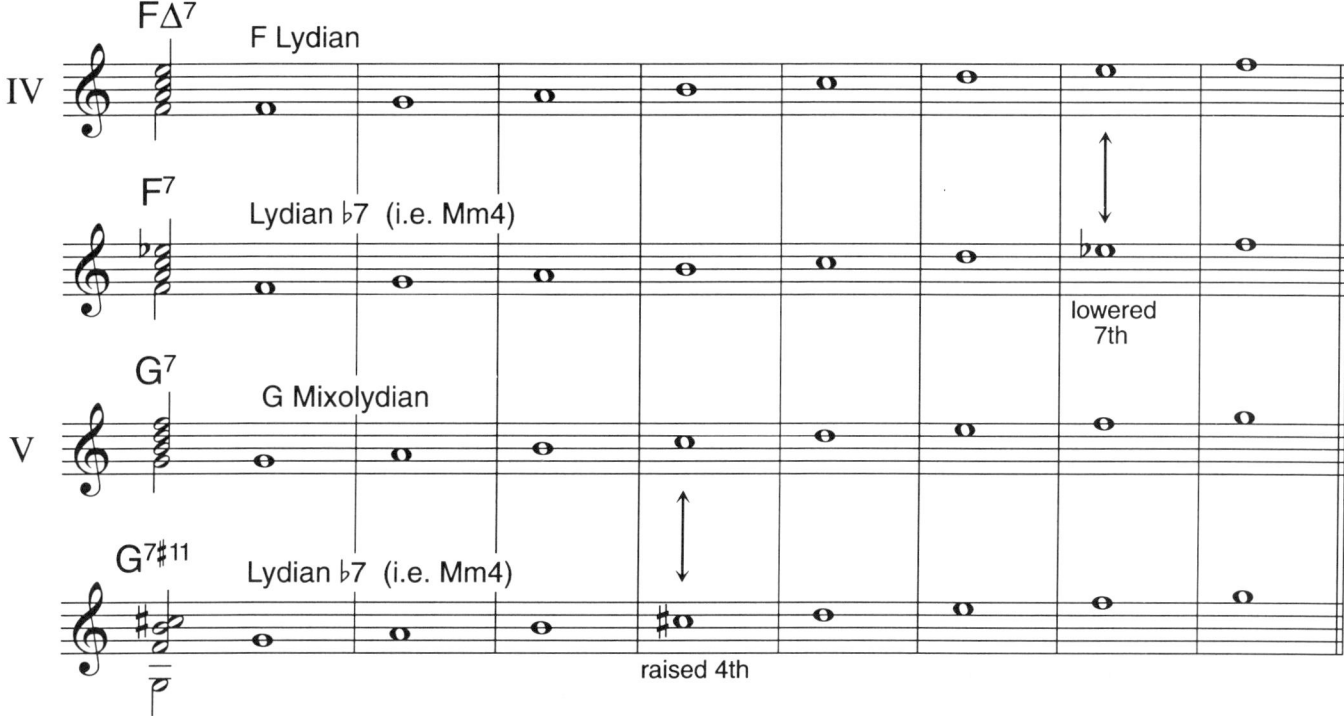

The last option for deriving a secondary dominant chord by altering a church mode involves lowering the 4th degree of the Locrian mode a half step. The result is the same Altered Dominant scale we encountered as Mm7 (Melodic minor from the 7th degree) in the chapter on minor tonalities, which (as I mentioned in the preceding paragraph) is one of the options for V7♭5 of III– that is superior to the altered Phrygian mode (example 55).

Example 55

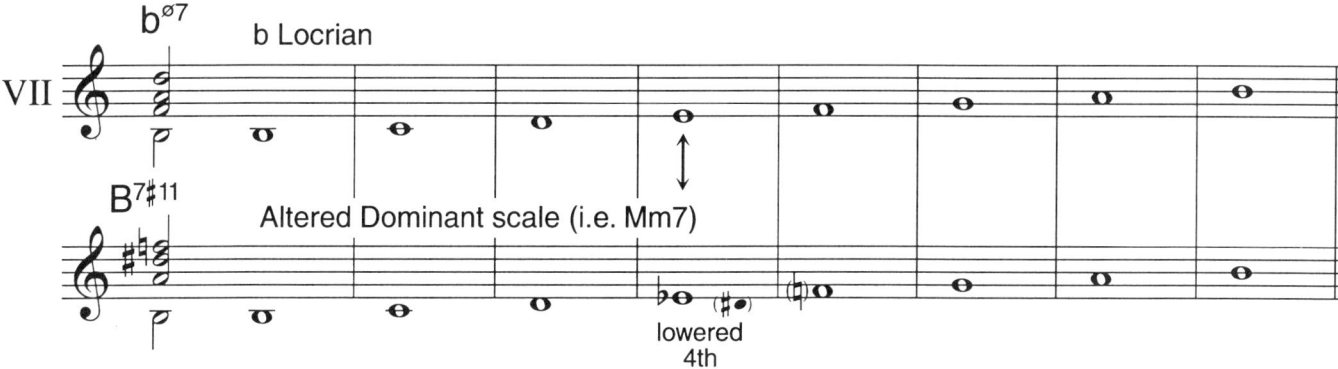

To recap: V7 of II is derived from Mm5, and V7 of VI is derived from Hm5 (example 56).

Example 56

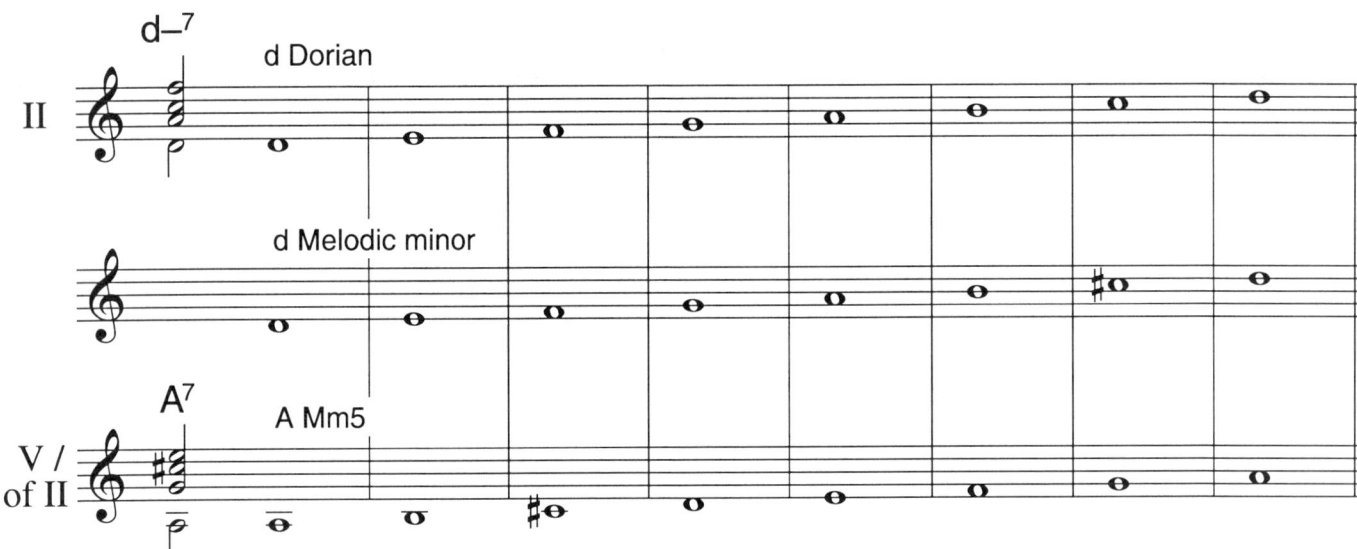

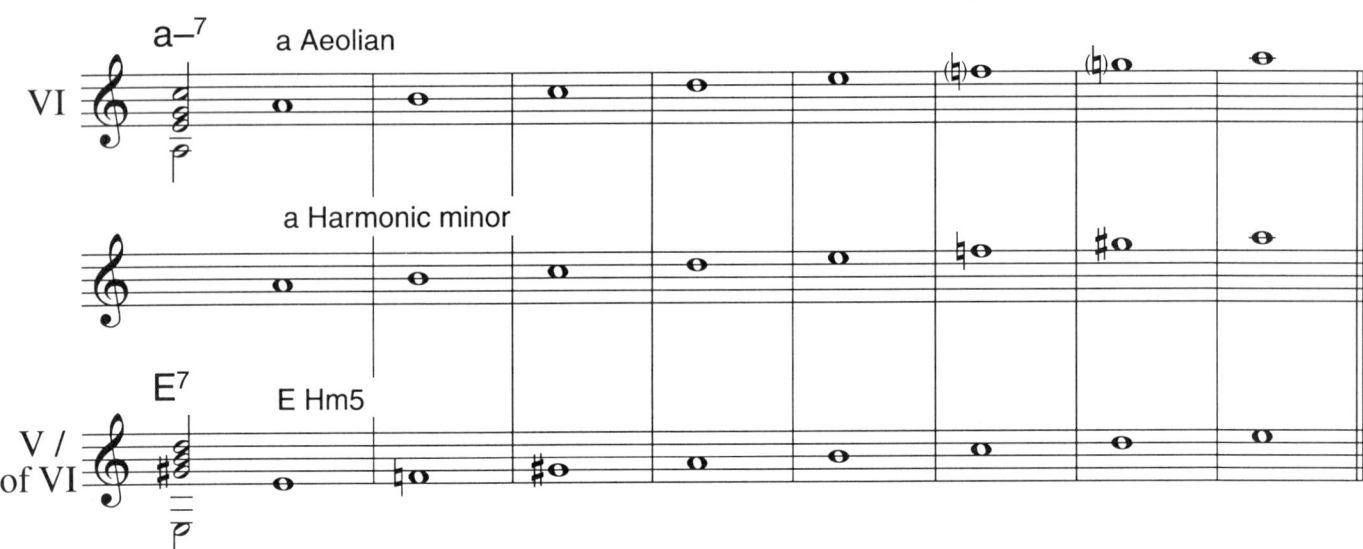

While V7 of III– can be derived by raising the 7th degree of the Phrygian mode, either the Lydian ♭7 scale (i.e., Mm4) or the Altered Dominant scale (i.e., Mm7) is a better option for defining this secondary dominant chord when it contains or infers ♭5 or ♯11. And if it (V7 of III) contains or infers ♮5 and ♭9, then Hm5 (the Dominant 7♭9 scale) is the best option, while Mm5 is the best choice if this secondary dominant chord contains or infers ♮5 and ♮9 (example 57).

Example 57

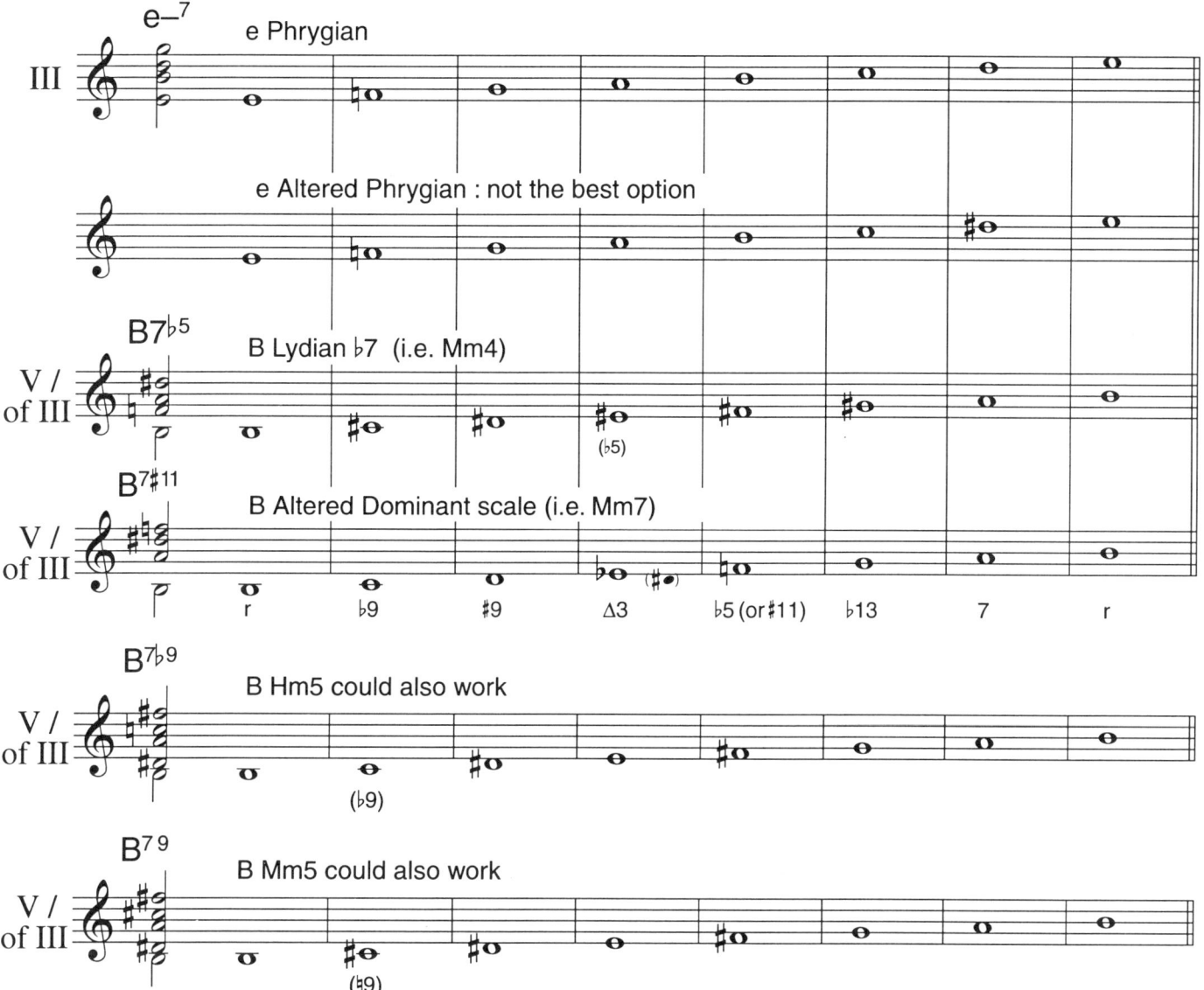

And similarly, both V7 of V and V7 of IV use Mixolydian just like V7 of I (where we first encountered Mixolydian; example 58).

Example 58

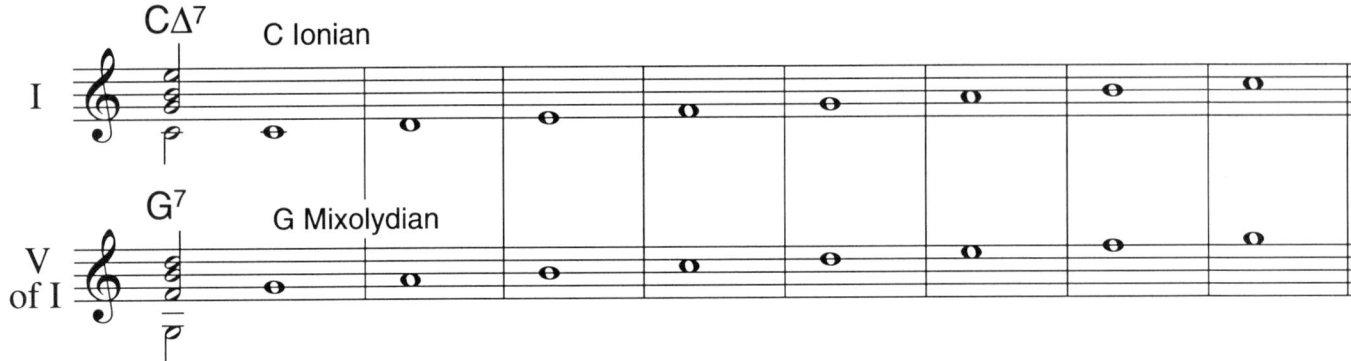

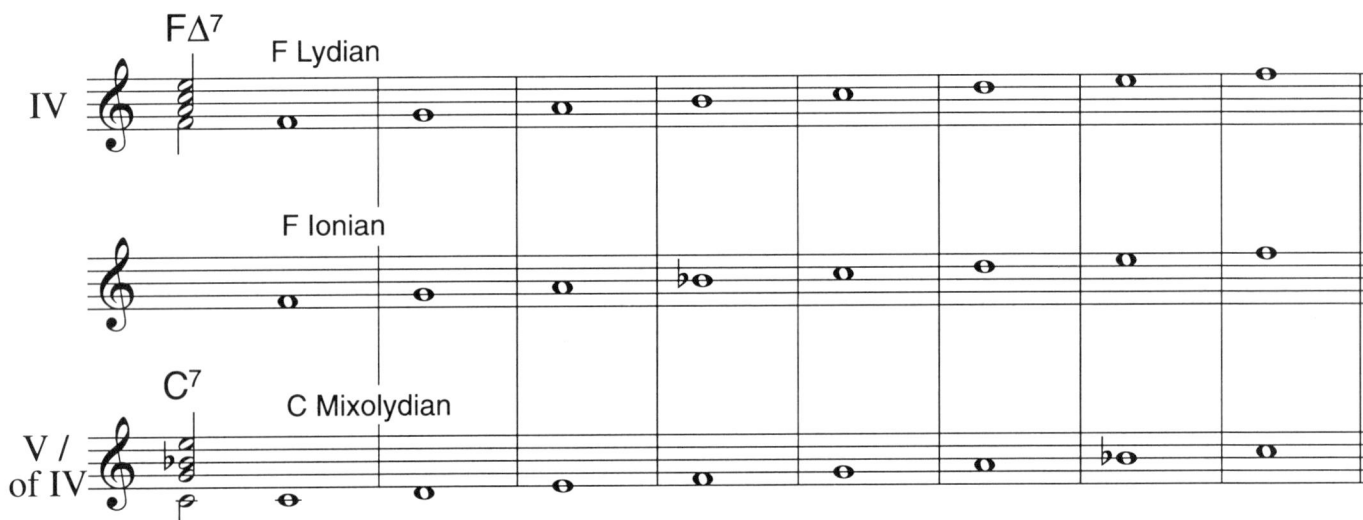

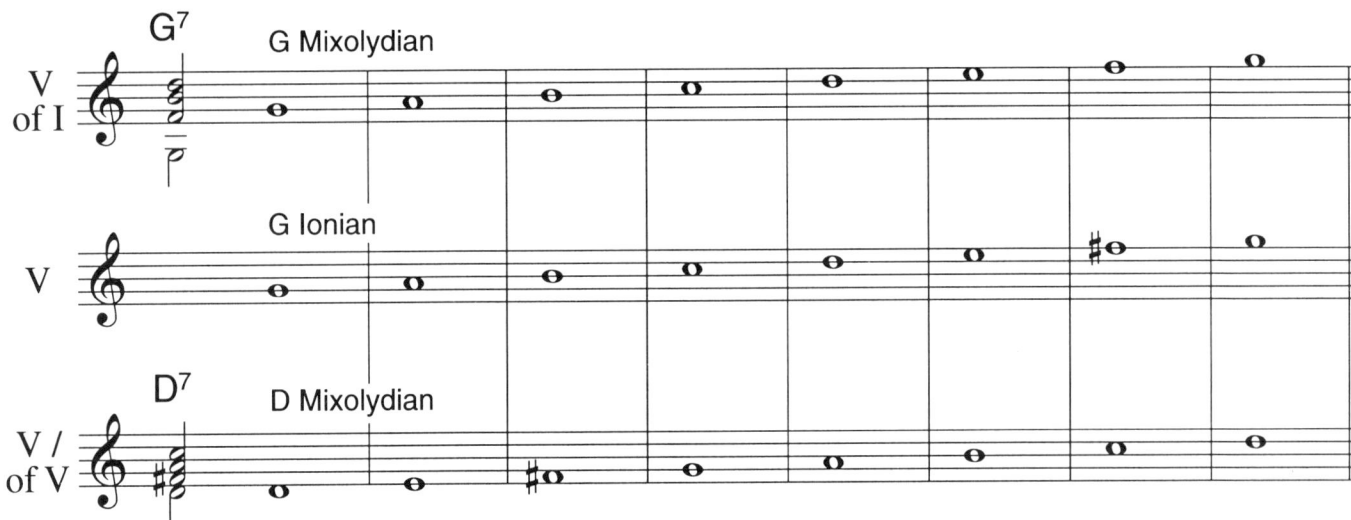

There is also the additional possibility of the Lydian ♭7 scale (Mm4) for V of IV and V of V, and even V of I in cases where either ♯11 or ♭5 is indicated (example 59).

Example 59

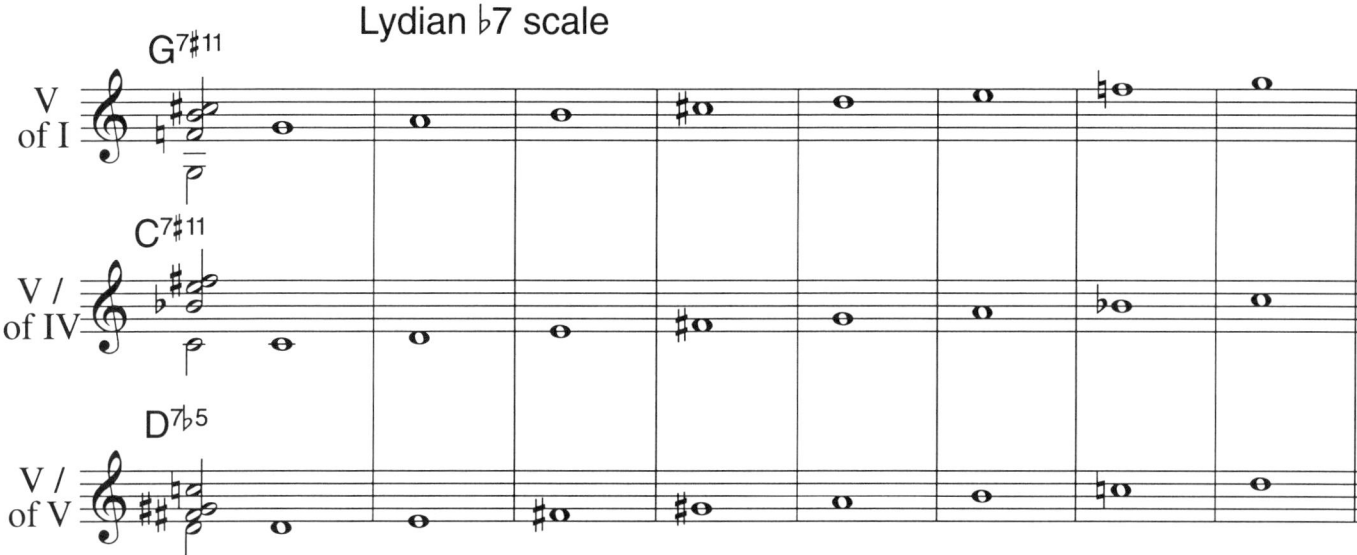

Even though I've shown these secondary dominant chords functioning as V7♭5 of IV, V7♭5 of V, or V7♭5 of I, these chords (i.e., V7♭5 or V7♯11) may resolve to minor chords or even other secondary dominant chords as well.

Some of you may have realized that raising the 3rd of either II–7, III–7, or VI–7, or lowering the 7th of either IΔ7 or IVΔ7, will convert these chords into dominant 7th chords which could function as secondary dominant chords (example 60).

Example 60

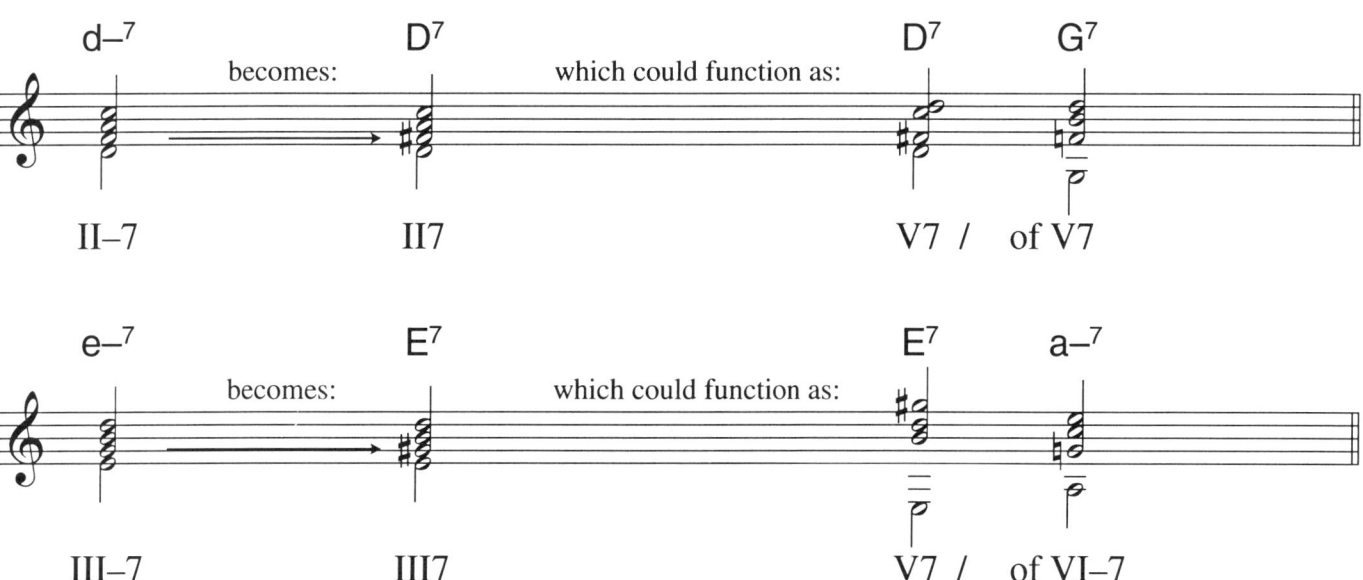

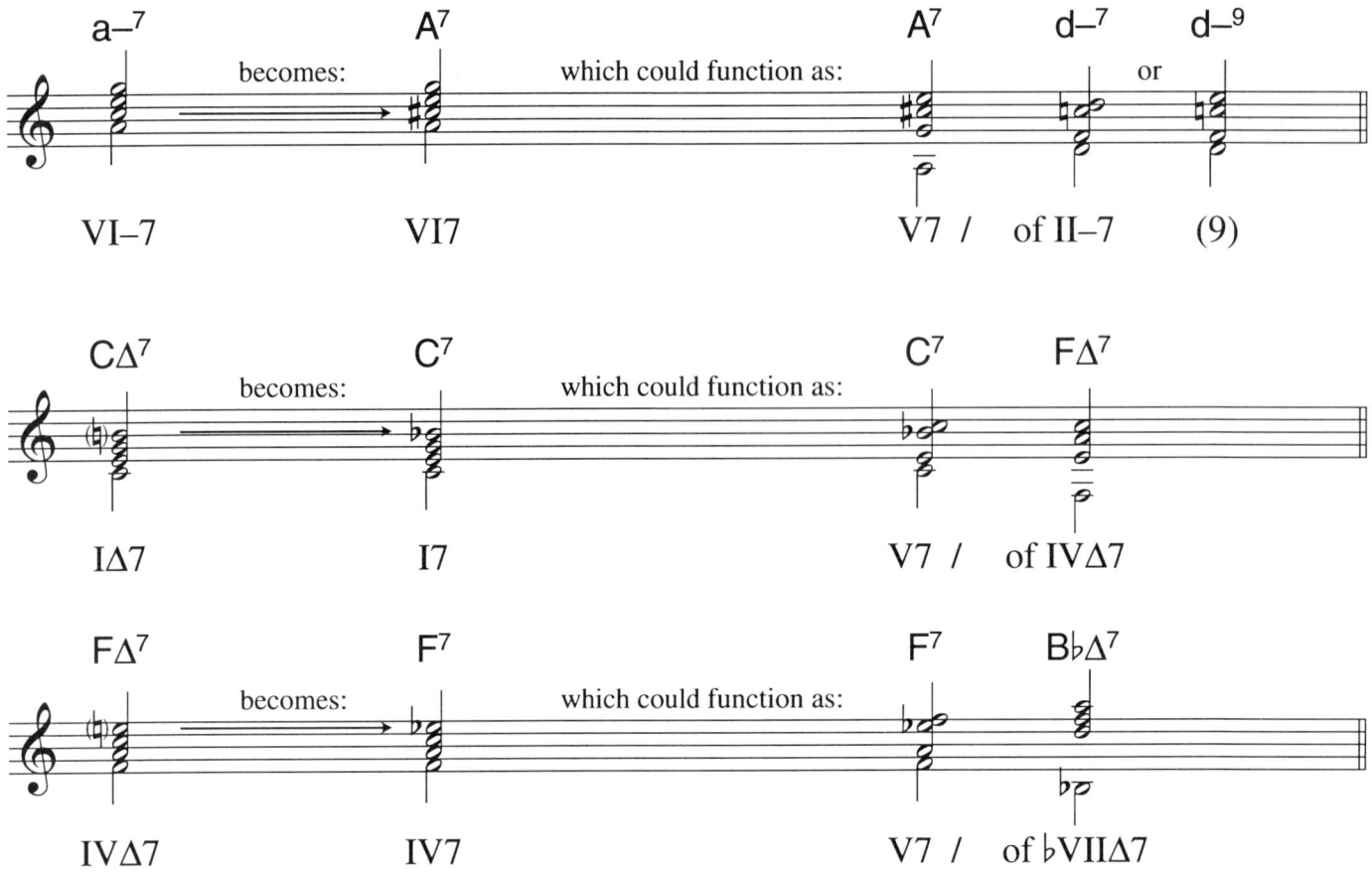

You can also create a dominant 7th chord by raising the 3rd of the VIIØ7 chord, resulting in a V7♭5 chord. Another way to convert the VIIØ7 into a dominant 7th chord would involve raising both the minor 3rd and the ♭5th a half step each. The resulting chord would be a dominant 7th chord, and either of these chords could function in a V of III capacity (example 61).

Example 61

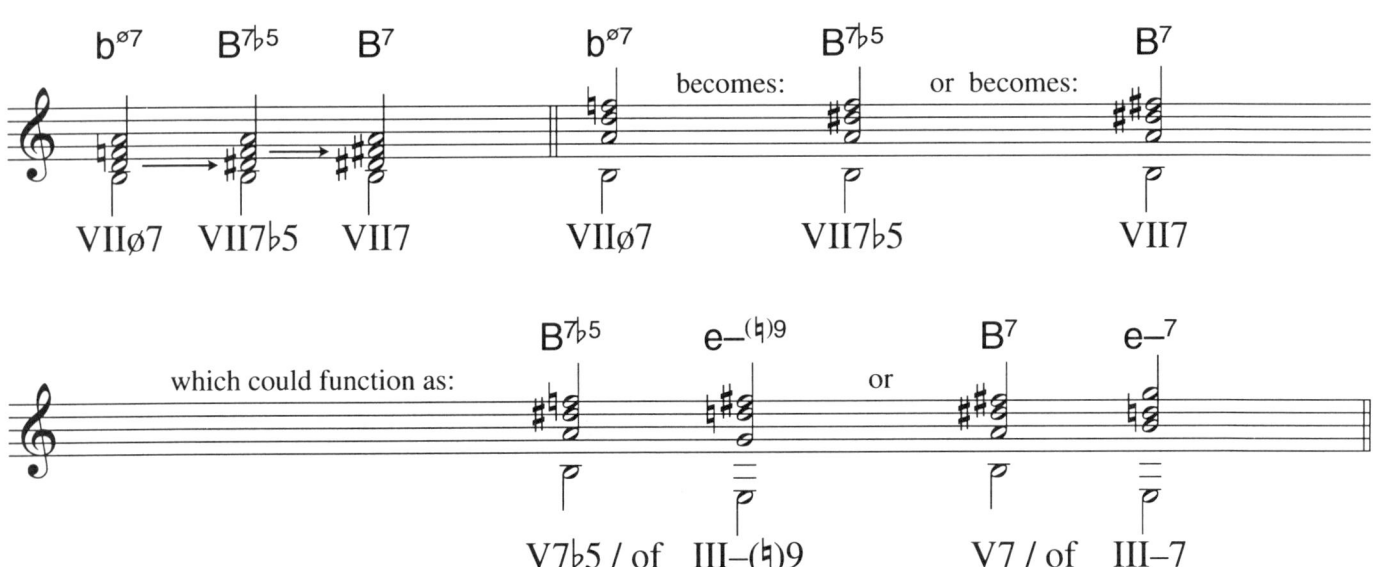

As you can hear from example 61, the V7♭5 chord works well when its ♭5th is voice led up a half step to the ♮9th of the chord of resolution, in which case it is questionable whether the chord of resolution is really functioning as III–. Since the 9th of the III– chord would diatonically be a ♭9 (which also happens to be the same note as the ♭5 of the preceding secondary dominant chord), there could be no such resolution of this dissonant voice in Phrygian. For this and other reasons, the V of III chord is often given a ♮5th, or the 5th is omitted altogether. When the V7♭5 does occur, it often functions as a substitute dominant 7th chord, in which case its harmonic function is best defined by the Lydian ♭7 scale (Mm4) or the Altered Dominant scale (Mm7). We will cover substitute dominant chords in more detail in the next chapter.

A secondary dominant chord is a dominant 7th chord whose root bears the same V to I relationship as that which diatonically occurs between the dominant and its respective tonic chord. But remember, as with all chords, secondary dominant chords may appear in any inversion and voicing which follows the guidelines of good voice leading. Consequently, there are times when the V to I root motion may be implied and not stated (example 62).

Example 62

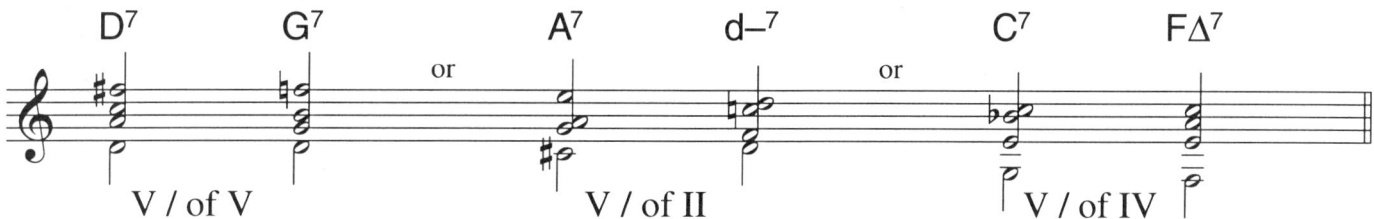

There are also occasions when the conversion of a diatonic chord into a secondary dominant chord by a process of chromatic alteration may result in a resolution that moves into another key. For example, if a IVΔ7 chord (say FΔ7 in the key of C) had its Δ7th dropped one half step, it would become an F7 chord which could resolve to B♭Δ, or b♭–, or even G♭Δ7 (as a deceptive cadence), all of which are clearly no longer in the key of C (example 63).

Example 63

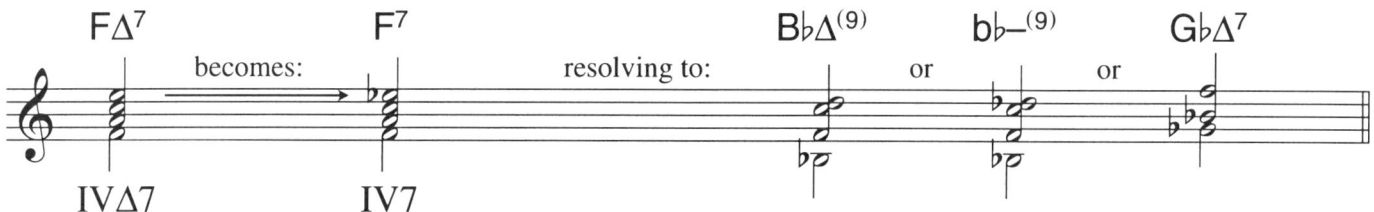

This same FΔ7 chord could also function as IΔ7 and, with the same half step alteration of its Δ7th degree (which again turns it into an F7 chord), could then function as V of IV. In fact, a series of just such one note alterations created the following famous four bar phrase from George Harrison's song "Something" (example 64).

Example 64

In example 64 I've added a 9th (voiced next to the 3rd) of the IVΔ7 chord, while in the original it is just a IVΔ chord. If you know this song, check out the next chord (in this key G7). It's another secondary dominant chord, V7 of V, which results from a process that alters two notes of the IVΔ chord. The octave of the root of the IV chord is raised one half step to become the Δ3rd of the V of V, and the root (of the IVΔ chord) walks down to become the root of the V of V. Or, using the IVΔ(9) that I used, the 9 moves down to become the Δ3rd of the V of V, the root of IV moves to the root of V of V, while the 3rd and 5th of IVΔ remain unchanged to become the 5th and 7th of V of V (example 65).

Example 65

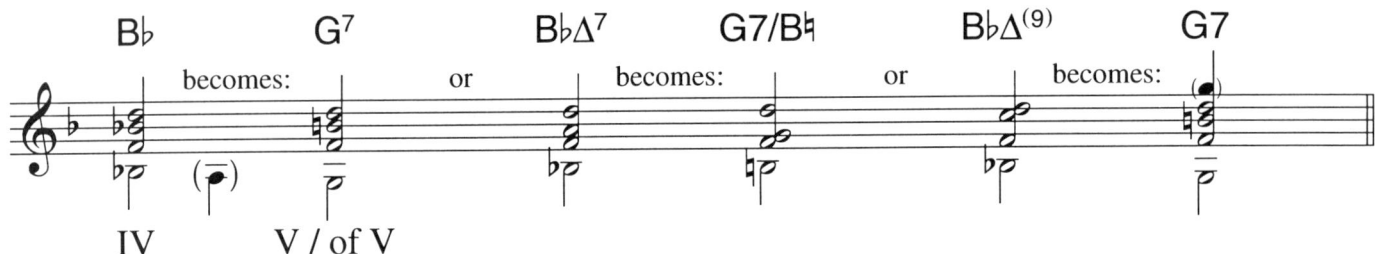

This demonstrates how small alterations can produce very interesting results. It also illustrates how good voice leading is the best way to generate musical sounding chord progressions.

Let's examine other examples of secondary dominant chords found in the standard repertoire.

In example 66 the first four bars of "All of Me" demonstrate one way to use V of VI. In fact, even the melody illustrates the shift from I to V of VI.

Example 66

In example 67, "There is No Greater Love" begins with the shift from I to V of III, which then moves to V of VI. There are often alternate chord changes used in tunes like this because their succession of sequential secondary dominant chords encourages the use of the substitute dominant 7th chords I mentioned earlier. For example, instead of the Bb△7 to A7 to D7 sequence I've used, you could use Bb△7 to Eb7 to Ab7, or chromatically even Bb△7 to A7 to Ab7, or Bb△7 to Eb7 to D7, all of which would work.

Example 67

Such sequential dominant 7th chords whose root motion (implied or stated) follows the cycle of 5ths (counterclockwise) are common, especially in the bridges (the B sections of AABA song forms) of rhythm changes (example 68).

Example 68

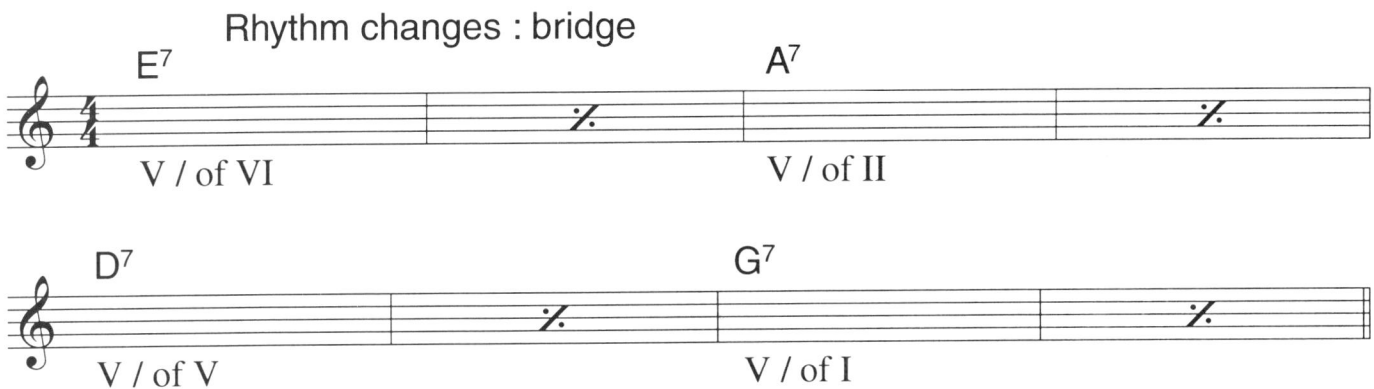

This covers examples for each of the diatonic possibilities for secondary dominant chords derived from the modes of the Major scale, except the rare V7 of VIIØ7, which could occur something like this (example 69):

Example 69

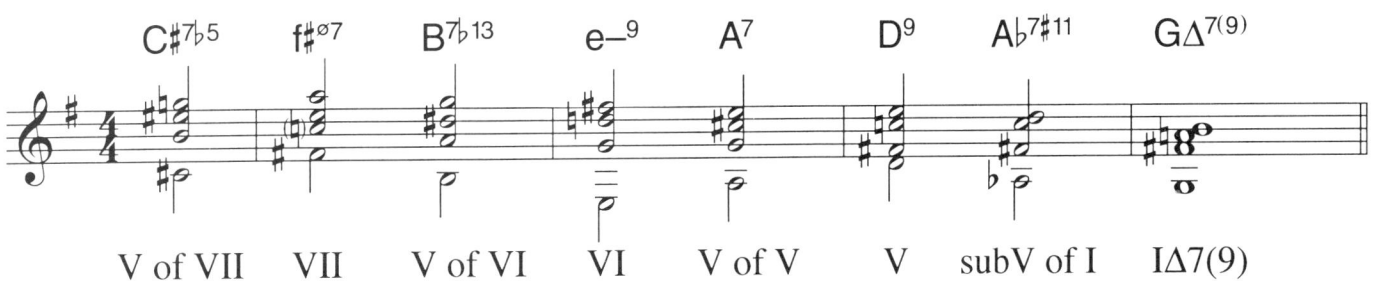

While technically the first chord from example 69 could be analyzed as V7(♭5) of VIIØ7, it only becomes convincingly so when the IΔ chord occurs at the end. There are many points during this progression where the chords could have moved elsewhere (for example, a different penultimate chord would move to another key; example 70), and, despite the V to I root motion which exists between the first two chords (C♯7♭5 and f♯Ø7), the different conclusion used in example 70 casts doubt on the veracity of interpreting C♯7♭5 to be V7 of VIIØ7.

Example 70

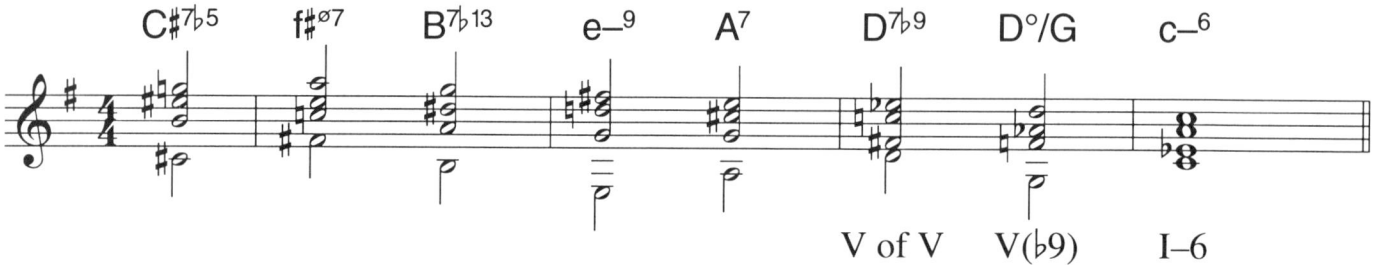

And if you combine the two four bar phrases of example 69 and example 70 together into one eight bar phrase, like the kind you might find for an A section in the AABA song form of many standards, then the c–6 at the end of example 70 sounds like the tonic, which casts an entirely different light on the other chords, including the C♯7♭5.

* * * * *

We can also derive secondary dominant chords for the diatonic chords found in the minor tonalities by any of the methods we employed to produce them for the diatonic chords of a Major tonality.

Since the harmonic function of an isolated dominant 7th chord may be interpreted in many different ways, we will employ the method of chromatic alteration of each of the seven "modes" of each minor tonality to produce their corresponding secondary dominant chord(s), thereby establishing a link to the harmonic function of each secondary dominant chord through its method of derivation. But keep in mind that just like the secondary dominant chords similarly derived in the Major tonalities, most of the secondary dominant chords this method yields can have multiple interpretations.

There is no need to reexamine Aeolian since we've already addressed it in relation to the Major tonalities, where it is identical to the descending form of the Traditional minor scale, and where the alteration necessary to derive a dominant 7th chord on its 5th degree (i.e., raising its 7th degree) would convert it into a Harmonic minor scale. Consequently we need only explore the secondary dominant chords derived from the "modes" of the Melodic minor and Harmonic minor scales. We will begin with Melodic minor.

It has already been established that the V chord in Melodic minor is a dominant 7th chord, so we can proceed to V of II– as derived from Mm2 by raising its 7th degree (example 71).

Example 71

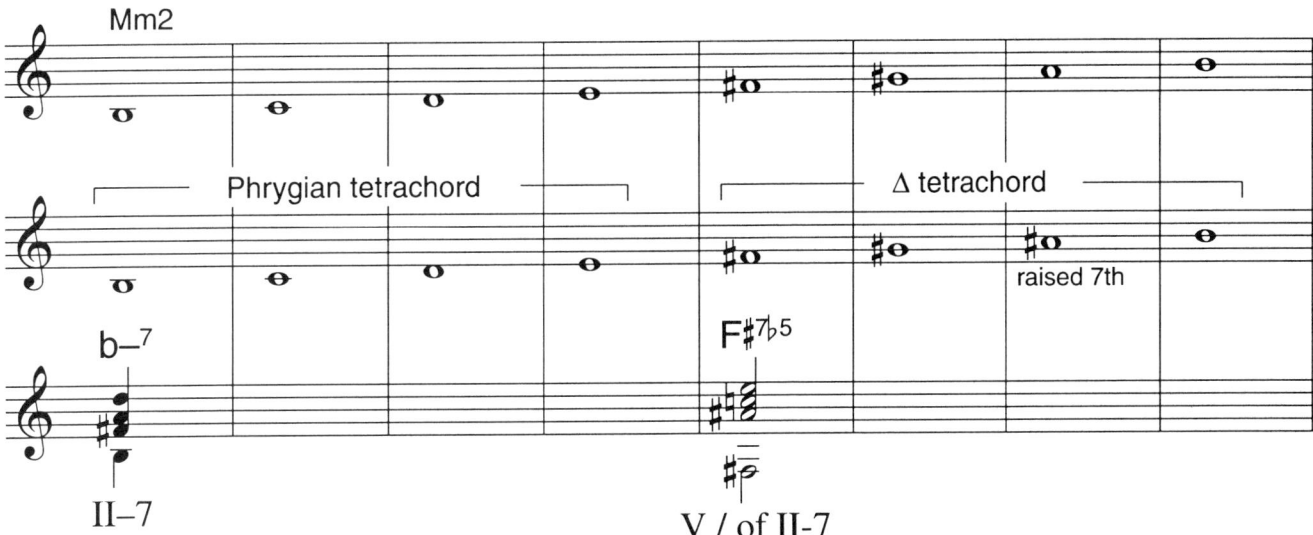

The altered Mm2, which produces a dominant 7th chord on its 5th degree, is essentially a Phrygian tetrachord combined with a Major tetrachord (or vice versa, if we begin on its 5th degree in concurrence with the root of this V of II– chord). While not as useful as the Lydian ♭7 scale or the Altered Dominant scale, this scale can work for a secondary dominant chord containing or inferring both ♭5 and ♮9, and either indicating ♭13 or resolving to a minor chord. The whole tone scale (which we'll address in the chapter on vagrant chords) could also work for V7♭5 of II–7.

Any of the possible alterations that would produce a dominant 7th chord on the 5th degree of Mm3 are problematic. Raising the 7th degree alone would give you a possible ♯V7 chord, resulting in a root motion that doesn't really resolve to the (natural) III+ chord of this tonality, and the raised 7th degree would become the same note as the tonic, so that would eliminate our leading tone with this option. While lowering both the ♯4th and ♯5th degrees will produce a V7 of III chord which could resolve to the III+ chord, the root of this V7 of III chord conflicts with the ♯5 of the III+ chord. And the resulting scale (when lowering the 4th and 5th degrees) has become an Ionian mode (or Mixolydian when starting on the root of V7 of III chord; example 72).

Example 72

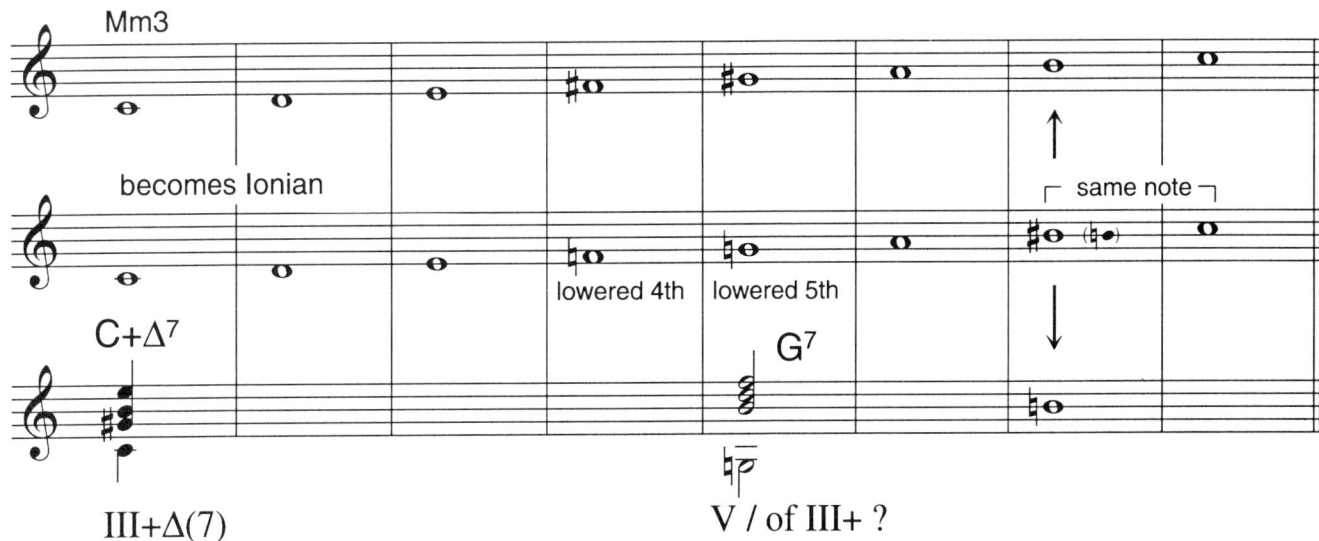

Both lowering the 4th degree and raising the 7th degree of Mm4 are required to produce a dominant 7th chord on its 5th degree. But it's hard to distinguish this V of IV in Melodic minor from a V of V in Major, because the chord of resolution in each case is another dominant 7th chord, and the two alterations of Mm4 necessary to derive V7 of IV convert it into an Ionian mode (which is a Mixolydian mode if we start at the root of the V of IV chord, the same scale we'd be likely to use for V of V in Major; example 73).

Example 73

Raising the 7th degree of Mm5 will produce a dominant 7th chord on its 5th degree, which also functions as V of V. But what distinguishes this scale from other options is that it is a Major tetrachord combined with a Harmonic minor tetrachord, making it a workable choice for either V7♭9♮13 chords, or some of the polytonal chords we will encounter later (e.g., G♯/B, which is B7♭9♮13), both of which either contain or infer ♭9 and ♮13 on a dominant 7th chord. Such a chord could resolve to any number of chords, not just another V chord (example 74).

Example 74

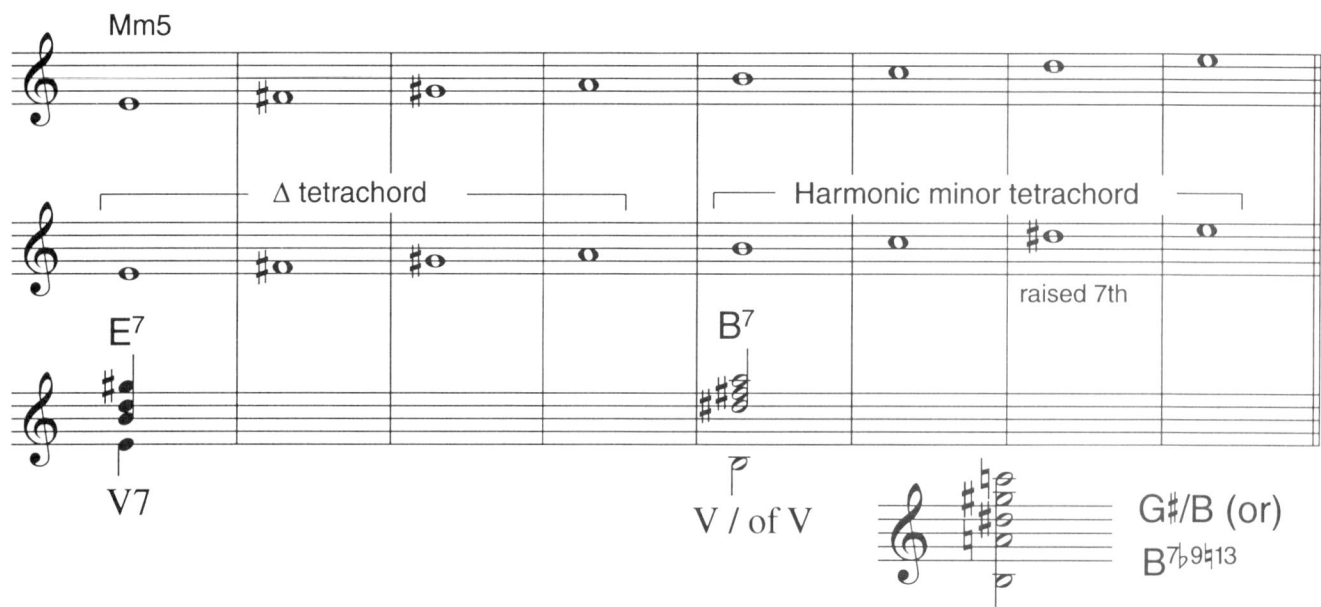

84

Raising both the 5th and 7th degrees of Mm6 is required to produce a dominant 7th chord on its 5th degree, resulting in a Harmonic minor scale, which is actually the Dominant 7th ♭9 scale (Hm5) when we use the root of this V of VIØ7 chord as our starting note (example 75).

Example 75

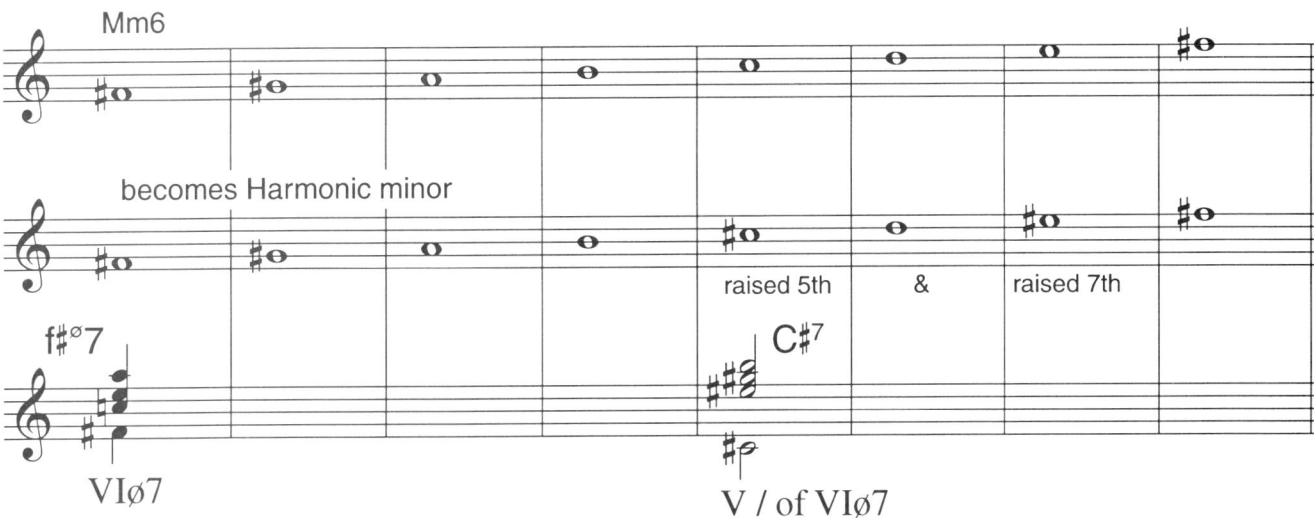

The alterations required to derive a V7 of VIIØ7 chord from Mm7 involve raising the 4th, 5th, and 7th degrees. The resulting altered Mm7 scale combines a Locrian tetrachord with a Harmonic minor tetrachord and can be a bit unruly to use (example 76).

Example 76

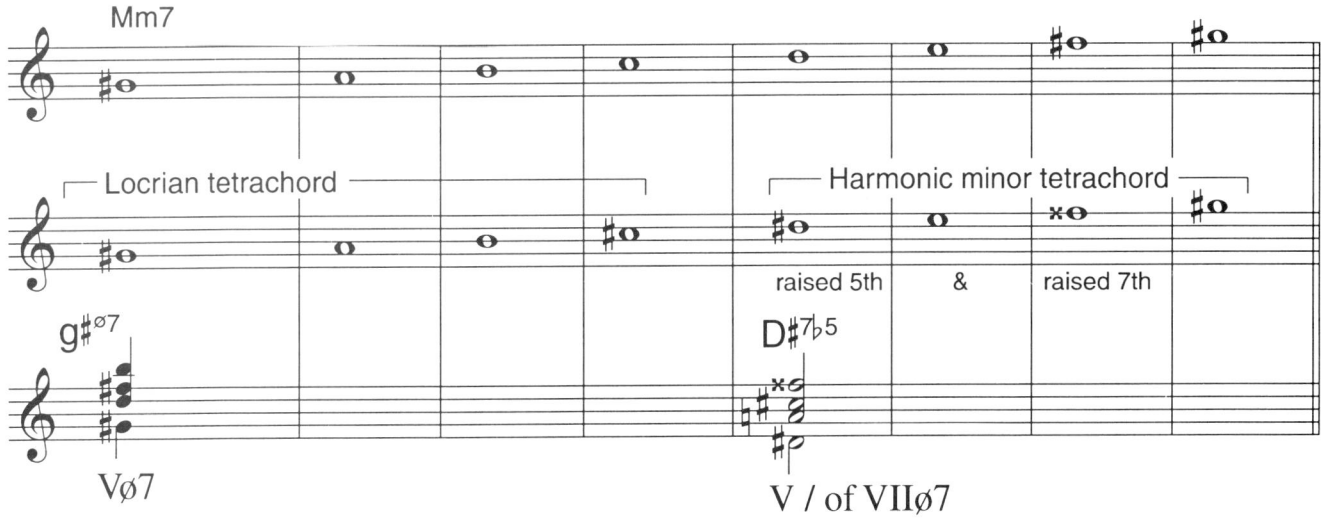

Let's now apply the same process to the modes of the Harmonic minor scale in order to derive secondary dominant chords from this tonality as well. As with the Melodic minor scale, the chord that diatonically occurs on the 5th degree of the Harmonic minor scale is already a dominant 7th chord, so no alteration of this scale is required to produce V7 of I– in this tonality.

Moving on to V of IIØ7 as derived from Hm2—here we must raise both the 5th and 7th degrees of Hm2 to derive a secondary dominant chord, resulting in the same V7♭5 of II and the same corresponding altered mode we encountered on Mm2 when we raised its 7th degree. Both modes are comprised of a Major tetrachord combined with a Phrygian tetrachord (when starting on the root of the secondary dominant chord). But their respective chords of resolution are different, and this poses an interesting problem that we will address at the end of this chapter. For the present, it's important to realize that Hm2 altered to produce V7 of IIØ7, and Mm2 altered to produce V7 of II–7, are both intervallically identical scales (example 77).

Example 77

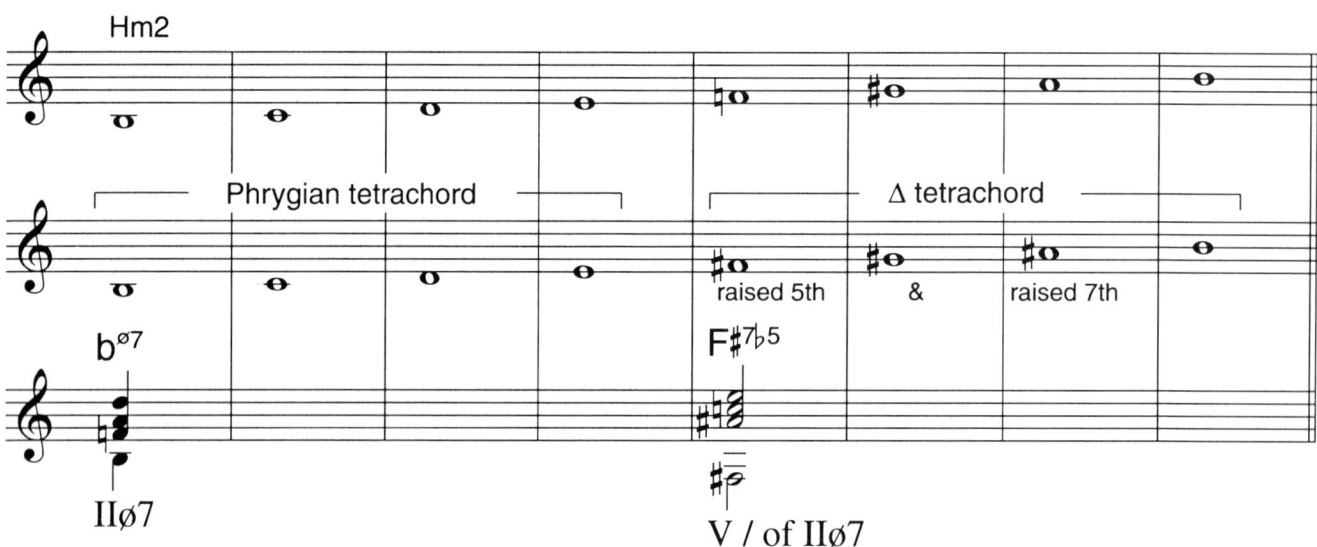

The only alteration required for Hm3 to yield a dominant 7th chord on its 5th degree is the lowering of its 5th degree a half step, thus converting this mode of the Harmonic minor into a Major scale, which we all know has a dominant 7th chord on its 5th degree. As with the other tonality that might have an +Δ7 chord for its tonic chord (i.e., Mm3), the note which makes this "mode's" tonic chord augmented in the first place needs to be altered in order to produce a dominant 7th chord whose root is a perfect 5th above the root of its chord of resolution, thereby throwing the stability of such a tonality (as derived) into question. This progression does occur, but usually as if it were V7 of IΔ or V7 of IVΔ, with the Major chord of resolution being altered by raising its 5th to produce the +(Δ7th) chord. In any event, the scale for the V7 chord in each case is usually the same Mixolydian (Ionian from the 5th degree) that we used for the V7 of III+Δ7 in example 72 (example 78).

Example 78

To derive a dominant 7th chord from the 5th degree of Hm4, we must lower the 4th degree and raise the 7th degree, thus converting Hm4 into a Melodic minor scale which, as has been previously demonstrated, has a dominant 7th chord on its 5th degree, making its corresponding mode the same Mm5 we've used for several other applications (example 79).

Example 79

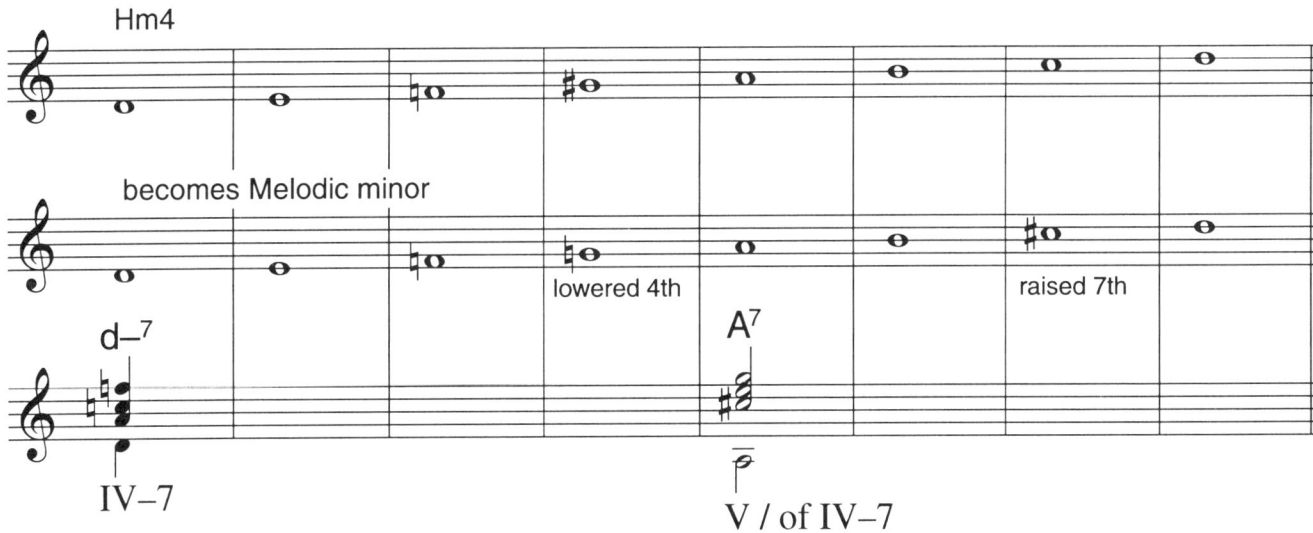

Raising the 7th degree of Hm5 not only gives us a secondary dominant chord (V7♭5 of V7), it also creates a very exotic scale that is a combination of two Harmonic minor tetrachords. This particular scale is to flamenco, Middle Eastern, and much of the music of the Mediterranean region what the Major scale is to Western European music. It is highly evocative in and of itself. Its unusual intervallic structure can sound like an arpeggio of a Major 7th chord whose chord tones are each successively approached from a half step below, creating the effect of two alternating adjacent Δ7th arpeggios one half step apart. While not common in jazz, it is occasionally used to create an effect, especially where its evocative Eastern influence is appropriate. However, its applicability for secondary dominant chords is questionable (example 80).

Example 80

The minimum alteration required to produce a V7 chord from Hm6 is the lowering of the 4th degree to create the ♭7 of this secondary dominant chord. But this chord would also have a ♯5 (i.e., the unaltered 2nd degree of Hm6), which is not a problem in and of itself. However, the resulting scale resembles two disparate elements randomly joined, in that the first four notes taken as a group (1, ♯2, Δ3, and ♮4) sound more like a blues lick than a tetrachord, while the remaining four notes are a Major tetrachord. The whole tone scale (which we will address later) could also be used for such a V7♯5 (or V+7) of IVΔ7 chord.

Another solution, which requires an additional alteration to produce a V7 chord for Hm6, lowers the 2nd degree as well as the 4th, resulting in a V7 chord with a ♮5th, but this process converts Hm6 into a Major scale (i.e., Ionian mode), which, as we all know, when starting on its 5th degree, would be the same Mixolydian mode we've often used elsewhere for secondary dominant chords (example 81).

Example 81

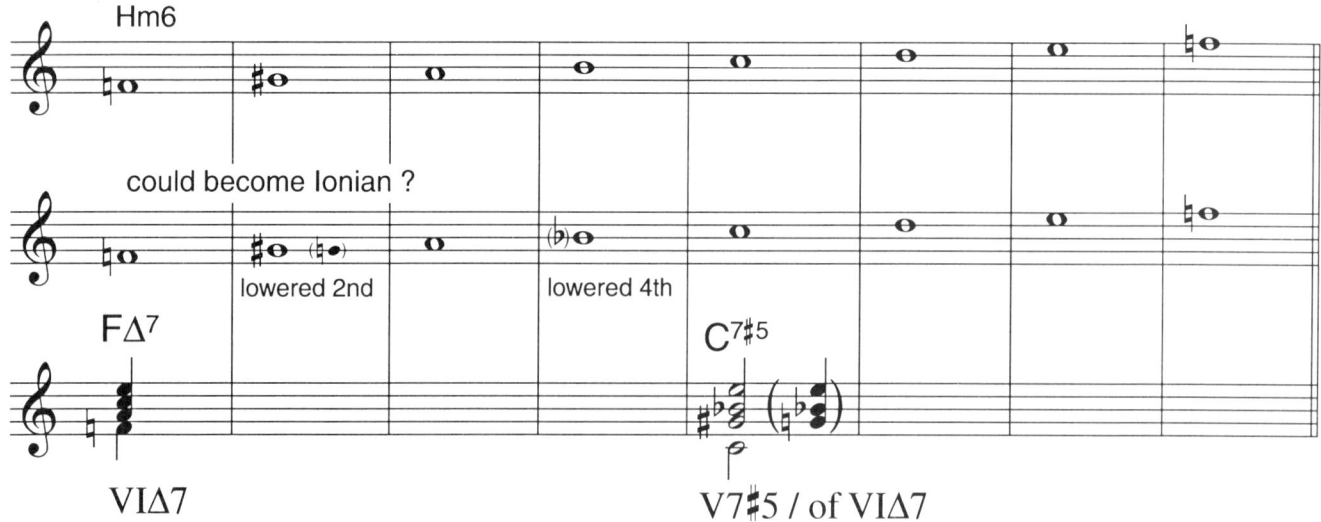

88

Converting Hm7 into a scale from which we can derive a dominant 7ᵗʰ chord on its 5ᵗʰ degree is the most problematic of all. It requires a minimum of three alterations to produce a V7♭5, and four alterations to produce a V7♮5. If we raise the 4ᵗʰ and 5ᵗʰ degrees a half step, and raise the 7ᵗʰ degree a whole step, the results produce a V7♭5 chord from a scale made of a Phrygian tetrachord combined with a Harmonic minor tetrachord, which is intervallically identical to the altered Phrygian from examples 52 and 57, and just as awkward to use. However, if we add the additional alteration of raising the 2ⁿᵈ degree a half step, the result yields a V7 (♮5) from a Hm7 scale which has been converted into a Harmonic minor scale.

I personally believe that having to alter four of the seven notes of any scale in order to derive any result exceeds the bounds of credibility and calls into question the system that requires such methods. But before we scrap what we've worked so hard to achieve, let me remind the student that all systems have their exceptions. V7 of any O7 chord is going to be a problem wherever it may be encountered (which is very rarely), and it's even more of a problem for those who attempt to derive these two chords from the same tonality. This is due in part to the unique character of all O7 chords. I previously alluded to Schoenberg's ideas regarding these chords, which he put in a classification he called "vagrant" chords, and we will cover this in more detail in the chapter of the same title later in this book. But for now, just consider the total lack of stasis these O7 chords produce, and realize that while the secondary dominant chord also creates tension that yearns toward release (or resolution), when the V7 chord resolves to an even more tension-filled chord, it calls out for continued motion toward some kind of resolution. And this is how you are likely to encounter a V7 of VIIO7, or V7 of any O7 chord in most music, including jazz, which means the highly altered Hm7 scale which I've created in example 82 for V7♭5 of VIIO7 may not be the best solution to define the harmonic function of such a dominant 7ᵗʰ chord, even when it rarely occurs. This scale is intervallically identical to the altered Mm7 scale found in example 76 and just as unruly to use, while the other scale in example 82 (i.e., for V7♮5 of VIIO7) is the same Hm5 (i.e., the Dominant 7♭9 scale) available for V7 chords in a variety of contexts (example 82).

Example 82

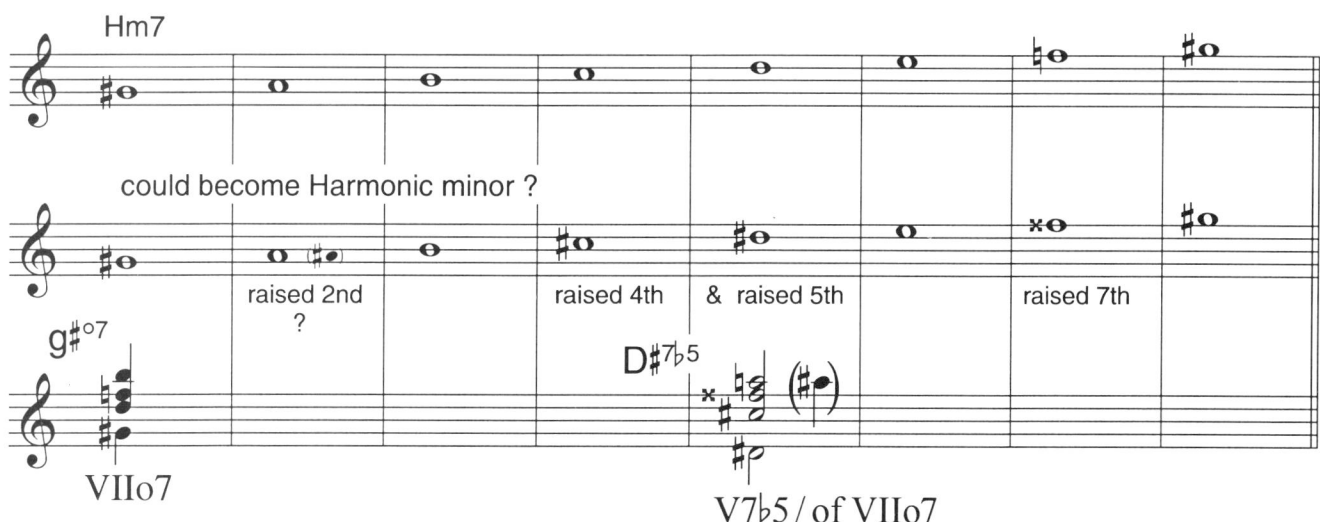

Some of you may have noticed that the alterations required to create secondary dominant chords result in V7 chords that often contain notes that conflict with notes found in their chords of resolution. When we attempt to reconcile these conflicts, the results can be unworkable hybrid scales that lack any coherent sense of tonality. And the workable scales this process yields more often than not turn out to be one of the same five scales that worked for secondary dominant chords derived from Major tonalities, which don't always reconcile the conflicts either. For instance, the alterations required to convert Mm4 into the Ionian mode which produces the V7 of IV7 chord in example 73 results in a scale containing a *C♯* functioning as the Δ3rd of the A7 secondary dominant chord, and this *C♯* apparently conflicts with the *C♮* found as the ♭7 in the D7 (IV7) to which it resolves. These conflicts are largely due to the fact that secondary dominant chords originally evolved either to produce a sense of tonality for chords other than the tonic chord of a key, or to make a stronger move to them by altering their mode of origin to produce a secondary dominant chord whose Major 3rd was intended to function as a leading tone, which would then be voice led to the root of its chord of resolution. These secondary dominant chords didn't often resolve to 7th chords, and when they occasionally did, the 7th in the chord of resolution rarely conflicted with the Δ3rd of the secondary dominant chord. Or where it could conflict, as in either the case of V7 of V7, or V7 of IV7, the apparent conflict would be confined to one voice moving chromatically (e.g., the *C♯* [or more likely *D♭*] moving down to the *C♮* as found in the aforementioned A7 to D7 from example 73). Many of these conflicts could be avoided if the chords of resolution were not 7th chords. But some jazz musicians have had a propensity for habitually overusing 7th chords, making every chord of resolution a 7th chord. There is no reason that the resolution of tension cannot be delayed or prolonged. And secondary dominant chords that resolve to 7th chords are often effectively employed in just such a manner in jazz, as they move through various tonalities before cadencing. This means that while a particular secondary dominant chord may have been derived from one tonality, it is not necessarily required to resolve to that tonality. So we are quite likely to encounter secondary dominant chords resolving to 7th chords in jazz, in which case one scale doesn't have to be (and often won't be) compatible with both the secondary dominant chord and its chord of resolution. This solution also accommodates the highly malleable character of dominant 7th chords in general. Remember how the same secondary dominant chord resulted from alterations to Mm2 and Hm2 and how each resolved to a different chord? One was V7 of II–7 in Mm2, while the other was V7 of IIØ7 in Hm2.[15] Well, virtually all dominant 7th chords can have multiple viable resolutions. So we'll often find that a secondary dominant chord will appear to be going one place, only to be reinterpreted, or its chord of resolution reinterpreted, in effect going someplace other than where it appeared to be heading. Schubert frequently did this to great effect in his music and in the process poignantly alluded to life's vicissitudes.

Since all secondary dominant chords are dominant 7th chords of some kind, the general characteristics of this family of chords apply more or less (tempered only by context) to all of them. Among the foremost qualities dominant 7th chords share is their malleability and the sense of motion they can create. With this in mind, I want to provide you with a reference chart that contains some guidelines to follow when selecting chord scales for V7 chords that appear to, or actually do, have multiple options.

In example 83 I have provided you with a reference guide of the five most useful scales for secondary dominant chords, in the form of an intervallic comparison of these five chord scales, like the ones we've used throughout this book. The numbers above each note compare the scale degrees of each scale to one another, using the Major scale as our basis for comparison (as always). The numbers below certain scale degrees indicate the function of these indicator notes as **available tensions** or **altered chord tones**. The chord on the left of each example shows a possible voicing containing some of the available tensions that distinguish each particular V7 chord's tonality from the others. And the remaining chords in each example show likely resolutions that correspond to each secondary dominant chord when functioning in a manner that could be defined by the chord scale indicated for each example. While the guide doesn't cover every possibility, it covers most of what you'll encounter in the types of jazz this book deals with, and it addresses all the chord-scale possibilities for secondary dominant chords you'll encounter in my compositions from the second half of this book.

---

[15] See p. 86 example 77 (V of IIØ7 from Hm2) and p. 83 example 71 (V of II–7 from Mm2).

Example 83 – Secondary Dominant Reference Guide

I encourage you to explore the other five scales we derived in this chapter, which I left out of the reference guide.[16] I only find two more to be useful (which I'll include below in example 84), but you should use your own judgment. I've left the two scales below out of the secondary dominant chord reference guide because they are more likely to be derived in a completely different manner than the five that are included, and they're often used in situations unrelated to secondary dominant chords. The Eastern sounding altered Hm5 comprised of two consecutive Harmonic minor tetrachords found in example 80 can be derived by placing the arpeggios of two adjacent Major 7th chords one half step apart in an alternating succession, while the chord scale previously addressed in example 74 (altered Mm5) could be produced by arranging the chord tones of a dominant 7♭9♮13 chord linearly and filling in the one remaining gap between the 3rd and 5th degrees with a passing tone from either the tonality in which the chord occurs (i.e., key of the moment) or its chord of resolution. There are only two possibilities anyway, either ♮4 or ♯4, and choosing ♮4 completes this scale (example 84).

Example 84

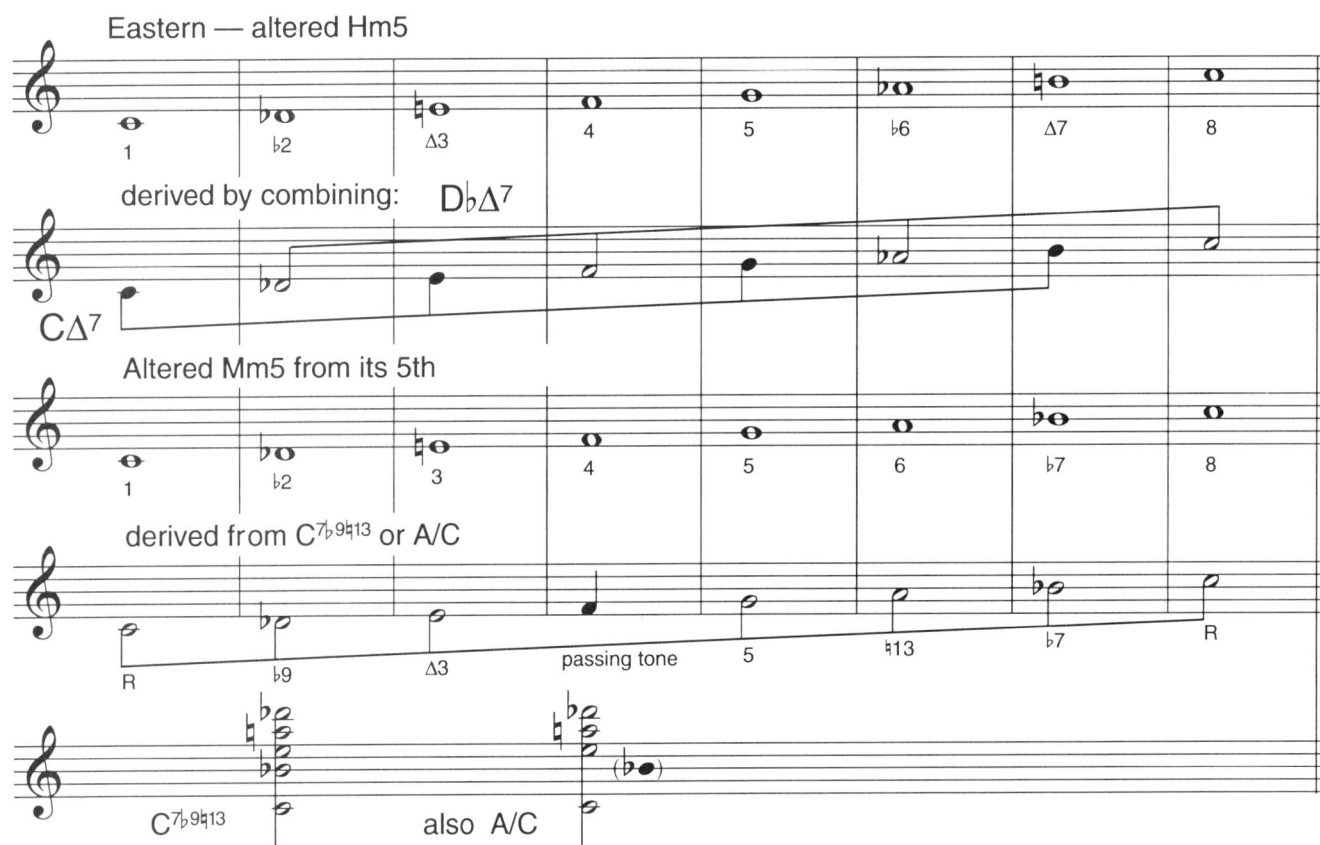

As with all chords, when improvising on or composing with a dominant 7th (secondary or otherwise), you can use its **chord tones**, plus the **passing tones** from the scale which best defines its harmonic function, some of which could also function as **available tensions**. You may also use **chromatic approach tones** outside of its appropriate scale, which would resolve in stepwise fashion to either its **chord tones** or its **available tensions**. In other words, the chromatic scale in its entirety is available, provided you can hear the relationships between the consonant and the dissonant notes and how to resolve the latter into the former. This principle applies to the substitute dominant chords we will examine and explain in the next chapter as well.

---

[16] Concerning the remaining scales derived in this chapter, both the altered Mm2 (example 71) and the altered Hm2 (example 77) are intervallically identical scales comprised of a Phrygian and a Major tetrachord combined, while of the four eastern sounding scales—the altered Phrygian (examples 52 and 57), the first version of altered Hm7 (example 82), the altered Mm7 (example 76), and the altered Hm5 (example 80)—I only find the altered Hm5 to be of much use, leaving the moderately useful altered Mm5 from its 5th degree (example 74) which I've included with Hm5 in example 84. In some music dictionaries I've seen the altered Hm5 scale called "the gypsy scale" and its origins related to Hindu and Turkish music.

Chapter 5: Substitute Dominant Chords

A substitute dominant 7th chord, such as the ones I mentioned in the last chapter, is a dominant 7th chord that can substitute for another dominant 7th chord, as the name implies. The reason this substitution is possible is because these two dominant 7th chords have two crucial notes in common. They both contain the identical chord tones required to form the augmented 4th interval characteristic of all dominant 7th chords (the Δ3rd and the ♭7th). However, the respective functions of each chord's Δ3 and ♭7 are inverted. In other words, the 3rd of one becomes the 7th of the other, while the 7th of one becomes the 3rd of the other. The significance of the augmented 4th interval to the relationship between these two chords doesn't end there, for the root of the substitute dominant 7th chord is an augmented 4th away from the root of the dominant 7th chord for which it can substitute as well (example 85).

Example 85

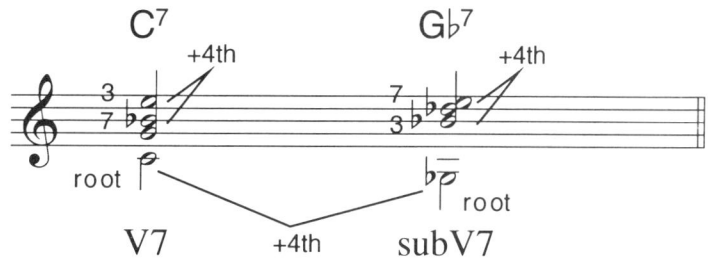

The reason I did not need to indicate the direction (either up or down) when referring to the augmented 4th distance between the roots of the substitute dominant 7th chord (G♭7 as in example 85) and the chord for which it can substitute (C7 as in example 85) is that the interval of an augmented 4th divides the octave into two equal parts, meaning that unlike other intervals, the distance (and therefore the intervallic relationship between the notes which constitute the interval) remains constant even when inverted (example 86).

Example 86

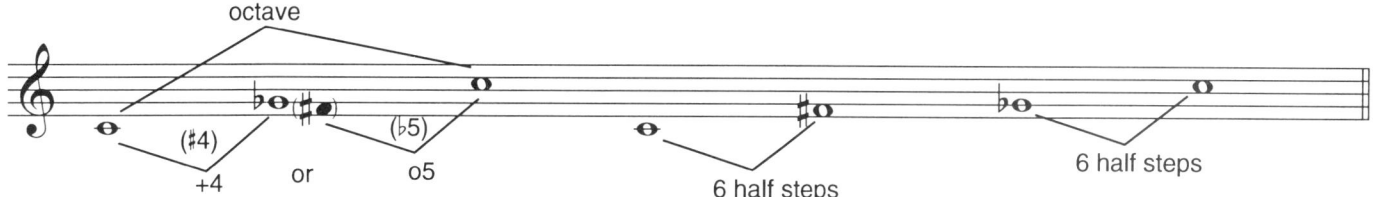

This (augmented) +4th or (diminished) O5th interval represents a distance between two notes of six half steps when measured by the smallest unit available in our musical system and has had a checkered past. The use of the tritone (as it is sometimes called) was even prohibited during the Middle Ages and the Renaissance. But without it a dominant 7th chord would lack the means of creating its inherent sense of motion or urgency. In fact, the sense of motion that is innate to the tritone is in part responsible for some of the problems we encountered in the preceding two chapters (e.g., the problematic Locrian dominant modal cadence [modal chapter, example 47] and a few of the secondary dominant chords which proved unwieldy, like V7 of VIIO7 [secondary dominant chapter, example 82]). Because the tritone yearns toward resolution so strongly, it can create a compelling sense of motion even out of the context or tonality from which it was derived. Consequently, a substitute dominant 7th chord whose root is a tritone away from another dominant chord (primary, secondary, or otherwise) may either resolve to the chord of resolution of the dominant 7th chord for which it is substituting, or it may resolve to a chord whose root would be a perfect 5th below its root (implied or stated). This is because the 3rd and 7th which this shared tritone represents can be interpreted in two different ways in this context, creating in turn two different root motions (implied or stated) for each tonality of resolution for each interpretation (example 87).

Example 87

There are in fact other possible resolutions of a substitute dominant 7th chord (as with all dominant 7th chords) and other possible interpretations of the function(s) of the tritone, but we will address the former in the subdominant minor chapter and will explore the latter in the chapter on vagrant chords.

As I mentioned in the preceding chapter, songs that employ sequential dominant 7th chords whose root motion moves around the cycle of 5ths (counterclockwise), like those in example 88, invite the use of substitute dominant 7th chords.

Example 88

The two seven-bar phrases in example 88 illustrate how substitute dominant 7th chords and the dominant 7th chords for which they can substitute contain the same Δ3rd and ♭7 (though inverted), despite their differing roots that are a tritone apart. This not only allows for the kind of substitution(s) I suggested for a tune like "There Is No Greater Love" (secondary dominant chapter, example 67), it also offers great latitude when substituting a sub V7 for the V7 in II V sequences. And II V sequences are one of the most prevalent ways we encounter dominant 7th chords in all kinds of jazz. We will explore II Vs in more detail in the next chapter. For now it's important to realize how interchangeable dominant 7th chords whose roots are a tritone apart are. In fact, dominant 7th♭5 chords whose roots are a tritone apart can actually be (and usually are) inversions of each other, which makes sense, considering the fact that the distance between the root and the ♭5 of such chords is also a tritone, which would of course also be invertible, just like the tritone existing between the Δ3rd and ♭7 of these interchangeable dominant 7th chords. Check out how the four chords in example 89 all contain the same four notes. And notice how the function(s) of these common tones differ(s) within the context of each chord.

Example 89

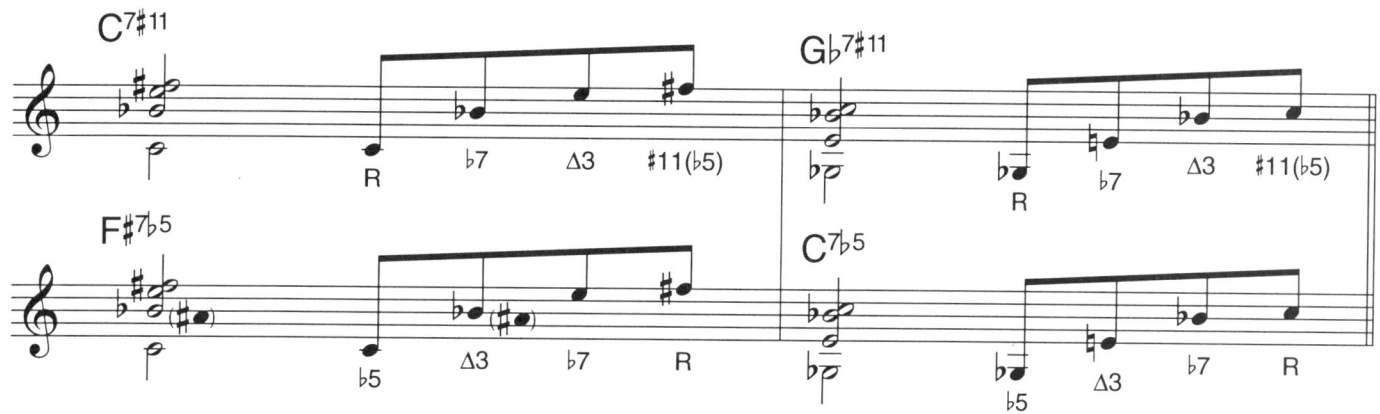

Substitute dominant chords like the chords in example 89 can resolve to any of the many chords that other dominant 7th chords can resolve to, which means their harmonic functions are contextually determined. This brings us to the options for chord scales for substitute dominant 7th chords. As I mentioned in the preceding chapter, dominant 7th chords with ♭5s often function as substitute dominant chords and are best defined by either the Lydian ♭7 scale (Mm4) or the Altered Dominant scale (Mm7). And as with other chords which can have multiple interpretations, the presence or inference of the indicator notes that distinguish these two scales from one another is the prime means for determining which to use. So let's make an intervallic comparison of these two scales (example 90).

Example 90

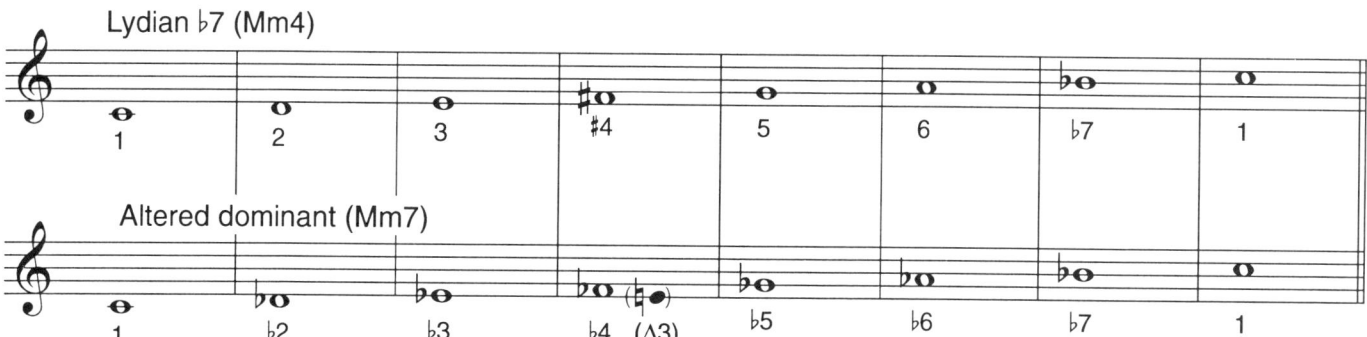

While the occurrence of such indicator notes as ♭9 (i.e., ♭2 8VA) versus ♮9 (i.e., ♮2 8VA), or vice versa, would seem to indicate one scale over the other, it's easy to confuse these two scales when comparing them, because of an interesting anomaly that reveals itself when we examine the Lydian ♭7 scale in comparison with an Altered Dominant scale whose roots are a tritone apart (example 91).

Example 91

As you can hear and see from example 91, both the C Lydian ♭7 scale and the F♯ Altered Dominant scale contain the same notes, which makes sense since they are both "modes" of the g Melodic minor scale, and the substitute dominant chords they could accompany (i.e., C7♭5 and F♯7♭5, as found in example 89) are inversions of each other. The same applies to the C Altered Dominant scale and the G♭ Lydian ♭7 scale from the second half of example 91, which both also contain the same notes, as they are both "modes" of a d♭ Melodic minor scale, and they could also accompany either G♭7♭5 or C7♭5. So how do we apply the indicator notes to determine which scale to use? We have to compare scales whose roots are identical, as in example 90. Don't compare the scales whose roots are a tritone apart, because these scales may come from the same tonality, in which case they will obviously have the same scale tones even if their respective functions appear to be different. When you encounter the ♭9, ♯9, or ♭13 on a substitute dominant 7th chord, you use the Altered Dominant scale built on the root of the substitute dominant 7th chord. And when you encounter the ♮9 and ♮13, you use the Lydian ♭7 scale built on the root of the substitute dominant 7th chord (example 92).

Example 92

I know it is difficult to distinguish these tonalities from one another at first. But the differences aren't so subtle in most of the contexts in which they occur. I'll clarify some of this in the next chapter on II Vs. I suggest that you sing each of the scales from examples 90 and 91 while you play the appropriate chord as found in example 92, because this can really help you to hear the differences more clearly.

In example 93 I've given you four different ways to use substitute dominant 7th chords for a sequence of secondary dominant chords taken from the same song we used in example 67 of the last chapter, "There Is No Greater Love."

Example 93

"There Is No Greater Love"

© Symes & Jones

1st option

2nd option

3rd option

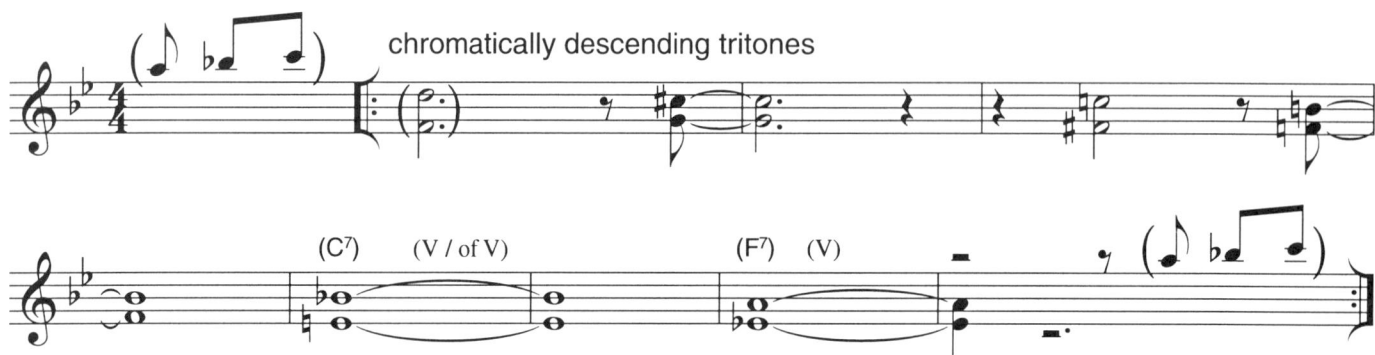

One possible way to interpret the harmonic analysis of the first four bars of "There Is No Greater Love" would be to see the IΔ chord (BbΔ) as the point of origin (and, as actually happens in the tune, the final destination as well), with the other chords, in particular the V7 of II chord (which ends each of the four options of our example) as signposts or way stations along the harmonic journey which the chords represent. In example 93 I've chosen four common options for traversing the distance between the I chord and the V of II chord, each of which employs a different series of dominant 7th chords as our vehicle or mode of transport. These four options demonstrate quite clearly how the chromatically descending tritone motion that occurs between the 2nd, 3rd, and 4th chords remains the same in all four options. Only the root motion and the resulting inversion of the function(s) of the notes of each tritone change. In fact, the rest of the first A section of "There Is No Greater Love" proceeds in much the same manner, moving on from V of II to V of V, and then to V of I.

We could also use substitute dominant 7th chords for the V of V and the V of I chords which conclude the first A section of "There Is No Greater Love"'s AABA song form. Many jazz musicians do employ such substitutions when blowing on this tune, but sub V of V and sub V of I may not be the best choices during the melody, and if we use sub V7 chords for all the secondary dominant chords in this or any song, we've only succeeded in making the unusual banal and predictable.

There are times when you will encounter the application of other methods of harmonic analysis for substitute dominant 7th chords. For example, in the second option from example 93, the Eb7 chord, which I interpret as sub V of III, could be interpreted as the IV7 chord, and the Ab7, which I interpret as sub V of VI, could be viewed as bVII7. I don't favor this method, because it fails to account for these chords' actual harmonic function, something which, while cumbersome, is crucial, especially initially as the student strives to acquire the facility necessary to deal with such substitutions as they often happen in performance, i.e., with no advance warning. And understanding a sub V7 chord's actual harmonic function is crucial, because if you expect an A7, but the bass player plays an Eb, or the pianist plays an Eb7, you have to react. One is more likely to arrive at the appropriate choice when the chord in question's harmonic function is recognized and understood. Ultimately this has to be an aural process, so learn to hear these chords and recognize their harmonic functions not just on the page, or on the fingerboard, but with your ears, for that is where true understanding will occur.

Chapter 6: Two Five Progressions

One of the most frequently used chord progressions in jazz is the II V sequence, which, as its name implies, is a combination of two chords occurring in succession which are modeled on the chords that diatonically occur on the 2nd and 5th degrees of a Major scale (example 94).

Example 94

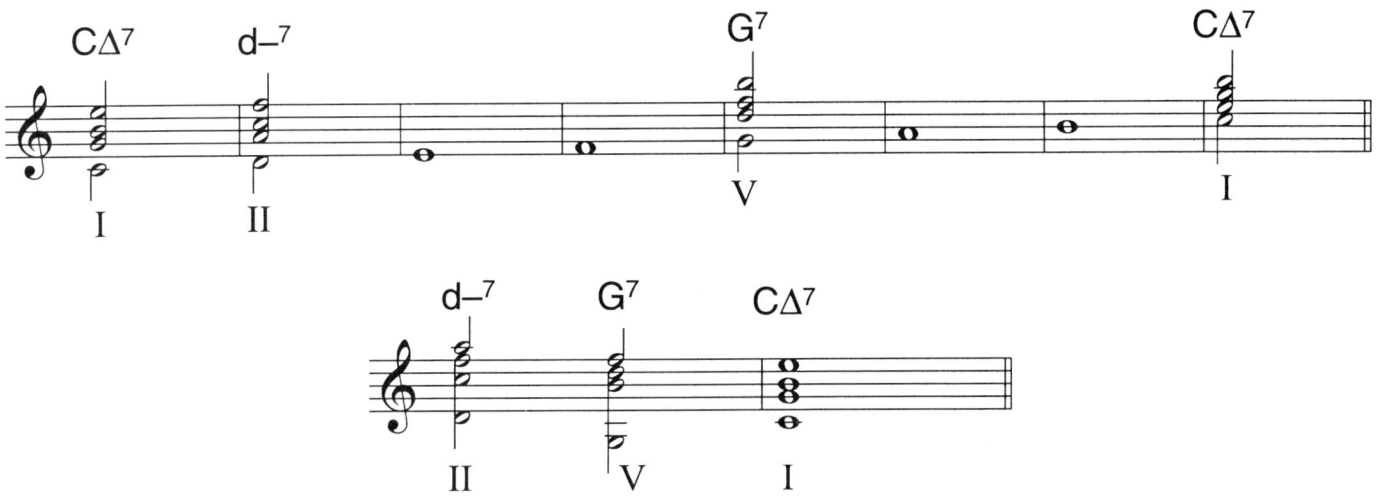

II V progressions don't always resolve to the I chord, however. Each of the secondary dominant chords we previously constructed for the non-tonic chords of both the Major and minor tonalities can be preceded by a II chord, and each of the II chords which precede the V chords in these "secondary" II V progressions can be either –7 or Ø7. These "secondary" II V progressions can then resolve to any of the chords that secondary dominant chords can resolve to (example 95).

Example 95

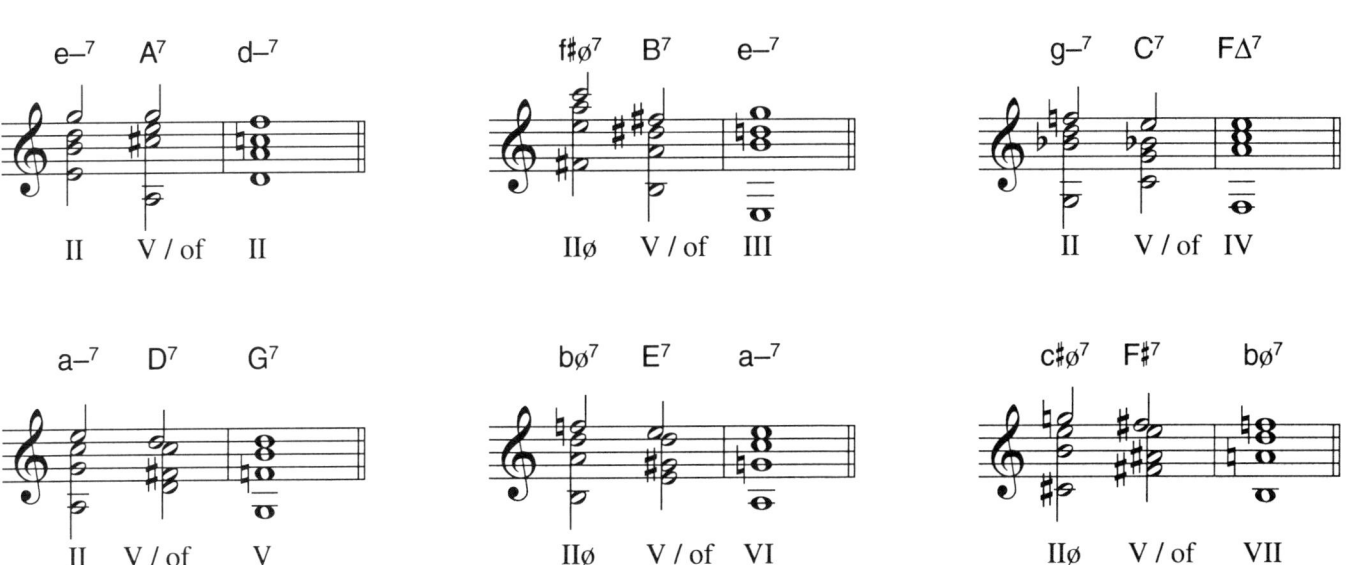

Example 95 shows the "secondary" II V progressions as derived for the non-tonic diatonic chords in the key of C Major. Just like the secondary dominant chords whose intervallic structures and upper structures vary, the II chords which precede them also vary in both the intervallic structure of their chord tones (i.e., some have ♮5, others ♭5) and the tensions occurring in their respective tonalities. Some of these tensions work on –7 and Ø7 chords, such as ♮9 and ♮11 (and even ♮13, though it is problematic in a II V progression, because it prematurely sounds the note which is the Δ3 of the V chord). While others, such as ♭9, are too dissonant to use on –7 and Ø7 chords. And ♭13 confuses the issue in a II V context, because it tends to make the II chord sound more like an inversion of the ♭VII chord, while ♯11 is either superfluous or misleading because it is the same note as the ♭5 which already occurs in Ø7 chords. Jazz musicians tend to favor the options that can accommodate the greatest number of workable available tensions on these II chords.

As you can hear and see for yourself from example 95, there are only two options for II chords (in a II V context), either –7 or Ø7, but as with most of the other chords we've dealt with, they each have multiple possible interpretations. In example 96 I've given you the five most useful chord scale options for II chords functioning in II V contexts as you're likely to encounter them in jazz (example 96).

Example 96

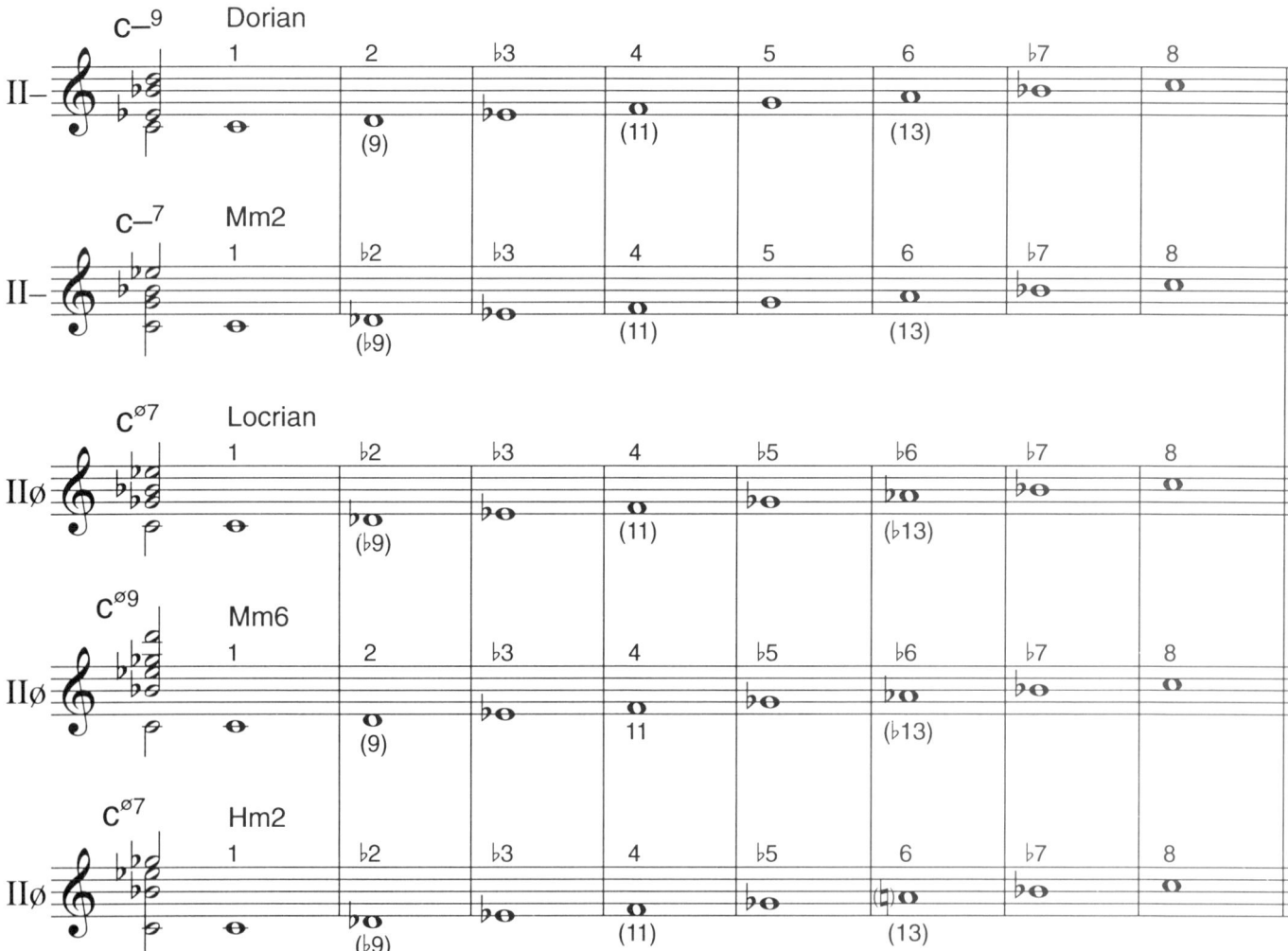

Some of you may wonder why I am referring to the cØ7 chord that corresponds to Locrian in example 96 as IIØ instead of VIIØ7, as it would diatonically occur in a Major tonality (D♭ Major in this case). If you remember the descending form of the Traditional minor scale, which is the same as Aeolian, then you'll know the answer: because b♭–, which would be the VI– chord in D♭ Major (whose corresponding mode is b♭ Aeolian), can be interpreted as

I– (as it would be in relation to the descending form of the b♭ Traditional minor scale), which means cØ7 would become IIØ (in the descending form of this scale), and its corresponding chord scale would be c Locrian (which is b♭ Aeolian from the 2nd degree).

A close examination of the intervallic structure of each chord scale from example 96 reveals that only Dorian (for –7 chords) and Mm6 (for Ø7 chords) can accommodate both ♮9 and ♮11, the two most useful available tensions for II chords in II V progressions. But the other three, Locrian, Mm2, and Hm2 do also occur. When you find the ♮9 or ♮11 on a –7 chord either as an available tension on the chord itself, or in the melody, or by inference, then Dorian is your best choice. These same indicator notes (♮9 and ♮11) in relation to any Ø7 chord would imply the Mm6 scale.

As I mentioned earlier, we can also derive "secondary" II V progressions from Melodic minor and Harmonic minor by adding a II chord to each of the secondary dominant chords we previously derived for each of the non-tonic diatonic chords of these two minor tonalities. In example 97 we'll examine the results that this process yields.

Example 97

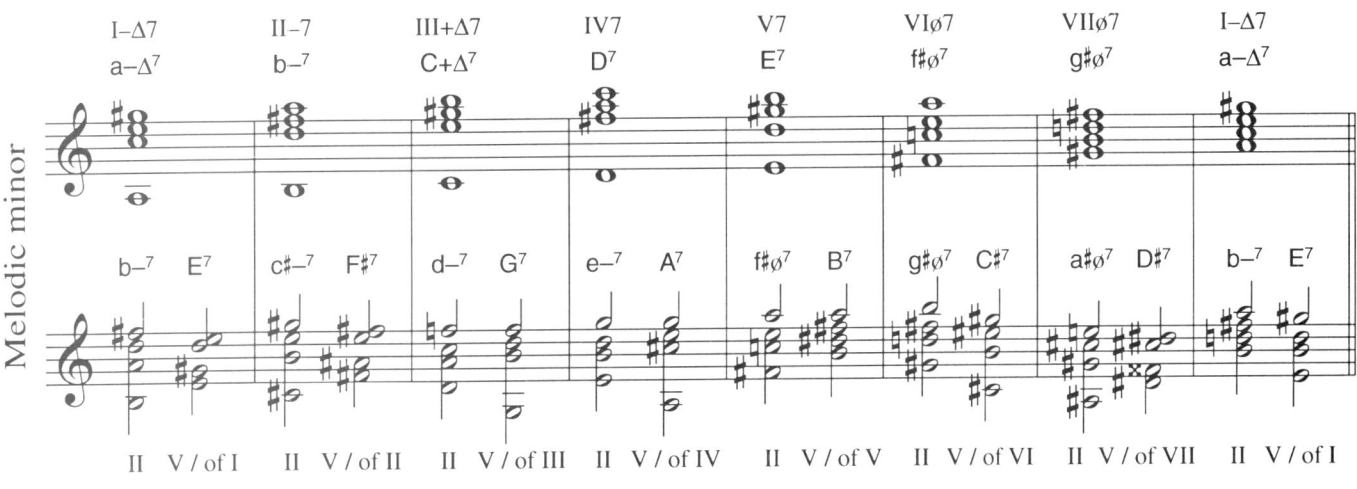

A close examination of example 97 reveals that every II chord of each "secondary" II V progression is again either –7 or Ø7, just like those occurring in the "secondary" II Vs derived from a Major tonality. This is because, like secondary dominant chords which don't have to resolve to the tonality of their derivation, the II chords that precede them may come from one tonality, yet resolve or move to another. In fact, in all II V contexts the II chords obviously move to a V7 chord of some kind. So one could correctly surmise that these II chords exist solely for the sake of the V chords which they precede. Consequently, the key to understanding their harmonic function is often inexorably linked to that of the secondary dominant chords which they accompany in II V progressions. And just like the secondary dominant chords that these "secondary" II chords precede in II V progressions, the key indicator notes within the chord tones of each II chord are ♮5 versus ♭5. However, unlike dominant 7th chords, which can accommodate a wide range of available and altered tensions, –7 and Ø7 chords can only usefully accommodate ♮9 and ♮11 in a II V context, again rendering Dorian (for –7 chords) and Mm6 (for Ø7 chords) the most useful chord scales for II chords in these "secondary" II V progressions derived from the minor tonalities. We will also find Locrian, Mm2, Hm2 and in some cases even Phrygian or Aeolian are workable, but not quite as flexible as Dorian and Mm6. Another reason for the recurrence of the same scales for these II chords no matter what tonality they are derived from is that like the secondary dominant chords which they precede in II V progressions, the alterations to their "modes" of origin required to create them transforms their "parent" tonalities into either an unworkable hybrid scale or one of the same five chord scales we ended up with for the II chords in the "secondary" II V progressions derived from a Major tonality (as shown in example 96).

We will also find substitute dominant 7th chords used in the context(s) of II V progressions. There are four basic approaches for II Vs, as I've shown in example 98. Two involve substitute dominant chords, and one uses the relative II chord of the substitute V combined with the chord for which the sub V can substitute.

Example 98

The four basic approaches for II V progressions are: (1) the standard II–7 V7, (2) II–7 sub V7, (3) sub II–7 sub V7, and (4) II of sub V to V. Remember that the II chords in each option can be either –7 or Ø7 chords. Each II V progression can resolve to any of the chords any dominant 7th chord can resolve to. I've shown four possible resolutions for each approach. All in the first staff (letter A) resolve to Δ7 chords; all in the second staff (letter B) resolve to minor chords; all in the third staff (letter C) resolve to dominant 7th chords; and all in the fourth staff (letter D) resolve to Ø7 chords. There are other possible resolutions, but the ones I've given you in example 98 are quite representative of what you'll encounter in jazz.

The first two options are pretty self-explanatory, i.e., II V and II sub V, but again remember, these II chords could be either II–7 or IIØ7. The third and fourth options may not be quite as obvious to some of you. The third option, sub II sub V, merely adds the relative II–7 (or IIØ7) to the substitute dominant 7th chord. For example, if G7 is V, then Db7 is sub V7, and the relative II–7 for Db7 is ab–7, just as the relative II–7 for G7 is d–7. The fourth option, II of sub V to V7, takes option 3 and replaces the sub V with the V7 chord for which it was substituting (in options 2 and 3). This fourth option is not as common as the other three, but it illustrates how flexible II V progressions are, which is in part why they are so frequently used.

If we interpret the II V progressions from the first staff letter A of example 98 in relation to Gb as opposed to C, they acquire entirely different harmonic functions: ab–7 to Db7 is now a standard II V, while ab–7 to G7 becomes II sub V, and d–7 to G7 becomes a sub II sub V, while d–7 to Db7 becomes II of sub V to V7.

Similar reinterpretations of these II Vs can be applied in relation to the other resolutions in example 98 (i.e., not just those resolving to IΔ). And the interpretations of some of the chords of resolution are in fact malleable as well. For example, any of the V7 chords which the II Vs resolve to in the third series of resolutions (3rd staff/letter C of example 98) could be interpreted as other secondary dominant chords (say V of II), or they could be interpreted as the IV7 chord found in a Melodic minor tonality, or as often occurs, they could be interpreted as the IV7 chord of a blues. And the Ø7 chords found in the fourth series of resolutions (fourth staff/letter D of example 98) could be interpreted as either VIØ7 in Melodic minor, or as VIIØ7 in Major, or Melodic minor. In fact, the Ø7 chord is often used where one would expect to find the –7 chord in II V progressions, because it can suggest an additional relationship to a tonic Major chord through the subdominant minor region.

Jazz musicians often play the last A section of the standard "Stella by Starlight" as a series of IIØ7 Vs beginning on the b5th of the key. The chords of this sequence function as IIØ7 V7 of III, moving to IIØ7 V7 of II, then to IIØ7 V7 of I, before resolving to IΔ(7). In effect, as IIØ7 V7 of III arrives at a chord whose root corresponds to III, this III chord is transformed into another IIØ7 as part of the IIØ7 V7 of II that follows (example 99).

Example 99

Excerpt from "Stella by Starlight"

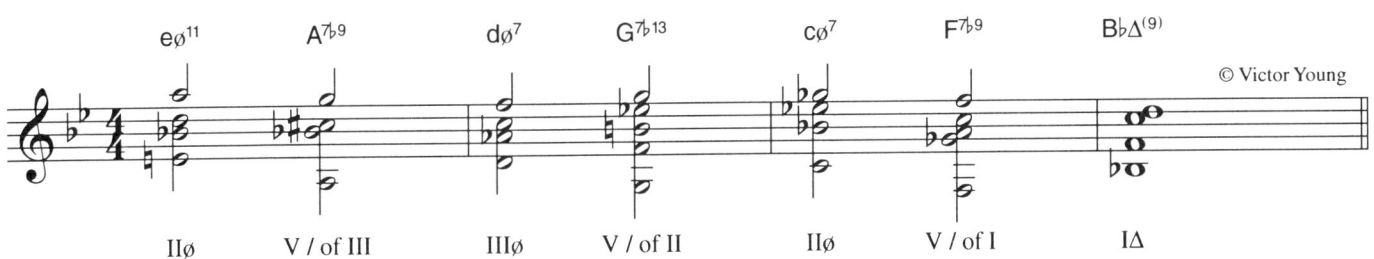

I've applied a process of diminution to the duration of the chord changes in example 99, reducing an eight bar phrase from the original song to a four bar phrase. This process in no way alters the relationships between the chords, while it illustrates them in half the space.

There is an interesting aspect of the penultimate bar in example 99: during the final IIØ7 V7 of I, the melody contains the key indicator note necessary to suggest a subdominant minor relationship to the tonic (IΔ) chord (i.e., G♭). This note is also the same note that distinguishes IIØ7 from II–7 in this key. And using the IIØ7 chord to suggest the subdominant minor region is another effective way either to establish or reinforce the tonic Major tonality of this song, as you can see and hear for yourself in example 100.

Example 100

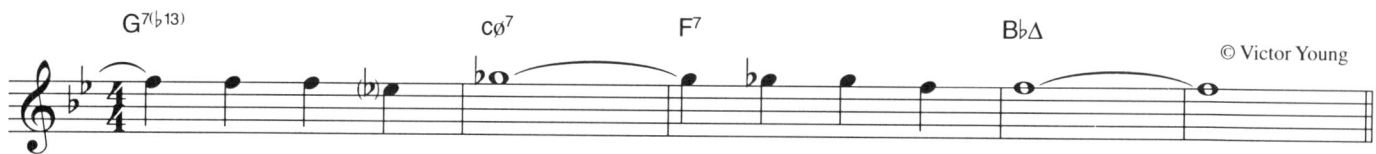

© Victor Young

We are going to cover the subdominant region in the next chapter. But first I am going to apply each of the four basic II V approaches from example 98 to the cadential phrase which concludes "Stella by Starlight": 101A is the standard IIØ7 V7 to IΔ7 used by most jazz musicians at this point of the song; 101B is IIØ7 sub V7 to IΔ7; 101C is sub IIØ7 to sub V7 to IΔ7; and 101D is sub IIØ7 to V7 to IΔ7.

Example 101A

Example 101B

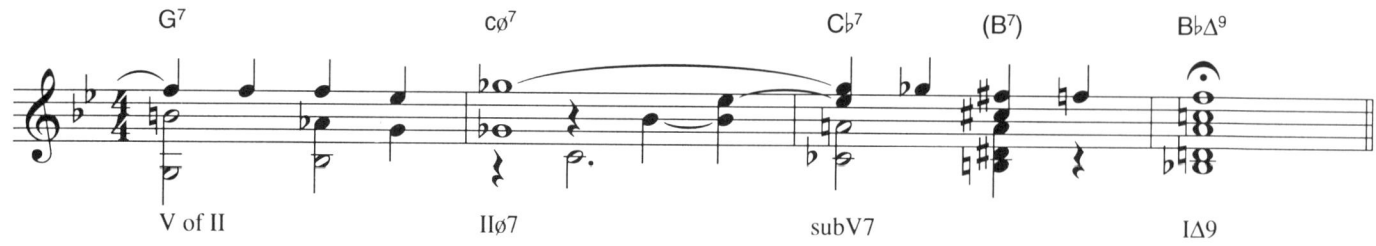

104

Example 101C

Example 101D

While these four reharmonizations of the cadential phrase of the last A of "Stella By Starlight" technically work, only the first two (101A and 101B) are in keeping with the character of the song when used in context. The last two reharmonizations (101C and 101D) only marginally work if preceded by another substitute dominant chord (sub V of IIØ7, i.e., D♭7), while preceding this sub V (of II) with its relative IIØ7 (i.e., sub IIØ7, which would be a♭Ø7) would not really work, because the melody at this point in the song would render redundant the move from sub IIØ7 to sub V7. And these last two reharmonizations do not improve upon either of the first two. But, as always, I encourage you to openly explore all options and use your own judgment if and when it is sufficiently developed that you can rely upon it.

Chapter 7: Subdominant Minor

Each of the scale degrees of a Major tonality can be identified by either the appropriate Roman numeral designation we've employed throughout this book, or by one of a corresponding series of titles. We have already used some of these titles, such as tonic for I and dominant for V. The entire series is as follows: I = tonic, II = supertonic, III = mediant, IV = subdominant, V = dominant, VI = submediant, and VII = subtonic (example 102).

Example 102

CΔ⁷	d–⁷	e–⁷	FΔ⁷	G⁷	a–⁷	bø⁷	CΔ⁷
Tonic	Supertonic	Mediant	Subdominant	Dominant	Submediant	Subtonic	Tonic
IΔ7	II–7	III–7	IVΔ7	V7	VI–7	VIIø7	IΔ7

These terms may also be applied to the chords built on each of their corresponding scale degrees, just like the Roman numerals. Consequently, a subdominant minor chord would be a chord built on the IVth degree that contains a ♭3 as a chord tone. This minor 3rd chord tone would be the ♭6th scale degree when measuring from the root of the relative tonic chord. (In the key of C this ♭6 would be A♭, the minor 3rd of an f– chord.)

There are three ways to derive a subdominant minor chord from the modes which correspond to Major triads: lowering the 6th degree of Ionian, lowering the 6th degree of Mixolydian, or lowering the 4th and 6th degrees of Lydian each produces a minor Δ7th or minor 6th chord on the 4th degree of these altered scales. However, without also lowering the 7th degree of Ionian and Lydian, the resulting scale, which some refer to as "Harmonic Major," is a bit unruly and rarely used. And once the 7th degree is lowered, all these altered scales become Melodic minor scales (from the 5th degree). And the Melodic minor scale is usually the best option for subdominant minor chords (example 103).

There are times when you'll encounter a minor chord that appears to be derived from the 4th degree of a Major tonality, yet it contains or indicates the ♭7th (as opposed to the Δ7th or Δ6th) as a chord tone, for example, an f–7 chord adjacent to a CΔ7 chord. But the resulting –7th chord is more likely part of a II V progression than a true subdominant minor chord, because the ♭7 (e♭ in the case of our f–7 chord) undermines the Δ3rd of our IΔ chord (E♮ in the case of our CΔ7 chord), calling into question the applicability of any subdominant minor to I Major relationship between these two chords. One reason for this ambiguity is that diatonic –7 chords naturally occur on the 4th degree of two minor tonalities: Aeolian and Harmonic minor (example 104).

Example 103

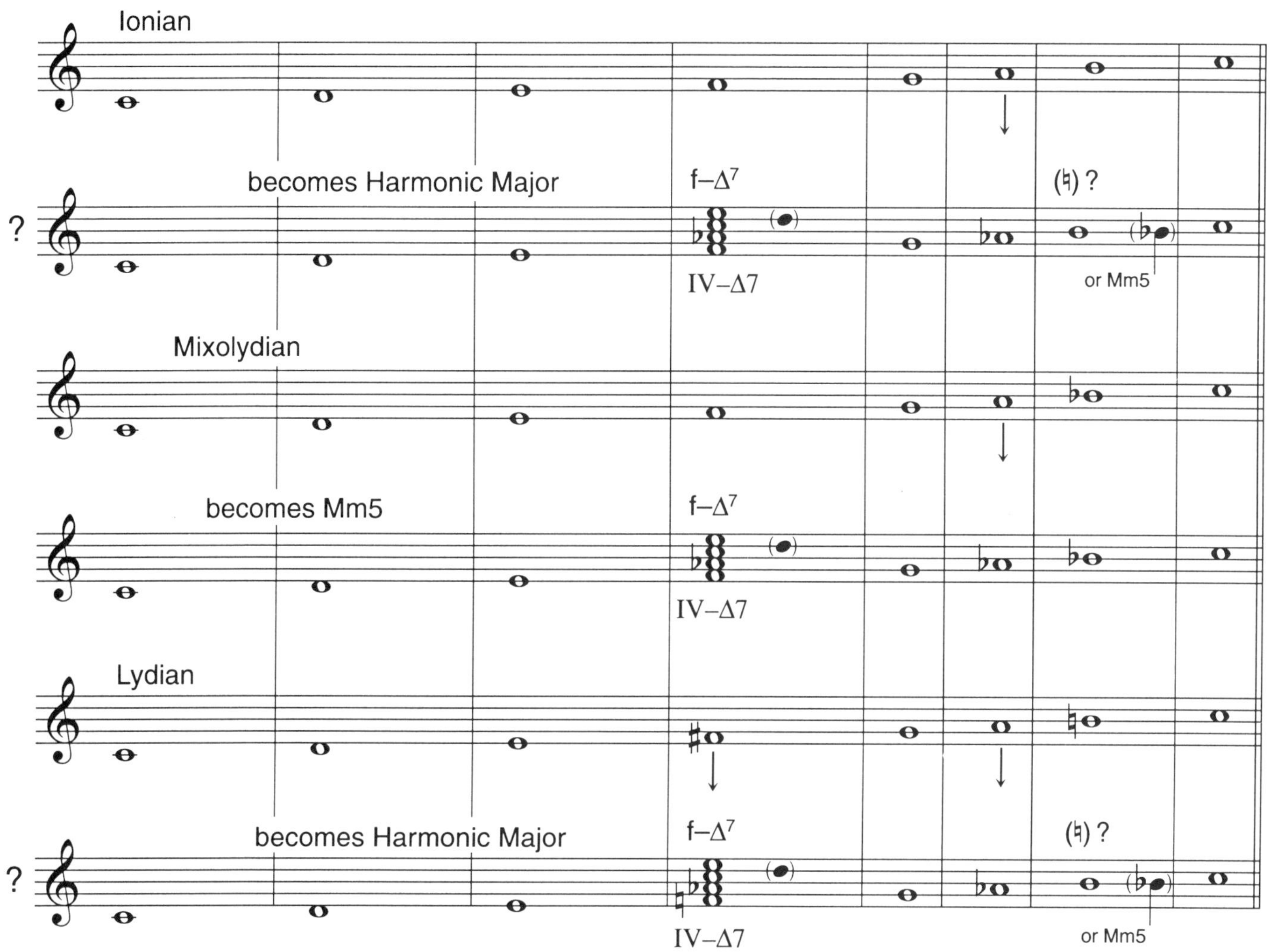

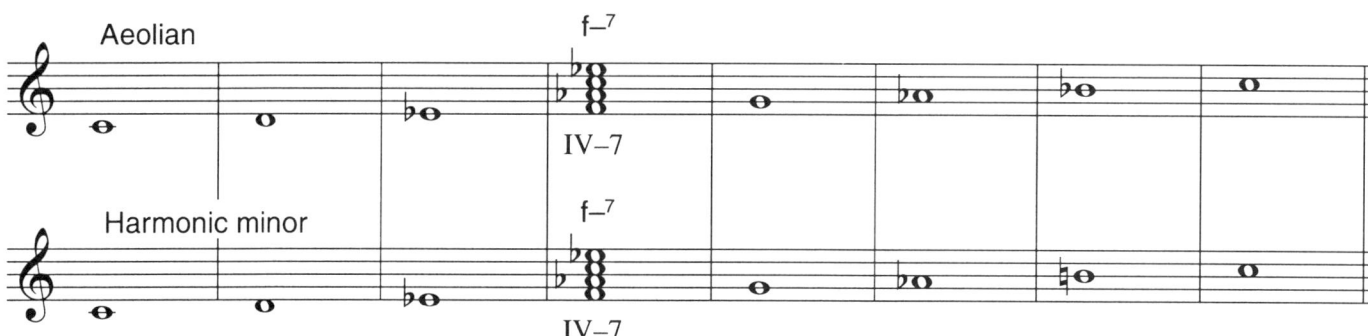

Example 104

While the IV–7 chords found in example 104 technically meet the definition implied by the name, in practice the subdominant minor chord, and chords from the subdominant minor region which contain the –3rd of the subdominant minor chord and can therefore substitute for it, tend to function in a manner that reinforces or sheds new light on the Major tonality a 4th below, particularly this Major tonality's tonic chord. And, as previously mentioned, the ♭7 of these IV–7 chords undermines the Δ3rd of the tonic Δ chord whose root is a 4th below.

Remember the last three chords that constituted the final cadence from "Stella by Starlight" at the end of the last chapter (example 100)? The cØ7 chord contains a $G\flat$ (the –3 of an eb– chord, which is the subdominant minor chord of B♭Δ, the tonic IΔ chord of the song). The F7♭9 also contains the same $G\flat$ (♭9) as well, and this IIØ7 V7 progression then cadences to B♭Δ functioning as IΔ. And cØ7 is also an inversion of eb–6, which is a subdominant minor chord of B♭Δ. Notice the lack of any $D\flat$ (the ♭7 of eb–) in the chords in example 105.

Example 105

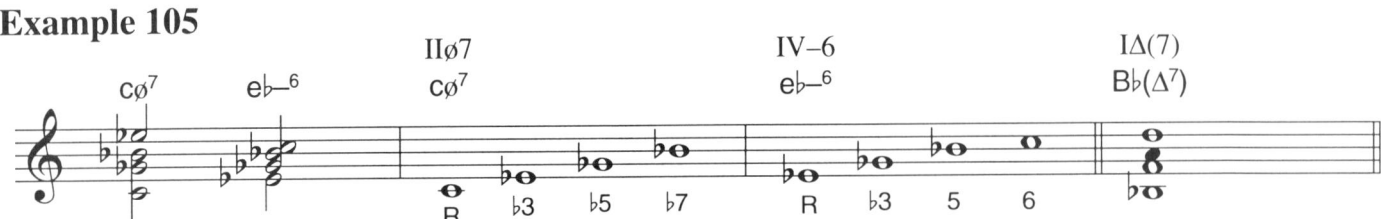

The example taken from "Stella by Starlight" illustrates how the subdominant minor chord and chords taken from its tonality which are either inversions of this IV– chord or contain the –3rd of this IV– chord enhance and reinforce a relationship between their respective tonalities. This is due in part to the fact that the relationship between these two tonalities is four steps apart on the circle of 5ths. This distance not only divides the circle of 5ths into three equal parts (see Major chapter, examples 9 and 10), but it also sets up an interesting relationship between the tonic of one key and the relative minor chord of the other. If we start with the key of C Major and move four counterclockwise steps around the circle of 5ths, we arrive at the key of A♭ Major. The relative minor of A♭ Major is f–, which is the subdominant minor of CΔ, and the tonic Δ triad in the key of C Major can also function as V (or a secondary V) of this subdominant minor chord, meaning the reinforcing nature of this relationship works both ways (example 106).

Example 106

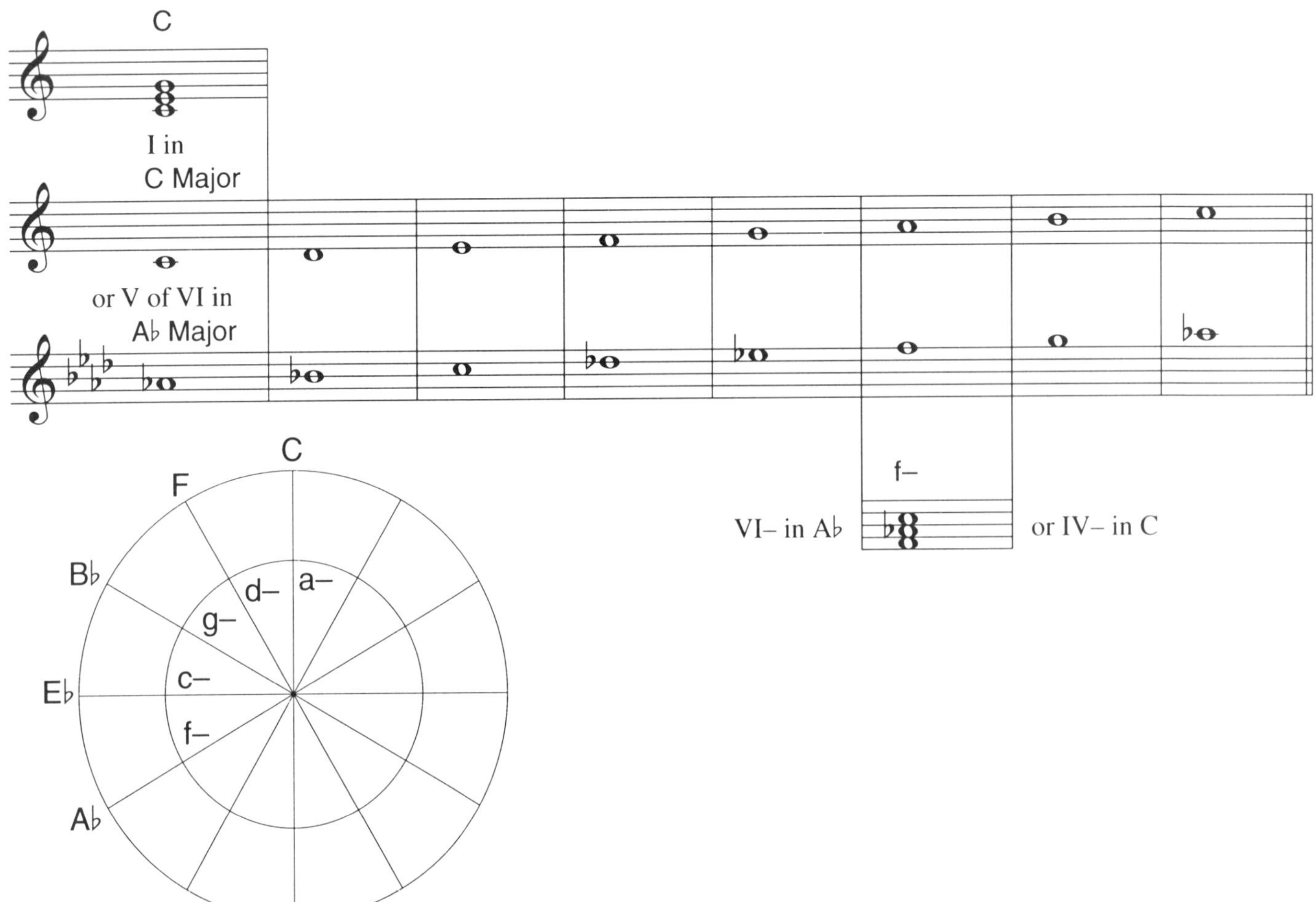

The use of the subdominant minor chord began and evolved in classical music, where these chords were not usually 7th chords, so the IΔ triad could and did function as the V of the subdominant minor chord, just as the subdominant minor chord could function as an altered IV in relation to the IΔ chord.

In jazz, as we know, we often encounter 7th chords where a triad would suffice, and the IV minor chord is no exception. When we either directly encounter or can infer the existence of the Δ6th and Δ7th degrees in relation to the subdominant minor chord, then the best chord scale choice is Melodic minor. Conversely, when we encounter or can infer ♭7, then Dorian is a likely candidate, while ♭6 and ♭7 indicate Aeolian. But remember, these −7 chords are unlikely to be functioning in a true subdominant minor capacity. There are rare occasions where Harmonic minor is plausible, but its (augmented) +2nd interval seems particularly out of place in the subdominant minor context. And Phrygian is even more alien in a subdominant minor context (example 107).

Example 107

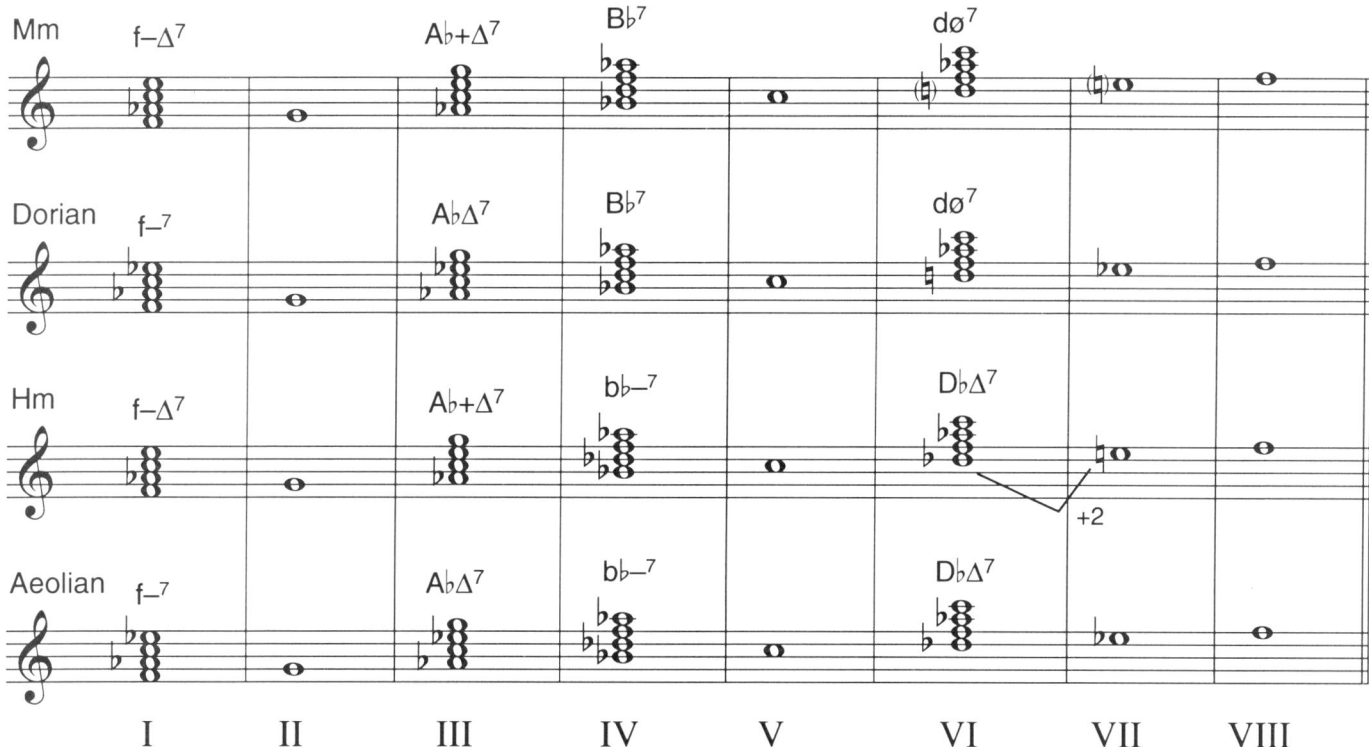

As you can see as well as hear from example 107, for each of the four minor scales, there are four chordal options that contain the key indicator note for the subdominant region (i.e., the ♭3rd of the scale or the −3rd of the subdominant minor chord). The four chords from each scale are often used as either direct substitutes for the subdominant minor chord, or as part of a deceptive or delayed cadence (example 108).

Example 108

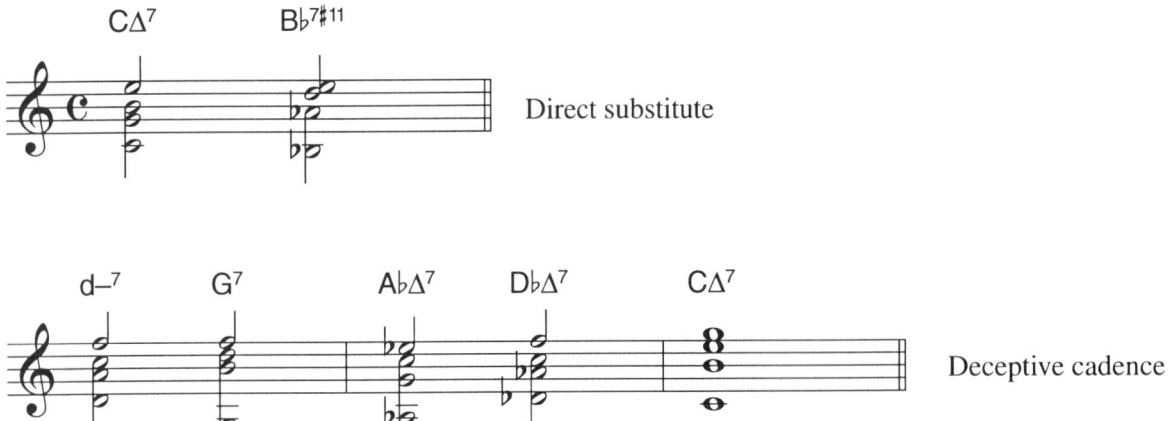

Direct substitute

Deceptive cadence

The first progression from example 108, IΔ7 to ♭VII♯11, is a common vamp which substitutes the ♭VII♯11 for a IV–Δ7 chord, in effect playing the subdominant minor region against a tonic Major tonality. The second progression uses a II–7 V7 to set up an expected cadence to the I chord, but instead deceptively goes to ♭VIΔ7 and then to ♭IIΔ7 (both of which contain the subdominant minor indicator note, i.e. A♭) before fulfilling the expectation which was delayed by the deceptive cadence.

In the first example the B♭7♯11 would use a Lydian ♭7 scale, which is in fact Melodic minor from the 4th degree. In the second example the ♭VIΔ chord would use the Lydian scale to define its harmonic function in this context, because it is most likely derived from a move three counterclockwise steps around the circle of 5ths from the IΔ chord which it delays, meaning it is related to the key of E♭ Major, making it IVΔ7, and therefore Lydian, while the D♭Δ7 is derived from a move four counterclockwise steps from the key of the IΔ7 (i.e., C Major), making it IVΔ7 of A♭ Major and therefore also Lydian (example 109).

You could also credibly treat the ♭VIΔ7 (A♭Δ7) and the ♭IIΔ7 (D♭Δ7) as if they are both derived from the same tonality (i.e., A♭) which occurs four counterclockwise steps away from C. But this approach removes the ♯11 available tension from the ♭VIΔ7 chord because it is now Ionian, not Lydian. And as I've previously stated, jazz musicians, especially since Art Tatum and Charlie Parker, tend to favor options that accommodate the widest spectrum of available tensions. This is not noted in order to imply that you must adhere to their methods. But you need to be aware of these methods and recognize them when you encounter them. It is also historically important to honor the innovations of our musical ancestors, for we stand on the shoulders of these giants when we strive to attain new musical heights.

Example 109 shows the I, IV, and VI chords for each of the first five keys moving counterclockwise around the circle of 5ths. It also contains these chords spelled out in the three keys which are pertinent to the deceptive cadence contained in example 108. Further examination reveals two additional possibilities for f–: the first is in the key of E♭ (which would be three counterclockwise moves away from C), where f– is II–; the second is in the key of D♭ (five counterclockwise moves away from C), where f– is III– (refer to example 10 of the Major chapter to confirm all of the possibilities in all twelve keys).

110

Example 109

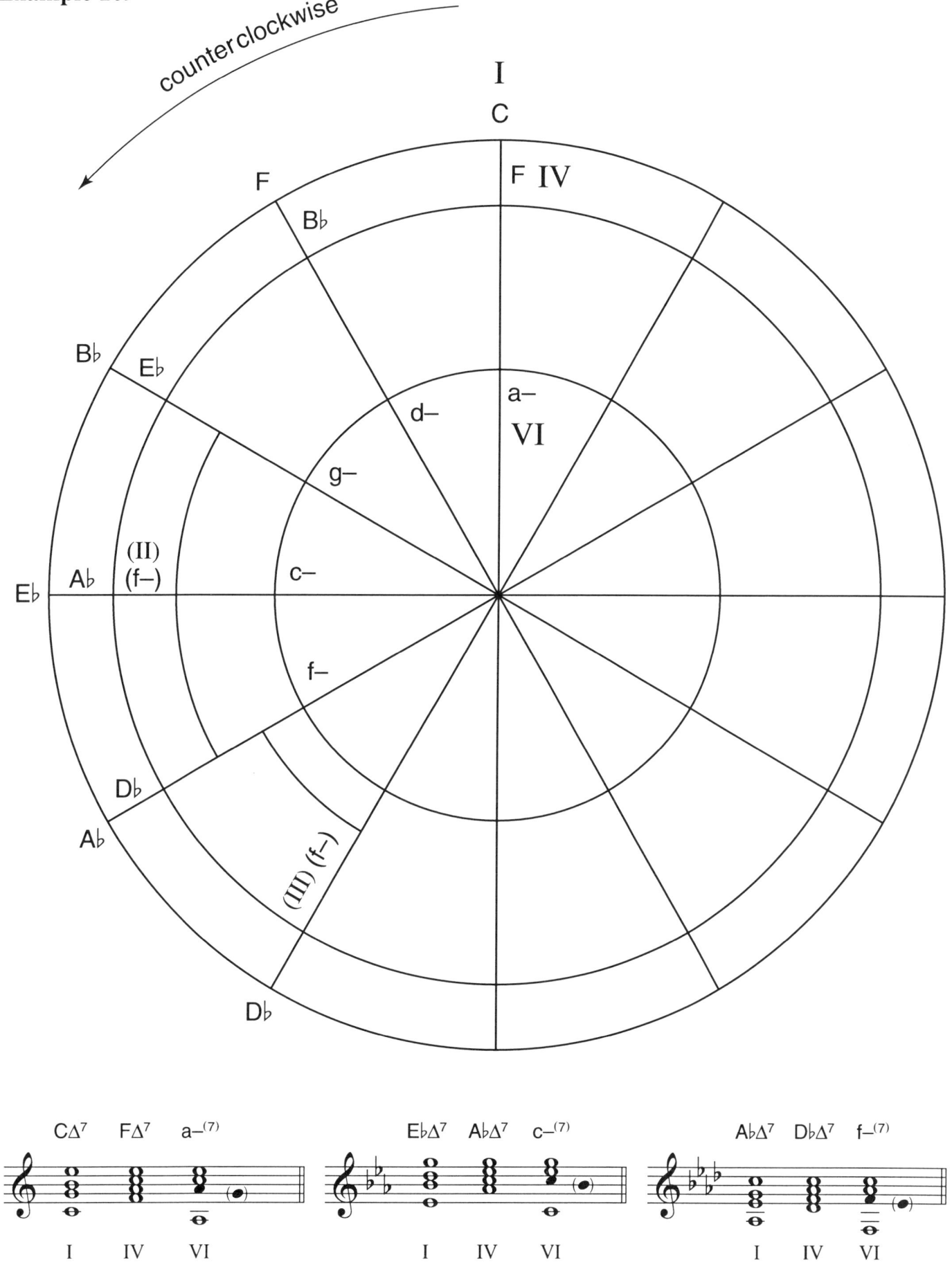

This covers all of the possibilities for f– in relation to CΔ, but when we add the other chords that contain the indicator note *A♭* within each of the tonalities where f– diatonically occurs, we have quite a resource to draw from. Remember, however, that many of the minor chords that diatonically occur in these keys are –7th chords and consequently need to be either left as triads or voiced as –6th chords or converted to –Δ7 chords to function as true subdominant minor chords.

To recap: The subdominant minor chord is a minor chord built on the 4th degree, historically the 4th degree of a Major tonality. However, in current usage in both jazz and pop music, many variants occur, including chords which contain the –3rd of the subdominant minor chord as a chord tone, even though they may not be minor chords. The key to listen for is the indicator note, which would be the **–3rd of the subdominant minor chord**. This note can also be heard as the ♭6th of the Major tonality that the IV– chord would be subdominant minor of (for example *A♭* in the key of C Major). Any of the chords containing this indicator note may substitute for the subdominant minor chord, and in doing so can suggest a subdominant minor relationship to the tonic chord (i.e., IΔ chord). This process in turn reinforces the primacy of the tonic (IΔ) chord.

Chapter 8: Vagrant Chords

I was first introduced to the term "vagrant chord" when I studied counterpoint with Paul Caputo. Arnold Schoenberg refers to vagrant chords throughout his *Theory of Harmony*, and he demonstrates them by example in a variety of contexts before explaining them in detail in his chapter entitled "At the Frontiers of Tonality."

Space limitations prohibit my covering all aspects of these chords in this book, or even covering the many that Schoenberg addresses in his *Theory of Harmony*. Schoenberg's presentation is problematic for us, because he employs the figured bass method of chordal representation, which one virtually never encounters in jazz.[17] So I am going to paraphrase the concepts regarding vagrant chords and generally use the standard nomenclature found in jazz (i.e., chord symbols such as **d♭O7** or **C+7**) to represent them.

The most intrinsic quality associated with vagrant chords is their extreme harmonic flexibility; they can in fact resolve almost anywhere. Consequently, until they do resolve, it is so difficult to determine where they come from that they appear to be homeless, hence the use of the term "vagrant." Like secondary dominant chords, they can be derived from alterations to diatonic chords.

The first type of vagrant chord we will address is the diminished 7th (O7th) chord. We already briefly discussed O7th chords in the section on minor tonalities (pp. 45–46), where their unique intervallic structure (i.e., consecutive minor 3rds) was noted. O7th chords occur diatonically only on the 7th degree of the Harmonic minor scale (example 110). However, O7th chords can be derived by chromatic alteration of the chord tones of diatonic chords from other tonalities (much like the way we derived secondary dominant chords—more about this later).

In the minor tonality section of this book, I explained how O7th chords can be treated like (or substituted for) dominant 7th♭9 chords whose roots are either omitted or replaced by the ♭9th of the dominant 7th♭9 chord. Due to the two tritone intervals (i.e., the one existing between the root and the ♭5th, and the one existing between the –3rd and O7th), these O7th chords can resolve to a multitude of other chords, in effect behaving like dominant 7th chords on steroids, making them extremely harmonically flexible. The symmetry of their construction (i.e., consecutive –3rds) means that any of their chord tones can function as their root, and each inversion is intervallically identical, allowing four different interpretations of each O7th chord. This also means that there are in actuality only three possible O7th chords in our twelve note musical system; they are: *aO7*, *a♯O7*, and *bO7*, because *aO7*, *cO7*, *e♭O7*, and *f♯O7* are all inversions of each other, just as *a♯O*, *c♯O7*, *eO7*, and *gO7* are all inversions of each other, and *bO7*, *dO7*, *fO7*, and *a♭O7* are all inversions of each other, bringing us to *cO7*, which is an inversion of the *aO7* we began with (example 111).[18] This makes perfect sense when you consider the fact that a minor 3rd interval divides the chromatic scale into four equal parts (3 x 4 = 12).

---

[17] The system of figured bass, also called thorough bass (from the old spelling of through bass), is a method of representing chordal accompaniment (usually keyboard, but also applicable to lute or guitar) that gives the bass note only; the chord voicing is to be improvised above the bass note with the aid of symbols that represent the intervals of the voices above the bass note. For example, six-four over a bass note of G♮ would indicate the second inversion of either CΔ or c–, depending upon the key signature. Figures indicating the intervals of the 3rd, 5th, and octave (3, 5, and 8) are often omitted, assuming these will be added at the player's discretion as needed. Chromatic alterations are indicated by accidentals accompanying the symbols, assuming the player understands which interval is to be altered. This system has fallen into disuse, especially outside of the realm of classical music education. It is rarely even used in classical composition today; rather it has become a tool for analysis in classical theory, where it is combined with Roman numerals (e.g., I$^6_4$, which would represent the I chord with the 5th in the bass). Like the Roman numerals we use for harmonic analysis in jazz, this method of representation requires additional contextual information (i.e., the key) to understand and interpret its symbols properly.

[18] You could in fact begin with any O7th chord and then move chromatically up (or down) to the next two O7th chords to create a set of three "prime" O7th chords. All other O7th chords would then be inversions of one of these three "prime" O7th chords.

Example 110

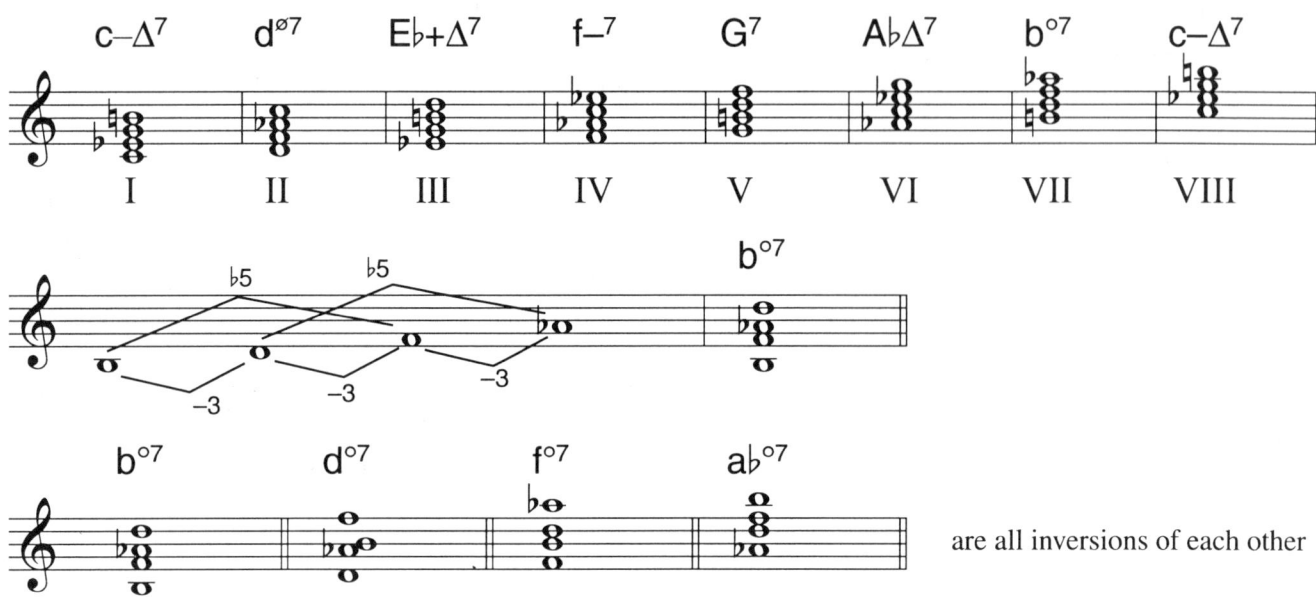

Harmonic minor

are all inversions of each other

Example 111

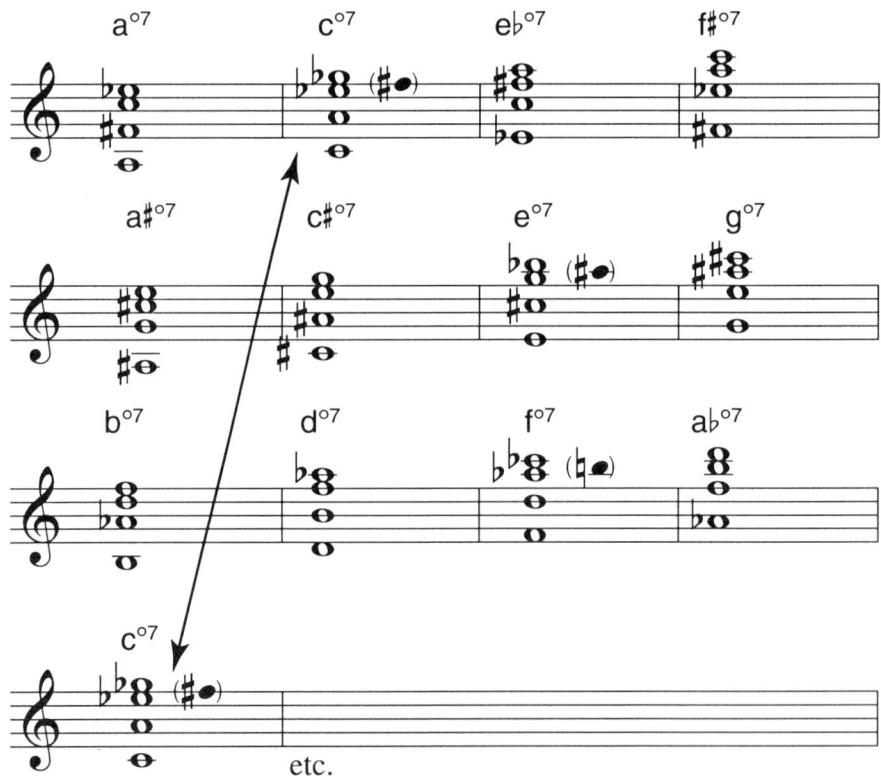

etc.

O7th chords' symmetry of construction affords us guitarists an interesting schematic that can be superimposed over the entire fingerboard to facilitate visualizing our instrument in a manner that lets us rapidly find not only these O7th chords, but others which can be produced by one- or two-note alterations to the O7th chord that can be moved so easily around the fingerboard. For example, drop any note of any O7th chord by a half step, and this note becomes the root of a dominant 7th chord (as has already been alluded to). Conversely, raise any one note of a O7th chord, and this raised note becomes the ♭7th of a Ø7th chord, or raise any two non-tritone notes by one half step, and these two raised notes become the 5th and the ♭7th of a −7th chord. Conversely, if we lower any two non-tritone notes of a O7th chord, these two notes become the root and the −3rd of a −7th chord. And if we lower the root of a O7th chord while raising its O7th, the lowered note becomes the root, and the raised note becomes the Δ7th of a Δ7th chord. Example 112 demonstrates these procedures.

Example 112

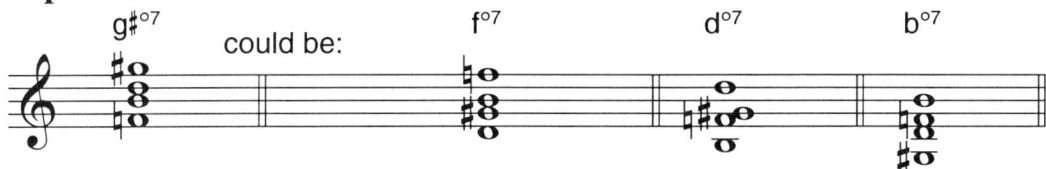

Drop one note by ½ step and each could also become:

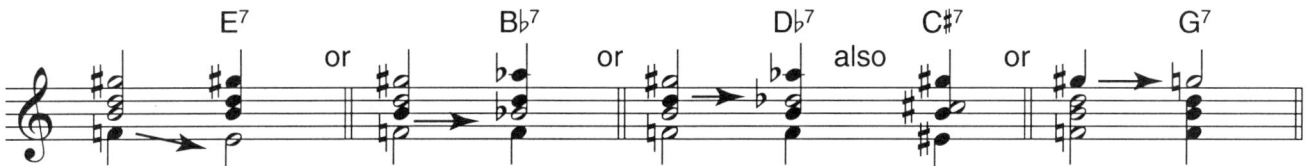

Raise one note by ½ step and get:

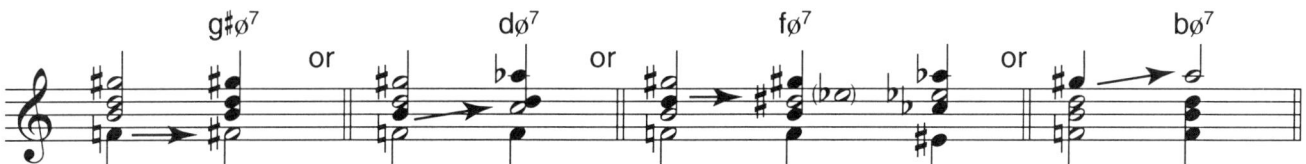

Raise two non-tritone notes by ½ step and get:

Lowering two non-tritone notes by ½ step yields:

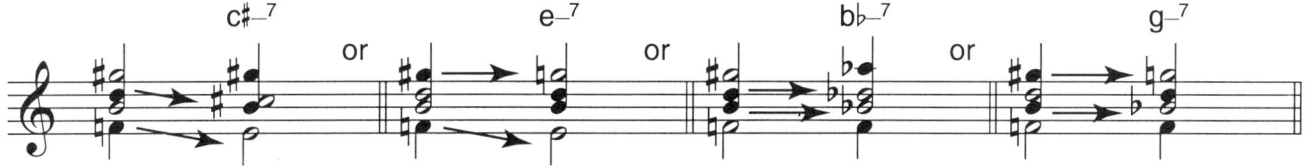

Lowering the root by ½ step while raising the o7th ½ step produces:

While the chords these processes yield are not vagrant chords, I think you can see the added benefit that is provided by employing the symmetry afforded by the O7th chords from which they are derived as a tool for visualizing the fingerboard from a different perspective. I encourage the serious and inquisitive student to explore this further by taking any O7th chord voicing that is playable on the guitar[19] and applying to it the various one- and two-note alterations demonstrated in example 112. Then take the same O7th chord voicing and move it up (or down) a minor 3rd to the next inversion, applying the same alterations while examining and comparing the results.

Returning to vagrant chords: another type of vagrant chord is the augmented chord (+), which is based on the + triad, whose intervallic structure is also circular in nature (just like the O7th chord). In other words, any chord tone of an + triad may function as its root, and all closed position inversions will be intervallically identical. Each + triad is constructed of three notes which are spaced a Δ3rd apart. Much like the –3rd interval (the building block of the aforementioned O7th chord), which divides the chromatic scale into four equal parts, the interval of a Δ3rd (the building block for the intervallic structure of all augmented triads) also divides the chromatic scale into equal parts, in this case three, meaning that there are essentially only four augmented triads. They are: C+, C♯+ (or D♭+), D+, and D♯+ (or E♭+). All others are an inversion of one of these four, i.e., E+ and G♯+ are inversions of C+; E♯+ and A+ are inversions of C♯+ (or D♭+); F♯+ and A♯+ are inversions of D+; and G+ and B+ are inversions of D♯+ (or E♭+). Augmented triads occur diatonically only on the third degree of Melodic minor and Harmonic minor scales (example 113). But like O7th chords, augmented triads (and + chords) can be derived from diatonic chords by the same process of alteration we employed previously to create secondary dominant chords.

Example 113

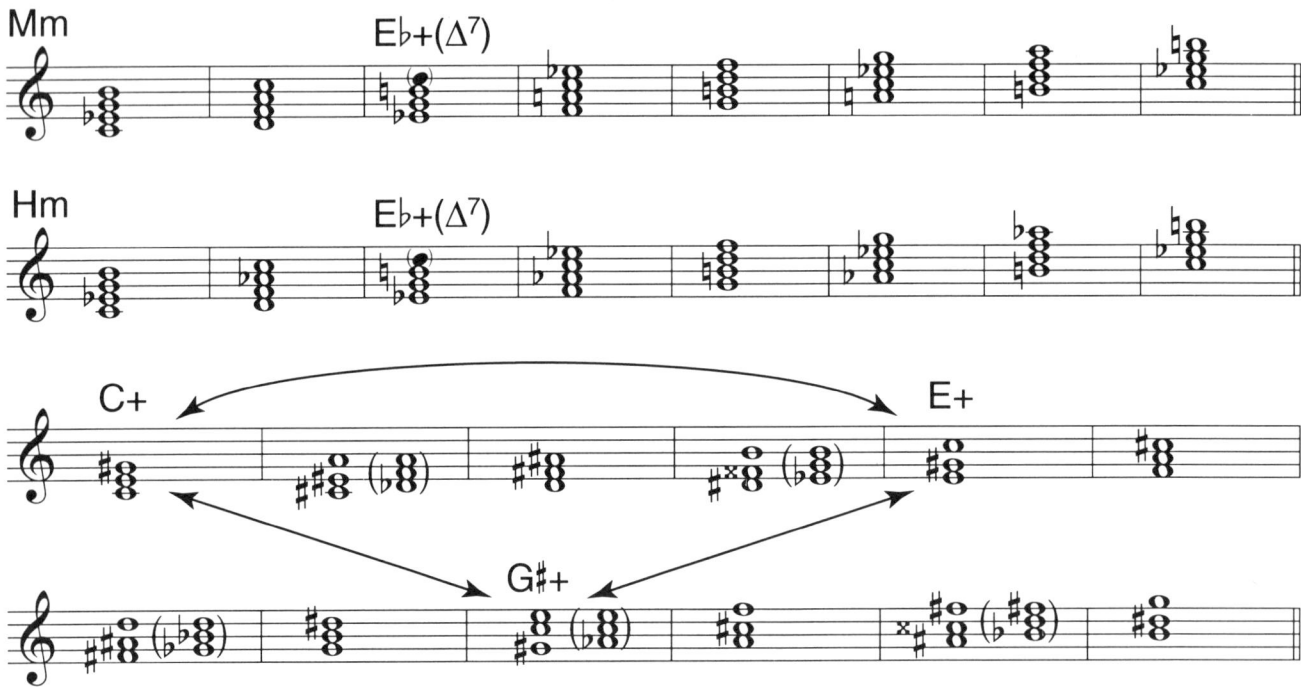

[19] Most of the playable voicings will be either drop 2 or drop 3 voicings (as is the case with many of the voicings playable on the guitar). Drop 2 voicings are created by placing each note in closed position below the melody note and then dropping the 2nd voice (i.e., the alto) down one octave (see end of example 110 and all of example 112 for more illustrations of drop 2 voicings). Conversely, drop 3 applies the same process to the 3rd voice (i.e., tenor; see example 111 for more drop 3 voicings). Hence the names drop 2 and drop 3.

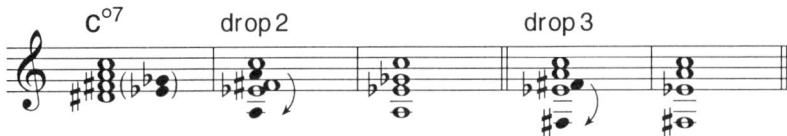

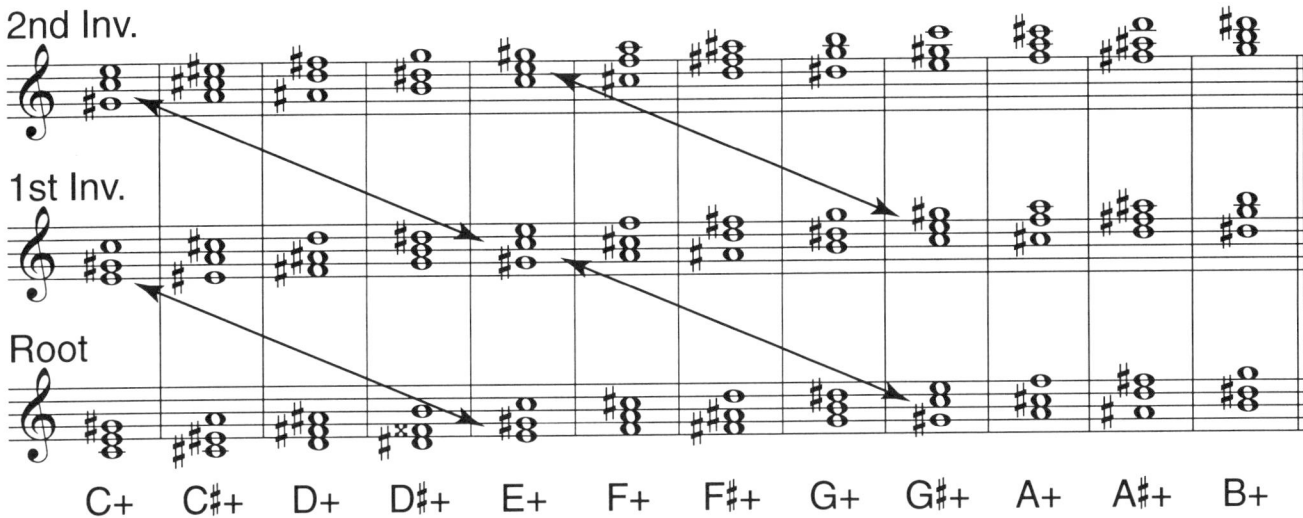

The symmetry of these + triads' construction offers yet another opportunity to superimpose a schematic over the guitar fingerboard. And like the one which the O7th chords afforded us guitarists, one-note alterations of + triads will also yield other chords which are easily located when viewed from the perspective of the symmetric schematic these + triads provide. For example, drop any one note of any + triad, and this note becomes the 5th of a major triad. Or raise any one note, and the raised note becomes the root of a minor triad (example 114).

Example 114

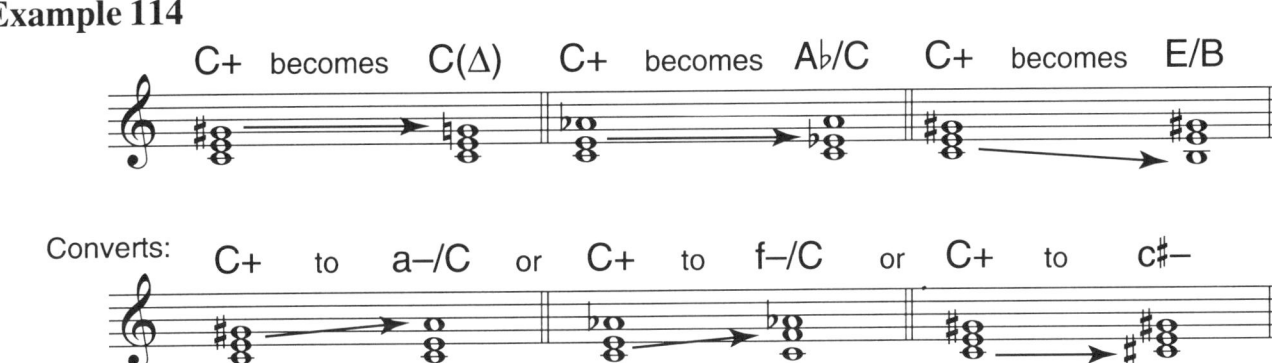

I've provided these digressions in order to encourage the serious student to explore the possibilities afforded by O7th chords and + triads for visualizing the guitar fingerboard in new and novel ways. But as with the chords that this alteration process yielded for O7th chords, these Major and minor triads produced by one-note alterations to an + triad are not vagrant chords! However, consider this: the chords and triads that can be so easily found on the fingerboard by altering the symmetrically constructed vagrant chords (i.e., O7th chords and + triads) are the very same diatonic chords and triads whose alteration could produce the O7th chords and + triads, not occurring diatonically, in the first place. In other words, we are reversing the process by which non-diatonic O7th chords, and non-diatonic + triads are derived when we alter them to produce chords and triads (that commonly occur diatonically), in effect returning them to what they were before they were converted into vagrant chords.

* * * * *

Many of the secondary dominant and substitute dominant chords we've already addressed are sufficiently malleable to be considered vagrant. But there is no need to cover the same material repeatedly, and while the former (secondary dominant chords) fit the description under extraordinary circumstances, the latter (substitute dominant chords) can often function as vagrant chords and occur in situations where they manifest harmonic tendencies that we've yet to address. These are what Schoenberg calls the + six-five, + four-three, + two, and + six chord (using figured bass nomenclature), which he considers to be derivations of the II chord (in either Major or minor). But if you check these chords out (as found in example 115), you can hear and see for yourself that they are essentially different inversions of a sub V of V7.

Example 115

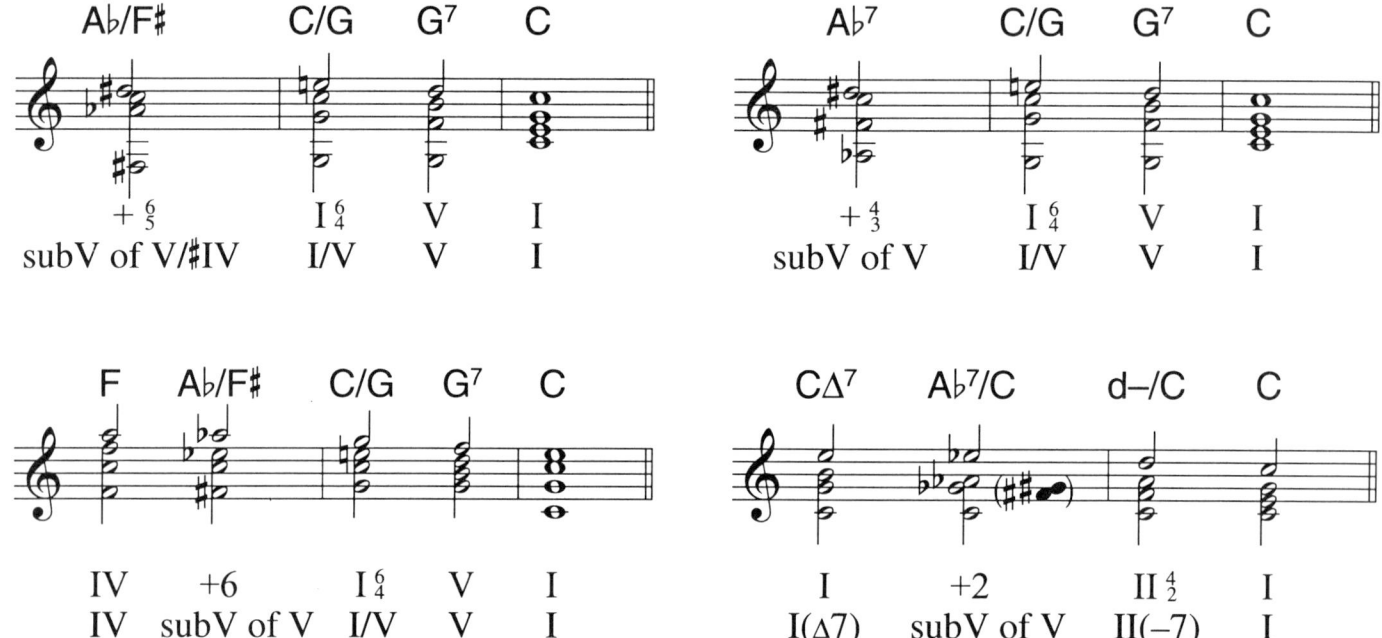

In example 115 I've given you four ways to represent different treatments of a sub V of V chord: two have the ♭7th in the bass (i.e., + six-five and + six), one has the root in the bass (i.e., + four-three), and one has the 3rd in the bass as part of a progression over a pedal (i.e., + two). The four options in example 115 demonstrate that the most accurate way to notate these progressions is to write out the voicings. Example 115 also shows the advantages and liabilities of the other methods, making it pretty clear that next to actually writing out the voicings, writing the chord symbols (above each staff) is the second best approach. This is the nomenclature for representing chords that you'll most often encounter in the real world of gigs as a jazz musician.

Example 115 also demonstrates that these sub V of V chords would all use the same Lydian ♭7 scale that any other sub V7 of V going to V or I/V would be likely to use. Finally, example 115 illustrates something that has not yet been emphasized, namely that these chords contain two leading tones: one up (i.e., *F*♯), and one down (i.e.,*A*♭), which is they key to why they work. Ideally, each leading tone would be voice led in accordance with its natural tendencies (i.e., in contrary motion to the same note [either in unison or an octave apart], as they are in the first three options in example 115), but since jazz musicians often use 7th chords where other simpler chords would not only suffice, but would be more effective, we are likely to encounter one of these leading tones moving in parallel motion to a note other than the one its nature would indicate (example 116).

Example 116

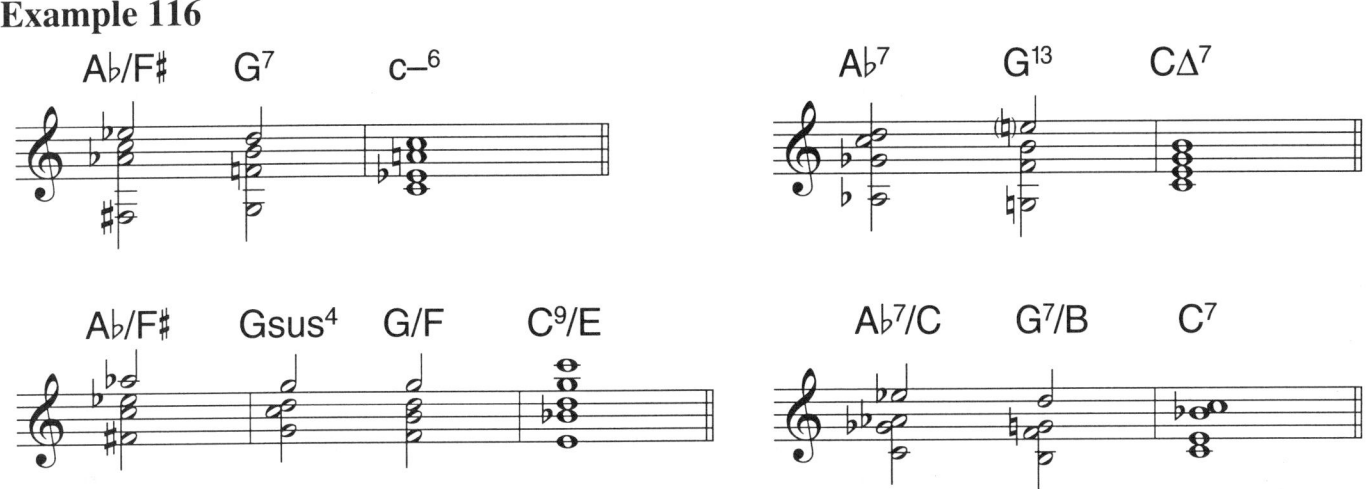

Example 116 shows some ways you'll encounter these "vagrant" substitute dominant 7th chords in a jazz context. They don't differ that dramatically from one another, except for the voice leading of the *Ab* to *F♮* in the first option (tenor voice), and the *Gb* to *F♮* in the second and fourth options (also tenor voice), while the third option actually voice leads the two leading tones in accordance with their natural tendencies (i.e., in contrary motion to two *G♮*s an octave apart in the outer voices).

I hope by now it has occurred to some of you that all of these vagrant chords can not only be derived from alterations to diatonic chords (just like secondary dominant chords). But, in fact, vagrant chords can often function as if they are either secondary dominant chords or substitute dominant chords, or substitutes for and/or alterations of secondary dominant chords or substitute dominant chords. Because just like all the secondary dominant and substitute dominant chords previously addressed, these "vagrant" chords (especially those that are intervallically identical to different inversions of dominant 7th chords) can resolve to any of the multitude of chords any dominant 7th chord can resolve to.

Remember how a O7th chord can function as a dominant 7th b9 chord (whose root is omitted or replaced by the b9)? Well, some + chords, especially those containing a b7th, either are or function as if they are dominant 7th chords (i.e., diatonic, secondary, or substitute). These dominant 7th chords either have their 5ths raised by a half step or contain the available or altered tension b13. And these chords are usually notated as dominant +7 or dominant 7♯5, or dominant 7b13 (e.g., C+7, or C7♯5, or C7b13).

Example 117

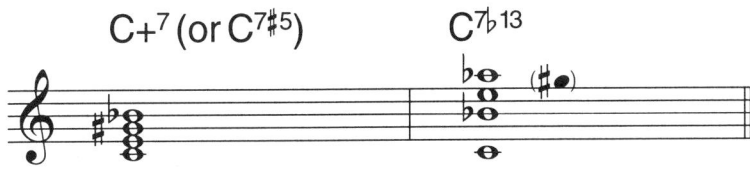

All of this brings us to how to deal with these vagrant chords when we encounter them in a jazz context. Since they often function in a dominant 7th capacity (i.e., secondary or substitute), or as a replacement for or an alteration of a dominant 7th chord (i.e., O7th and +7th), many of the scales we've previously used to define dominant 7th chords' tonalities are going to work to define the harmonic functions of these vagrant chords as well. Here are some guidelines to follow when dealing with vagrant chords (i.e., indicator notes to listen and/or look out for).

As I already mentioned in relation to the vagrant chords from examples 115 and 116, whose first three examples are all inversions of a sub V7 of V either resolving to I over V (as in example 115) or resolving to V (as in example 116), the best scale choice is the same Lydian ♭7 scale (i.e., Mm4) that we've discussed in both the secondary dominant chord section, and the substitute dominant chord section for dominant 7th chords containing or indicating ♯11 or ♭5. This might not be obvious to some of you, because none of the options in examples 115 and 116 actually contains the Lydian indicator note within the voices of the vagrant chord for each option (i.e., first chord of options 1 and 2, and second chord of options 3 and 4 in example 115, and first chord of all four options in example 116). But remember that V of V in C (Major or minor), even resolving to V of IV as in options 3 and 4 of example 116, would be D7. And A♭7 would be the substitute dominant chord for this D7. Which means that the *D♮*, which would be the Lydian indicator note, is inferred in this context for the A♭7 functioning as sub V7 of V even if it is not sounded!

Whenever you are in doubt as to which chord scale to use, you can always construct a scale by arranging the chord tones of the chord in question linearly (in closed position) and then filling in the spaces between the chord tones with passing tones from the adjacent tonalities. For example, if we take the A♭7 chord as found in examples 115 and 116 and linearly arrange its chord tones, which are *A♭, C, E♭*, and *G♭* (or *F♯*), then fill in the spaces between the thirds of the chord tones with passing tones that fit the tonality of either the chord preceding or the chord following our chord in question (A♭7), we can find or create a workable chord scale for this chord (example 118).

Example 118

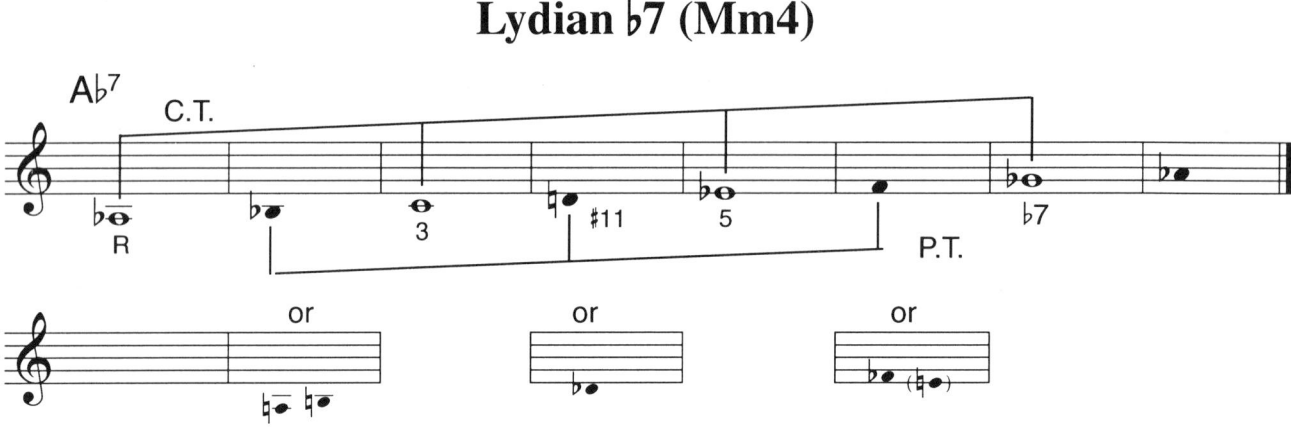

Lydian ♭7 (Mm4)

The resulting scale clearly demonstrates that A♭ Lydian ♭7 is the best scale choice in this context, and that only on the 2nd, 4th, and 6th degrees are there even any other variables. The results of using these other variables are not very convincing in this context because they produce: A♭ Mixolydian if we use *D♭* for the 4th degree; or d♭ Melodic minor from the 5th (i.e., A♭Mm5) if we use *D♭* for the 4th degree and *E♮* for the 6th degree; while using *A♮* for the 2nd degree, *D♭* for the 4th degree, and *E♮* for the 6th degree produces A♭Hm5 (i.e., d♭ Harmonic minor from the 5th degree), none of which really works. This only leaves *B♮* for the 2nd degree unaccounted for. This note, which would be ♯9 in relationship to the A♭7, is hard to rectify with the sub V7 of V as found in examples 115 and 116, because it prematurely sounds the leading tone of key, which is also the 3rd of the V chord of which this A♭7 is sub V. If ♯9 were indicated or sounded, it would require the same Altered Dominant scale Mm7 (i.e., a Melodic minor from the 7th degree) we previously used for similarly altered dominant 7th chords. But as you can hear and see in example 119, we have lost one of our chord tones if we use this scale (i.e., ♯5 has replaced ♮5).

Example 119

Altered Dominant (Mm7)

This still leaves us with the Lydian ♭7 scale as our best choice for the options in which A♭7 (functioning as sub V of V) occurs, as illustrated in the four types of vagrant chords found in examples 115 and 116. We can also use the Altered Dominant scale when the altered tensions of ♭9, ♯9, and ♭5 (i.e., ♯11) or ♯5 are indicated. Which means that the guidelines concerning chord scales for this variety of vagrant chord (i.e., different inversions of sub V7 of V) are the same guidelines we used to determine what chord scale to use in examples 90, 91, and 92 in the chapter on substitute dominant 7th chords in this book.

Virtually all dominant 7th chords with either ♯5 or ♭13 may be treated like +7th chords. However, it is important to distinguish between the variety of + chords containing ♭7 and the type of + chords that diatonically occur on the 3rd degree of the Melodic minor and Harmonic minor tonalities, because those occurring diatonically in minor tonalities would have a Δ7th (not a ♭7th). When we encounter +Δ7th chords, they often function as a substitute for a subdominant minor chord, while the +7th chords we will encounter are likely to function in one of the many ways that we've already addressed for dominant 7th chords.

Augmented (+) 7th chords (i.e., those with a ♭7th) could use either the Altered Dominant scale (Mm7), or the Dominant 7th♭9 scale (Hm5), or the Mm5 (Melodic minor from the 5th degree), as we've already covered in the secondary dominant chords derived from minor tonalities section (see p. 91, example 83, the Secondary Dominant Reference Guide for Mm7, Hm5, and Mm5). This is due to the fact that the ♭13 (or ♯5) that makes these chords augmented in the first place is also the minor 3rd of each Tonic I– chord from the two tonalities that could yield such +7th chords on their 5th degrees (i.e., Mm and Hm).

There is, however, another chord scale option for augmented dominant 7th chords, and that is the Whole Tone scale, which, as the name implies, is constructed entirely of notes that are spaced one whole step apart (example 120).

Example 120

Whole Tone Scale

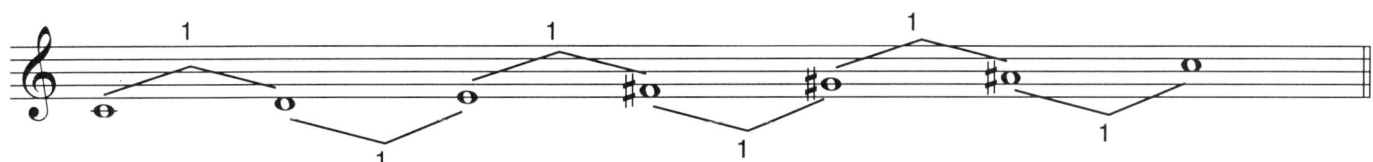

The symmetry of this scale nicely mirrors the symmetry of + triads themselves, for if we build chords from this scale, they are all going to be + triads and/or +7th chords. And if we extend these chords diatonically into their upper structures, we get ♮9 and ♯11 as well (example 121).

Example 121

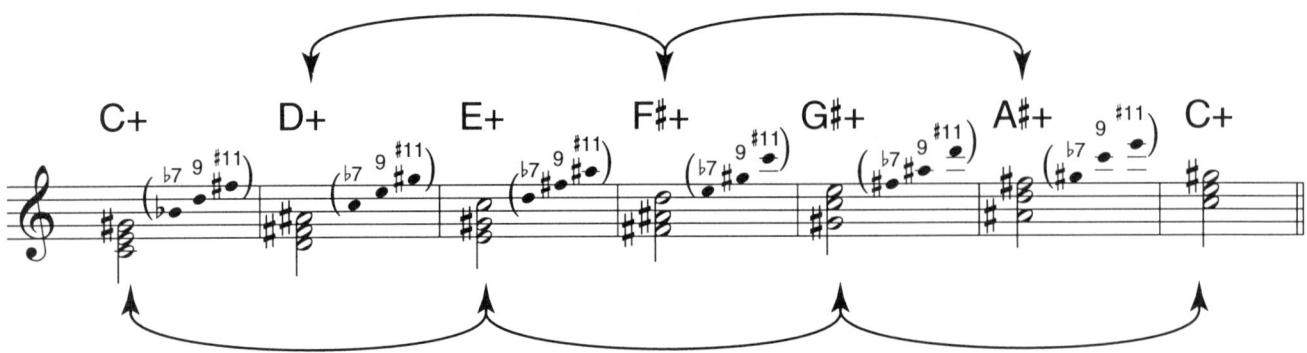

Example 122

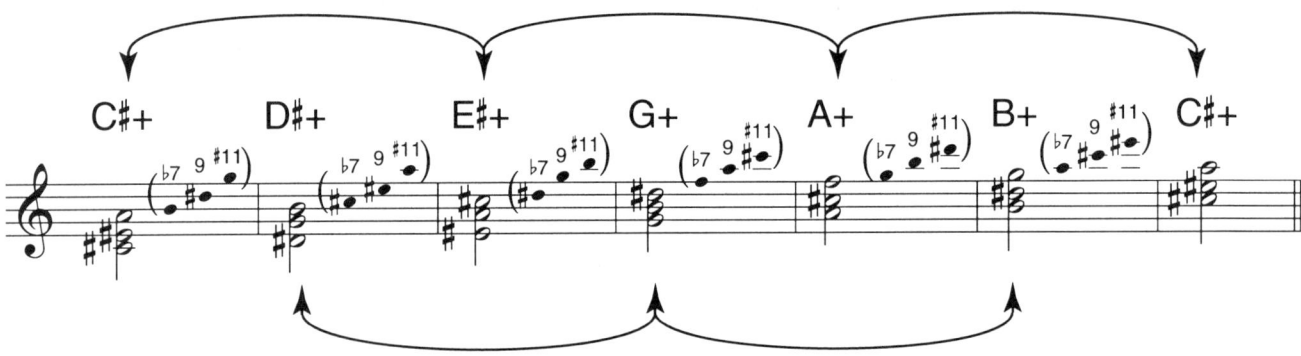

Not only are the upper structures of these + triads themselves + triads, as you can see from example 121, but each is also an inversion of the + triad built on the adjacent scale degree (and vice versa), because there are in effect only two possible + triads that this scale (or any whole tone scale) can produce, in this case: C+ and D+, since all the others produced by this scale are inversions of one of these two (i.e., C+, E+, and G♯+ are inversions of each other, just as D+, F+, and A♯+ are inversions of each other).

And if you remember from our previous discussion of + triads, there are only four + triads that exist in our musical system, due to their symmetric intervallic construction (i.e., consecutive Δ3ʳᵈs), meaning that if each Whole Tone scale contains two of the possible four (which, along with the inversions of these two, constitute all of the options for diatonic construction of + triads within a Whole Tone scale), then there can only be two Whole Tone scales which can be accommodated by our twelve tone musical system: C Whole Tone and C♯ (or D♭) Whole Tone, in effect making all other Whole Tone scales modes of one of these two![20]

If you compare the + triads and potential +7ᵗʰ chords constructed in examples 121 and 122, you'll see that all available possibilities are accounted for. All of which means that when we encounter either an +7ᵗʰ chord or a dominant 7ᵗʰ chord containing or inferring either ♯5 or ♭13 combined with ♮9 and ♯11, then the Whole Tone scale built upon its root is a good scale to use. Conversely, if all other indicator notes are the same (i.e., ♯5 or ♭13 and ♮9), but ♯11 (or ♯4) seems out of context, or clearer still, ♮4 or ♮11 are indicated or inferred, then the music will be better served if we employ the Mm5 scale that was introduced in the minor tonality chapter (example 123).

[20] In a manner similar to the O7ᵗʰ chords previously addressed, you can begin on any pitch and then ascend (or descend) by one half step to create the two "prime" Whole Tone scales (of which all others would be modes), and ascend or descend three consecutive half steps to create the four "prime" + triads of which all others would be inversions.

Example 123

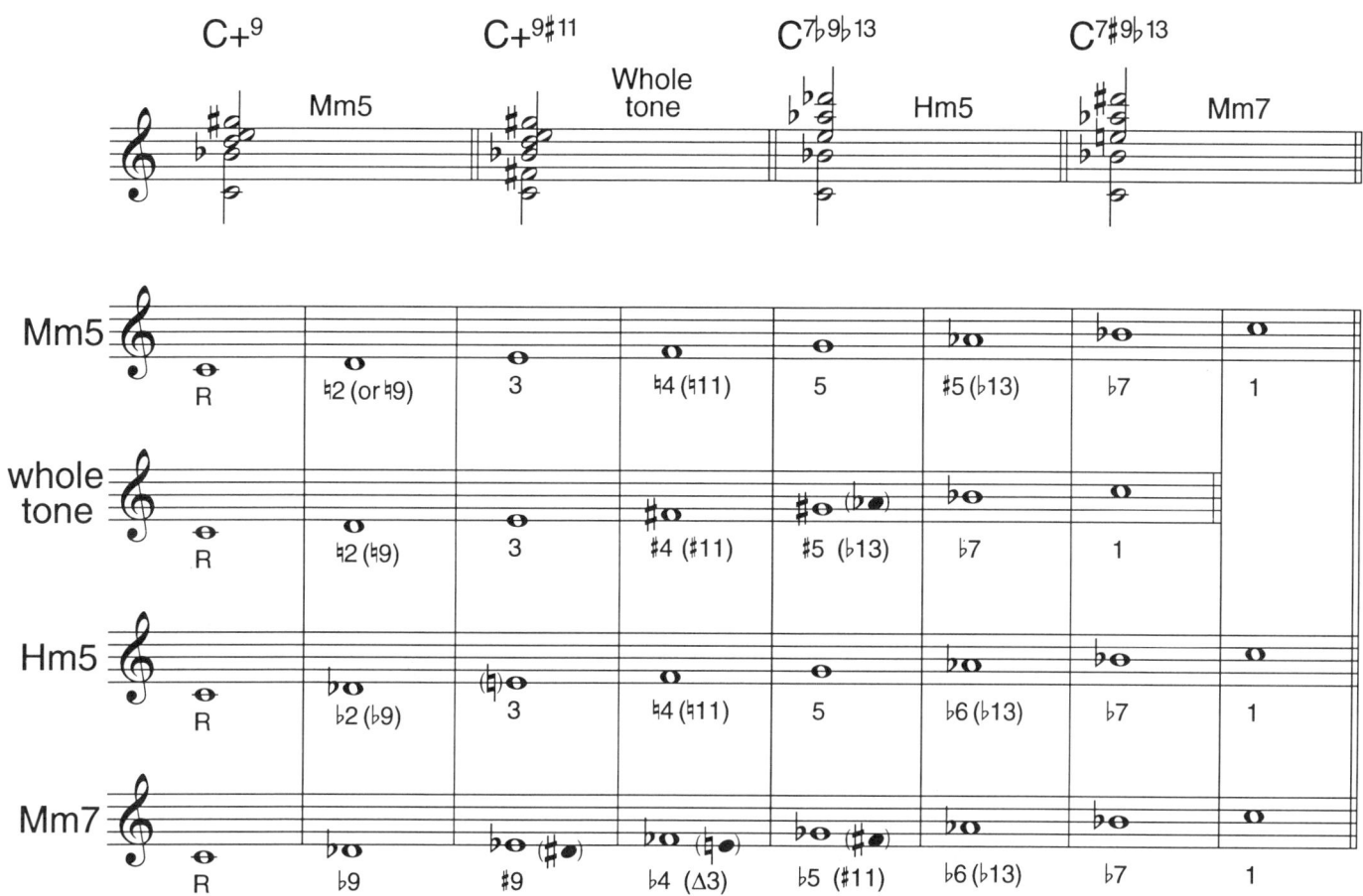

The first two options in example 123 distinguish between C+9, with no ♯11 inferred, and C+9♯11, while options 3 and 4 address differences distinguishing two dominant 7th chords that can be interpreted as + (due to their ♭13s), one with a ♭9 (i.e., C7♭9♭13) that infers no ♯9, and one which contains ♯9 (i.e., C7♯9♭13).

There is only one remaining scale option for + triads containing or inferring ♭9 and ♭13, and that is the scale that I call the eastern-altered Hm5, which is constructed of two consecutive Harmonic minor tetrachords, and which occurs in flamenco, klezmer, and other eastern-influenced music but rarely occurs in the context of vagrant, or secondary dominant, or substitute dominant chords as they occur in jazz, because of this scale's Major 7th (versus ♭7th) scale degree. (For more on this scale, refer to examples 80 and 84 in the secondary dominant chapter.)

Of course there are the diatonically constructed +Δ7 chords that exist on the 3rd degree of both the Harmonic minor and Melodic minor tonalities. But they aren't vagrant, as they occur diatonically, and they use the modes of their parent tonalities that correspond to their scale degree (i.e., Mm3 and Hm3, depending upon the context in which they occur).

This brings us back to the O7th chords we began this chapter with, and the question of how to address improvising over them when we encounter them in a jazz context. When a O7th chord is functioning as a dominant 7th♭9 whose root is omitted, then the best solution is to use the Dominant 7♭9 scale (i.e., Hm5) whose starting note corresponds to the omitted note of the the dominant 7♭9 chord. The best way to identify a O7th chord functioning this way is to observe its root motion, because the root of the O7th chord operating as a dominant 7♭9 chord is going to function as the leading tone and is therefore likely to resolve in stepwise fashion upward. But remember the root of such a O7th chord may not always be in the bottom voice as it is in example 124!

Example 124

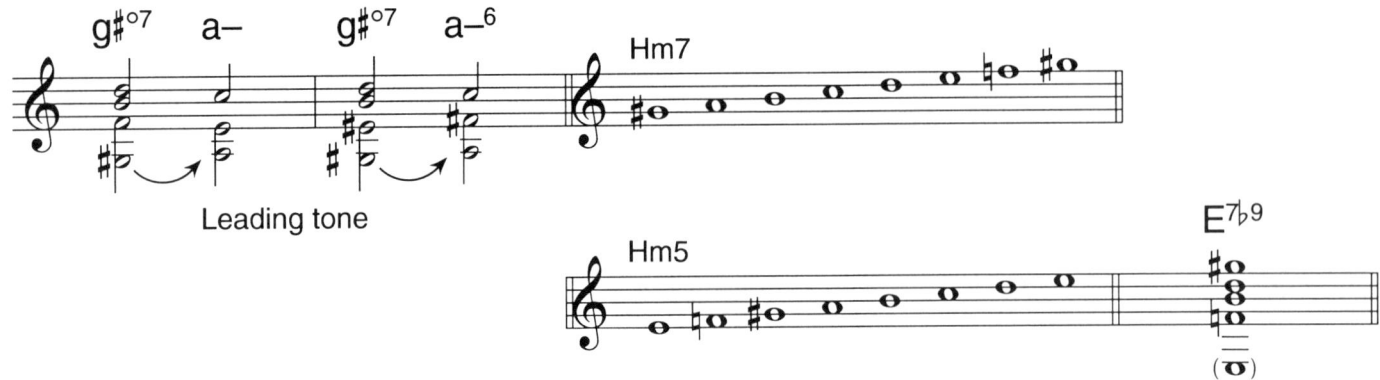

As you can see from example 124, the chord scale for the E7♭9 contains the same notes as the scale for g♯O7, which one would expect, since both scales are modes of *a* Harmonic minor: one is *g♯* Hm7 and the other is *E* Hm5. This makes all the more sense when you consider the fact that g♯O7 does diatonically exist as the chord built on the 7th degree of *a* Harmonic minor, and when you remember that the V chord in Harmonic minor contains a ♭9 (when extended into its upper structure). So why have we gone through all of this rigamarole to arrive at what is essentially a diatonic O7th chord? Because, as I mentioned earlier, these O7th chords may be derived from alterations to virtually any of the chords diatonically built on any degree of any tonality, much like the secondary dominant chords that we previously constructed. Meaning that the g♯O7 found in example 124 might be merely a VIIO7 resolving to I–, but it could also be any number of other O7th chords functioning as a secondary dominant 7♭9 chord whose root is omitted, and whose 3rd is being interpreted as the leading tone that resolves upward to the root of a diatonic minor chord, e.g., V7♭9 of III– in the key of F Major (as in the first option in example 124), where this g♯O7 chord might pass between II– (g–7 in the key of F) to get to III– (a–), in which case it might also be analyzed as ♯IIO7, even though it is functioning as a V7♭9 of III–.

While all of this may seem confusing, the source of the confusion lies in the fact that not all harmonic analysis is insightful enough to actually account for a chord's true harmonic function. When I was a student at Berklee, these "passing" O7th chords were all treated the same whether they resolved up or down. For example, g♯O7 passing from g–7 to a–7 was analyzed the same as a♭O7 passing from a–7 to g–7. Some of you may ask what difference this error makes. Well, I think Schoenberg is right in considering the g♯O7 chord passing between g–7 and a–7 as a variant of E7♭9, but I think the harmony professors at Berklee were right in considering the a♭O7 passing between a–7 and g–7 as what they called a passing O7th chord. But neither analysis fits both situations (example 125)!

Example 125

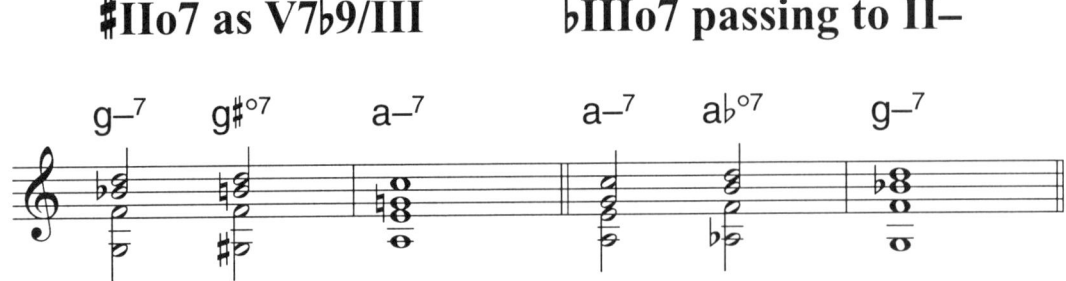

The g♯O7 chord from the first option in example 125 (g–7 **g♯O7** to a–7) can convincingly be linked to an E7♭9 chord, which could be functioning in a V7 (♭9) of III– capacity in the key of F Major. But it is very hard to find a dominant 7♭9 chord that could be convincingly linked to the a♭O7 chord as it occurs in the second option (i.e., a–7 **a♭O7** to g–7), because none of the corresponding chord scales for any of the four dominant 7th chord options for a♭O7 (i.e., G7, B♭7, D♭7, or E7) really convincingly defines the a♭O7 chord's harmonic function in this or similar situations. And when you consider how chromatic alterations of virtually any of the diatonic chords in either Major or minor can produce O7th chords whose harmonic function cannot be linked to any dominant 7th chord, it becomes pretty clear that a scale other than the Dominant 7♭9 scale is going to be required for such passing O7th chords.

And it just so happens that such a scale exists in two versions. It is called the Symmetric Diminished scale. The Symmetric Diminished scale is similar to the Whole Tone scale in that its intervallic construction is symmetrical, as its name implies. If we construct a scale for a O7th chord using the same technique we've previously employed for any chord whose chord scale is in doubt, we will arrive at one of these two Symmetric Diminished scales. Because, as you recall, the method we use when in doubt involves aligning the chord tones in closed position linearly, then filling in the spaces between the chord tones with passing tones (remember most scales are comprised of alternating chord tones and passing tones). Applying this approach to cO7, we get *C, E♭, F♯,* and *A* as our chord tones, and since each chord tone is a minor 3rd apart, there are only two options for passing tones between the equally spaced chord tones: we must use either a whole step or a half step. Once either interval is chosen, the resulting scale becomes a sequence of alternating whole steps and half steps, or vice versa, because the distance between the passing tone and the second chord tone will be the one that we didn't choose to begin with. In other words, if we begin with a whole step, the sequence for the entire scale will alternate whole step / half step, etc.; conversely, if we begin with a half step, the scale structure will alternate half step / whole step, etc. (example 126).

Example 126

The two types of Symmetric Diminished Scale

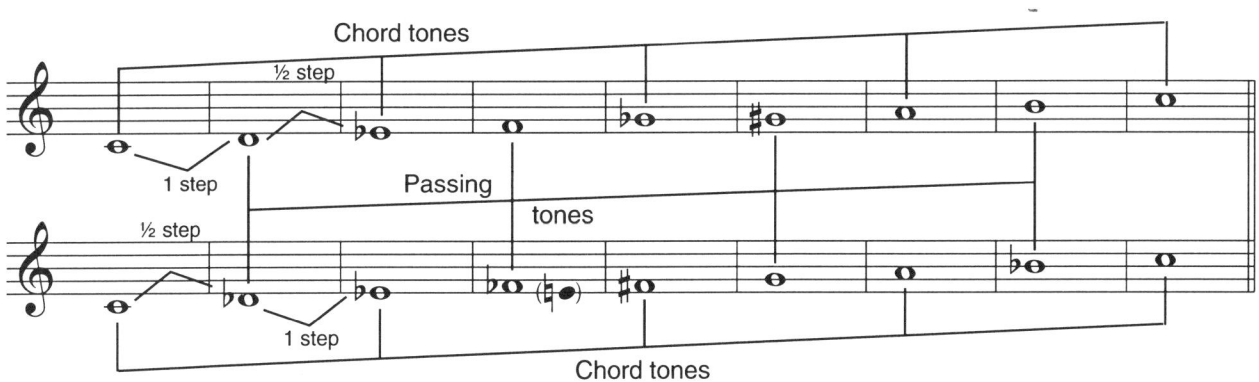

It is always desirable to have an audible relationship between the chord and chord scale. The symmetry of either of these two Symmetric Diminished scales nicely mirrors the symmetry of the O7th chord itself. I suppose that is the reason for maintaining one of these two options for passing tones consistently throughout each scale. Whatever the reason, these scales work well, especially for passing O7th chords resolving downward. They also are quite effective with isolated O7th chords, and/or O7th chords that occur for longer durations (i.e., not just one or two beats, as is often the case with passing O7th chords found in jazz). And they can be superimposed over certain altered dominant chords.

Determining which Symmetric Diminished scale to use can present some difficulties, because these scales are almost as malleable as the O7th chords whose harmonic function(s) they are intended to define. In contexts where the O7th chords really are passing between two other chords, we can't really expect the passing tones from these Symmetric Diminished scales to come exclusively from the tonalities of the chords either preceding or following the O7th chord, meaning that the key to the workability of these scales is the resolution of the dissonant pitches into the consonant pitches, not just within the context of the Symmetric Diminished scale / O7th chord relationship, but within the context of the chord progression in which the O7th chord occurs (e.g., a–7, to abO7, to g–7). O7th chords are themselves so dissonant and can accommodate such a large number of available and/or altered tensions that it can often be more illuminating to consider the dissonant to consonant resolution from the perspective of the Symmetric Diminished scale's relationship to the tonality that the passing O7th chord is moving to (example 127).

Example 127

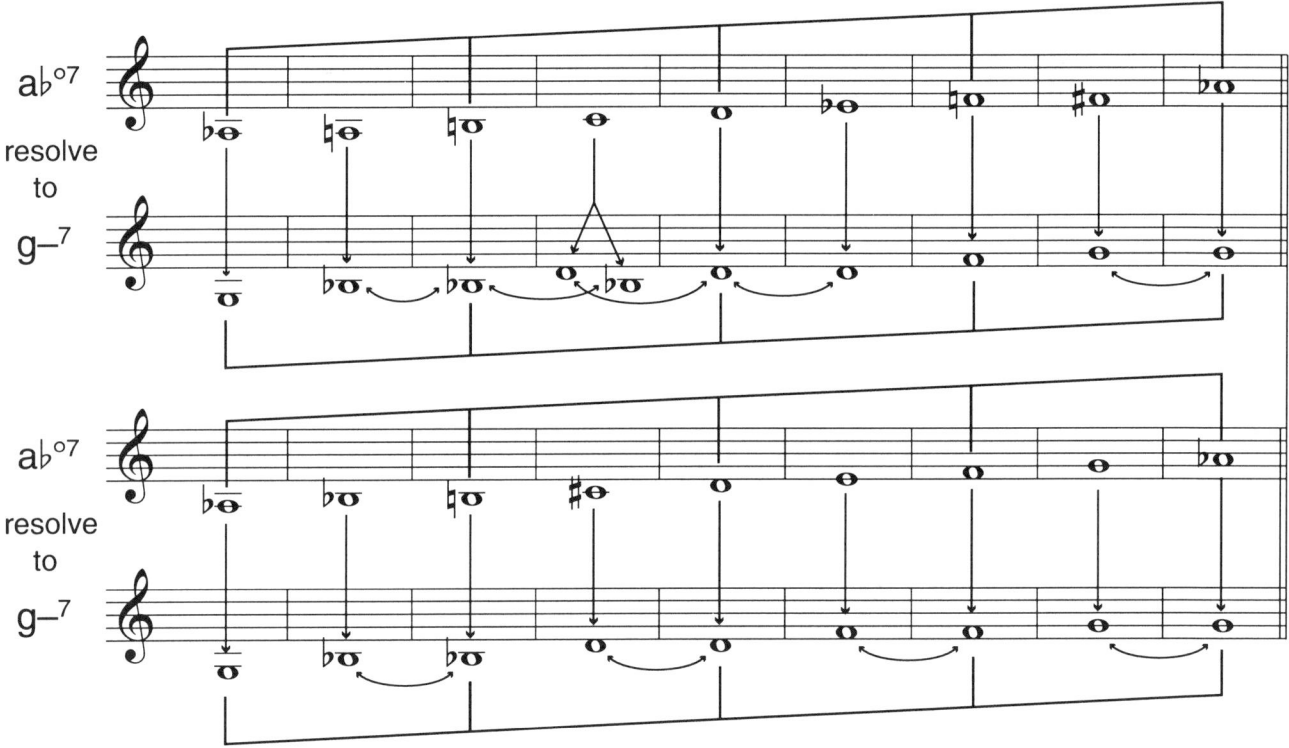

While example 127 illustrates possible resolutions for the chord tones of an abO7 chord to the chord tones of a g–7 chord (as found in the second option of example 125), it also demonstrates some possible resolutions for the passing tones from each of the two Symmetric Diminished scale options in the same context. This approach is a bit unorthodox, but I feel that it illustrates why the whole step half step option is superior in the context of a passing O7th chord moving down to any –7th chord, i.e., because only one scale tone is not a chord tone of either the abO7 chord or the g–7 chord, and that note, C♯, is a chromatic approach tone to D♮, which is one of the two notes that are common to both chords (i.e., D♮ and F♮).

Conversely, the half step whole step option is superior if we have a passing O7th chord resolving down to any Δ7th chord, for similar reasons. In this case, only two notes, C and E♭ are not chord tones of either abO7 or the GΔ7 to which it resolves. Each of these two notes is a half step above a chord tone in the chord of resolution (i.e., B♮, the 3rd, and D♮, the 5th of GΔ7), and they both suggest the subdominant minor region (c– is the subdominant of GΔ) where an inversion of the abO7 (i.e., bO7) diatonically occurs on the VIIth degree of one of its possible parent tonalities: c Harmonic minor (example 128).

Example 128

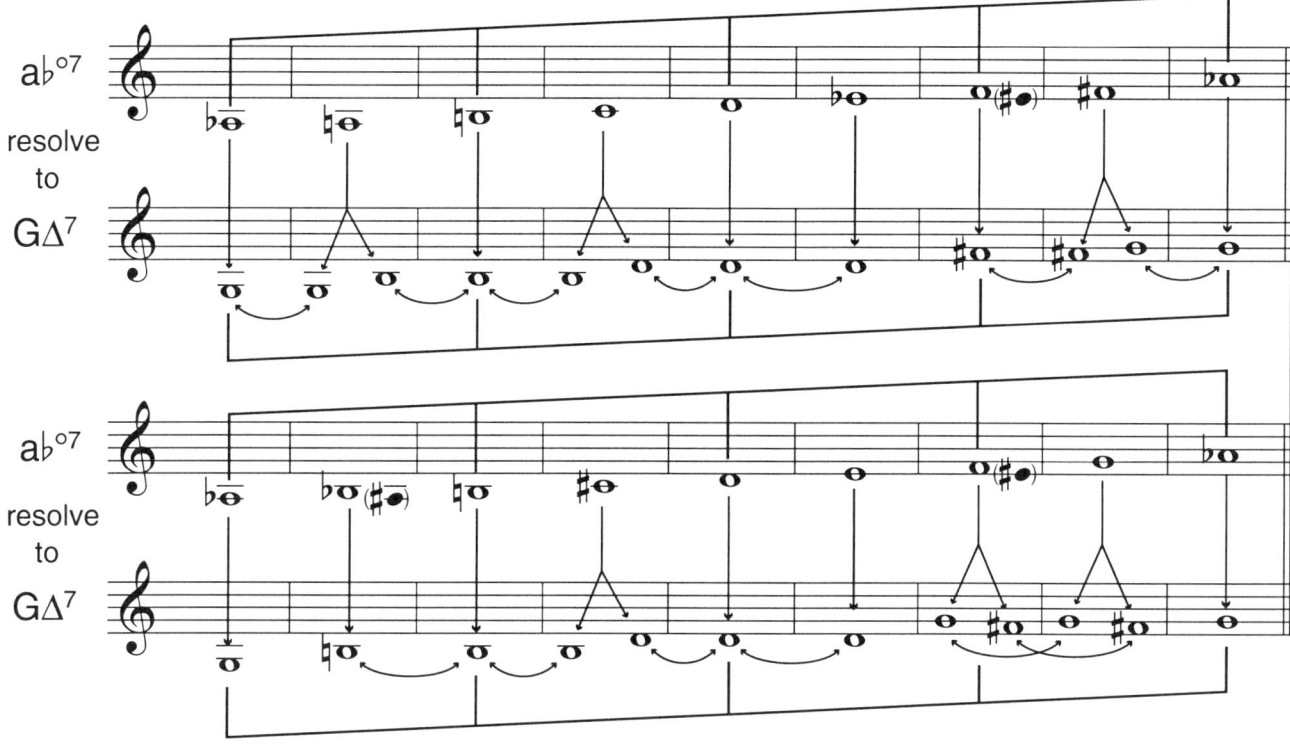

Having explained what I feel are the best options for employing the Symmetric Diminished scales for passing O7th chords resolving down to –7 chords or down to Δ7 chords, I must say that either option can be made to work in each case, as the other resolutions in examples 127 and 128 illustrate. I encourage the serious student to explore these options in more detail on your own, or with the guidance of a qualified and knowledgeable teacher, then decide for yourself. Ultimately your ears and your own aesthetic judgment must be your guide.

Before we move on to a reference guide for chord scale applications for vagrant chords, there is one remaining aspect of O7th chords and their relationship to Symmetric Diminished scales that we need to address. It may have occurred to many of you that some of the awkwardness of resolution for the passing tones found in Symmetric Diminished scales is due in part to the fact that these passing tones themselves also form O7th chords, making all of the diatonic chords constructed from these Symmetric Diminished scales O7th chords. And much like the + triads diatonically constructed from the Whole Tone scale, the O7th chords diatonically constructed within any Symmetric Diminished scale will all be inversions of the O7th chords found on one of the first two degrees (example 129).

Example 129

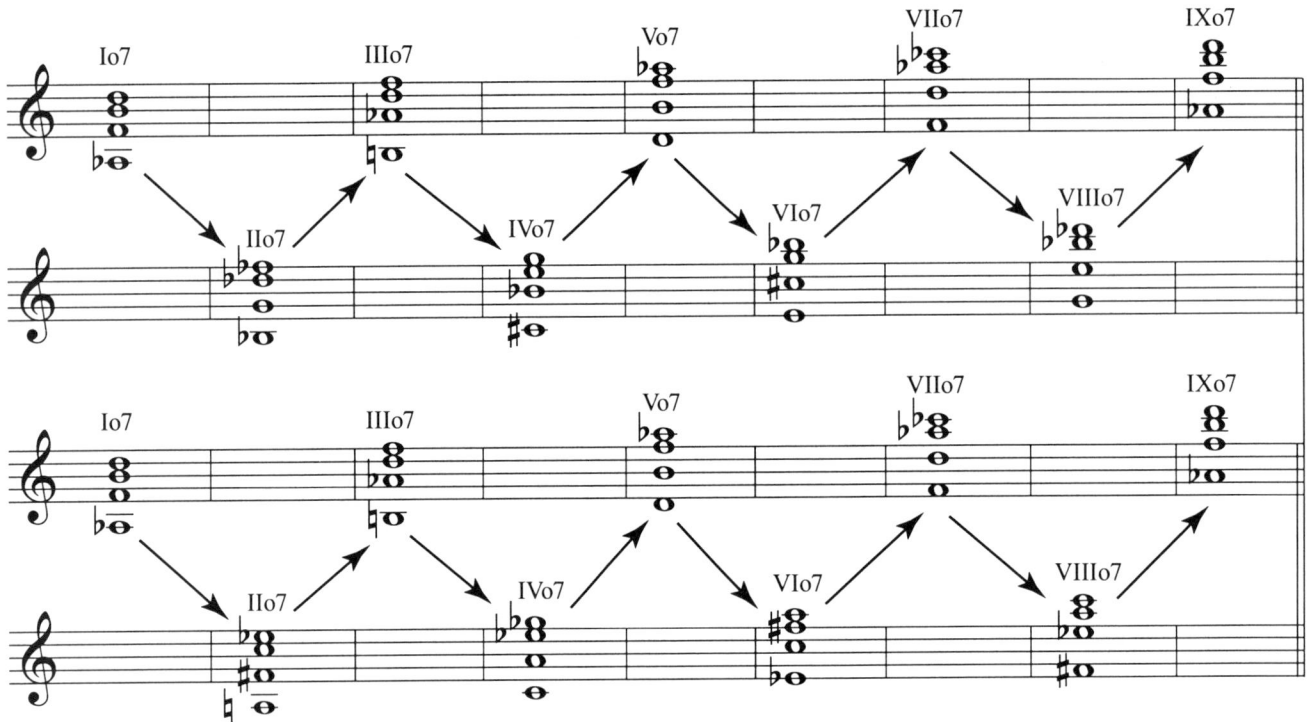

The chords built on the 1st, 3rd, 5th, and 7th degrees are all inversions of each other, just as the chords built on the 2nd, 4th, 6th, and 8th degrees are inversions of each other. This is true of both scale options found in example 129. You should also recall that our twelve note musical system can only produce three O7th chords that are not an inversion of one of the three "prime" O7th chords, meaning that since each of the forms of the Symmetric Diminished scale can diatonically accommodate two O7th chords and their subsequent inversions, there must be additional duplication somewhere, because 2 x 2 = 4, and 3 x 4 = 12, which when multiplied by the two versions of the Symmetric Diminished scale would equal 24, which is unworkable since we don't have a quarter-tone system—we have a semi-tone system that can't accommodate 24 different roots for O7th chords.[21] The explanation for this apparent anomaly lies in the fact that each form of Symmetric Diminished scale can in fact be a mode or version of the other. For example, half step whole step starting on *B♮* contains the same notes as whole step half step starting on *C♮* (example 130).

---

[21] As we all know, there are only twelve tones in our musical system. Each of these twelve notes could be the root of a O7th chord (although only three will not be inversions of one of any three whose roots are consecutive half steps apart, as has already been noted). However, virtually every one of the twelve tones of the chromatic scale can be named enharmonically (e.g., *B♮* could be called *C♭*, etc.). But, enharmonically (re)naming the twelve notes of the chromatic scale doesn't really produce the twenty four different roots for O7th chords that our math yields when we fail to take into account the duplication within the two types of symmetric diminished scales themselves, because in effect the enharmonic spelling is more about note function within specific tonalities than it is about producing new pitches in a tempered (chromatic) scale.

Example 130

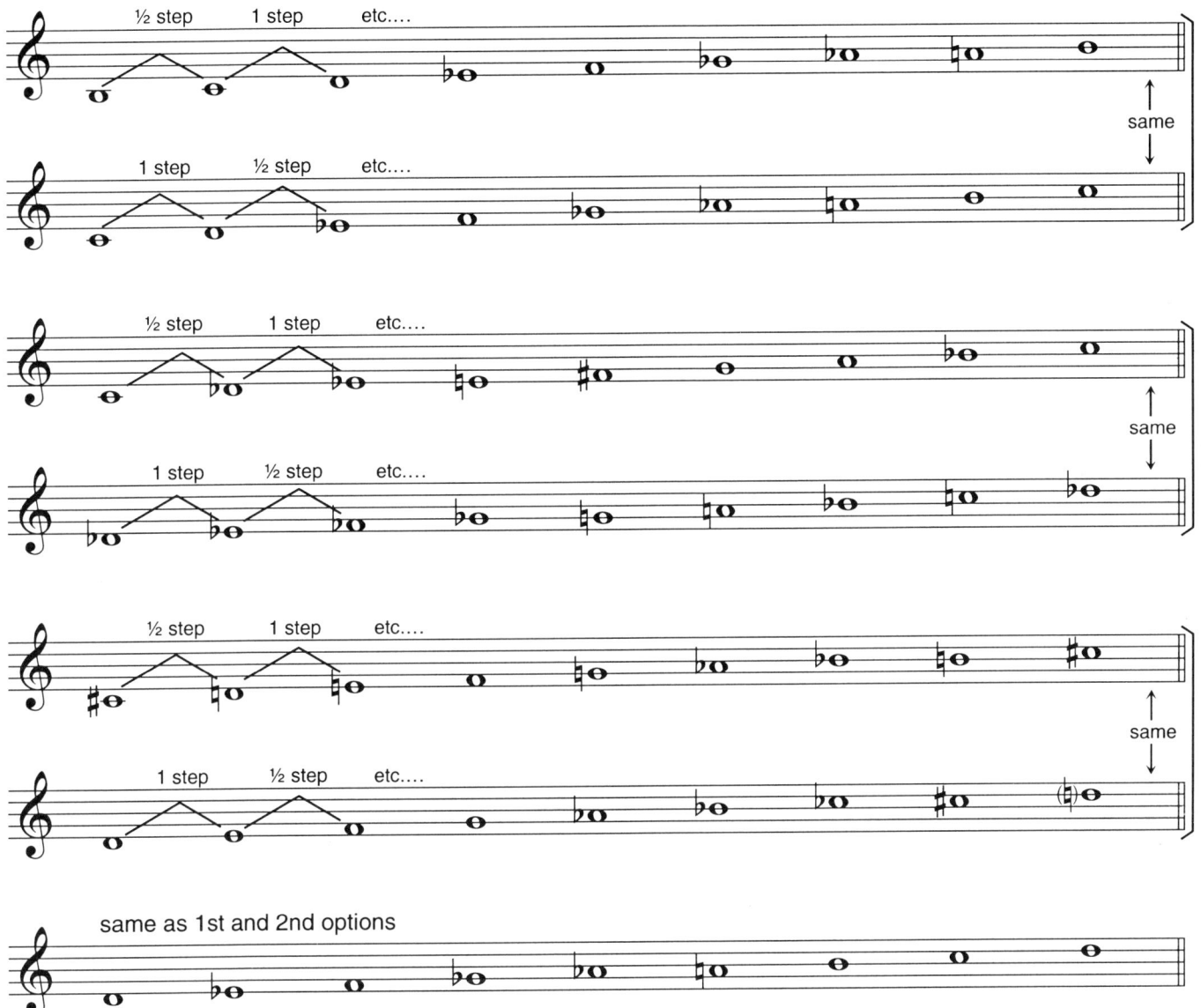

I hope it is obvious to everyone by now that any starting point can be used to begin the series of three consecutive O7th chords or Symmetric Diminished scales that would constitute a complete set of "prime" O7th chords (of which all others would be inversions), or a complete set of "prime" Symmetric Diminished scales (of which all others would be modes).

All of this may seem a bit confusing at first, so I am going to give you a reference guide to help you determine which chord scale to use with various "vagrant" chords. Remember that the contextual determining factors that affect the harmonic functions of all chords can be even more crucial to defining the harmonic functions of vagrant chords, due to their inherent ambiguity (example 131).

Example 131

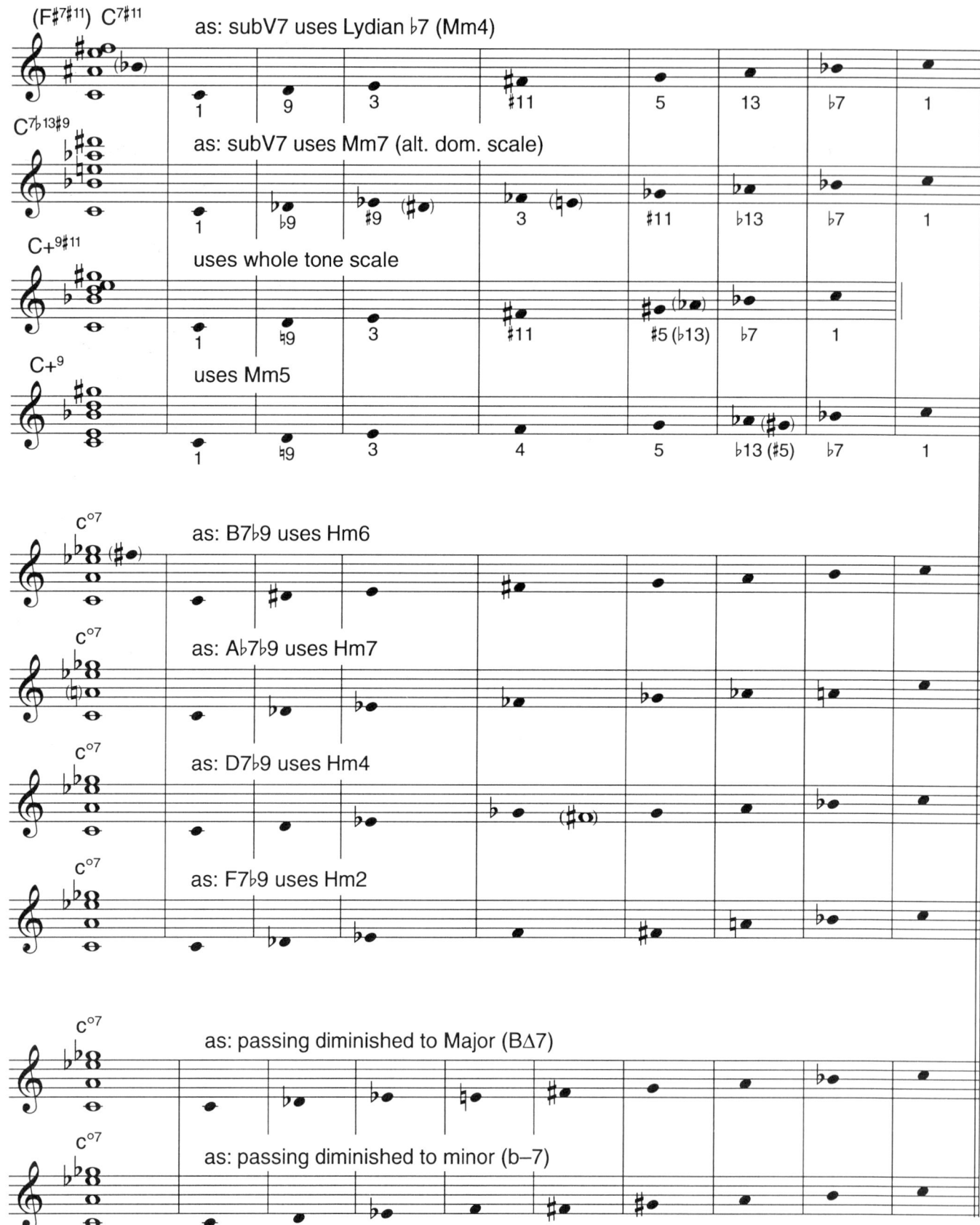

As with all of the chords we've dealt with, you can use the entire chromatic scale in relation to any of the vagrant chords addressed in this chapter. Just remember that the same guidelines for the breakdown of the twelve notes of the chromatic scale also apply to vagrant chords. In other words, you can use: (1) **chord tones**, (2) **passing tones** from the scale that best defines the chord's harmonic function within the context in which it occurs, (3) **available** and/or **altered tensions**,[22] which are often some of the same passing tones 8VA from the chord scale used to define the chord's harmonic function, and (4) chromatic **approach tones**, which will approach the chord tones and/or available or altered tensions chromatically from either above or below. These approach tones are dissonant and must resolve. This is the part that is a bit harder for vagrant chords, because the vagrant chords themselves are often so dissonant and/or can accommodate such a wide variety of dissonant tones that careful listening is required in order to intelligently use and master the additional dissonances these chromatic approach tones represent within the context of this frontier of tonality.

The three following exercises illustrate ways of constructing lines on three different vagrant chords using tools we've discussed. Exercise 27 targets the chord tones of a cO7 chord by approaching each chord tone with the passing tone from above and a chromatic approach tone from below. Since the passing tones are each a whole step above the chord tone, and the approach tones are a half step below each chord tone, the notes of this exercise come exclusively from a whole step / half step Symmetric Diminished scale built on the root of the cO7 chord. In fact, each note from exercise 28 is also taken exclusively from the whole step / half step Symmetric Diminished scale built upon the root of the cO7 chord. However, exercise 28 demonstrates how lines constructed from this scale work on dominant 7th chords with altered tensions (note the symmetry of the line itself). Exercise 29 employs a chromatic approach tone below and a passing tone above to approach the chord tones of a C+7 chord. Like the passing tones in exercise 27, the ones in exercise 29 are each a whole step above the chord tones they approach, meaning that these passing tones all come from a C Whole Tone scale. But unlike exercise 27, the chromatic approach tones in this case are outside of the tonality of the chord over which this line would be played.

---

[22] The term "altered tension" is a bit of a misnomer here, because the chord scale that best defines a vagrant chord with an altered tension would contain this "altered" tension, in effect making the altered tension an available tension. But since you will encounter this term in reference to altered dominant 7th chords, I've used it. An altered dominant 7th chord is a dominant 7th chord containing two or more altered tensions. This term evolved, as did many of our chord symbols, to enable one to play a chord that contains as many correct notes as possible while avoiding incorrect ones, without requiring that the player understand the chord's relation to the key in which it occurs. So taking the dominant 7th chord (regardless of harmonic function) as the basis, any tension which would not diatonically occur on a "normal" V7 chord (i.e., Mixolydian tonality) would be considered altered, hence the term. I personally feel it is better for the composer or the arranger to write chord symbols that contain the specific tensions (altered or otherwise) that they want. But since this is not a universally accepted approach, you will encounter C7 alt. to represent C7♭9♭13 or C7♯9♭13 or C7♯9♯11 or C7♭9♯11. Since each of these chords contains two altered tensions, they technically meet the definition of the term altered dominant chord. However, you can see how the application of this term lacks specificity.

Exercise 27

Exercise 28

Exercise 29

Exercises 27 and 29 bear a close relationship to their respective chords and each chord's respective chord scale, because each note in exercise 27 (i.e., both the passing tones above and the chromatic approach tones below), and the passing tones above in exercise 29, are scale tones. And while the notes from exercise 28 come exclusively from a C whole step / half step Symmetric Diminished scale, the harmonic function of each note can be related to the B7#9#11 chord as follows: root, ♭7, #9, ♭9, #11, Δ3, ♭13, ♮5, root, ♭7, etc. This all demonstrates how malleable these chords and their respective chord scales are. It is important to realize that the different functions and/or interpretations of the same notes even in the same or similar contexts (as represented in exercises 27 through 32) are in fact audible phenomena, not just theoretical constructs.

If we use chromatic approach tones from above combined with a passing tone a whole step below to target the chord tones in exercise 27, we will find that these notes now form the other Symmetric Diminished scale (i.e., half step / whole step from the root of cO7; exercise 30).

Exercise 30

We could also approach each chord tone chromatically from above and below as illustrated in exercise 31.

Exercise 31

And we can extend the method of approaching targeted chord tones into the upper structure of a chord as I've done with the C+ chord in exercise 32.

Exercise 32

The C+9♯11 found in exercise 32 could also be notated as B♭+/C+ or D+/C+. This method of chordal representation is often called a polytonal chord, and polytonal chords are the focus of the next chapter.

Chapter 9: Polytonal Chords

The term polytonal means many keys or tonalities occurring simultaneously. This phenomenon rarely occurs even in modern music. The term polytonal is often incorrectly applied to any chord that is represented by a chord stacked over a bass note (e.g., C/E). But many of the chords that are represented by such chord symbols are in fact merely inversions, consequently they contain a chord tone other than the root in the bass. While other chords represented by such chord symbols may have a chord stacked over a bass note that comes from a different tonality such as A/C, even these are not truly polytonal. It would be more accurate to call them bitonal. Be prepared to have to decipher both terms, as they are often indiscriminately interchanged in common usage, leading to some confusion. It is crucial to be able to distinguish quickly between an inversion such as G/B (where a chord tone other than the root [in this case, the Δ3rd] is in the bass), and a chord that is essentially one triad or chord stacked upon another, such as F♯/A7. This F♯/A7 is an example of how our chord symbol nomenclature has evolved into a shorthand designed to facilitate the player's recognition that the upper structure of an A7♭9 ♮13 chord is in fact intervallically identical to an F♯ triad (i.e., F♯ is both the root of the F♯ triad and the ♮13th of A7; C♯ is both the 5th of the F♯ triad and the 3rd of A7; and the 3rd of the F♯ triad [A♯] is also the ♭9 [B♭] of the A7 chord; example 132).

Example 132

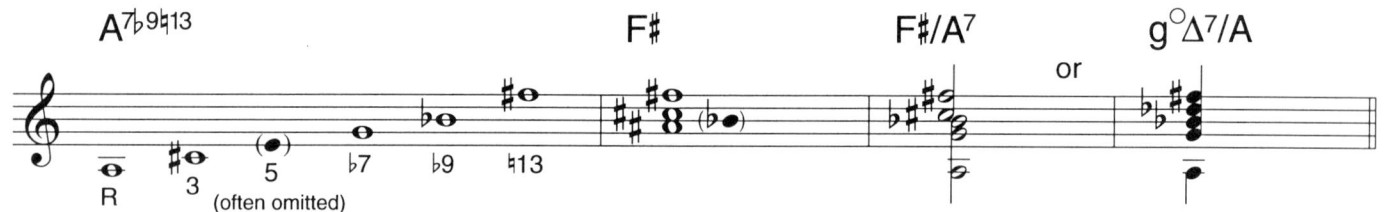

This same chord could also be represented as gOΔ7/A, because the F♯, D♭ (or C♯), B♭, and G♮ form a gOΔ7 chord.

All of this illustrates that the workability of this method of chordal representation is predicated upon the player's ability to recognize the individual components and then assemble them on the fingerboard.

Like any new word added to an already existing vocabulary, one must learn to recognize and use each of these bitonal or polytonal chords one at a time. The first step requires us to distinguish between the inversions of chords we already know and the bitonal chords constructed by stacking chords we already know upon one another or over a bass note from a different chord, key, or tonality. This is no easy task at first.

For those of you who are not readily familiar with all of the inversions of the diatonic chords and triads in all Major and minor tonalities, the problem can be even more daunting. So the first thing to do when one of these chords stacked above a bass note is encountered is to determine whether or not the bass note is a chord tone. If it is, then such a chord is merely an inversion (example 133).

Example 133

The chords from example 133 demonstrate possible voicings for root position and each subsequent inversion for all the diatonic 7th *chord types* occurring in Major and minor tonalities (excluding O7th, for reasons explained below. All of the voicings are drop 2, except the ones with the 7th in the bass, which are drop 3.).

As with our previous "intervallic" comparisons, each chord has *C* as its root. However, it is imperative that you explore all the inversions of all 7th chords in all twelve Major and minor keys, because you will encounter them in all twelve keys, especially in jazz.

Some of you may have noticed that I only provided the root position and two subsequent inversions for a O triad (all drop 2). This is because a O triad can have inversions in which a note that cannot be interpreted as the root can occur in the bass, while (as previously discussed), any note of a O7th chord can function as its root. Inversions of chords from the two families of chords whose intervallic structures are cyclical (i.e., O and +) can be difficult to represent as chords stacked above a bass note, and it is often misleading or redundant to do so. Take as a case in point the +7th chords in example 133, which could all easily have different chord symbol representations. For example, the first inversion of C+7, **C+7/E**, could easily be represented as E+♯11, just as the second inversion, **C+/G♯**, could be G♯+♮9, and the third inversion, **C+/B♭**, could be either G♯+/B♭ or E+/B♭.

The key to understanding these and all "accurate" chord symbols is an awareness that the chord symbol itself tells you what notes need to be included. All of our chord symbols are designed to guide you in choosing the correct notes while excluding incorrect ones, but they don't all aid you in interpreting their harmonic functions. So while I've called the last chord in example 133 C+/B♭ (which is accurate), I've done so in keeping with the pattern for each "chord set" in example 133; that is, the last inversion of each set has the 7th in the bass (excluding the O triads for the reasons stated above). But representing this voicing of this chord as G♯+/B♭ might be easier to read, because the + triad stacked above the bass note is a closed root position G♯+ triad (which we all know by now is an inversion of C+). In any event, any inversion of any voicing of a C+ triad stacked over a B♭ bass note would fulfill the minimum requirements of the chord symbol: C+/B♭. However, musicality would add the additional requirement of good voice leading to and from any such chord, and employing the appropriate chord symbol (which is contextually determined) could clarify its harmonic function. I believe it is possible to employ our chord symbols in a manner that better suggests a chord's contextual harmonic function while encouraging proper voice leading by the knowledgeable player; however, space restrictions force me to leave that topic to a future volume.

This brings us to what I prefer to call **bitonal** chords. As the name implies, components of these chords come from two different keys, tonalities, or chords. Due to the tertiary nature of the harmonic system that jazz inherited from Western European classical music, most of our chords are constructed in ascending thirds. As noted in Chapter 1, these tertiary structures form the chords and triads that are the basis for most of our harmony. Continuing this tertiary construction process into the upper structure of our chords produces the 7ths, 9ths, 11ths, and 13ths we've already covered, but, taken as units themselves, these upper structures also form triads and chords in and of themselves. This is not really surprising, because any structure built in consecutive ascending 3rds from any pitch is likely to produce a triad or chord of some kind, especially if we limit our choice of notes to those which would be diatonically available. Consequently, many of the diatonic 7th chords we've previously addressed contain diatonic upper structures that form easily recognizable triads and chords. As a result of the common recognition of this fact, many jazz musicians use bitonal chord symbols such as D/C to represent a chord such as CΔ9♯11♮13. Example 134 illustrates some of the possibilities for this first type of bitonal chord, namely, "diatonic bitonal chords."

Example 134

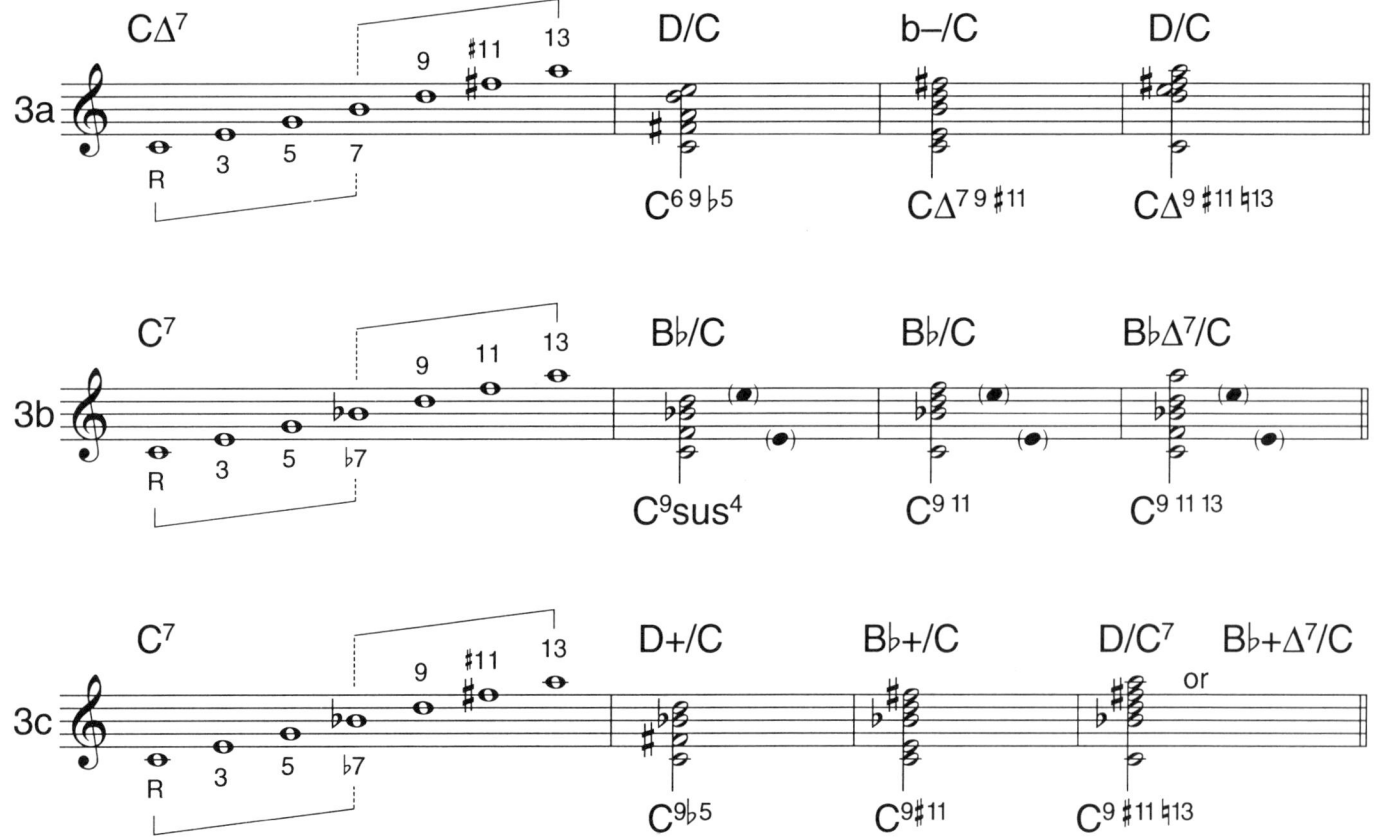

137

While not every possibility is addressed in the chords from example 134, I have covered possible voicings of bitonal chord symbols for each of the seven basic types of 7th chords that you are likely to encounter in jazz compositions. Some are quite common, such as those in 3a, and 3b; some are quite rare, such as the whole tone chord from 3g, and the Gb+/cO from 3i. In addition to providing a possible voicing for each chord, I've given you the bitonal chord symbol above and the standard chord symbol below each voicing to illustrate how some bitonal chord symbols are easier to decipher than standard chord symbols, while others are so convoluted that they are impractical.

I want to draw your attention to an aspect that these voicings illustrate which has only been demonstrated by inference so far: namely, the necessity for omission of certain chord tones. Since our instrument has a relatively small number of strings, the number of voices we can play simultaneously is limited, as we obviously can't play more notes at the same time than the number of strings can accommodate. And it is not very practical to voice lead more than four or five notes simultaneously on the guitar anyway, meaning that we cannot accommodate all of the chord tones and available tensions in a seven note chord such as C9♯11♮13 or D/C7, nor would it necessarily sound better if we could. So often notes are omitted or a tension is substituted for a chord tone that might be inferred. In fact, we've already been doing this with many of the 7th and 9th chords that are presented in "guitar friendly" voicings from previous chapters in this book. I'll cover this in more detail and offer some guidelines for choosing which notes to omit later in this chapter. But first let's examine some of the voicings in example 134. The first and third bitonal chord symbols in 3a are identical (though the standard chord symbols and the voicings differ) and occur quite commonly. I think these bitonal chord symbols are generally easier to recognize than their equivalent standard chord symbols. However, they don't indicate all the notes to be included as clearly as do the standard chord symbols below each voicing. Both types of chord symbol require guitarists to choose which chord tones to omit in order to accommodate their upper structures. I've omitted the 5th in all three voicings and raised the Δ3rd an octave, taking advantage of the availability of the open high *E* string in the first and third voicings.

The dominant 7th chords from 3b come from a Mixolydian tonality and therefore contain ♮11. These chords commonly occur and are often represented with the bitonal chord symbols placed above each voicing. They may function as and be represented as sus 4 chords. However, if the omitted Δ3rd were included, something that the bitonal chord symbol suggests is possible (this can be achieved by again using the high *E* string), they would not really be standard sus 4 chords. The use of both Δ3 and ♮4 together in a voicing is not as common, but does occur when the 3rd is either placed above the 4th, creating a rich Δ7th interval, or when the 3rd is placed next to the 4th, creating a minor 2nd interval that adds some spice to the voicing (especially if used in the middle voices). Using the ♮4th above the Δ3rd doesn't work in this context, because the resulting ♭9 interval is too harsh and out of character with the rest of the chord.

The dominant 7th chords from 3c are derived from the Lydian ♭7th scale (Mm5), which accounts for the ♯11. Both types of chord symbol work here, but both also require choices of omission.

Examples 3d and 3e address the inherent differences between minor chords derived from Dorian (3d) and those derived from Melodic minor (3e). You can judge for yourself the workability of the different chord symbol representations.

The Ø7 chords found in 3f demonstrate the first signs of the limits of our attempts to relate both the chord and all available tensions to one tonality. As we know from our previous examinations of Ø7 chords, the differences between the three possible chord scale options revolve around the indicator notes: ♭9 vs. ♮9, and ♭6 vs. ♮6. To accommodate both the chord tones and the upper structure as they occur at the beginning of 3f, we would need a hybrid tonality, because only Mm6 can accommodate the ♮9, and only Hm2 can accommodate the ♮13 (i.e., ♮6 8VA); neither can accommodate both, and Locrian can't accommodate either. I personally feel the ♮13 to be of little value here, because although it is possible, it prematurely sounds the note that the ♭7 of the Ø7 chord would likely resolve to (i.e., *A♮* if c∅7 resolved to F7 or B7). For most ∅7 chords I feel the standard chord symbols are superior, as they can nicely accommodate both the chords and their upper structures if extended no further than the 11th, which is the practical limit of ∅7 chords' upper structures in most contexts.

The last three examples, 3g, 3h, and 3i, address chord symbol representations of voicings derived from triads or chords whose intervallic structures are cyclical in nature, and they all further manifest the problems that began to occur with the ∅7 chords from 3f. Several are of interest, however. While the standard chord symbol representation for C9♯11 in 3g works better than B♭+/C or its other interpretations, the whole tone chord at the end is merely an inversion of the whole tone scale itself, because the distance between each voice is a minor 7th (which results from inverting the whole step interval from which the scale is built). So determining its root is arbitrary at best, since any note of the scale could be the root, in theory. And no chord symbol is likely to ensure a composer or arranger that a player would play such a voicing. Only writing it out would achieve this result.

The other two interesting anomalies occur with the bitonal representations of c○Δ79 as either G♭+/c○ or E♭+Δ7/C (in 3i). In each case the bitonal chord symbols use what are essentially their chordal opposites to represent these voicings, i.e., an + chord (stacked upon a bass note or upon a ○ triad) to represent a ○ (Δ7) chord. While these representations are possible, they stretch the system to such a degree that they can be misleading.

However, I feel that both the g♯∅7/C and the E9/C (in 3h), as well as the B/C (in 3i) successfully represent the actual voicings corresponding to each of these bitonal chord symbols.

All of this further illustrates the flexibility of both the chords themselves and the various methods of representing them. It also further illustrates how demanding the music that employs them can be for the player. This is why I am covering these aspects in as much detail as I am. Both those who write and those who play these chord symbols need to be clear about what they mean, and I'm afraid that is not always the case for either the writer or the player. Just remember both "stacked" bitonal and standard chord symbols are supposed to tell you, the player, which notes need to be included and, by inference, which to exclude. These symbols often require you to omit certain tones, and some symbols are simple enough that you can also add tensions that are not contained in the chord symbol. But you can only do this if you clearly hear what is available. This is why understanding a chord's harmonic function is so crucial. Because whether or not you can function at the level of hearing and understanding concurrently, understanding is still the only guide you can use. So acquire it!

Now let us address the last type of bitonal chord. While the name "polytonal" seems more applicable here, these chords also tend to exist in only two tonalities, with the rare exception only proving the efficacy of my preference for the term bitonal. These chords tend to be dominant 7th chords whose upper structures form triads or other chords that appear to come from a tonality completely alien to the chord or bass note upon which they are stacked, like the F♯/A7 previously mentioned in this chapter (example 132), or the G♯/B we briefly addressed in the secondary dominant chord chapter of this book (p. 84, example 74), or the A/C from later in the same chapter (p. 92, example 84). While some of the chords from example 135 (those from 3f, 3g, and 3h in particular) would also seem to fit this description, the tonalities related to their derivations are far more common than the hybrid tonalities required to possibly yield the chords from this last category of "polytonal" chords.

Example 135

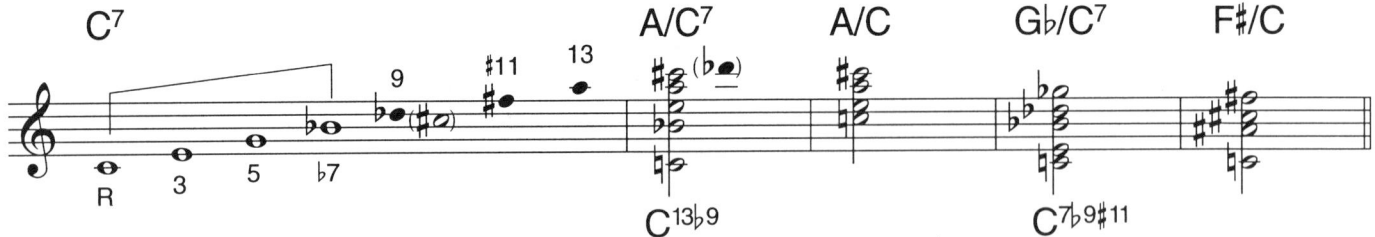

As you can see from example 135, there are only two such chords. I know this seems a bit anti-climactic after such a lengthy explanation, but since in reality all of the bitonal chords involve a method of chord symbol representation that is viable because the upper structures of the chords represented form recognizable triads and/or chords stacked above a bass note or another chord, and we guitarists (as well as most pianists in practice) omit some "expendable" chord tones, the results are usually simple triads voiced above a chord or bass note. While example 135 doesn't really cover every possibility, it represents the two most common bitonal chords whose upper structures form a Major triad that bears only the remotest relationship to its bass note.

In example 136 I've taken the four basic triad types, i.e., **Major**, **minor**, **Augmented**, and **diminished**, as the basis for an experiment that moves each triad type voiced above a constant *C* bass note, to demonstrate my point. Each triad is moved up chromatically to cover all twelve possibilities for Major, minor, and diminished, and the four possibilities for Augmented. I've placed bitonal/polytonal chord symbols above, and standard chord symbols where possible below each of the resulting voicings. This does in fact cover all of the possibilities for triads voiced above a C♮ bass note (however, not all inversions are covered). I think you can see for yourself that only four of the forty possibilities cannot be represented by standard chord symbols. These four are likely to occur in the context of a chord or chords moving over a pedal tone in the bass. Even these four "questionable" voicings can be accommodated by one of two methods of chord symbol representation. And if we add a Major 3rd above the *C* pedal for f♯–/C, it can be represented by the standard chord symbol C 13, ♭9, ♯11; similarly, adding the same E♮ to g♯–/C means it can accurately be represented by the standard chord symbol C+Δ♯9. While the last two "questionable" voicings this experiment yields (fO/C and bO/C) can only be realistically represented with bitonal chord symbols, even these two can be constructed diatonically in a c Harmonic minor tonality.

The O and + triads present some interesting anomalies. (1) Remembering that there are only four "prime" possibilities for + triads that would not be an inversion of one of the first four, and observing that the bass note is common to all of the chords in example 136, three of the four possibilities for + triads voiced over a *C* pedal are also diatonic 7th chords occurring in other tonalities, and the fourth is an inversion of the standard + chord which begins this series. (2) Regarding the O triads voiced over a *C* pedal in example 136, four of the twelve are dominant 7th chords (three with ♭9, one without); three are O triads that have *C* as a chord tone (cO7, aO7, and f♯O); one is a O7th chord (e♭O7/C is a cO7th chord); one is a Ø7th chord (because f–6 is an inversion of dØ7); one is the same C+Δ79 chord that I commented on before, noting the unusual fact that we had used a g♯O/C to represent it; and the last two (fO/C and bO/C) were addressed at the end of the preceding paragraph.

Example 136

As with virtually all of the examples and exercises in this book, the chords in example 136 need to be explored in the eleven other "keys," that is, using each of the remaining eleven tones of the chromatic scale as the constant pedal in the bass for each series of possibilities. Both the 2nd inversion and the root position need to be investigated for the Major and minor triads as well. No one can acquire mastery of these chords without undertaking such an exploration. I leave it to the serious student to do so, either on his or her own, or with the assistance of a qualified teacher.

Before we turn to some advice about how to improvise over these "bitonal" or "polytonal" chords, I want to give you some thoughts and/or guidelines regarding the omission of expendable chord tones required to play these chords (particularly on the guitar).

I believe it likely that the implementation of bitonal chord symbols was facilitated by the aforementioned common recognition among many jazz musicians that the upper structures of these chords form easily identifiable triads, or chords, and that the use of these bitonal chord symbols is necessitated by the uncertainty (especially among players of intermediate or lesser skills) as to what notes to omit when confronted with a chord that could potentially contain seven or eight notes if spelled out and/or played in its entirety. When you encounter D/C, you don't have to worry about choosing to omit or include the 5th of the CΔ chord, or even the 3rd of the CΔ chord for that matter. If you include the *D, F♯,* and *A* (of the *D* triad) over a *C* bass note, you've adequately addressed the minimum requirements of this chord symbol. However, if the same chord were represented as CΔ13♯11, or CΔ9 13♯11, then you would have to decide which four or five tones are the most in need of inclusion.

All of this gives you some insight into how and possibly why bitonal chord symbols entered our nomenclature in the first place, and if you reflect a bit further, it also gives you some insight into how to choose which notes to omit, because no one that has any idea of what they want you to play would write a straight CΔ7 chord (even in a Lydian tonality) if they wanted to insure that you would include the 9, ♯11, and 13. Conversely, one shouldn't include tensions in a chord symbol that one doesn't expect the player to play, the point being that if the tensions are included in the chord symbol, they should be there for a reason. There are only two reasons. The first is the one you must assume is operative unless some aspect of the music indicates otherwise, namely, that these tensions need to be included in your chord voicing(s) even if doing so requires you to judiciously omit one or more chord tones. The second reason can be problematic, as it justifies the inclusion of these tensions within a chord symbol solely for the purpose of clarifying a chord's harmonic function. For example, CΔ7 may be either Ionian or Lydian, but CΔ7♯11 or D/C can only be Lydian. I don't advocate this second approach as a general rule, because it can be misleading. But be prepared to deal with it, as you'll likely encounter it, especially when you're given "homemade" chord charts by some well-meaning singer or instrumentalist who transposed the chords of a song from a lead sheet into a key that they are comfortable with, omitting the melody, assuming you don't need it, and then adding every tension inferred by the melody to the chord symbols to help clarify what only needs clarification due to the omission of the melody. This is not a problem with chord charts written by knowledgeable arrangers, because their chord symbols can be relied upon to include only the tensions they want you to include in your voicings.

Returning to the choice of omissions: unless the 5th is altered (i.e., ♭5 or ♯5), it is usually the most expendable. And if you are playing with a bass player, he or she is going to be playing the root, or whatever note is indicated as the bottom voice, so you can usually also safely omit that note in such circumstances. This brings our potential seven note voicing down to a manageable five notes. There are times when even the 3rd can be omitted, but you should avoid doing this unless all other methods have been tried and have failed. Even then, consider losing a tension before omitting the 3rd, unless of course the chord symbol(s) indicate(s) the 3rd is expendable, for example, in cases such as C711 or C11 or C sus 4, where the 11th or 4th is generally intended to replace the 3rd. The 3rd is often the most crucial note, because it differentiates between Δ and –. This "rule of necessity" is really the guiding principle for the choices of omission. You want to include the notes that define the chord. If someone else has the root, or bottom voice covered, you don't need to double it and potentially get in his or her way. The root infers the 5th (as it is the 1st overtone); therefore, unless it is altered, it can safely be omitted. The 3rd defines whether a chord is Δ or –. The 7th defines whether a Δ chord is dominant 7th or Δ7th, whether a minor chord is –7th or –Δ7th, and it differentiates between OΔ7th, O7th, and Ø7th, so these notes (i.e., the 3rd and the 7th) are generally the last to be omitted.

The chord symbol(s) should clearly delineate what tensions to include. Some notes, however, are inferred. For example, C9 is a dominant 7th chord with a ♮9th; the 7th is inferred by the presence of this 9th. Conversely, CΔ9 would infer the presence or availability of a Δ7th due to the presence of its 9th. The basic principle here is that the presence of any part of the upper structure or any available tension infers the presence or availability of those diatonically occurring below it. In other words, 13 infers 11, 11 infers 9, and 9 infers 7. Of course, this implies that you the player understand enough about a chord's harmonic function to know which tensions are available and/or practical. For instance, CΔ13 would imply Δ7, 9 and 11, but which 11th is available? ♯11 is only available in Lydian, while ♮11 (which is available in Ionian) will sound awful against the Δ7th of the chord, so it's not really practical.

The same basic concepts apply to all of the chords based on minor triads as well. For example, c–9 infers the ♭7. While you would need c–Δ9 (which is uncommon) to infer the Δ7th, it is better to use c–Δ79, or even G/c–. And again, the presence of other upper structure tones infers those below, so c–11 infers ♮9 and ♭7. In this case the ♭3rd is not as expendable, because without it you have no way to differentiate between c–11 and C11, which is based on a CΔ triad or chord whose 3rd is replaced by 11 (or 4). c–13 infers ♮11, ♮9, and ♭7, although the ♮13 is often problematic for –7 chords for the reasons previously addressed. c–Δ11 is possible but unlikely, because any time you have the Δ7 and the ♮11 together, they create a O5th interval, which suggests a dominant 7th chord (in this case, G7). It would be better to write this chord as either c–Δ711, which would infer the ♮9, or as G7/c–, but this latter bitonal chord symbol illustrates why this chord is impractical in the first place. cØ9 would infer the ♭7, but it is customarily written out as cØ79, while cØ711 would infer the ♮9. And cØ713 extends the upper structure into the realm of impracticality for the reasons previously mentioned.

Both O and + chord symbols usually clearly indicate the tensions to be included, because it is so hard to omit any of their chord tones without obscuring what type of chord they are. Example 137 illustrates some of the options for the seven basic types of 7th chords (omitted notes are in parentheses, and questionable tensions are indicated as quarter notes).

Example 137

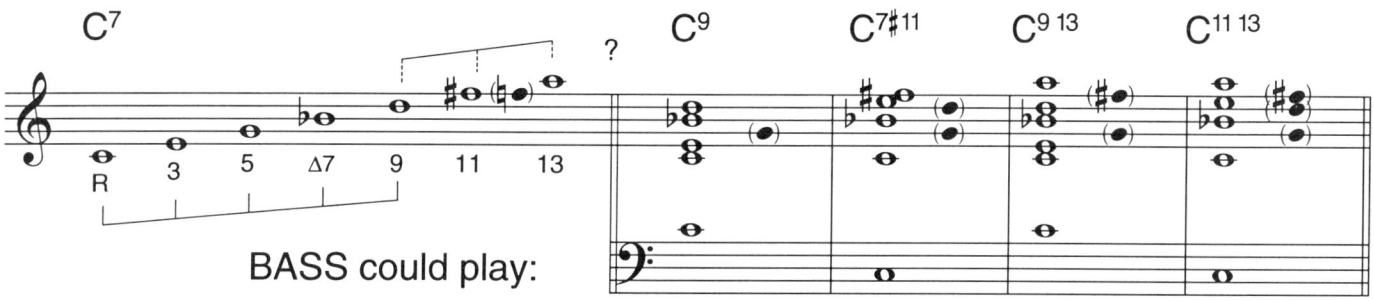

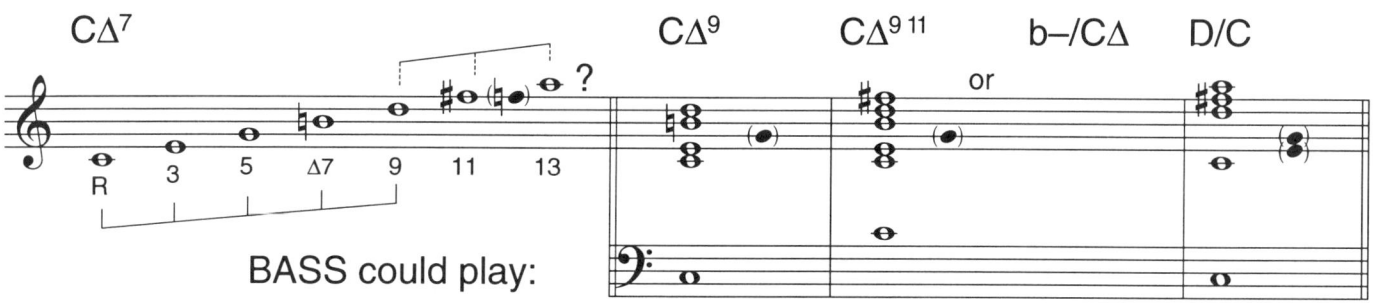

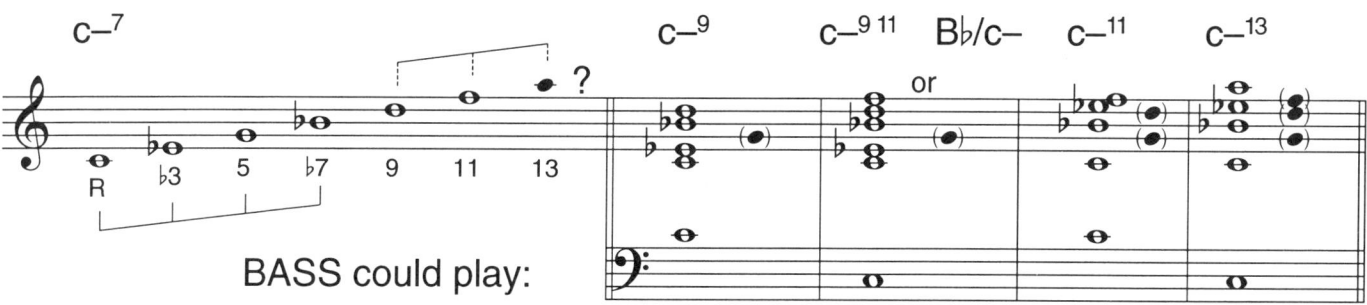

143

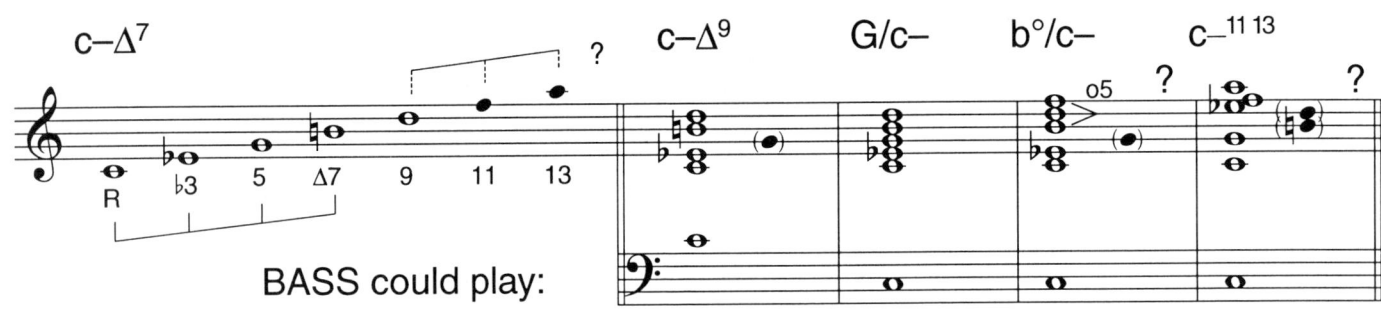

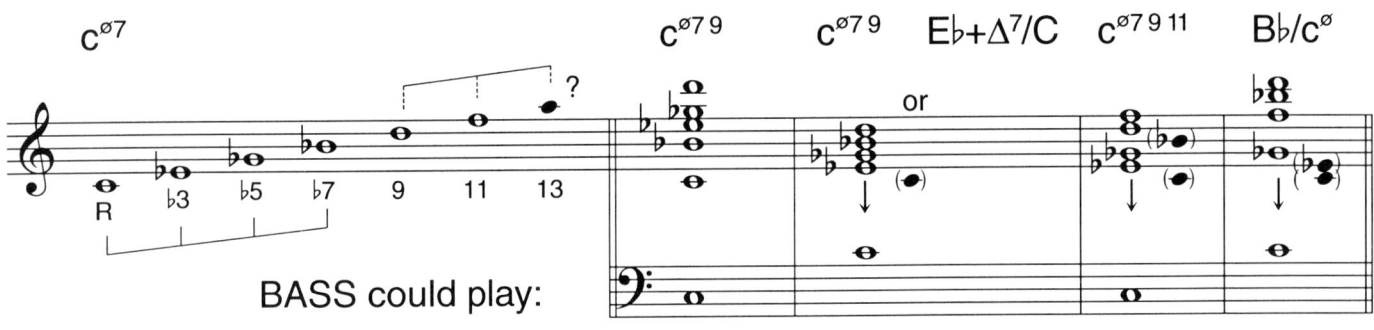

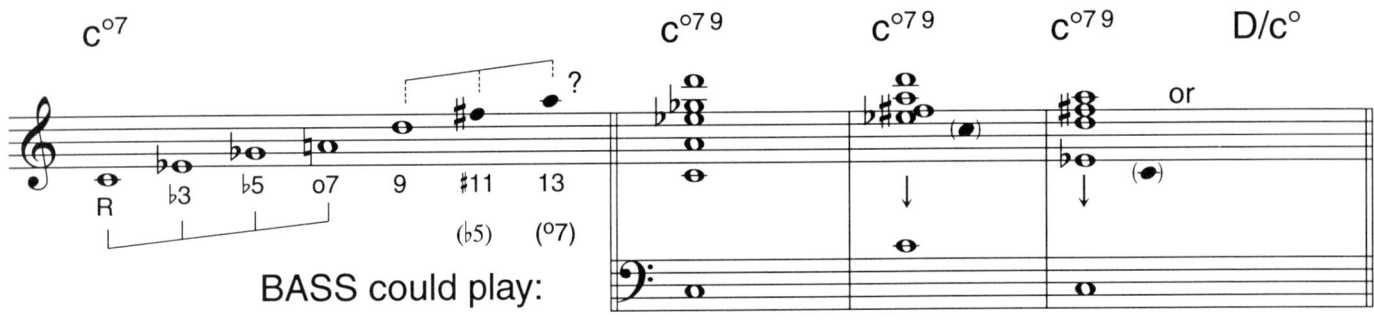

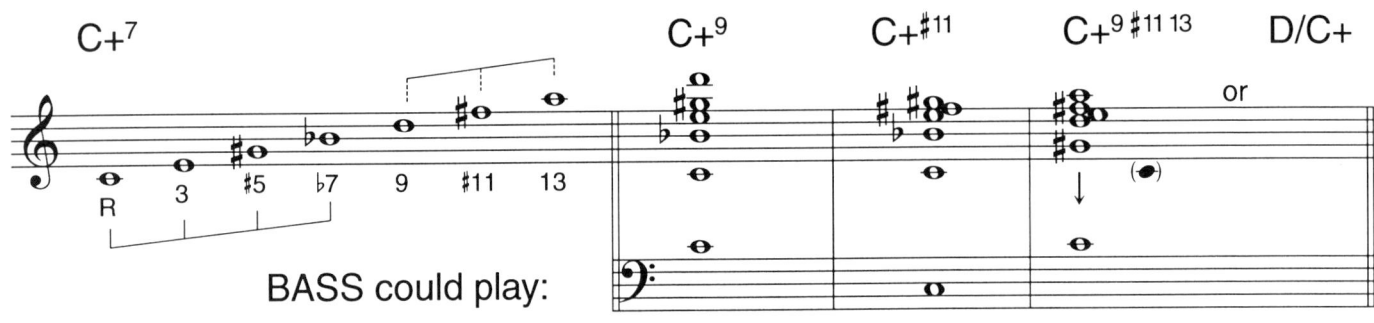

This brings us to a discussion of some guidelines for improvising over these chords. I hope that it has occurred to most of you that the inversions of triads and chords which are notated as "stacked" chords require the same chord scale(s) that they would use in root position.

While those chords found in example 134 (i.e., "diatonic bitonal chords") are all derived from the individual tonalities that can accommodate both their chord tones and their upper structures, a linear arrangement of the pitches of both results in each actual chord scale for most of these "bitonal" chords. The only exception is the Ø7 chord and its upper structure, which can even be accommodated within one tonality if we avoid using the problematic ♮13th.

Example 138

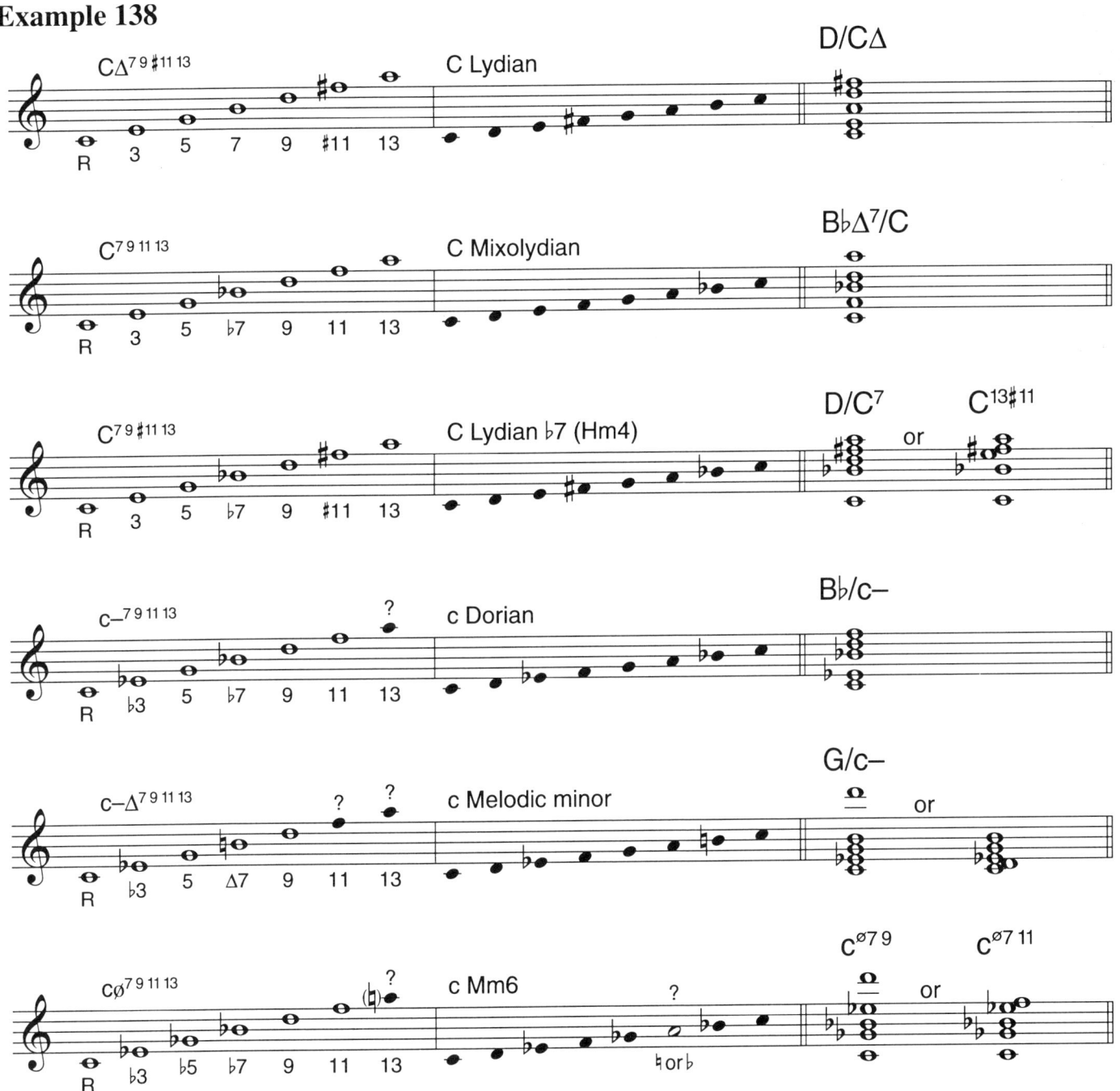

All of the "bitonal" chords in example 138 can be diatonically "derived" from scales we have already covered. However, difficulties arise when extending the upper structures of minor chords up to the 13th (because the +4th or O5th interval created between the 13th and the −3rd can suggest a dominant 7th chord). We encounter similar problems when including both Δ7 and ♮11 within any chord (also producing a O5th interval), or when extending Ø7 chords up to the ♮13th.

The one remaining problem area involves the last chord from example 138. This O7♭9 chord does occur, but its harmonic function can be hard to define, even in context. This is due to the ♭9 interval existing between its root and its ♭9th. The O7th chord's extreme dissonance is responsible for its ability to accommodate the ♭9th as a tension. But as the bitonal chord symbol (e♭Ø7/C) illustrates, it is still a problem, because if the ♮13th is a problem on a Ø7th chord, it is even more of a problem in the bottom voice, and the fact that we can represent a O7th chord with a Ø7th chord symbol illustrates how potentially confusing the ♭9 tension can be on a O7th chord. But if you do encounter such a chord, then the half step / whole step Symmetric Diminished scale is a good chord scale option.

This brings us to a discussion of strategies for improvising over the types of "bitonal/polytonal" chords found in example 135, i.e., those whose upper structures form triads and/or chords that come from tonalities that are only distantly related to the chords or bass notes upon which they are "stacked." Often the only possible way to create chord scales that can accommodate both the chord tones and all of the tones of the upper structures of these bitonal/polytonal chords involves fabricating "hybrid" tonalities like the altered Mm5 formed from a Major tetrachord and a Harmonic minor tetrachord (which we previously used in the secondary dominant chapter for constructing G#/B; p. 84, example 74). Therefore, many jazz musicians often blow over these chords by playing predominantly around the pitches of their upper structures, in effect creating the "bitonal" or "polytonal" relationship between what they play in the upper structure and what the accompanying musicians play under them with the basic chord(s).

Example 139

Example 139 provides the basic chord and its upper structure on the far left of each of the first two staffs in the form of an arpeggio that represents the raw material from which both the chord voicings and the lines that follow are constructed. The lines each illustrate how one might play around the pitches of the upper structures of the chords to their left. Notice the use of the chromatic approach tone *D#* to approach a note which is common to both the A Major triad and the C7 chord in the first line (i.e., *E♮*). And notice how the same *D#* functions a bit differently in the second line, that is, to approach the same *E♮* in a scalewise manner. In fact, all of the notes except the *D#* from each of the two lines in example 139 come from either the upper structure (these are generally the target notes) or the "chord below" (whose tones either approach the notes of the upper structure or are common to both).

147

The rest of example 139 illustrates some possible chord scale options for these bitonal/polytonal chords. You can use a hybrid scale formed by combining both the basic chord (in this case, C7) and its upper structure (i.e., notes from an A Major triad). You can see that the only note in this hybrid scale that is not a chord tone of one of the two chords indicated by the bitonal chord symbol is the F# in parentheses. This note would be #11 in relation to the C7 (i.e., bottom half of the bitonal chord). This F# is also the only note that distinguishes this hybrid scale from the altered Mm5 found earlier in example 139. This altered Mm5 scale could also work as long as you avoid the #11, which this scale cannot accommodate (and which isn't actually implied by the chord symbol A/C7). I think you'll generally find these two scales to be of more use for the first type of bitonal/polytonal chord in example 139 (A/C7) than the second type. The second type (Gb/C7 or F#/C) is better defined by the Altered Dominant scale (from *C*) if it is not extended beyond the #11. If it is extended to the ♮13th, then the best scale option is the half step / whole step Symmetric Diminished scale, which could also work for the first type of chord (A/C7). Explore all of these options for yourself, and make your own discoveries and conclusions—that is part of the adventure of our music.

Of course, as with all other chords, you can use the notes of the entire chromatic scale with any of the chords we've covered in this chapter. Just be sure to clearly hear and treat the upper structures as what they are, namely, available or altered tensions that just happen to form recognizable triads or chords. And be careful not to confuse the triads and chords formed by these upper structures with the chords upon which they are stacked.

To recap:

(1) Some of the chords which are represented by "stacked" chord symbols are merely inversions containing a chord tone other than the root in the bass, such as Eb/G or f#Ø7/C.

(2) Some chords represented by "bitonal" chord symbols are comprised of triads or chords formed from upper structures which are voiced over chords that come from the same tonality from which these upper structures were derived (i.e., they are diatonic), such as: Bb/C or D/C.

(3) And some "bitonal/polytonal" chords contain triads or chords voiced over another chord or bass note coming from a distantly related tonality, such as: F#/A or A/D#.

You may find yourself in unfamiliar territory when first trying to hear your way into using the upper structures of these chords, because some (especially the "bitonal/polytonal" chords) can seem to move quite outside of the tonalities that precede and/or follow them. So proceed at your own pace and be sure to check out the recordings of some of the masters who have paved the way for all of us in their use of these adventurous harmonies.

Chapter 10:
Quartal Harmony and Voicings in Fourths

There is one remaining area of harmonic phenomena that you'll encounter in jazz (as well as other music), which I'd like to address briefly before we turn our attention to the compositions and transcriptions of improvised solos that illustrate the practical application of the material covered in this book. The harmonic devices to which I refer are the chords voiced in consecutive ascending 4ths.

Some have proposed an entire harmonic system based on triads and chords constructed in 4ths. They call this system "quartal" harmony, as opposed to tertian harmony, which is a harmonic system that is based upon chords constructed in 3rds. The analysis of tertian harmony has been the guiding principle for this entire book, because it has also been the modus operandi for the development of most of western harmony throughout its history. Those who advocate replacing the tertian harmonic system with a quartal harmonic system attempt to justify jettisoning more than five hundred years of musical history because one single harmonic structure built in ascending consecutive fourths can accommodate all twelve notes of our chromatic scale before the onset of any duplication of pitches, a feat that no tertian structure can achieve.

Example 140

Ironically this all-inclusive quartal harmonic structure brings us back to where we began: the fundamental tone and its overtone series. Because if you invert the 4th upon which the quartal system is based, the result is the same 5th upon which the Pythagorean system is based. And a linear arrangement of the first seven notes of this structure built in ascending 5ths yields the scale upon which the tertian system is based.[23] And if we continue to ascend in 5ths, we can create a structure that will also accommodate all twelve notes of our chromatic scale before the onset of pitch duplication occurs.

---

[23] Of course, as you can see for yourself in example 141, the 7th note is an *F♯*, which makes our scale Lydian, not Major (Ionian). This, in fact, is one of the primary principles upon which George Russell's famous *Lydian Chromatic Concept of Tonal Organization for Improvisation* is based. But that is yet another system for explaining what we've already largely covered. Just remember that Pythagoras didn't have a tempered scale, so all of the 5ths in his system weren't equidistant, making the sixth note closer to B♭ than B♮ (as it is in the actual overtone series found in Example 1 Model 2, p. 8). Consequently, the seventh note (which is a 5th above the 6th note) would be closer to *F♮* than *F♯*. In any event, even in the quartal system, all chords are not voiced exclusively in perfect 4ths, as you'll see. So, like all musical systems, this quartal system must also be capable of accommodating alteration if it is to account for what actually occurs in our music.

Example 141

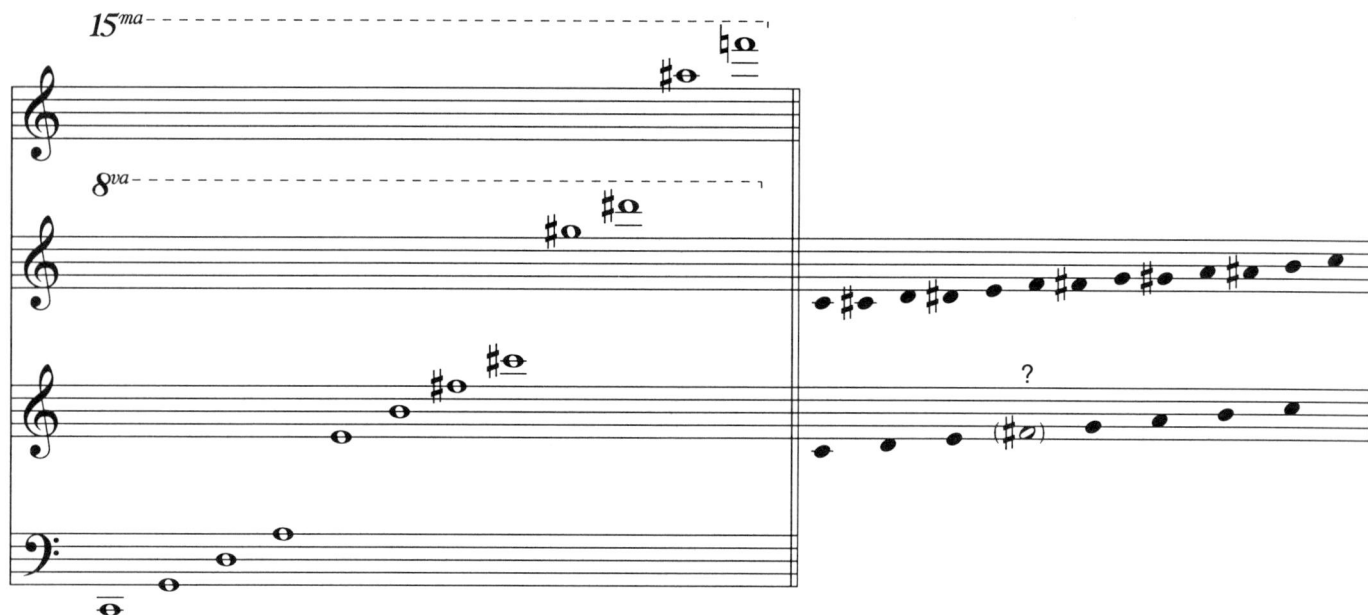

Not only does an inversion of the interval upon which the quartal system is based yield the same scale upon which our old tertian system is based, but virtually all voicings in 4ths can be accommodated by our old tertian harmonic system. And voicings in 4ths are the prime manifestation of the quartal harmonic system that we are likely to encounter in jazz.

If we examine chords voiced in 4ths, like, for example, the one(s) used to answer the bass line in Miles Davis' tune "So What," we find that they are essentially both minor 7th chords with the 11th (or 4th) voiced in the tenor voice. And as we've previously demonstrated, if a minor 7th chord in a Dorian (or for that matter Aeolian, or even Phrygian) tonality is extended diatonically into its upper structure, after the 9th, we arrive at the ♮11th. So these voicings in 4ths can quite easily be diatonically derived from tonalities clearly rooted in our tertian harmonic system.

Example 142

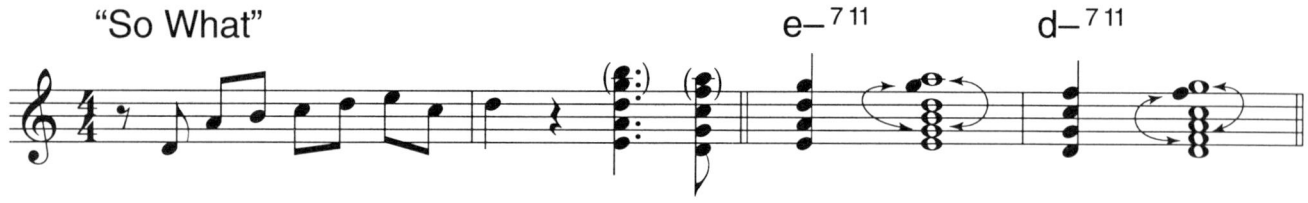

These voicings in 4ths from "So What" are created by reordering the placement of certain chord tones, in effect interchanging the 5th and the 11th while including the ♭7th and raising the minor 3rd one octave. Notice the Major 3rd created between the top two voices. This, too, is a type of 4th—a O4th—more about this later. If the 5th were omitted, the resulting four-note voicing would be constructed entirely of perfect 4ths.

Since our instrument is tuned predominantly in perfect 4ths, voicings in 4ths are quite easily played on the guitar. These guitar-friendly voicings are readily available on any group of three or four, and even five or six adjacent strings.

Example 143

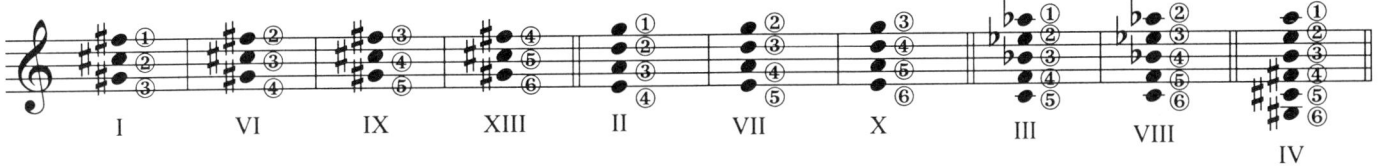

However, voicings in 4ths most commonly occur in four note voicings (on the guitar), where they function as part of a chord in conjunction with another instrument playing the rest of, or part of the rest of, what is required to complete the chord.

In fact, voicings in 4ths have a chameleon-like character, because they are often sufficiently incomplete in and of themselves that they can assume any number of identities. These identities are often provided by the bass note placed beneath them. Check out the voicings in example 144 and observe how many different harmonic functions the same voicing in 4ths can have.

Example 144

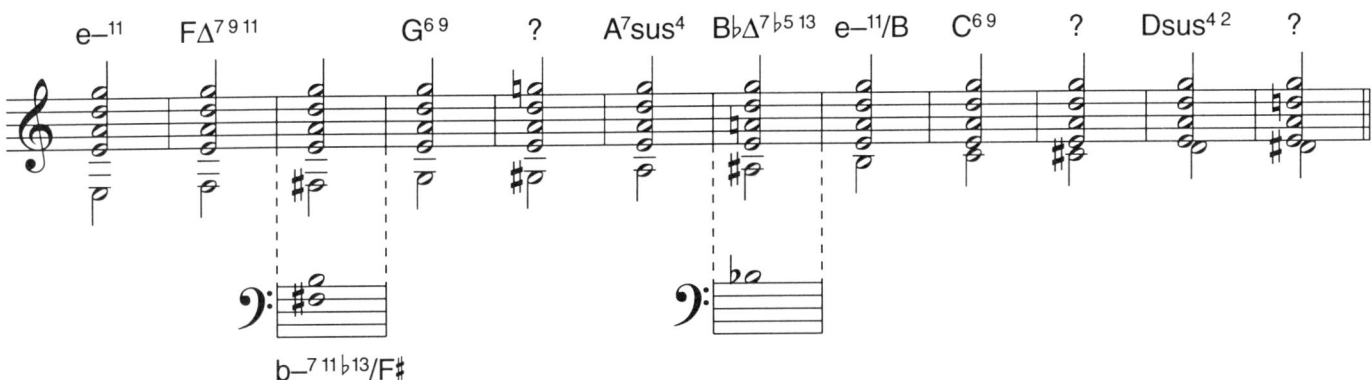

As you can see, only three of the chords voiced in 4ths from example 144 are difficult enough to name that they require the question mark that I've placed above them. Another one has the chord symbol below the voicing. The chord symbol for this chord (b–7 11 b13/F♯) would only work if an additional 4th were added between the *F♯* in the bottom voice and the four note voicing common to all the chords in example 144 (as I've done in the bass clef), making it now intervallically identical to the last voicing in example 143.

You could easily apply this process of using each note of the chromatic scale for the bass note of each of the voicings in example 143 as well. This gives you some idea of how ambiguous these chords can be on their own.

During much of western harmony's evolution, the 4th has been considered a dissonance. While not the harshest of dissonances, it still differs in nature from the traditionally consonant intervals. Much of the meaning in our music is expressed through an ever-changing interplay between consonance and dissonance. I feel it is unreasonable to expect audiences to relate to new music with no reference to their previous musical encounters. While I'm not advocating pandering to an audience whose expectations have little or no musical or aesthetic refinement, I am cautioning against assuming that anyone can come to a musical experience as a blank slate. We all view the things we encounter in our lives through the "veil" of our previous encounters, and music is not excluded from this fact of life. You may write the greatest poem ever written, but if you write it in Sanskrit, don't expect many people to read it. In other words, our sense of what is and what isn't dissonant is there. Whether this sense is innate or a cultural construct may be the subject for an interesting debate, but it exists, and consequently both musicians and the audience have to deal with it. Since the 4th itself was historically treated as a dissonance, chords built exclusively in 4ths can be difficult to employ convincingly as chords of resolution, especially within the context of harmonic sequences comprised entirely of other chords voiced in 4ths.

Chords voiced in 4ths can add an open quality to the harmonic content of our music that is often quite appealing. But like many other things in life, too much of a good thing may not be so good. The open/ambiguous nature of some chords voiced in 4ths fits nicely with the aesthetic ideals of certain kinds of music, like the modal jazz of the late 1950s and early 1960s. Since modal jazz was striving for an openness that was the antithesis of the cluttered harmonic obstacle courses prevalent in much of the jazz of the time, open sounding voicings were a nice fit. But listen to any of a number of the musicians who indiscriminately embraced this approach, voicing every chord of an old standard (whose beautiful changes needed no improvement) in 4ths, and you'll quickly hear the silliness of a universal application of this technique. It's as if those who exclusively used chords voiced in 4ths were striving for a musical personification of "Kant's imperative."[24]

My advice is to develop your own judgment to the point where you can rely upon it. Meanwhile, use these chords voiced in 4ths like any other ingredient or spice in a well-prepared meal, that is, judiciously.

Since some of you may not be sure how to improvise over chords voiced in 4ths, let me offer some guidance. If they are occurring in a modal context, then you would obviously use the appropriate mode. For example, Miles Davis's "So What" is Dorian, so that's the mode you would use. However, since virtually every chord we've covered can be constructed in some form that would be predominantly voiced in 4ths, chords voiced in 4ths often function just like many of the other chords we've already covered. Once you determine the harmonic function of a chord voiced in 4ths, then you would apply the appropriate chord scale for that chord. Just remember that, like most other intervals, a perfect 4th can be altered and still remain a 4th. For example, if you raise the top note of a perfect 4th interval by a half step, the result is an +4th, which is intervallically identical to a O5th. Conversely, if you lower the top voice of a perfect 4th by a half step, the result is a O4th, which is intervallically identical to a Δ3rd.

Example 145

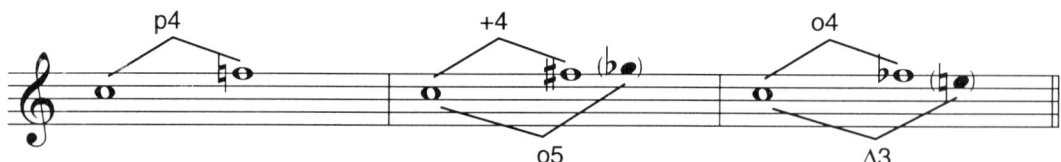

---

[24] Immanuel Kant's categorical imperative has several versions. The best known is: "Act only on that maxim which you can at the same time will to become universal law" (*A Dictionary of Philosophy*, ed. by Antony Flew, revised second ed., [New York: St. Martin's Press, 1979], 191).

Example 146 is designed to illustrate how the Major and minor (Melodic minor and Harmonic minor) tonalities, and subsequently the modes of each, can all produce diatonic chords voiced in 4ths.

Example 146

Major

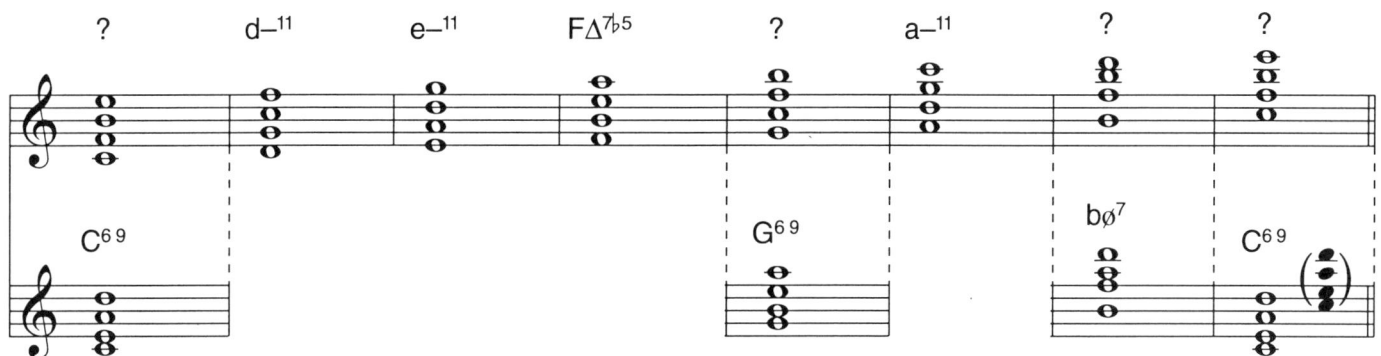

Melodic minor

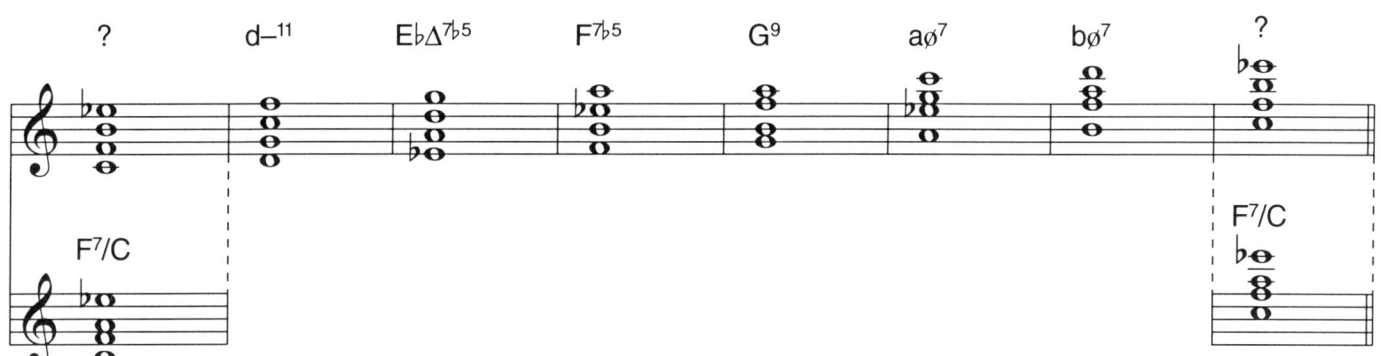

Harmonic minor

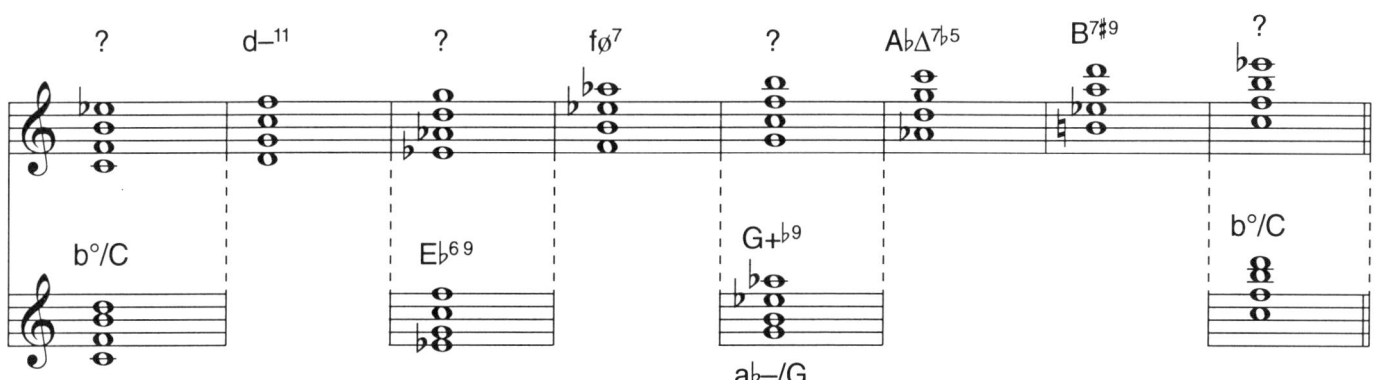

I've not directly included each of the diatonic chords voiced in 4ths for each mode of each of the three types of scale in example 146, but they are inferred, because each mode would obviously contain the chords that are common to its parent tonality, albeit in a different order. Nevertheless, example 146 illustrates how easily the tertian harmonic system can accommodate voicings in 4ths, especially when using O4ths and/or +4ths, as well as perfect 4ths. And while not every possibility is covered here, most of the chords voiced in 4ths that you'll encounter in a jazz context will resemble the chords in example 146, because most jazz tunes and virtually all standards are tonally oriented and based on tertian harmony. So the chords voiced in 4ths found in these situations are either derived from tertian harmony or can be accommodated by it. This is due in part to the ambiguity inherent in most chords voiced in 4ths, which in effect lets them be, within the limits of musical credibility, what we want them to be. So undertake the adventure of exploration that is part of the joy of jazz, and check out as many possibilities as you can. And remember that while most of the examples and exercises from the theoretical portion of this book are in the key of *C*, do take the time to explore all of the material presented in the remaining eleven keys.

Remarks on Method of Presentation

The first half of this book is an explanation of the various harmonic phenomena that you'll encounter in the compositions that comprise the second half. The material in the second half is representative of what you'll encounter in the jazz compositions that you'll play in the real world as a gigging jazz musician.

The method of presentation in the first half of this book follows a simple model: a natural occurrence is observed and analyzed. This occurrence then becomes the prototype for the explanation of musical phenomena derived from it, beginning with the fundamental tone, which gives rise to the overtone series, which yields the scale that forms the raw material from which the triads and chords are constructed. This prototype is then imitated in other tonalities, and the results are analyzed. This method is not original to me. In fact, Schoenberg employs much the same approach in his *Theory of Harmony*, and it seems only fitting to conclude this portion of my book with Schoenberg's explanation of his methods in acknowledgement of how indebted to him I am, and in the realization that his explanation of his methods may help to clarify my own: "The development of the harmonic resources is explained primarily through the conscious or unconscious imitation of a prototype; every imitation so produced can then itself become a prototype that can in turn be imitated."[25]

---

[25] Arnold Schoenberg, *Theory of Harmony*, trans. Roy E. Carter (Berkeley and Los Angeles: University of California Press, 1983), 385.

Part II:

Application / The Compositions

Chapter 11: The Blues

There are many factors that contributed to the development of jazz. Primary among them was the opportunity for the mixing of different cultural influences that the New World provided. In the early 20th century no city facilitated this cultural-musical cross-pollination better than New Orleans. One of its native sons, Louis Armstrong, was among the first to bring a blues-based sensibility to his interpretations of the popular songs of the day. In September of 1924, Fletcher Henderson persuaded Louis Armstrong to leave King Oliver's band (then working in Chicago) to join his band in New York City. In doing so Mr. Henderson successfully brought together one of the nation's finest orchestras, whose repertoire largely consisted of well written arrangements of popular songs, with Armstrong, one of the prime proponents of the blues-based approach to interpreting popular songs.

Many musicologists mark this confluence of a blues-based sensibility and popular song forms as the seminal event that codified the jazz approach. Despite his enormous musical talents, I'm not convinced that Mr. Armstrong was the sole instigator of this approach, because others were following a similar path. Among them was another musician from New Orleans: soprano saxophonist Sidney Bechet. During the mid-1920s Bechet was working in Claude Hopkins' band accompanying Josephine Baker's review, which was based in Paris and touring throughout Europe. This took him out of the U.S. spotlight during the time Louis Armstrong was in Henderson's band, and consequently lessened the impact of Bechet's innovations on players in the United States. Whomever the musicologists choose to credit, it is clear that the blues-based sensibility that Mr. Armstrong's music exemplifies is at the heart of jazz music. For while there may well be great improvising musicians that don't play the blues well, there have been no great jazz musicians that can't play the blues well.

The blues represents many things to many people, but the common thread that ties them all together is a rich and flexible harmonic platform comprised of the relationship between three chords: the I, the IV, and the V.

The compositions in this chapter are designed to demonstrate many varieties of the blues, particularly as jazz musicians have played the blues. First let's examine the three chord-twelve bar platform that constitutes the genome of the blues.

Example 147

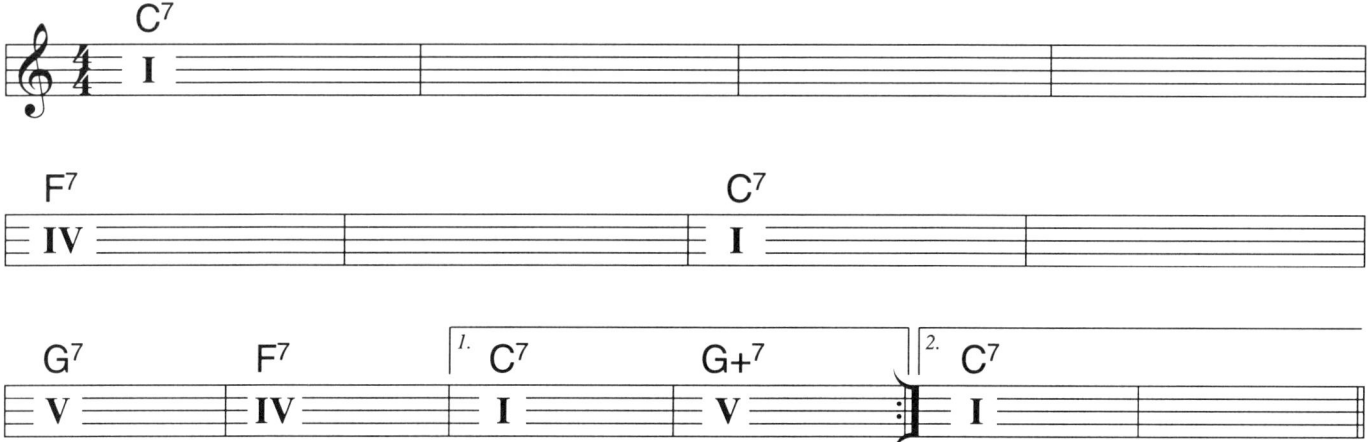

The chord progression in example 147 is a rudimentary twelve bar blues. The first thing the observant among you will notice is that each chord is a dominant 7th chord. Usually dominant 7th chords occur diatonically only on the Vth degree, except in Melodic minor (where they also occur on the IVth degree). Yet the I chord in most blues progressions is frequently a dominant 7th chord (as it is in example 147). There is no clear explanation for this. It is possible that the circular nature of this repeating twelve bar progression led to the gradual conversion of the I chord into a dominant 7th chord that in effect could function as V of IV and thereby lead better to the IV chord that follows. It is just as likely that the Africans that were forcibly brought to the Western Hemisphere during the African diaspora heard the ♭7th differently than did the Europeans, because the Africans didn't have a tempered scale. And if you remember Example 1 Model 2 (p. 8), you'll recall that the sixth overtone (i.e., the 7th note of Example 1 Model 2) is in fact ♭7, not the Δ7th which the tempered scale produces. Consequently, the Africans would have likely treated this ♭7 differently than the Europeans did, making it potentially easier for them to credibly hear a dominant 7th chord as the tonic of one of their tonalities. (Such a tonality might resemble Mixolydian.)

While both of these explanations are speculative, each alludes to the ways that folks from different cultures may use the same device(s) differently. These explanations also illustrate how the cultural-musical cross-pollination which occurred in the New World may have fostered what I'm calling a blues-based sensibility. In any event, this blues-based sensibility has informed every aspect of jazz from its inception through its ongoing evolution.

The other thing to check out about the rudimentary twelve bar blues progression in example 147 is that the first and second endings are each comprised of two different two bar phrases. The first ending is the simplest of "turnarounds," which, as the name implies, is a phrase designed to turn or send the music back to the top. The second is designed to be final, i.e., the most rudimentary of cadences.

Now let's check out an actual blues composition. "Blues Etude 1" is a simple blues for solo guitar that is comprised of two parts occurring simultaneously. Part 1 is the bottom part and functions as the bass line, with the notes of this part beamed down. Part 2 is comprised of the chords, triads, and lines that form the top part. The notes of this part are beamed up. In example 148 I've separated the two parts into two different treble clef staffs, and placed the harmonic analysis of the I, IV, and V above the bass part, while the more elaborate chord symbols which correspond to the top part are placed above the voicings and lines that comprise the top part.

Example 148

The fingerings in "Blues Etude 1" are one possible option. Explore others for yourself.

Blues Etude 1

© Ken Hatfield 2001

Further analysis of both "Blues Etude 1" and example 148 reveals that even in such a simple blues, many of the harmonic devices addressed in the first part of this book occur. Let's examine some of them. During the first and the third bars of the four bar phrase which corresponds to the Roman numeral I region, we find D6 moving to C6, each in identical first inversion voicings moving over the identical bass line, making the phrase: D6 to C6/E, followed by the chromatic move in the bass, which converts the C6/E into C6/E♯, which may be interpreted as C6/F♮, which is also intervallically identical to an FΔ7 chord. Except for the FΔ7, this phrase is a variant of a Mixolydian dominant modal cadence, and even the FΔ7 which is created through the chromatic motion in the bass line can be explained by the leading tone function of the E♯ (which is why I didn't notate it as F♮ in the music), because it leads to F♯, the note to which E♯ functioning as a leading tone should resolve. We can also interpret this E♯ as F♮, which in this key is one of the most common blues notes: that is, the ♭**3rd** whose presence conveniently converts the C6 voiced above it into an FΔ7 chord. The first four bars are really two "antecedent and consequent" phrases, meaning that if we consider bar 1 to be the question, then bar 2 is its answer, just as bar 3 could be the question, and bar 4 its answer. The chords voiced in the top part of bar 2 and the first two chords of bar 4 are identical root position voicings. Only the bass line and a difference in the alto voice (of the third chord) distinguish these two different answers to the same question (posed in bars 1 and 3) from one another. However, the last chord of bar 4 is a sub V(13) of the G6 which begins the next two bar phrase that corresponds to the Roman numeral IV region. The bass line also sets up a motif which is an important part of this simple blues. In particular, the bass line in bar 2 employs a blues lick comprised of the three note phrase which concludes the bar to create a motific expectation which is fulfilled by the imitation a 4th lower in bar 4. However, the last note of this imitation is placed in the top voice of the sub V of IV chord that ends bar 4 (i.e., *F♮*, functioning as the 13th of the A♭13 chord). This sub V(13) of IV then resolves to the IV chord of our blues (G6).

Bars 5 and 6 correspond to the Roman numeral IV region of this blues. Bar 5 is intervallically identical to bar 1, though transposed down a 5th to correspond to the IV chord region of this blues. (Remember inverting an upward 4th yields a downward 5th.) However, the last two chords of bar 6 suggest the whole tone tonality that corresponds to the +7 chord which is functioning as V(+7) of I. This V+7 brings us back to the reprise of bar 1, whose chords are voiced 8VB. This all occurs while the bass line in bar 7 remains identical to that in bar 1. Bar 8 continues the motion begun in bar 7, and in the process briefly passes through the subdominant minor chord (g–) on its way to another substitute dominant 7th chord, i.e., B♭13 functioning as sub V(13) of V.

This sub V of V leads us to the last four bars of our twelve bar blues. This section begins with root position voicings of two chords which mirror those we began with. These chords are transposed down a 4th to correspond to the V chord region of our blues (again, remember that inverting an upward 5th yields a downward 4th). The third chord of bar 9 (A♭13) is yet another substitute dominant 7th chord (again sub V of IV) which moves to the region corresponding to the second IV of this blues, and again uses two chords that mirror those previously used, though in root position this time. All this occurs prior to ending bar 10 with a blues lick that sets up the turnaround the first time (i.e., first ending), and sets up the final cadence the second time (i.e., second ending).

Bar 11 uses simple two-part counterpoint in contrary motion to suggest a variant of the harmonic cliché: I to V of IV, to IV, to sub V of V, to I/V (for more about this form of sub V of V, see chapter on vagrant chords and the +six-five, +four-three, +six, and +two chords, p. 118, example 115).[26] This harmonic cliché in turn sets up another question which is answered by the turnaround in the first ending, and is answered in the second ending by an open voicing of the famous phrase with which Count Basie often ended tunes.

[26] This is the actual harmonic cliché:

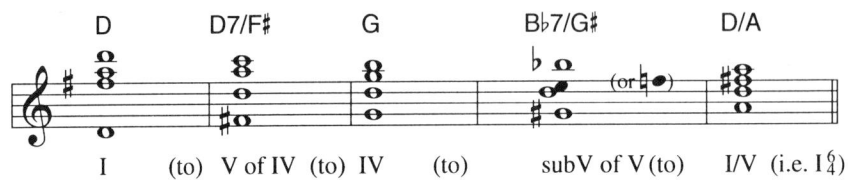

The next blues we will examine, "Pinky's Blues," is an example of a type of blues that employs more harmonic motion to move between each of the three "prime harmonic regions" (i.e., I, IV, and V) common to all blues.

The first four bars correspond to the "prime Roman numeral I region" of this blues; however, there is far more harmonic motion here than there is in the blues of example 147. The move from I7 (in bar 1) to IV9 (in bar 2) is a common way to break up the harmonic monotony of four consecutive bars comprised of the same chord. The four chords in the fourth bar of "Pinky's Blues" are a harmonization of the bass line designed to lead to the IV chord region. Notice the passing diminished 7th chord (c#07) functioning as #IIIO7. This passing diminished chord is passing between first inversions of two diatonic chords (i.e., Ab/C and Bb/D; for more about passing O7th chords, see vagrant chord chapter, pp. 124–130, examples 124–131). If you are uncertain about the diatonic relationship between these two chords, remember that if Bb is I, then Ab is bVII, because this is essentially a Mixolydian tonality.

Example 149

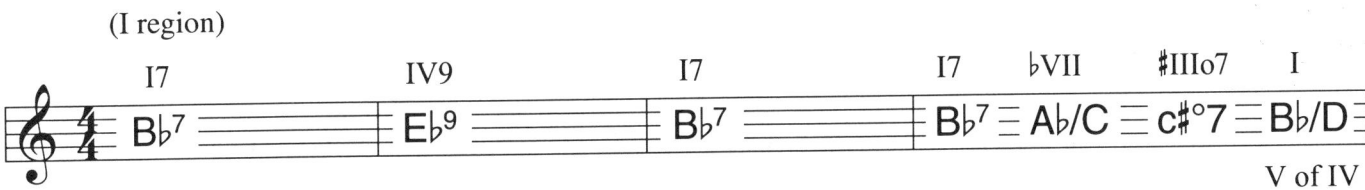

The next two bars (5 and 6) of "Pinky's Blues" correspond to the "prime Roman numeral IV region" of this blues. Bar 5 is obviously the IV7 chord. Bar 6 uses two different inversions of another passing O7th chord, namely #IVO7, to pass between IV and I (remember both bbO7 and dbO7 are inversions of eO7). Normally, this harmonic cliché would be: IV to #IVO7 to I/V, but to avoid direct motion to octaves in the outer voices (i.e., bass and melody), and to set up the bass line upon which the harmonic motion of bars 7 and 8 are based, I've employed these two different inversions of the passing O7th chord in bar 6 to return to the I chord in root position. Bars 7 and 8 again use a diatonically harmonized bass line to lead from the I chord to a secondary IIØ7 V7 of II, which in turn sets up the final four bar phrase of this blues.

Example 150

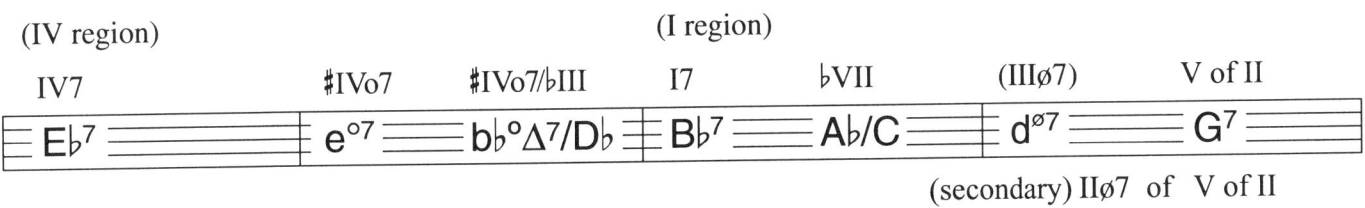

The last four bar harmonic phrase of "Pinky's Blues" is really two phrases. The first interpolates a IIØ7 chord between the V of II chord in bar 8 and the V (of I) chord in bar 10. As previously discussed (in the II V chapter), II chords may precede and/or accompany any V chord, and these II chords may be either –7 or Ø7 chords.

The gb in the melody of bar 9 (which occurs for thematic reasons) requires that the II chord must be a Ø7 chord as opposed to a –7 chord. All of this corresponds to the "prime Roman numeral V region" of this blues.

The final two bars, which constitute the second phrase of the last four bars of "Pinky's Blues'" basic blues form, are a classic turnaround. This turnaround is based upon a bass line that we will encounter a lot in jazz. This bass line outlines the roots of four diatonic chords—I, VI, II, and V—but the chord voiced over the bass note which corresponds to VI is really a secondary dominant chord, i.e., V of II. While the harmonic function of this V of II is the same as the one previously encountered in bar 8, both its chord of resolution and its actual voicing are quite different. In fact, the voicing of the V of II chord in bar 11 is a bitonal/polytonal chord just like the first of the two types previously addressed in the polytonal chord chapter of this book (example 135, p. 140).

Example 151

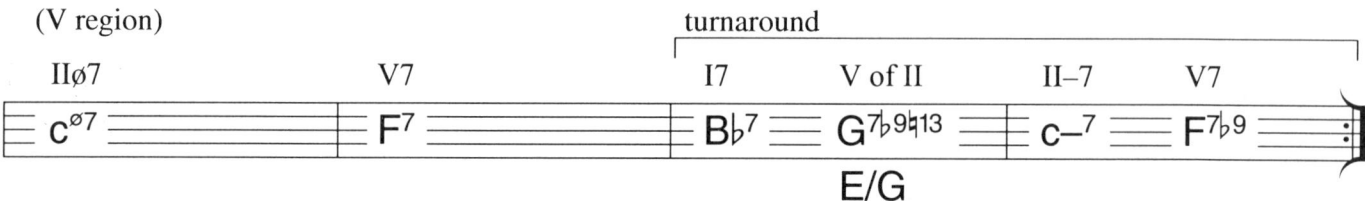

The coda of "Pinky's Blues" is played only on the second time through the out head, or recap of the melody. Though there are no improvised solos on the recorded performances of "Pinky's Blues" on the CD that accompanies this book, the out head would normally occur after the solos. The coda is in the form of a common "tag." A tag is a harmonic phrase which extends a cadence before ending. This is often achieved by harmonically "treading water." In this case, we "tread water" by passing between a II V and a secondary II V of the II V, which produces a cadence to the tonic I chord of this *Bb* blues. The last two bars are a more sophisticated treatment of a common blues ending which dates back at least to the time of Robert Johnson.

Example 152

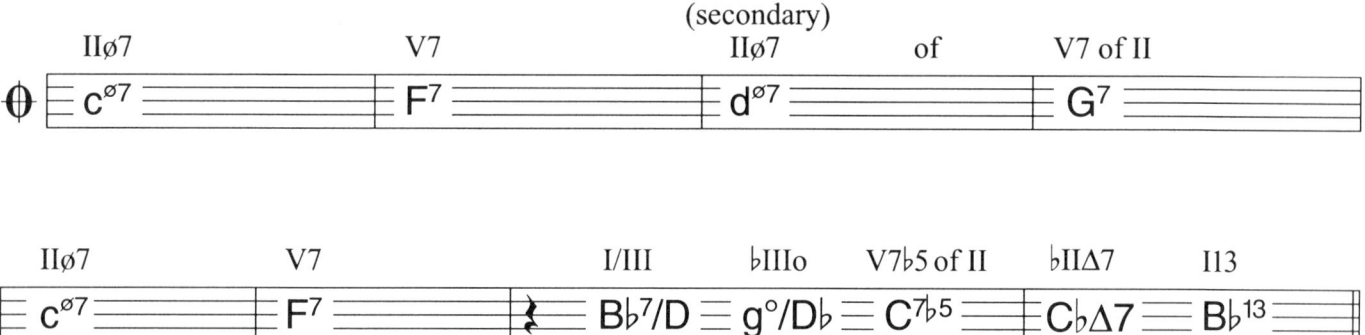

Pinky's Blues

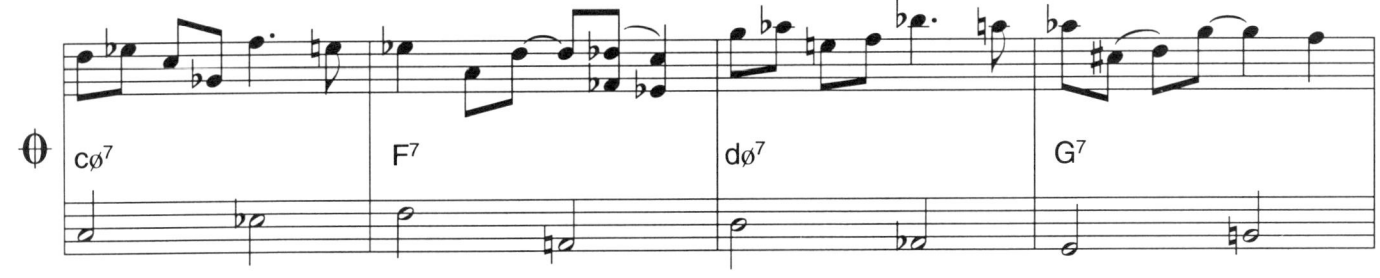

Examples 149 through 151 are the harmonic analyses of the three four-bar phrases that constitute the chord changes of the twelve bar blues form for "Pinky's Blues." Example 152 is the harmonic analysis of the eight bars that constitute its coda.

The first version of "Pinky's Blues" (p. 163) is a lead sheet presentation of the composition (with a bass line). This is the version upon which the harmonic analysis is based, and it resembles the kind of lead sheets jazz musicians often use.

The second version of "Pinky's Blues" (p. 164) is a solo guitar arrangement of the composition that the lead sheet represents. This is but one version of how a player might approach creating a solo rendition of "Pinky's Blues." I encourage you to create your own.

Pinky's Blues: Solo Guitar Arrangement

© Ken Hatfield 2003

The next blues we will check out is "Riff for Brother Jack." I composed this blues in memory of my former employer, the great jazz organist Jack McDuff. McDuff was one of the best blues players and one of the swingingest musicians of his generation. In keeping with his ebullient personality, "Riff for Brother Jack" is not a sad blues.

This twelve bar blues is based on a repeating four bar riff. A riff is a musical figure of short to medium duration (often repeating) that is comprised of notes that are either harmonically neutral, or are readily capable of multiple harmonic interpretations. By harmonically neutral, I mean that the notes of such a riff can fit over a number of different chords with little or no alteration. The relationship between a riff and the various chords by which it could be "harmonized" is analogous to the outline of a figure, such as might be found in a child's coloring book, and the various colors that could be used to fill in the space within the line drawing (example 153).

Example 153

The four bar phrase upon which "Riff for Brother Jack" is built is comprised of two two-bar sections. Each two bar section functions like an answer to the question posed by each of the differing "two chord hits" which precede each two bar section of the riff. The various "two chord hits" present the changes of the blues in the form of the question that is answered by the applicable two bar section of the "harmonically neutral" riff. The riff repeats three times during each exposition of the head (because 3 x the 4 bar riff = the 12 bars of the blues form; example 154).

Example 154

The second time through each head, the riff is harmonized a third below. This is an arranging device that McDuff often employed for the two front line instruments (saxophone and guitar) of his band which he called the Heating Unit (example 155).

Example 155

The lead sheet of "Riff for Brother Jack" on the next page is identical to the actual lead sheet I gave to the musicians for the recording of this tune (track 10, *Phoenix Rising*, ACM 9512). Except for the specific rhythmic placement of the "two chord hits" and the melody riff, much of what you hear on the recording developed from each player's contributions during the rehearsals and the recording. For example, the bass line walking in halftime which occurs during the second time through the head before the solos, and both times after the solos, was something that bassist Hans Glawischnig came up with while we were playing the tune down during the first rehearsal. Drummer Duduka da Fonseca responded by altering what he was playing to accommodate the new bass line, resulting in what you hear on the recording.

This interactive process continues to an even greater degree in the solos and trading of "fours" that follow.

A transcription of my solo begins on p. 168. It is followed by four choruses of "4s," i.e., the alternating four bar phrases that the drummer and I trade. This trading of four bar phrases occurs over the blues form, meaning that when I blow, I am doing so over the chord changes that correspond to whatever part of the cyclical twelve bar blues form I find myself in, as the entire band follows the form of the solo changes found in the bottom three staves of the lead sheet (pp. 167–168).

Riff for Brother Jack

© Ken Hatfield 2001

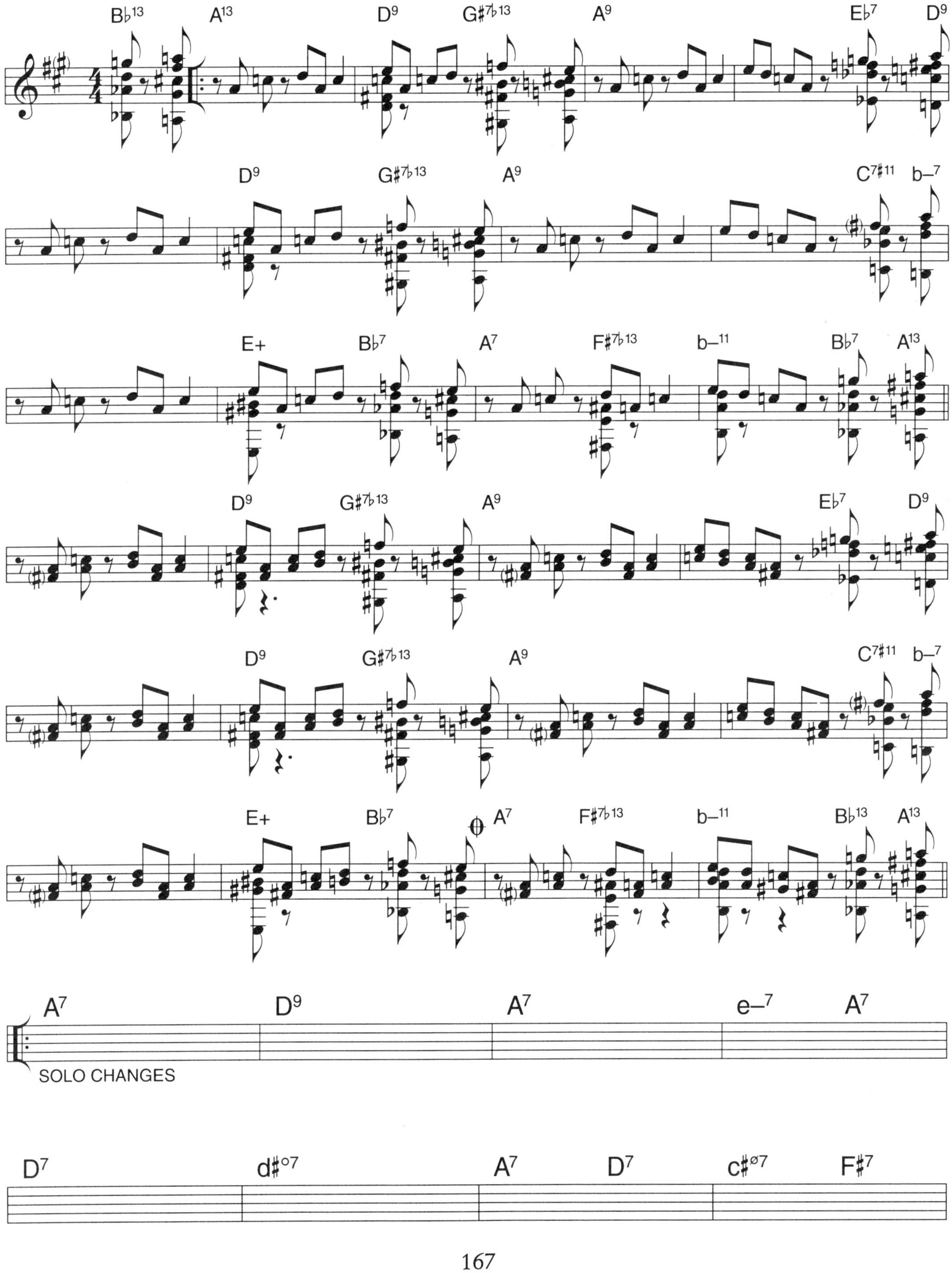

D.C. al Coda

Analysis of solo from "Riff for Brother Jack"

Let's examine how some of the musical devices explained in the first half of this book are employed in my improvised solo from "Riff for Brother Jack."

First chorus: The phrase which begins with the last two (16th) notes of bar 8 and concludes with the *g♯* occurring on the second beat of bar 10 is a series of three note groups that target the chord tones of the II–7 V7 progression that makes up bars 9 and 10. These targeted chord tones are approached from above and below with a combination of passing tones (above) and chromatic approach tones (below) in much the same manner as previously used in exercise 10 (pp. 34–35) at the end of the Major chapter, and exercise 19 (pp. 56–58) at the end of the minor chapter from the first half of this book.

Example 156

Second chorus: The second chorus opens with a variation of a Mixolydian dominant modal cadence as the idea for the first bar of the two bar phrase which begins this chorus (bars 13 and 14). This chordal relationship (between A6 and G6) is then continued in a line built from arpeggios of A7 and e–7 (remember G6 is an inversion of e–7) in the third bar of the second chorus (bar 15).

Example 157

The secondary dominant chord in the eighth bar of the second chorus, i.e., F♯7 (functioning as V of II), is actually voiced as a bitonal chord: D♯/F♯, which is an example of one of the two varieties previously discussed in the polytonal chapter (p. 134, example 132).

Example 158

The line beginning with the last eighth note of bar 21 (i.e., *g♯*) is constructed solely from chord tones of a g♯O7 chord which is functioning as a substitute for a dominant 7th chord, i.e., E7♭9 (as discussed in the vagrant chord chapter, p. 124, example 124).

Example 159

Third chorus: The third chorus begins with an idea based upon an A Mixolydian scale. The fifth bar of this chorus employs a string bend in the bottom voice of a three note voicing. This effect is achieved by holding both the *d* and the *a* with the little finger while bending the e♮ up to f♯ (or as close to f♯ as you can get) with the third finger.

Example 160

Bar 8 of the third chorus employs a secondary IIØ7 V7 of the II of the tonic key. When we arrive at this II–7 chord (in bar 9), a motif built upon the whole step between *C♯* and *B♮* is played as part of a double step (against *D♮*). This motif, which occurs in the bottom voice in bar 9, is then imitated in the top voice of bar 10 as the ♯9 and ♭9 are employed over the V chord.

Example 161

Fourth chorus: The fourth chorus begins by using the sub V of I that ends the third chorus to set up a motif built upon the relationship between the B♭13 and the A13 that resembles the Neapolitan relationship in classical harmony as well as a similar relationship in flamenco music. These two chords also allude to the "two chord hits" from the head. This is followed by a secondary II V of IV that sets up the IV chord region and the blues lick that follows.

Example 162

Bar 5 of this chorus uses double stops (in this case, 6ths) to form the pickups to a blues lick played in "tremolo style." While this tremolo technique comes from flamenco and classical guitar traditions, I've employed it here in a manner similar to the octave tremolos often used by jazz pianists such as Wynton Kelly to sustain the top voice or melody voiced over a chord. This blues lick-based idea then continues in bar 7 en route to its conclusion in bar 8.

Example 163

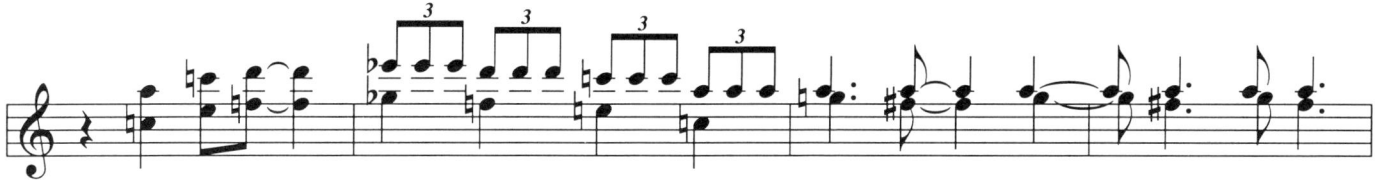

Fifth chorus: The fifth chorus begins with an arpeggio of an A7 chord that starts on its third. In its second octave, this arpeggio heads for the upper structure, i.e., the 9th (*B♮*), but as the chord changes from A7 to D7 in bar 2, this *B♮* is no longer 9 of A7; instead it is 13 of D7. The fourth bar continues this interplay between notes that can function as either chord tones or tensions for both D7 and A7 by rapidly arpeggiating each chord in succession.

Example 164

Bars 5 and 6 employ a motific riff whose common tones are only altered to accommodate the one note difference between the D7 chord (in bar 5) and the d♯O7 chord (in bar 6).

Example 165

Bar 7 uses another string bend against two sustained pitches to set up a secondary dominant chord (V of II) in bar 8, with a motif that continues into bar 9. Bar 10 uses the "blues note" ♭3 (i.e., *c♮*), voiced above a g♯O7 chord that is functioning as a dominant 7th (♭9) chord, to set up the blues lick voiced in 4^{th}s that brings the entire solo to its conclusion.

Example 166

Let's examine the improvised four bar phrases I traded with drummer Duduka da Fonseca.

The first four bar phrase uses two different Major 7th intervals superimposed upon an altered A7 chord as the primary motific device to create an antecedent and consequent riff-type phrase. The two Major 7th intervals occur between the Δ3rd and ♯9, and between the ♭7 and ♮13 of the A7 chord. This A7 chord is in effect used for the entire four bars. The alteration of the chord changes (i.e., omitting the D7 in the second bar) occurred because the bass player Hans Glawischnig reacted appropriately to what he heard me play. The final note I play in this "4" is the only note that is not part of this motif directly based upon the two Major 7th intervals. However, this note, e♭, is both a Major 7th above the ♮5th of the A7 chord, and also the note required to suggest the substitute dominant 7th chord for A7, which would also be sub V of the IV7 chord that would occur at the start of the drummer's "4," within the context of the blues form upon which we are playing.

Example 167

The third "4" (my second) begins with a repetitive triplet phrase built upon the upper structure of the b–7 chord (II–7) that occurs at this point in the solo changes of the blues form. The next bar morphs this phrase into a repetitive 16th note phrase that suggests the whole tone scale by its inclusion of a blues note that also functions as ♭3 in relation to the tonic chord of this blues (i.e., A7). This is superimposed over the V chord of the II V progression that makes up the first two bars of this "4." This phrase in turn sets up the blues lick built upon a combination of double stops and single notes that is played over the turnaround that comprises the last two bars of this "4." All of this sets Duduka up for his next "4" at the top of the second chorus of the blues form.

Example 168

My next "4" corresponds to the chord progression IV7 to ♯IVO7, to I, to V of II, and consequently employs devices that clearly outline these chords. The first bar uses the same type of string bend previously used in the third and fifth choruses of my solo. The next bar employs two different inversions of the passing ♯IVO7 chord. This is followed by a variation on the bent string lick used two bars earlier but altered to fit the I chord. The last bar pulls off from the g♮ above the 12th fret (i.e., ♭9) on the V of II chord to the open high E string (i.e., ♭7) as the F♯7♭9 chord is in effect arpeggiated, albeit in an unorthodox manner, taking advantage of a voicing possibility that really only makes sense when played fingerstyle.

Example 169

My next "4" begins back at the top of the blues form and is pretty self-explanatory, if you've worked through the first half of this book.

Example 170

Duduka's "4" on the second four bars of the blues form is followed by mine, which is based upon a blues lick that is superimposed on the II V that sets up the turnaround, the last bar of which is an E+7 chord arpeggio in triplets.

Example 171

My last "4" employs the same type of $\Delta 6^{th}$ chord voicings a whole step apart that were previously used in "Blues Etude 1" to suggest the two different Mixolydian tonalities that correspond to the changes at this part of the blues form (i.e., IV7 and I7). These chords are interspersed with voicings of the passing #IVO7 chord that leads to the I, which in turn sets up the V7 of II chord that leads to the sustained II–11 chord I used to create a harmonic background for Duduka to bring his final "4" to a close that could set up the band's return to the recap of the head of "Riff for Brother Jack."

Example 172

* * * * *

The next type of blues chord progression that I want to address is the minor blues. As the name implies, these blues occur in a minor tonality.

Being a blues, we will still find the I chord, the IV chord, and the V chord, in addition to the frequent use (by jazz musicians) of secondary dominant chords such as V of IV, and even substitute dominant 7th chords such as sub V of V. The basic blues progression in a minor blues is:

Example 173

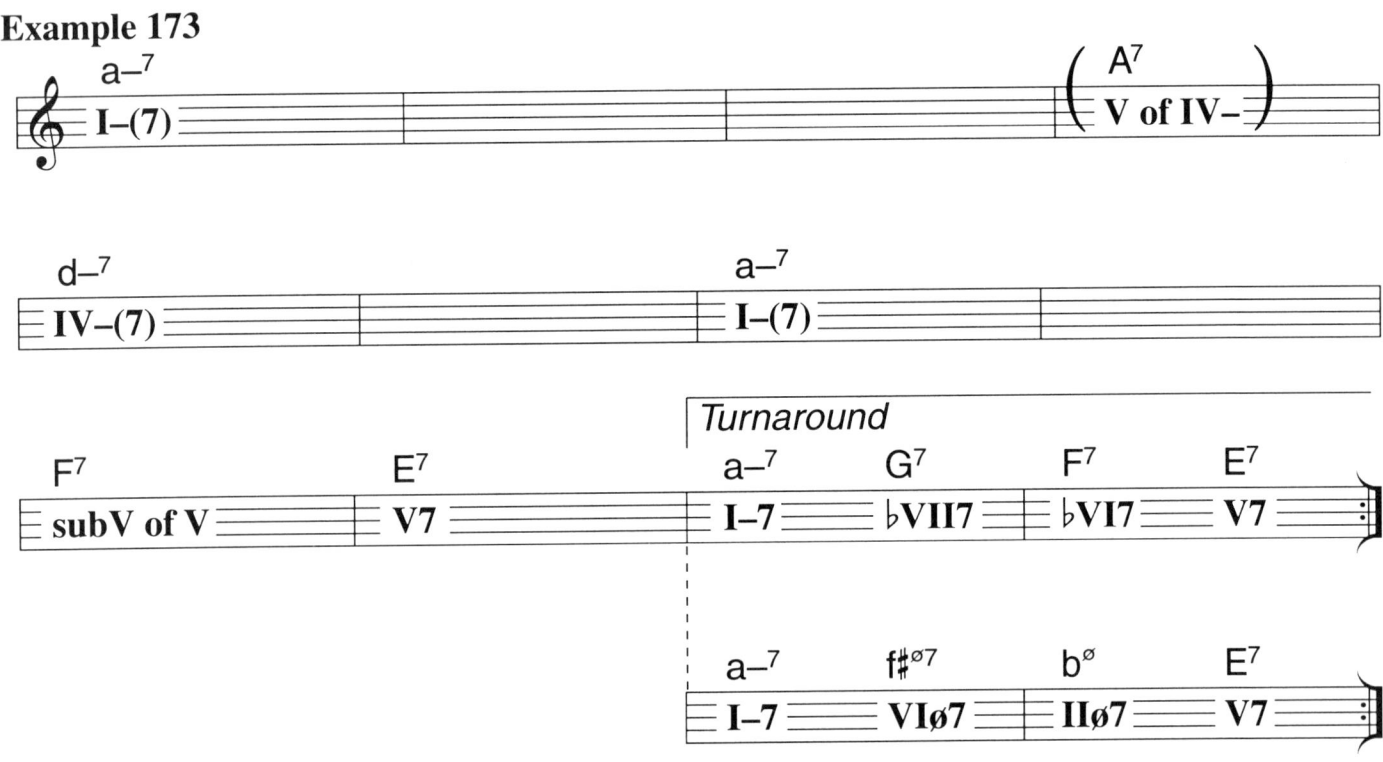

Some of you may recall how I alluded to the significance of the I IV V relationship(s) in both the Major and the relative modal minor tonalities in the modal chapter (bottom of p. 66 and top of p. 67). I briefly mentioned how the intervallic root relationship that manifests itself diatonically between the I, IV, and V chords is mirrored in the intervallic root relationships between the VI–, II–, and III– chords. Remember that the relative minor chord (i.e., VI–) can become the I (tonic) chord of a minor tonality, consequently, if VI– is I–, then II– becomes IV–, and III– becomes V–.

I believe it likely that the V– chord in such a relationship was gradually converted into a dominant 7th chord through a process of chromatic alteration similar to the one which converted the Aeolian mode into the Melodic minor scale (which we addressed in Chapter 2), resulting in the minor blues relationship of I–, IV–, and V7 that is the genre's foundation today. This I–, IV–, and V7 relationship does diatonically occur in the Harmonic minor tonalities, but most jazz musicians don't treat the I– chord of a minor blues as if it is Harmonic minor, and even fewer use Hm4 to define the IV– chord in a minor blues context, though Hm5 is often used for the V7 chords in minor blues.

The chord progression in example 173 is the basic minor blues progression that many jazz musicians use today. Like all blues, there are many variations of the minor blues progression, and this in part accounts for its widespread use. I've indicated one of the common variants in parentheses and have given two frequently used turnarounds. The first turnaround is built upon the descending bass line of the Aeolian mode which adheres to Schoenberg's guidelines for the descending form of the pivot tones in a minor tonality. The second turnaround is a minor version of the I VI II V progression we find in the turnarounds of many blues, such as "Riff for Brother Jack."

Let's check out some chord scale options that are commonly employed in a minor blues context:

Example 174

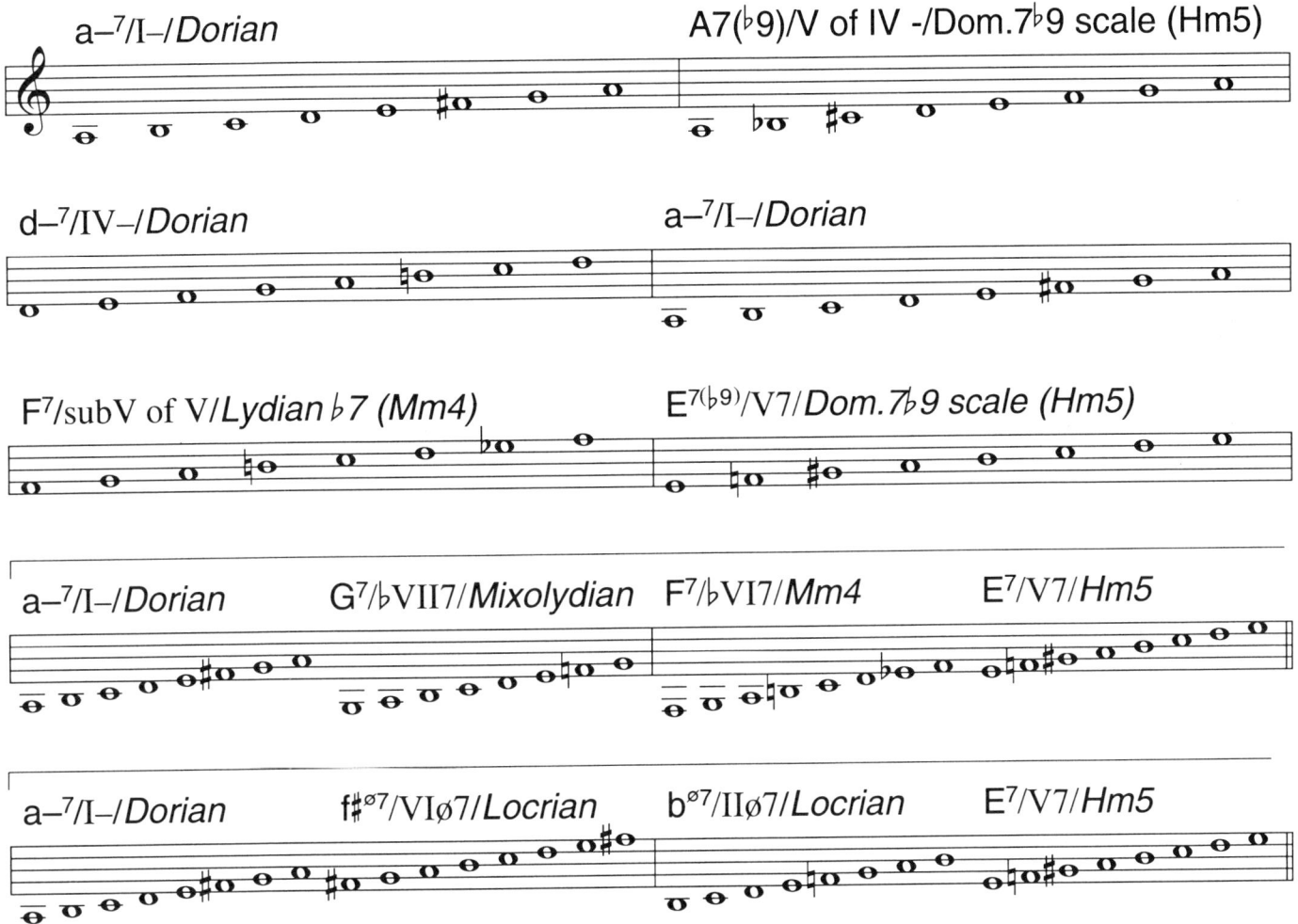

While these options don't cover all possibilities, they are representative of the scales that many jazz musicians use to approach blowing on minor blues. Of course, the use of arpeggios and chromatic approach tones will add other dimensions to one's improvisations, so don't limit yourself to scales alone.

The following tune, "Funkissimo," is a minor blues played in a half time groove that is one of the ancestors of swing. This rhythm is commonly called "second line," and it came to our music from West Africa via New Orleans. The "second line" rhythmic feel is often used by the musicians in the street parades of New Orleans, such as those occurring during Mardi Gras. It has influenced the evolution of R&B, funk, and jazz.

I strongly advocate the practice of transcribing solos by other jazz artists, because this has traditionally been a primary means of expanding one's understanding of the jazz vocabulary while simultaneously developing one's ear. Consequently, for the recording of "Funkissimo" (track 5), I've improvised two choruses for you to transcribe (the first line of each chorus is included to get you started), and we've comped two choruses for you to improvise on.

5

Funkissimo

To Solos

etc.

etc.

Now let's check out another minor blues, this time for solo guitar.

El Otro

D.C. al Coda

Fine

"El Otro" is a minor blues in § time in the key of *b* minor. It is the final movement of a suite I composed for solo guitar that was inspired by the short stories of Jorge Luis Borges. Like each of the work's seven movements, the title of the suite, "Borges and I," corresponds to the name of the short story that inspired it. The entire suite is composed rather than improvised, but "El Otro" is set up as if it could have been improvised. For example, the minor blues form occurs three times. The first time is very much like the "head," or exposition of the theme. (The theme is essentially in the bottom voice.) The second chorus is the development section, which follows both the minor blues form and its chord changes. This development section is not unlike an improvised chorus. It is, however, more contrapuntal than any of the pieces we've played so far. The contrapuntal nature of the second chorus is achieved by adding what resembles the improvised "voice" or "voices" above a paraphrasing of the thematic bass line. Classical guitar and fingerstyle technique are better suited to this type of playing than are steel string guitar and pick style playing. The third chorus is the recap of the head with a coda that extends the cadential ending to heighten the tension prior to conclusion.

When playing through "El Otro," pay close attention to the voicings and the application of a blues-based sensibility to the various contrapuntal devices used. You'll find that this piece embodies much of what we've covered thus far in this book.

* * * * *

There are so many variations of the harmonic structure(s) that can be accommodated by the basic blues form that it would be impossible to cover them all, especially in a book that is designed to address other subjects as well. However, there is one remaining type of blues progression that I would be remiss in omitting. These changes don't have a universally accepted name like minor blues changes or rhythm changes. I have heard them referred to as "New York blues changes," so I'll use that term for the sake of brevity. These "New York blues changes" continue the harmonic evolution that we can hear when we compare the changes of "Blues Etude I" to those of "Pinky's Blues." The harmonic evolution I'm referring to is the increased use of various harmonic devices to move between the basic I, IV and V regions found in all blues. "New York blues changes" primarily make the connections between these regions with a series of sequential II Vs and/or secondary II V progressions, such as those I mentioned in the modal chapter in reference to the Ø7 chord that corresponds to the Locrian mode (p. 62 last paragraph, and p. 63 example 47). These changes and/or variations of them are used in some famous jazz standards, such as Toots Thieleman's "Bluesette" and Charlie Parker's "Blues for Alice." When I worked with Jack McDuff, sometimes we used different blues changes for successive choruses of each player's solo, culminating with "New York blues changes" because they were the most harmonically complex.

It seems like a bit of a misnomer to refer to any such harmonically elaborate chord progression(s) as basic, but there are essential aspects of "New York blues changes" that most jazz musicians recognize as soon as they hear them, even if they don't all refer to them by a specific name.

The essential form and harmonic content of what I'm calling "New York Blues changes" are as follows:

Example 175 - New York blues changes:

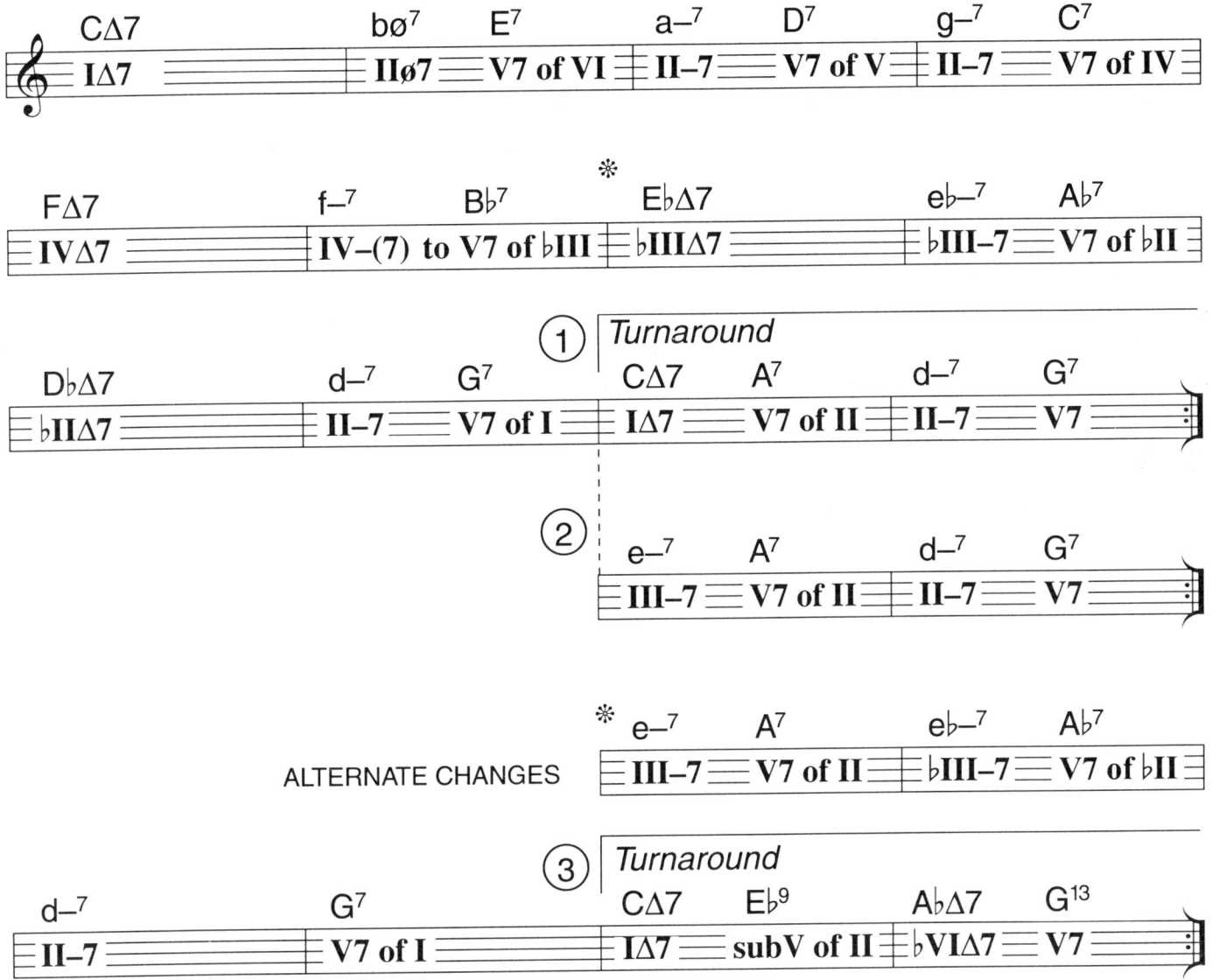

For those of you that have worked through the first half of this book, getting from I to IV by way of the sequential secondary II Vs (i.e., I to IIø7 V7 of VI, to II–7 V7 of V, to II–7 V7 of IV, to IV) is self-explanatory. But what follows may not be as clear to some of you. Going from IVΔ7 to IV–(7), to V7 of ♭III, is in effect a novel way of combining an allusion to the subdominant minor region with a continuation of the pattern of sequential secondary II Vs that got us to the IV chord, because f–(7) (the IV– chord) is also the relative II–7 of the B♭7 that is functioning as V7 of ♭IIIΔ.

In the first option: the changes then go to the relative IΔ chord of this secondary II V, i.e., ♭IIIΔ7 (E♭Δ7), which is also the relative Major chord of the tonic chord's parallel minor chord (i.e., E♭Δ is the relative Δ chord of c–, which is the tonic's [CΔ] parallel minor chord). In the alternate changes: the IV–(7) to V7 of ♭III more clearly relates to the subdominant minor region, because it is followed by the III–7 chord, which is a commonly used substitute for the I chord (as we'll see in the second turnaround).

In the first option the ♭III∆ goes to ♭III–, continuing the pattern of the previous two bars, i.e., converting a ∆7ᵗʰ chord to a –7ᵗʰ built upon the same root. This –7ᵗʰ chord then becomes part of another secondary II V, which in the first option goes to the secondary II V's relative I∆ chord. This chord also happens to be ♭II∆7 (another chord related to the subdominant minor region: see pp. 110–111, examples 108–109). The root of this ♭II∆7 chord is conveniently the same as the root of the substitute dominant 7ᵗʰ chord for the V chord that "normally" occurs at this point of a basic blues progression. This ♭II∆7 chord then moves to the II–7 V7 of the tune's tonic I chord, subsequently leading to one of the turnarounds. The second option, which moves from the III–7 (as part of another secondary II V) to V of II, is part of a series of chromatically descending II Vs that lead to the "primary" II V of the tonic I chord, which then goes on to one of the turnarounds.

I've provided three different turnarounds, and any of them will work with either of the options for the changes to a "New York blues"-type progression. This first turnaround is like the I to V of II, to II, to V (i.e., those built on a I, VI, II, V bass line) that we've already addressed. The second merely substitutes III–7 for I∆7, which, if you remember from our previous discussions of the upper structures of chords, you'll know is a possible substitution because of the many notes these two chords have in common. The third turnaround is yet another way to pass through the subdominant minor region, i.e., I to V of ♭VI (this V of ♭VI is also sub V of II). When we get to ♭VI∆, we've arrived at the relative Major of the subdominant minor chord (because, A♭ is I∆ if f– is VI–, and f– is the subdominant minor chord for the key of C Major).

The next tune we'll play and examine, "Moon over Astoria," is my take on "New York blues changes." The melody and my three improvised choruses are based on these changes.

Moon over Astoria

The Blues

D.C. al Coda

185

The following is a harmonic analysis of the melody of "Moon over Astoria." This melody is composed in a Post-Bop style, and, like many of the heads to jazz tunes from that era, it contains an array of the melodic-harmonic devices one would use to authentically improvise in this musical vernacular.

The method of analysis I've employed is essentially a means of defining each note's harmonic relationship to the chord upon which it occurs. So the first note ($D\sharp$) is the $\Delta 7^{th}$ of the first chord ($E\Delta 7$), followed by the $\Delta 3^{rd}$ of the $E\Delta 7$ chord ($g\sharp$), which is followed in turn by the 5th and the $\Delta 6^{th}$ (B and $C\sharp$). This $\Delta 6^{th}$ could also be interpreted as $\natural 13$. You'll notice that the last note of bar 1 (the $g\sharp$ approached by a grace note) has a tie attached to its harmonic indication below (i.e., $\frown 11$); this is because it is an anticipation. Sometimes these anticipations will be tied across a bar line or across two beats within a bar between chord changes (as occurs in bars 2 and 3), and at times they are followed by silence, as you'll see shortly.

Example 176

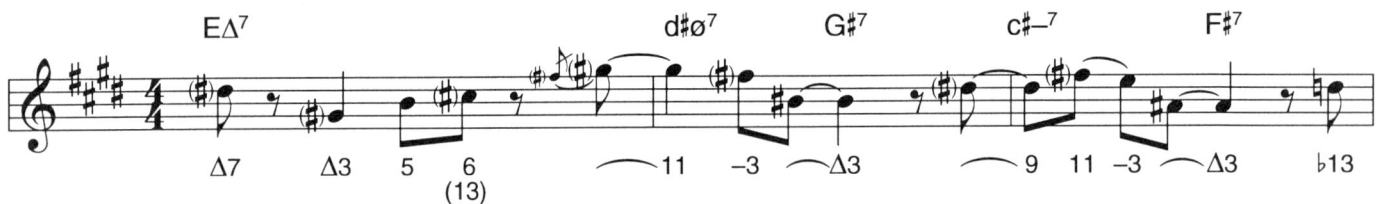

Bar 4 begins with a leap from the 9th down to the 3rd of the b–7 chord and ends with a resolution of the $\flat 9$ (of the E7 chord) to a note that would be the tonic of the E7 chord, but because the changes move to $A\Delta 7$ in the next bar, and the note that ends bar 4 ($e\natural$) is followed by silence (for $1\frac{1}{2}$ beats), this note is harmonically functioning in anticipation, as the 5th of the $A\Delta 7$ chord.

Example 177

Notice how the scalewise passages in bars 7 and 8 move between the 3rd and the root by passing through the 9th (which could also be analyzed as a passing 2nd) or, as occurs elsewhere, similarly move between adjacent notes (such as the first five notes of bar 8 or the last three notes of bar 5), applying scalewise motion to move between or target harmonically significant notes.

Example 178

Check out how the arpeggio that comprises bar 9 is preceded by a **chromatic approach tone** simultaneously functioning as the 4th of the C7 chord (in bar 8) and the leading tone to the root of the f♯–(7) chord (in bar 9; i.e., *e♯* is the same pitch as *f♮*). This *e♯* also chromatically passes from the Δ3rd of the C7 chord to the tonic of the f♯–7 chord, as it leads to the f♯–7(9) arpeggio that ascends into the upper structure, concluding with yet another anticipation that employs a note which is an available tension common to both chords (i.e., *g♯*, which is 9 of f♯–7 and 13 of B7). This in turn sets up the chromatic descending motif (*g♯, g♮, f♯*) that leads to the turnaround comprised of two similar scale-like descending motifs.

Example 179

I am leaving the harmonic analysis of the transcribed solo to you, the student. If you get in over your head and don't have access to a qualified teacher, just play through the solo for the time being, and listen to it periodically. Then, after you've gone through the rest of the book, come back to the analysis or any part of it that is giving you problems, because we will cover much of the same material from different angles throughout the book, and individual students may find that some explanations will be more illuminating than others.

Chapter 12: Rhythm Changes

The term "rhythm changes" refers to an entire category of tunes that are either derived from or based upon the chord changes to George and Ira Gershwin's composition "I Got Rhythm." I see this genre as a sub-species of the standard, because "I Got Rhythm" is a standard. Since most jazz musicians blow on the chord changes of the tunes they play, we are always looking for tunes whose changes are as comfortably navigable a harmonic platform as the blues are, meaning that we need to hear and feel such changes so clearly in our "mind's ear" that we can concentrate on improvising and interacting with our fellow musicians while playing. As the jam sessions that musicians frequented evolved from the swing of the big band era to the quartets, quintets, and septets of the bebop era, musicians began to want to demonstrate their prowess by increasing the difficulty of the changes they improvised on, in what were sometimes called "cutting contests." This required that those in the know shared a common harmonic vocabulary to call upon in order to ostracize any interloper whose skills were not up to par. So oftentimes those changes in which the knowledgeable musicians were well versed would be used. This is how rhythm changes and variations based upon them became almost as common and versatile a vehicle for improvisation as the blues.

Rhythm changes and tunes based upon them occur in a thirty-two bar song form comprised of four eight-bar harmonic phrases. These eight bar sections are of two varieties: A sections and B sections. This form is generally presented as AABA. This AABA form may have the last A augmented with an extension or tag as occurs in the original Gershwin composition. There are many variations on the A sections, and even some on the B sections. There are even variations of the form in minor tonalities.

The original chords for the A sections begin with changes based upon the bass line of the two bar turnaround of our blues from the previous chapter, i.e., I VI II V. This usually repeats to create the second half of the first four bars that make up half of each A section. There are then several ways to move away from the tonic tonality to set up either a cadence or a turnaround that completes each A section. The two most common involve progressions also built around bass lines. They are either: (1) I to V of IV/$\flat$7, to IV/3, to IV–/$\flat$3, to I/V, to V, to I, or (2) I to V of IV/3 to IV to $\sharp$IV O7, to I/V, to V, to I.[27] In the key of C, these would be: (1) C to C/B$\flat$, to F/A, to f–/A$\flat$, to C/G, to G7, to C, or (2) C to C/E, to F, to f$\sharp$O7, to C/G, to G7, to C.

There are many variations on these changes for the A sections, and the endings of each A section are designed to function differently. **A**[1] usually ends with a turnaround; **A**[2] ends with a cadence that can set up the **B** section; and **A**[3] usually ends with a cadence that is either final or can accommodate a tag ending or can send us back to the top of the song form. The **B** sections generally start on a secondary dominant chord whose root corresponds to the third degree of the tonic (Major) chord. This secondary dominant 7th chord functions as V of VI and in turn sets up a sequence of secondary dominant chords that move counterclockwise around the circle of 5ths leading to the V of I to get back to the **A**[3] section. It generally moves like this: V of VI, to V of II, to V of V, to V of I, which in C would be E7, to A7, to D7, to G7. Each chord lasts two bars, and this pattern not only facilitates the use of substitute dominant chords (such as those previously demonstrated in the substitute dominant chord chapter, p. 94, example 88)—it also facilitates the interpolation of II–7 or IIØ7 chords before each V or sub V(as demonstrated in Chapter 6, Two Five Progressions).

Before we check out compositions that demonstrate some of the variations, let's examine the basic rhythm changes upon which the variations that will follow are based.

---

[27] When I use "stacked" Roman numeral chord symbols in the harmonic analysis, they follow the same guidelines used for "polytonal" and "bitonal" chord symbols. However, these "stacked" representations occur in two forms. (1) A Roman numeral "stacked" above another Roman numeral means that both the chord and bass note above which it is voiced have significant harmonic functions in relation to the tonality in which they occur. (2) A Roman numeral "stacked" above an Arabic numeral means that the bass note's function is primarily in relation to the chord voiced above it. The latter form usually occurs as part of a harmonized bass line.

Example 180

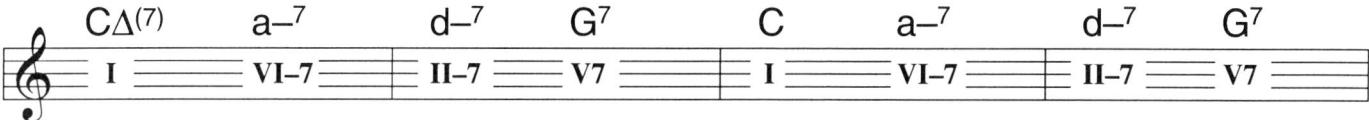

Example 180 contains the chord changes for the first half (i.e., four bars) of the **A** sections (they work for **A¹**, **A²**, and **A³**). As you can see and hear for yourself, this two bar I VI II V progression repeats to create the four bar phrase.

Example 181

Example 181 contains one of the two most common progressions used for the second four bar phrase (i.e., second half) of each **A** section. Notice the simple I to V turnaround of the first ending and how it differs from the second ending, and how similar it is to the last two bars of **A³**.

Example 182

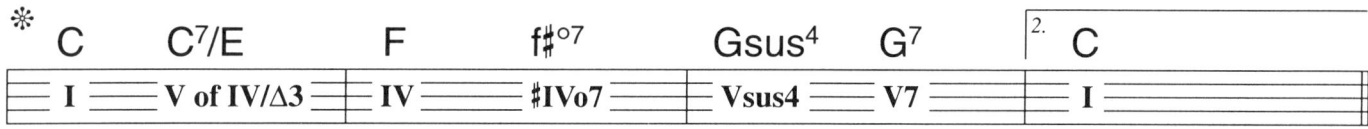

Alternate 2nd 4 bars of A *section*

Example 182 contains the other most common set of changes used for the second half of each **A** section. Compare the last two bars, which include the second ending, to those concluding **A¹** and **A³**.

Example 183

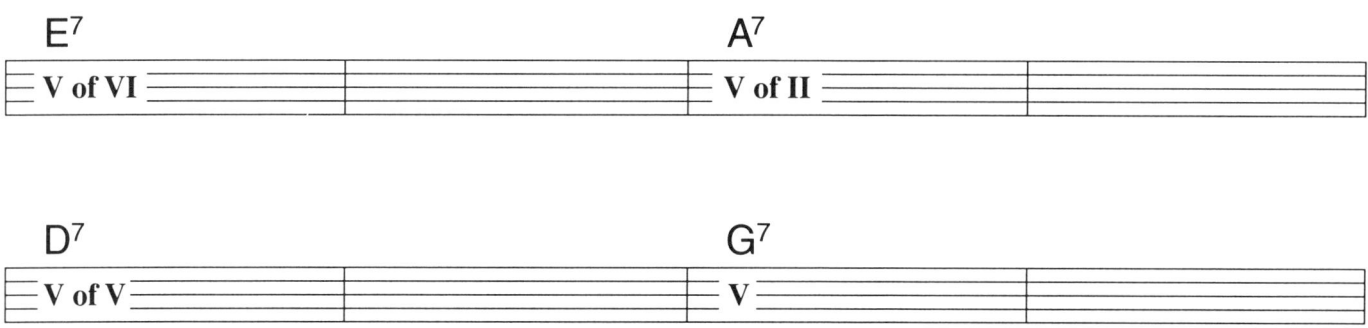

Example 183 contains the chord changes to the bridge (i.e., **B** section) of the AABA song form of rhythm changes.

Example 184

CΔ	a–7	d–7	G7		**2**
I	VI–7	II–7	V7		𝄎

C	C7/B♭	F/A	f–/A♭	C/G	G7	CΔ	(G+7)
I	V of IV/♭7	IV/Δ3	IV–/–3	I/V	V	I	V7

Example 184 contains the chord changes that comprise the eight bars of **A³**. In fact, isolated, these eight bars could be any of the **A** sections, with the exception of **A²**, because the V chord (i.e., last chord of last bar) doesn't set up the first chord of the bridge (i.e., **B**) very effectively, while it works well to turn the music back to the I chord at either the top (as is the case at the end of **A³**) or for the repeat at the end of **A¹**.

The entire set of basic rhythm changes is as follows, but remember that the alternate changes from example 182 can substitute for the changes in the second half of each **A** section, as long as we use the ending appropriate for each section's function within the form.

Example 185 – Basic Rhythm Changes

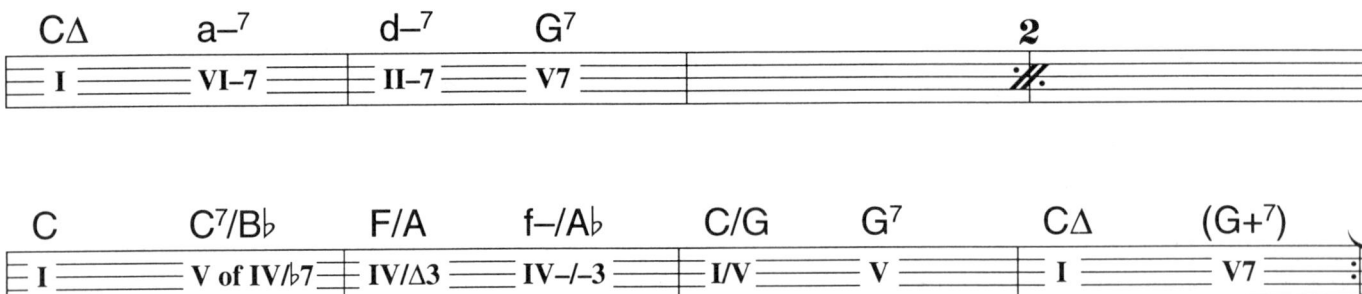

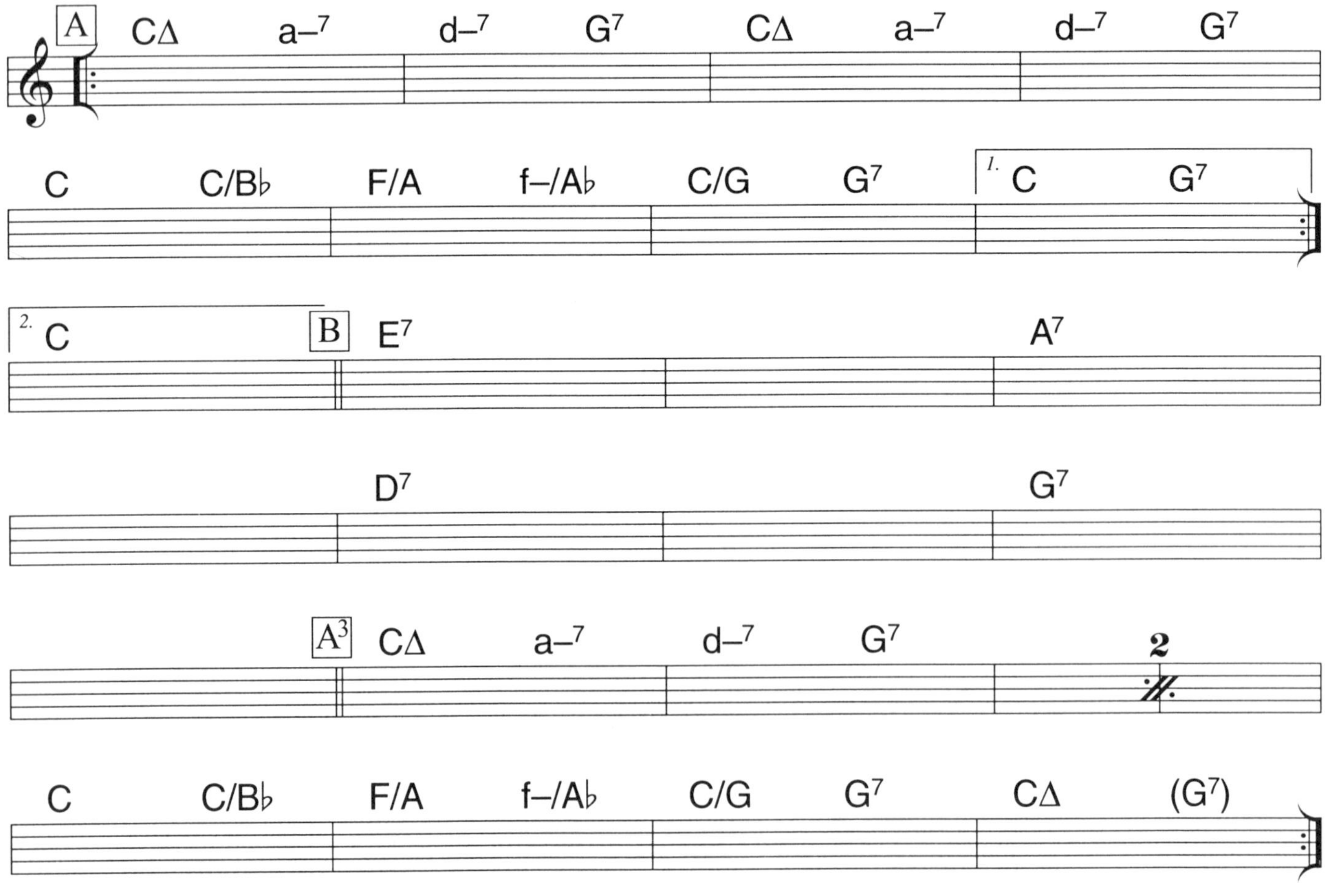

Before we turn our attention to an actual composition based on rhythm changes, I'd like to explain two aspects of my method of presentation for some of the tunes found in the second half of this book which might be confusing to some of you, namely those tunes without chord changes for the solo sections (transcribed or otherwise), and those tunes with solos that I've left for you to transcribe, in part or in whole.

Tunes like "Riff for Brother Jack" (from the blues chapter) and our next tune, "Prosodic Permutations" (rhythm changes), exemplify the basic harmonic platform for each of the genres that they represent to such a degree that, when you encounter such tunes in lead sheet form, you often find no solo changes indicated. Instead, you only find a designation such as "solos on blues," followed by the appropriate key, say "in A," as would be the case for "Riff for Brother Jack," or solos on rhythm changes (in the appropriate key, such as "in A♭"). Such a designation would follow the head, which in some cases may not have the changes either, it being taken for granted that the player would know them. So I've presented some of the tunes in a manner that parallels this approach. If this gives you problems initially, merely write the changes (which I have included with the melodies of each tune) above the bars allocated for the solos. For more elaborate variations on these forms I have included the solo changes.

Regarding transcriptions, even though this book is not an ear training manual, I feel obligated to reiterate the importance of developing the prime faculty by which we all perceive music. And, as previously noted, transcribing solos, whether on paper or only on your instrument, has historically been the preferred method for learning to play this music we call jazz. Even giants like Charlie Parker (who copied Lester Young solos from Count Basie recordings) and Wes Montgomery (who copied Charlie Christian solos from Benny Goodman recordings) learned this way.

So I've given you the opportunity to transcribe some of my solos. And despite the fact that (due to space constrictions) I've been unable to give you much guidance as to how to proceed in doing so, I encourage you to make transcribing solos part of your regular studies (and not just my solos, but especially those of other players whose music moves you). It may be difficult at first, but persevere, because it is well worth the effort. And if you need additional guidance, there are plenty of good books and teachers that can help you with this important aspect of your musical development.

Now to the next tune. "Prosodic Permutations" is written in the style of the rhythm changes tunes that came out of Kansas City during the late 1930s. Count Basie's famous "Jumpin' at the Woodside" is a classic example of this style. The bass line is related to boogie-woogie and stride piano styles; the chord changes are then superimposed over this bass line. While a riff style melody would traditionally be added to complete this type of composition, the melody I have composed is a little more involved than a pure riff-style melody, though my line can be construed as a variation on the riff style. "Prosodic Permutations" is presented in two versions. For the first one (track 8), I play the melody and improvise two choruses (the second of which I've transcribed, leaving the first for you to transcribe). In the second (track 9), you'll hear only the rhythm section, so you can play the melody and practice improvising over the two choruses.

Prosodic Permutations

© Ken Hatfield 2001

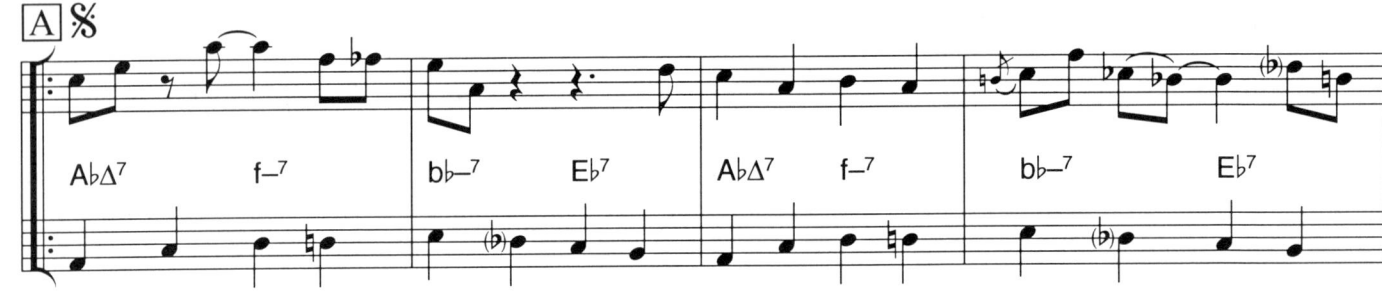

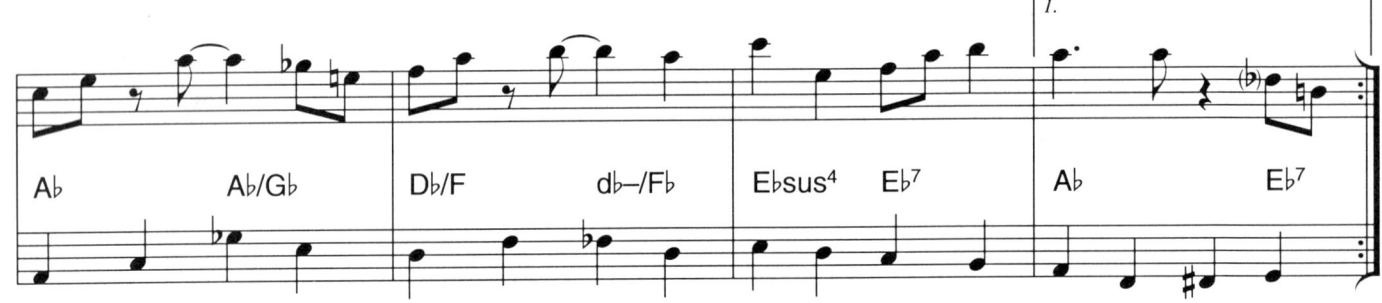

Solos on Song Form

Fine

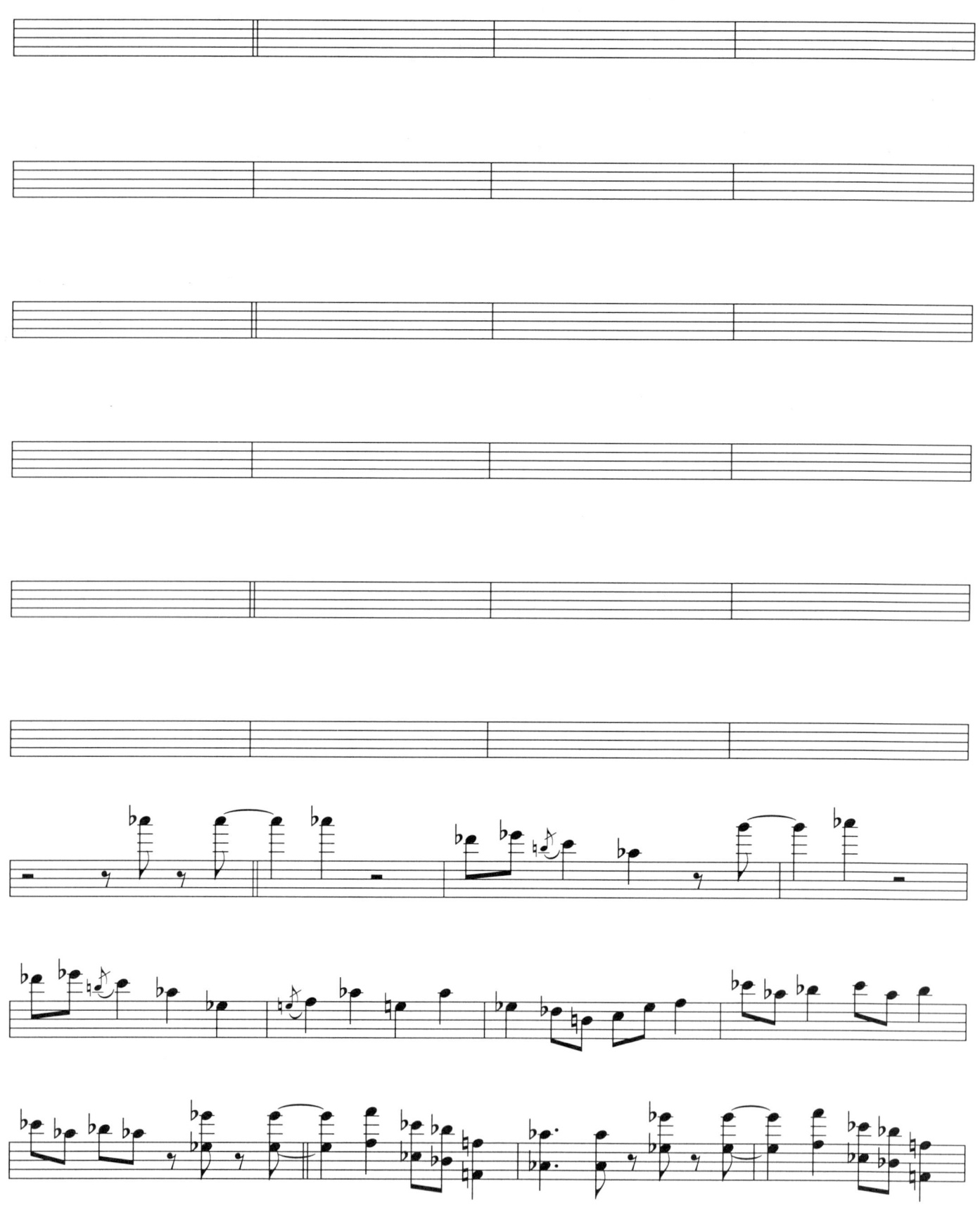

D.S. al Coda

Those of you who are unfamiliar with playing and reading from lead sheets may wonder why the codas from "Prosodic Permutations," "Riff for Brother Jack," and "Moon over Astoria" are not placed at the end of these compositions (as they are for "El Otro" and "Funkissimo"). The answer is that I've presented these tunes in the form that the musicians used for the recordings so that you can familiarize yourself with what you are likely to encounter on gigs. This form, commonly called a lead sheet, would not contain the transcriptions of the improvised solo(s), therefore, the coda is presented after the "head" (i.e., after the theme or melody). Since the blowing is based on the form and chord changes of each tune, for the musicians that recorded these tunes there was no need to include the bars that are allotted for the (transcribed) solos. The codas function as tag endings and consequently are placed at the end of what are in effect lead sheets. I did place the coda at the end of "El Otro" and "Funkissimo" because these tunes can be viewed in their entirety on two consecutive pages without a page turn.

* * * * *

Those of you who have worked through the first half of this book will have noticed a recurring theme regarding the various approaches that I've presented and their application to the two primary tonalities that our music inherited from Europe: Major and minor. Just as we encountered blues in both Major and minor tonalities, we will also find rhythm changes tunes in both Major and minor tonalities.

The next tune, "Necessary Appurtenances," is an example of a rhythm changes tune in minor. The first four bars of the **A** sections are pretty easy to see as I VI II V in minor, because the roots of these chords are I VI II V. However, the I and VI come from a different minor tonality than the II and V come from. This is because no one minor tonality can accommodate both VIØ7 and IIØ7 (i.e., aØ7 and dØ7). As we will see, it is not unusual to encounter commonly recognized root motion derived from one type of tonality reharmonized to create chord progressions in another type of tonality. In fact we've already encountered this phenomenon in the turnaround of "Pinky's Blues," where the chord corresponding to the VI in the I, VI, II, V root motion was converted to a V7 of II chord.

Example 186

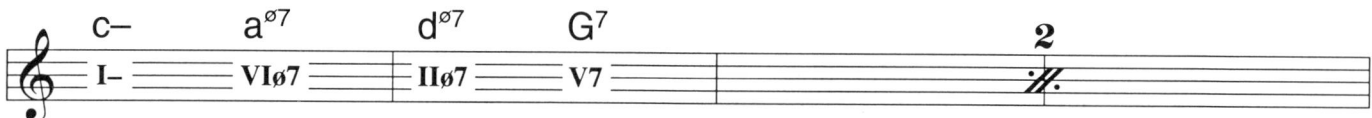

The second half of each **A** section is comprised of two two-bar phrases. (1) The root motion of the first mirrors the descending root motion corresponding to one of the two options for the same part of the rhythm changes in Major, but here the chords come from a minor tonality, and their root motion follows Schoenberg's guidelines for the descending pivot tones (i.e., the root motion comes from a descending Aeolian mode). (2) Like each of the two bar phrases that conclude the **A** sections of "Prosodic Permutations," the turnarounds for either **A¹** or **A²** of "Necessary Appurtenances" are designed to fulfill similar specific harmonic functions (albeit within a minor tonality): the first turnaround sends us back for **A²**, while the second leads us to the bridge (**B**).

Example 187

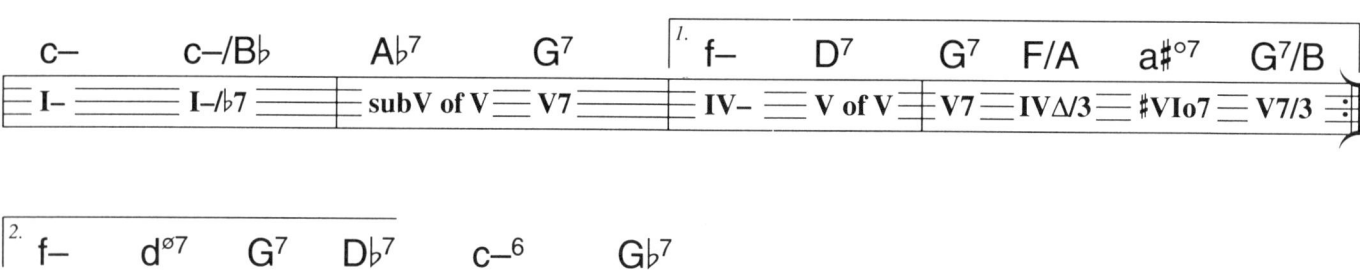

It is in the bridge sections of rhythm changes in minor tonalities that we first encounter a departure from an obvious correlation between the harmonic root motion and that of Gershwin's "I Got Rhythm," because here the bridge doesn't begin on a chord whose root corresponds to the third of the tonic chord. Such deviations are not unprecedented though, as those who recall the alteration of the basic I IV V we encountered in our minor blues progressions know (i.e., ♭VI functioning as sub V of V is interpolated before the V chord; see p. 176, example 173).

The **B** sections of minor rhythm changes often begin with a secondary II V of the chord whose root corresponds to the third of the tonic chord, a situation that does correlate to that found in Gershwin's "I Got Rhythm," because here we find a secondary II V of the relative Major, mirroring the secondary dominant of the relative minor which begins the bridges of Major rhythm changes.

There are many variations on the bridges for rhythm changes in minor tonalities. The one I've used bears a relationship to the blues because it begins on IV–, which is part of a secondary II V of IIIΔ, as part of a progression that leads to I–. This I– chord is then converted to V of IV–, leading to a repeat of the first two bars of **B** as we proceed to a secondary II V of V, which leads to the V of the tonic minor chord that gets us back to the **A** section. In the process, this bridge alludes to the blues by touching the IV–, the I–, and the V7 chords while it reinforces the minor nature of the song's tonality even as it passes through chords that it shares with its relative Major tonality.

Example 188

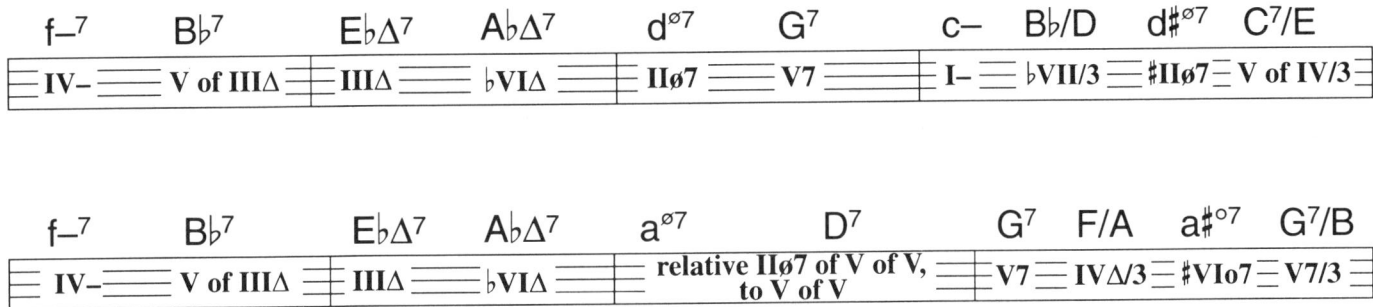

The last **A** (**A³**) mirrors **A¹** and **A²**, except for the two bar turnaround at the end. The coda is essentially a tag ending that extends the melody of the turnaround as it develops into a final cadence.

Example 189

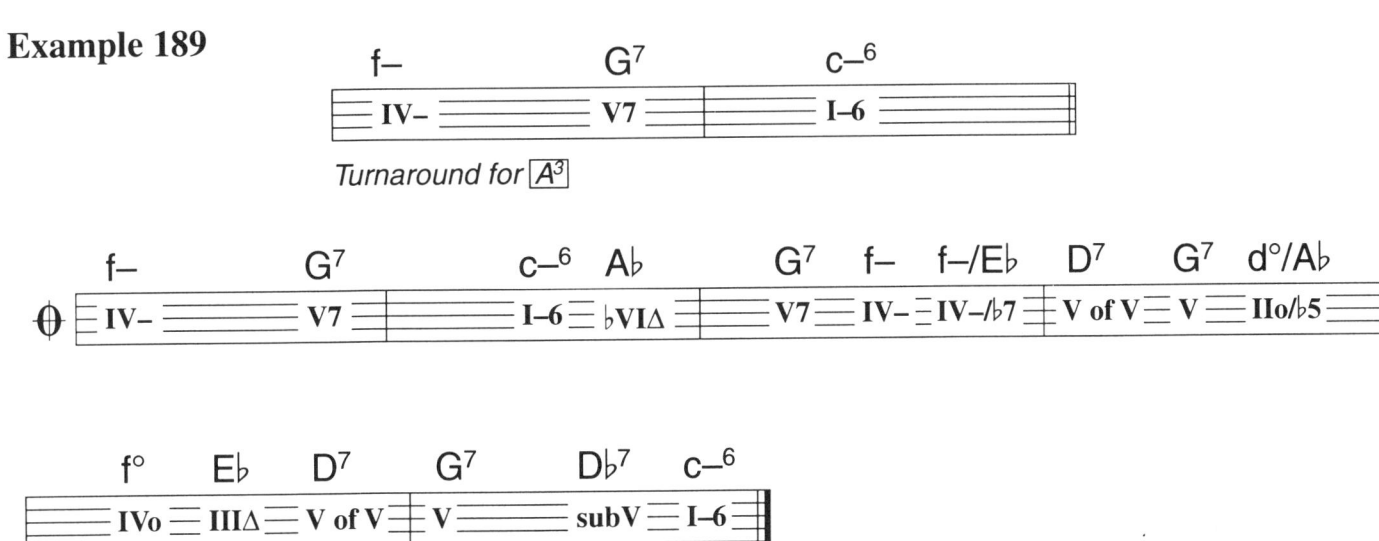

Necessary Appurtenances

© Ken Hatfield 2001

D.C. al Coda after solos on song form

Fine

(solo pickups)

We've talked a bit about chordal substitutions in this book. I'd like to draw your attention to two examples. The first one occurs on the first chord of the seventh bar of letter **A²** of the bass solo, where I played part of an A♭13 chord instead of the f– that would normally accompany this part of the tune. And in the last bar of my first four, I played a gØ7 instead of the d#O7 on the third beat, creating a II V of the tonic minor of the key to set up Jeff's drum four. These two examples illustrate how hanging a voicing below an improvised melody can facilitate the use of harmonic substitutions. This process is all the easier to implement when you're the only chordal instrument, as I was for this recording of "Necessary Appurtenances."

As long as one adheres to the "general road map" of the form, it is possible to divide the **AABA** form of rhythm changes into different sections and assign each section a different function. For the arrangement of "Necessary Appurtenances" I've applied just such an approach. Consequently, after my guitar solo (which is one chorus), the **AABA** form is divided into two sixteen-bar "halves." The first sixteen bars (i.e., **A¹** and **A²**) are used for the bass solo, while the second half (i.e., **B** and **A³**) is used by the drums and guitar to trade fours, much as the drums and guitar did over the entire blues form of "Riff for Brother Jack" (pp. 170, 174–175, examples 167–172). I've included the changes above each bar to illustrate how we follow the form even during Jeff's "drum" fours.

I've also transcribed my comping behind Hans's bass solo to help demonstrate how the comping follows the form and the changes as it responds to the soloist's ideas in an inobtrusive manner. Notice how what is omitted in order to leave room for the soloist to formulate and execute his ideas is as important as what is included. Some liken comping to adding the punctuation to the sentences that the soloist improvises. Remember, listening is the key to coming up with an appropriate comping response to a soloist's ideas, and never forget to follow the soloist when comping, because the soloist is leading.

* * * * *

When analyzing the various types of blues from the previous chapter, it becomes pretty clear that the evolution of the harmonic resources we encountered can be viewed as a progression from the simple to the complex. As noted on p. 182, this escalating harmonic complexity is achieved by implementing increasingly sophisticated means of traversing the space between the key harmonic signposts that define a specific genre. This process not only applies to the blues, but to other categories of harmonic progressions as well, such as rhythm changes. This evolutionary process is advanced at times through the use of devices such as substitutions and/or passing chords, as we will see in the next tune, "Yo Es."

Within the context of this evolutionary harmonic overview, if we consider "Necessary Appurtenances" (i.e., rhythm changes in minor) as the parallel to "Funkissimo" or "El Otro" (i.e., minor blues), then "Yo Es" can be considered the rhythm changes parallel to "Moon over Astoria" (which is based on what I call "New York blues changes").

Let's check out the chord changes for a more harmonically complex variation on rhythm changes and see how they evolved. You'll recall how the root motion of I VI II V is the basis for the first four bars of each **A** section for rhythm changes, and how this same root motion was employed in the turnarounds of blues such as "Moon over Astoria" and "Riff for Brother Jack." In the case of our turnarounds, the chord whose root corresponds to VI is often converted from minor to Major, and in the process becomes a secondary dominant chord that functions as V7 of II.

Example 190

I'd like to remind you of our previous discussion (pp. 123–125 in the chapter on vagrant chords) regarding diminished 7th chords and how they often function as or substitute for dominant 7thb9 chords, because this is the key to understanding the first two bars of the changes to "Yo Es." When viewed as a variation of the I to V7 of II option for the first bar of rhythm changes in the key of G Major, we can see that the g♯O7 in bar 1 of "Yo Es" is functioning as a substitute for an E7b9 chord. This interpretation is further bolstered by the fact that the g♯O7 chord resolves to the II–7 chord that the V7 of II would be expected to resolve to in the key of G Major, i.e., a–.

Example 191

The second bar employs a harmonic device similar to that used to get from IΔ to II–, in order to move from the II–7 chord in bar 2 to the III–7 chord that begins bar 3. This is accomplished via another diminished 7th chord that, like the previous example, is functioning as a secondary dominant chord; in this case we have ♯IIO7 functioning as V7 of III–.

Example 192

Bars 3 and 4 of the **A** sections contain the same variations of I VI II V that we encountered for the first optional turnaround of the New York blues changes that "Moon over Astoria" is based upon (p. 183, blues chapter, turnaround 2), because III– can and often does substitute for IΔ.

Example 193

The next two bars of each **A** section contain chords whose harmonic functions should be obvious to you by now: i.e., a secondary II–V7 of IVΔ, to IVΔ7, to sub V7 of VI. This last chord, sub V7 of VI, is also a substitution for the subdominant minor chord, because it contains the note necessary to suggest the subdominant minor region.[28] In the key of GΔ, this note is *eb*, i.e., the –3rd of the c– chord. This note is also the b7th of the F7 chord occurring for the last two beats of bar 6. I've analyzed this chord as sub V of VI, because it is both functioning in that capacity and suggesting the subdominant minor region. Both interpretations are supported by the turnarounds that follow, because III– is a substitute for IΔ, which reinforces the subdominant minor function of the F7 chord. And III– is also the relative II– of the V of II chord whose root corresponds to VI, which supports the notion that F7 is functioning as sub V of E7, with E7's relative II– (b–7) interpolated between the two chords.

Example 194

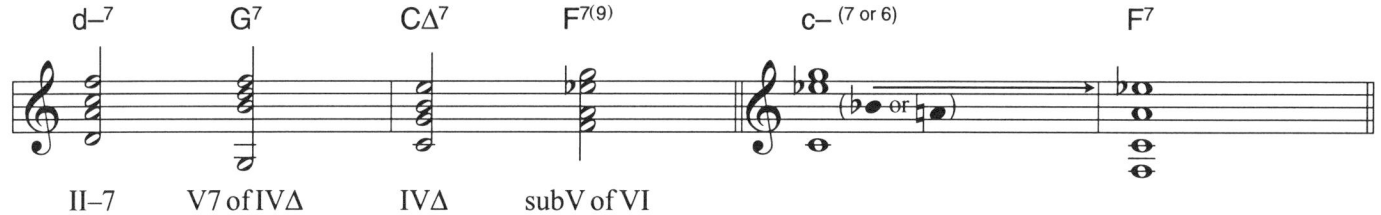

The turnarounds that conclude each **A** section should be self explanatory by now, because they are all variants of the basic I VI II V, with III– substituting for I, and VI converting to V7 of II. Both the turnarounds for **A²** and **A³** resolve to the I chord.

---

[28] For more on chords from the subdominant minor region, see Chapter 7.

Example 195

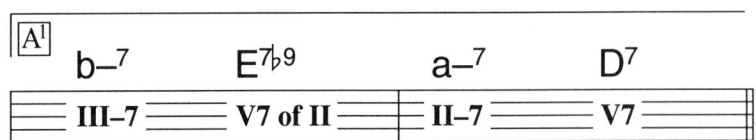

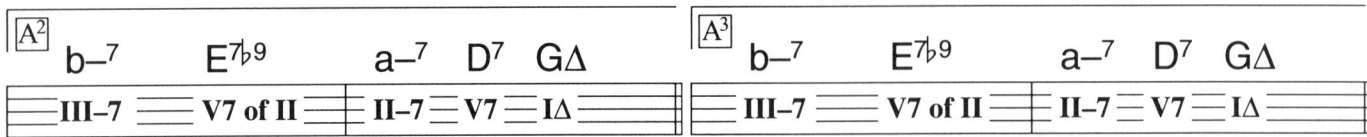

The bridge (**B**) sections of "Yo Es" follow the basic model of Gershwin's "I Got Rhythm," with three additional chords that are interpolated between the standard changes. They are: the sub V of the V of VI chord that occurs solely to break up the two consecutive bars of B7 that begin our bridge; this is mirrored by the sub V of the V of V chord used to break up the two consecutive bars of A7 otherwise occupying bars 5 and 6 of the bridge; and the last two bars use the relative II–7 of the V7 that normally occupies bars 7 and 8 of the bridge to precede the V7 chord that gets us back to **A³** (this same harmonic device was also used in the penultimate bar in the **B** sections of "Prosodic Permutations").

Example 196

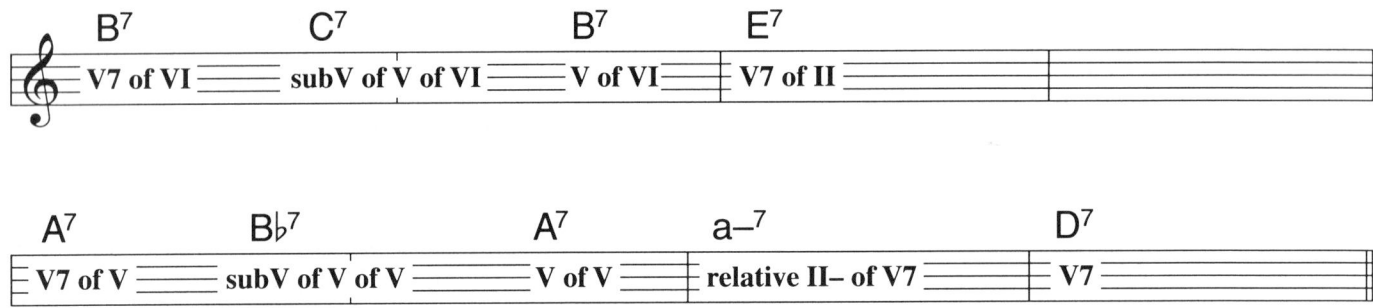

A³ is harmonically a mirror image of **A²**, and only differs from **A¹** in the last bar of the turnaround.

Example 197

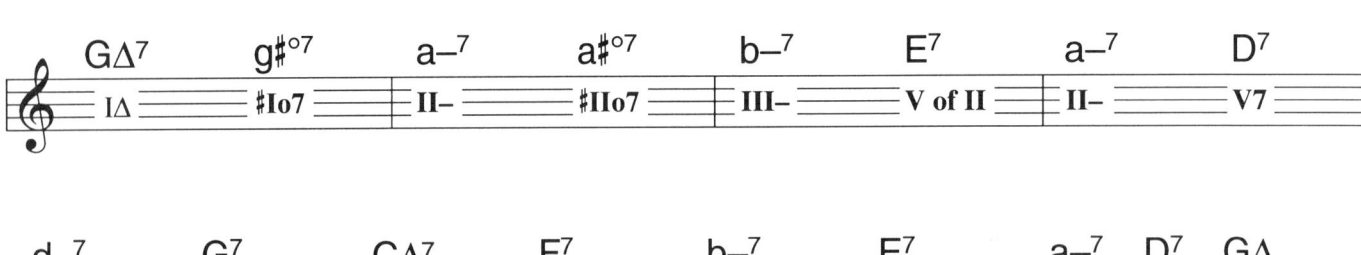

Yo Es

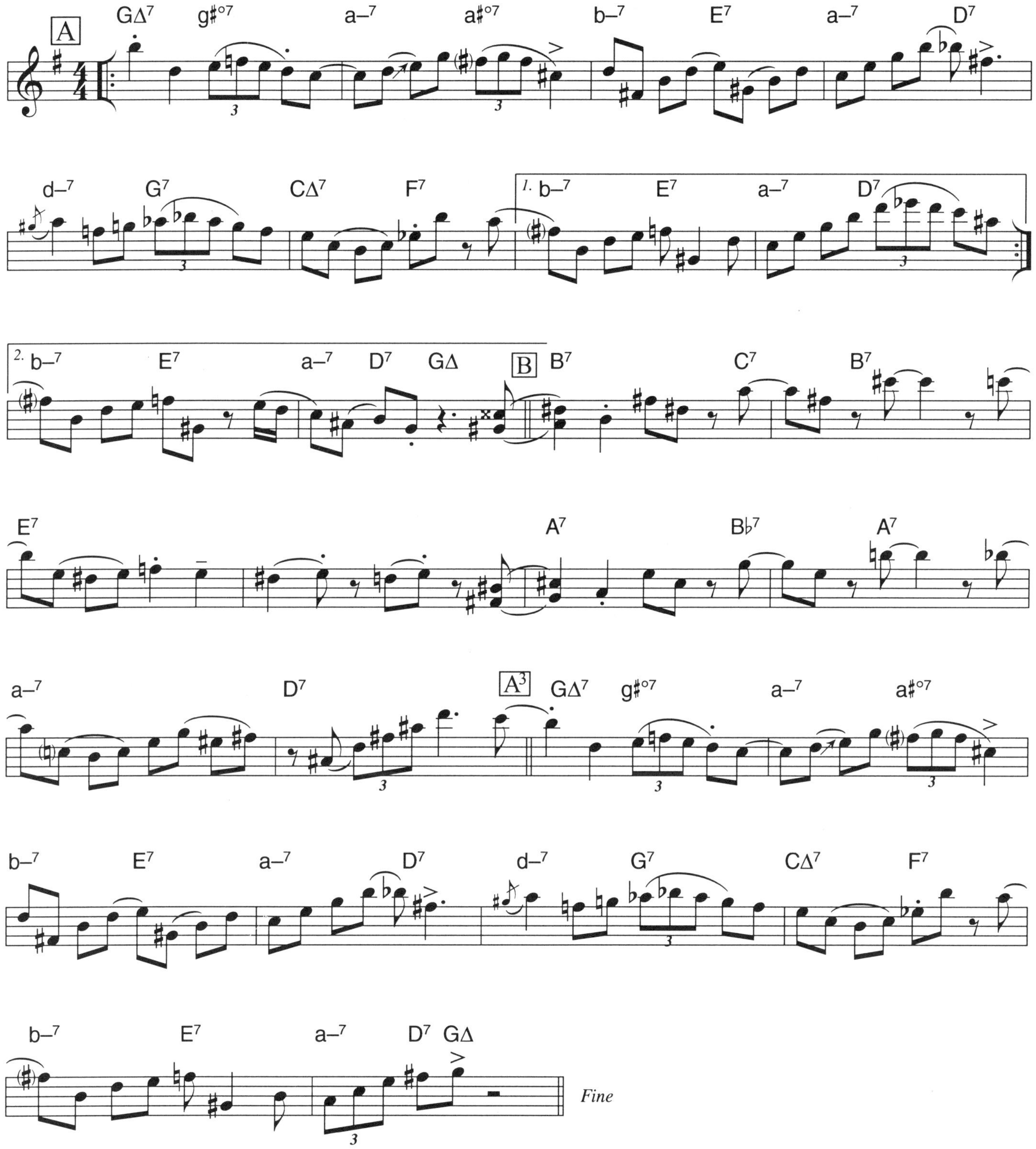

Piano Solo: 2 Choruses

Guitar Solo — First Chorus

Guitar Solo — Second Chorus

D.C. al Fine

Arco Bass Solo: 1 Chorus

The method of harmonic analysis used for my two improvised choruses of "Yo Es" is the same as the one I applied to the melody of "Moon over Astoria," i.e., each note is analyzed in relation to the chord over which it occurs. I've placed the entire analysis in context, under the actual solo transcription, with the chord changes placed above each bar to facilitate following the flow of ideas as they relate to the form and the chord changes.

While the improvised solos of "Yo Es" are based on the chord changes to the head of the tune, they also refer to the roots of the rhythm changes genre. Consequently, there are times when the comping differs from the changes for the head in response to what each soloist plays. For example, in the bridge (**B**) of my guitar solo the only sub V chord occurs during the second bar of the first **B**, and I play a line that suggests the relative II–7 of the V of VI that begins **B** of my second chorus, while we follow the original changes to Gershwin's tune elsewhere in the **B** sections. In response to what I play at the top of my second chorus, i.e., the tremolo in the top voice and the pull offs to the open G string as part of the blues lick in the bottom voice, both Hans and Salvador keep the harmony around GΔ for the first four bars of my second chorus, as they wait to hear where I go.

Much like the division of the form employed for the bass solo and drums-guitar fours of "Necessary Appurtenances," pianist Dom Salvador and I divide the form for the comping behind Hans Glawischnig's arco bass solo of "Yo Es." Salvador comps during the **A** sections, and I comp during the bridge (**B**).

One last point of interest before we move on to the "Standards" section. Many guitarists think they need fingerings and/or tablature in order to play a piece of music. While these tools can clearly be helpful, the need for them requires a level of knowledge of our instrument that non-guitarist composers and arrangers simply do not possess. No composer or arranger is ever expected to provide a trumpet player with fingerings or indications of lip positions and valve combinations, yet guitarists routinely resist weaning themselves from such remedial aids and, in doing so, ghettoize our beloved instrument. Because while practical knowledge of what is and what is not possible on an instrument is indeed a prerequisite for effectively writing for that instrument, it is unrealistic to require that composers acquire the thorough knowledge of the mechanics of playing individual instruments that is necessary to enable them to provide players with instructions for the physical execution of what they write. This situation is exacerbated by the expectation that composers learn a special means of musical representation that lies outside the purview of the common method(s) of musical notation familiar to all reading musicians. All of this contributes to composers' understandable reluctance to write for an instrument whose players either require or have the reputation of requiring such aids, and in the process this isolates guitarists from the larger community of our fellow musicians.

In theory I am not opposed to the remedial use of tablature and/or fingerings; I'm simply advocating that as guitarists grow and develop as musicians, they join the same world that other musicians inhabit. As a freelance musician in New York City, I often encounter horn players who are routinely expected to sight transpose parts from one key to another, as others in the same horn section spontaneously create harmony parts. And the entire group of horn players does all of this successfully, reading only from the same type of "concert" lead sheet that many so-called professional guitarists can't even sight read.

While other instrumentalists don't require fingerings or tablature at the professional level, they do often welcome phrasing markings such as those I've provided for the head and my solo for "Yo Es." When playing "Yo Es," try to play by first imagining the sound of each phrase. Since you have a recording, you may want to start by following the music as you listen to it. Then try to hear the phrases in your mind's ear as you look at the music without the recording. Then try to visualize each phrase in a place on the fingerboard that can accommodate that specific phrase, as you look at the music. Then try to read slowly through the music with your guitar, using the music notation and phrasing to guide you.

This process may be difficult at first, depending upon how dependent you are on tablature and fingerings, but if you include this kind of practicing in your routine, you'll find that you can move toward acquiring some of the same skills other instrumentalists possess, while improving your ability to phrase more musically. This is especially true if you combine these practices with solfège and transcription studies.

In the meantime, when you play through music that has no tablature or fingerings, such as what you'll encounter in fake books and lead sheets, remember that the phrasing and the fingerings are inextricably linked, meaning that a clear understanding of the phrasing of a line will reveal the fingerings, as there are often only a few workable possibilities. When considered in context, these few options can be further reduced to the single most practical one. Ironically, even though the phrasing will give you the fingerings, the reverse is not true, because the sound of the phrasing has to guide your playing, meaning that even the right fingerings can be phrased incorrectly. This may seem odd, but you are more likely to find both if you clearly hear the phrasing in your mind's ear and let this guide you toward finding a fingering that will facilitate the desired phrasing.

And remember to conceive the phrasing in relation to the overall shape of the song or solo. I've heard that Wes Montgomery compared playing the guitar to playing pool, because in order to excel at each, one must set up every move in relation to the preceding and following ones. While Wes couldn't read music, his phrasing was so extraordinary that he is one of the few guitarists whose playing influenced horn players and pianists, as well as guitarists.

Chapter 13: Standards

You will recall that at the beginning of the chapter on secondary dominant chords (chapter 4) I mentioned that many of the tunes of American popular music have become "standards." The vast majority of these tunes were written for Broadway musicals originally produced during a period spanning the 1920s through the 1960s. The legendary composers of many of these tunes, such as George Gershwin, Jerome Kern, Richard Rodgers, Harold Arlen, and Cole Porter, along with lyricists like Adolph Green, Betty Comden, Lorenz Hart, Ira Gershwin, and Sammy Cahn are recognized around the world. And even those who don't recognize their names recognize their musical creations.

It is difficult to define a standard in terms of harmonic structure and/or form, because there are no universal guidelines that delineate the genre like those that define the blues or rhythm changes. Ultimately, what makes a tune a standard is its acceptance by musicians as an effective vehicle for interpretation. This acceptance may take time and is often affected by changing perceptions, fashions, and cultural sensibilities. The tunes of the Brazilian composer Antonio Carlos Jobim are a good example of this. In the U.S., Jobim tunes like "Wave," "Corcovado" (i.e., "Quiet Nights"), and the ubiquitous "Girl from Ipanema" became standards overnight because both the audience and jazz musicians embraced them immediately, while masterpieces like "Retrato em Branco e Preto" (sometimes called "Zingaro") and "Fotografia" have only recently entered the repertoire of American jazz musicians and vocalists, despite the fact that these tunes were written in the early 1970s. And some Jobim tunes that are standards in his native Brazil, such as "A Felicidade" and "Chega de saudade," are so well known there that entire soccer stadiums full of people spontaneously erupt into singing the lyrics upon hearing the opening lines of these tunes, yet most Americans don't know these tunes at all.

My main point is that acceptance, particularly by the musicians who choose to interpret and perform the music, is what makes a tune a standard. The two prime factors influencing this acceptance are: (1) the purely musical quality of the song, i.e., the melody and the harmony, particularly regarding the song's fitness as a vehicle for instrumental performance; and (2) the popularity or recognition factor the song has historically had with audiences. This ongoing process of acceptance, which results in the incremental growth of the standard repertoire, is fueled more by the occasional discovery of overlooked gems from the past than by the addition of contemporary compositions that have yet to stand the test of time.

However, don't think that contemporary composers aren't still trying to write tunes that may become new standards, because in fact that is part of what many composers like myself are attempting to do. But the impetus to do so is necessarily different today, because the popular music of the last twenty-five to forty years differs radically from that of the "golden era" which produced most of our standards. Contemporary pop music has been dominated by singer-songwriters whose focus is naturally different from that of jazz musicians who perform songs as instrumentals. Musical structure and purely musical content are of secondary importance to most of these pop songwriters, who focus more on the lyrics, groove, and production qualities. Subsequently, the pop audience has learned to focus what little attention it has on these aspects of the music as well. I encourage anyone who doubts the veracity of what I'm saying to attempt instrumental renditions of some of the pop tunes from the last quarter century of American popular music. Take the words away, and it becomes blatantly obvious how poorly constructed most of these tunes are.

In all fairness to the singer-songwriters who created many of these songs, one shouldn't judge them by criteria they aren't concerned with. Their goals and skills differ from those of a composer like George Gershwin. That is why I believe that the impetus of any contemporary composer striving to create tunes that may become new standards is inherently different from that of the pop songsmiths of today. And while the musical goals of the contemporary composers who emphasize both melody and harmony may be much the same as the composers of yesteryear, there is no longer the kind of support system that once existed for the caliber of music created in Tin Pan Alley and the Brill Building, or during the heyday of the Broadway musical.

Consequently, jazz musicians who are looking for quality contemporary material to perform are left in a bit of a quandary. For unlike today, most of the well-constructed tunes that became standards from the "golden era" were already popular when jazz musicians began to play them. Since Louis Armstrong burst onto the scene, jazz musicians have chosen to improvise on popular songs so that the audience will recognize the tunes and therefore have a better understanding of what the musicians are doing. However, regardless of how well written a song may be, this strategy only works if the audience is familiar with the song being performed. Conversely, if the song is poorly written, with a weak melody and banal chord changes, there isn't much a jazz musician can do with it when attempting an instrumental interpretation, no matter how well known the song may be. These are the reasons why jazz musicians have performed and continue to perform so many standards and why they play so little contemporary pop music.

I know that I am generalizing, for the last forty years of American popular music has not been a complete wasteland. There have even been some tunes from that era that either have become standards or are well constructed enough that they deserve to be and someday may become standards. The Beatles, Stevie Wonder, Paul Simon, James Taylor, Jim Webb, Billy Joel, Walter Becker and Donald Fagen of Steely Dan, and Sting have all written some great tunes that were huge popular successes and can be credibly performed instrumentally. Henry Mancini, Burt Bacharach, Michel LeGrand, Stephen Sondheim, and Leonard Bernstein are master composers of the highest skill level that have each created tunes that are standards. Outside the U.S. Astor Piazzolla and Antonio Carlos Jobim have each composed some of the most original tunes of the twentieth century. But as numerous as these exceptions may appear to be, they are a small but extraordinary minority in comparison to the glut of "product" churned out by the corporate pop music machines that dominate the industry.

This is why studying the "golden era" of American popular music that produced most of the standards requires us to go back to music written before many of us were born. To those raised on more contemporary fare, these tunes can sound like "Muzak." But don't be fooled—the same tunes you may hear in the elevator have been vehicles for incredible improvisatory flights of fancy by the likes of Charlie Parker, Clifford Brown, Art Tatum, Thelonious Monk, and Wes Montgomery. If you want to be a jazz musician, you need to thoroughly check out this repertoire, because it is part of the lifeblood of our music. Remember that the mundane versions of these great tunes that are commonly presented aren't the best way to judge their caliber as compositions. So as you listen to the great jazz musicians, let them introduce you to these wonderful tunes.

There is a subspecies of the standard that some call the "jazz standard." These tunes are jazz tunes that have become standards via a process of assimilation similar to that which conferred the title of "standard" on many of Gershwin's tunes (i.e., acceptance into the common repertoire of professional musicians). Jazz composers such as Duke Ellington, Thelonious Monk, Horace Silver, Bobby Timmons, Dizzy Gillespie, John Coltrane, and Miles Davis have all contributed tunes to the jazz standard repertoire. And contemporary jazz composers such as Herbie Hancock, Joe Henderson, Wayne Shorter, Chick Corea, Joe Zawinul, and Keith Jarrett have created and continue to create tunes that either are or are destined to become jazz standards.

This brings us to the three tunes of mine contained in this chapter. I should really call these "standard wanna be" tunes, because they are still quite young and have yet to be embraced by enough musicians to be considered standards. However, they demonstrate various compositional devices discernable in many of the tunes that have become standards, such as the melodic inventiveness, thematic development, and harmonic sophistication traditionally associated with the Great American Songbook.

The form of my three tunes roughly mirrors the "chorus" sections of many of the songs from the Broadway musical genre that gave us so many of our standards. Originally many of these "show tunes" had a verse that was performed in a manner reminiscent of the recitative style inherited from early operatic performance practices, i.e., they were performed rubato, or tempo ad libitum. The verse was then followed by the chorus in tempo, which was often constructed in an **AABA** or **ABA** form. This chorus is the only part most jazz musicians play, employing its chord changes and form as the basis for their improvisations. This is also why jazz musicians often refer to each cycle through this form as a "chorus," because they are only blowing on the chorus. Now there are some very knowledgeable jazz musicians who do perform the verses as ad lib intros to these tunes. Musicians such as Howard Alden, Gene Bertoncini, Dick Hyman, Harold Mabern, and the late Tommy Flanagan have made an art out of this, but most jazz musicians don't even know the verses, and fewer play them.

My three tunes are in the thirty-two bar **AABA** form that we encountered for rhythm changes tunes in the previous chapter. "A Bit for Miss Fitt" (track 12) affords us the opportunity to check out some of the sophisticated harmonic devices one encounters in the standards of the Great American Songbook, as it lets us observe the two prime roles for the guitar in a jazz ensemble: accompanist and soloist. The guitar fulfills both of these roles in the arrangement of the head, as well as during the improvised choruses. This tune was originally recorded on my CD *Dyad* (track 8 of ACM-3482).

Let's look at a harmonic analysis of the chord changes from "A Bit from Miss Fitt." The changes (sans melody) are presented in example 198 with the harmonic analysis below each chord.

Example 198

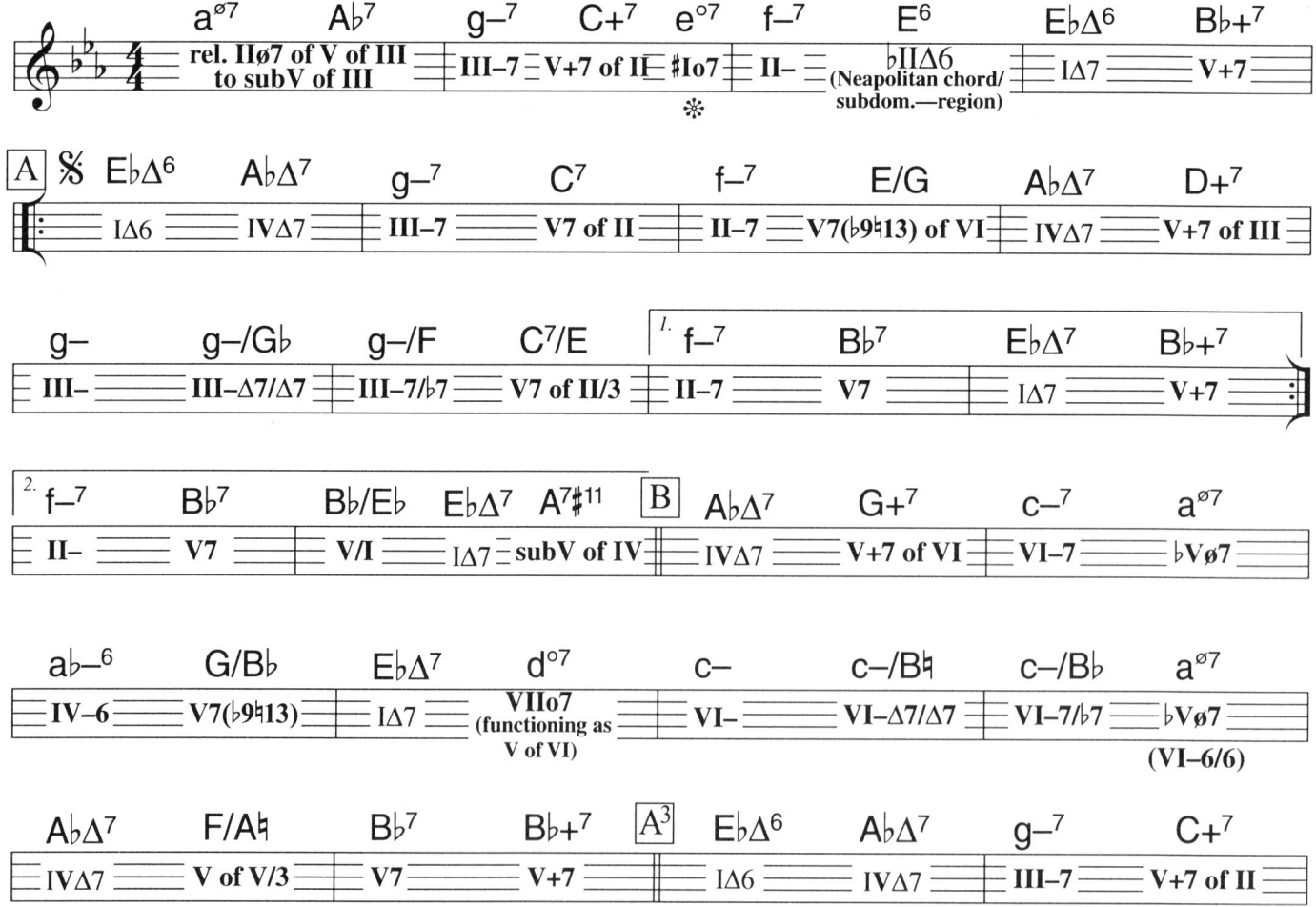

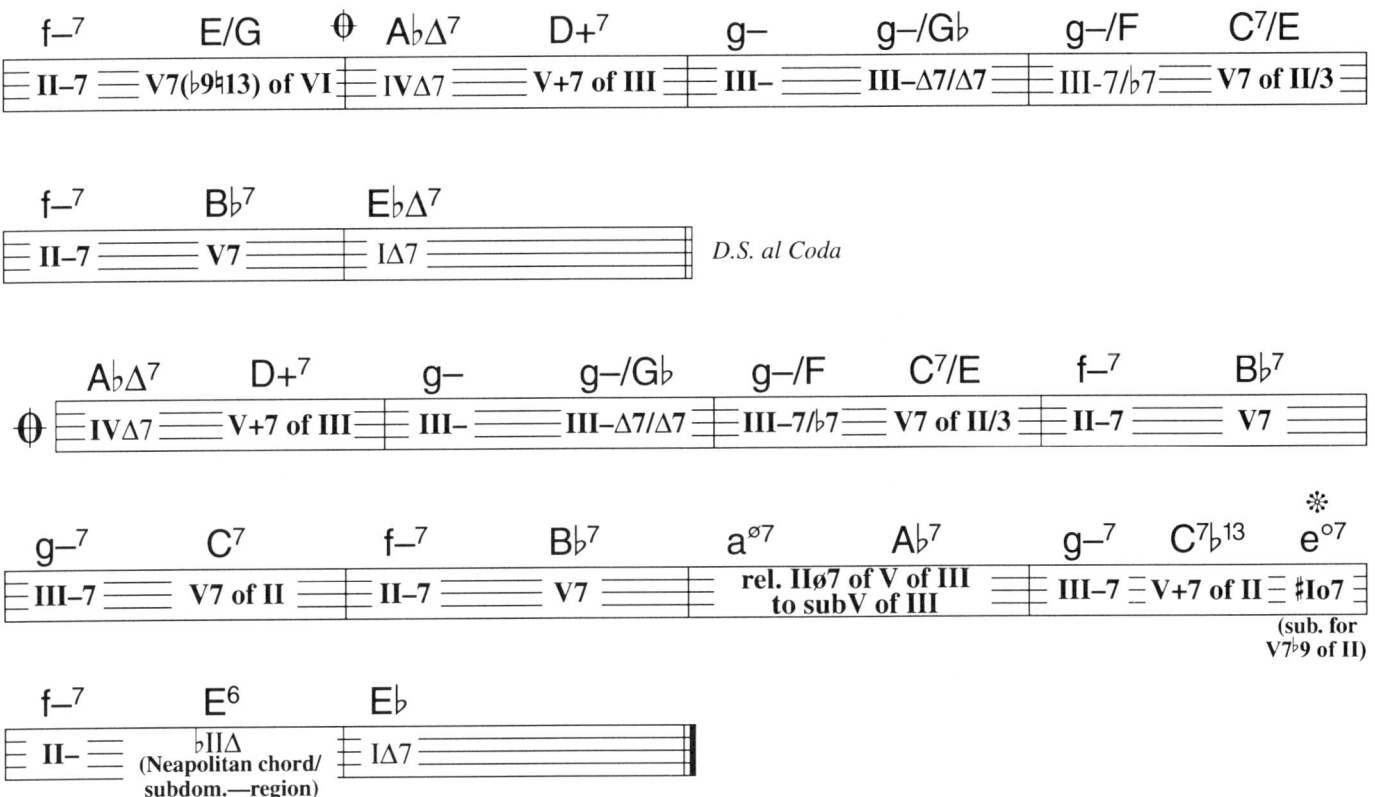

Now let's examine the actual tune and the recording of "A Bit for Miss Fitt." The front line combination of guitar and violin that this tune features has a long history in jazz, from Joe Venuti and Eddie Lang, to Django Reinhardt and Stéphane Grappelli, to John McLaughlin and Jerry Goodman in the Mahavishnu Orchestra, to contemporary pairings such as Bill Frisell and Jenny Scheinman, or Valentin Gregor and myself.

Val's performance on "A Bit for Miss Fitt" is a good example of how jazz musicians interpret the melody by adding and/or omitting certain notes and altering the phrasing by rhythmically displacing notes and/or accents. Notice how, during the bridges of the two heads in particular, the violinist not only alters what is written, but also varies each of his own two statements. Also check out how both the bass and guitar "interpret" their parts during the heads.

I've presented "A Bit for Miss Fitt" in a hybrid form that is a cross between a lead sheet and a score that contains the violin, guitar, and bass parts, so you can follow the interaction among the instruments while observing how the guitar's role varies throughout the tune, as well as how each player interprets his part. The guitar solo is a straight transcription whose harmonic analysis I leave to you, the student.

A Bit for Miss Fitt

Solo pickups

Fine

rallentando

Violin Solo: 31 bars

Each of the tunes and transcribed solos in the second half of this book was chosen to illustrate specific aspects of the harmonic concepts that were presented in the first half of the book. While many of the concepts mentioned in relation to one tune can often be applied to others, I have not explained them all in relation to each tune. I've chosen rather to limit the focus of each tune to a few concepts in order to avoid redundancy. I encourage you to explore each tune for examples of the concepts illustrated in the other tunes.

One underexplained aspect involves the various techniques employed in the voicings that I've played. Some aren't really voicings per se, but are rather a confluence of two or more parts, such as those used in "Blues Etude 1" or "El Otro." These polyphonic phenomena are generated by either voice leading or counterpoint. These are topics that lie on the periphery of the scope of this book and are consequently only briefly explained in the glossary of terms, though they are touched upon at several points in the book. The serious student should undertake a thorough study of these aspects of music.

I've also only briefly explained the commonly used voicing techniques known as "drop 2" and "drop 3" (p. 116, n. 19). These voicing techniques occur frequently in my solos in the standards chapter. A close examination of my solo from "A Bit for Miss Fitt" reveals that every bar from the last two measures of **A²** through the end of my solo is comprised predominantly of drop 2 voicings (except the octave phrase occurring in bars 5 and 6 of **A³**). These voicings are often spontaneously generated by hanging either a drop 2 or drop 3 voicing below a note in an improvised melody. Of course the most musical applications of these approaches are guided by good voice leading.

The music itself is the best illustration of these various techniques. I will draw your attention to their use when they occur in the next two tunes. I encourage you to go back and look for them in the previous tunes as well, once you begin to recognize them.

* * * * *

The next tune, "Stirrings Still" (track 13), was inspired by a short story of Samuel Beckett's. It is a ballad played with a quasi-bossa nova feel. This performance also comes from my CD *Dyad*.

There are times when a composer must be specific. Conversely, there are times, particularly in a jazz context, when one needs to leave the players more interpretive freedom. Jazz musicians are accustomed to creating "head arrangements" on the fly. They often do this by using tunes they all know well, whereas with new or unfamiliar material, they operate from lead sheets. The arrangement for "Stirrings Still" is an example of how musicians collectively interpret new material from a lead sheet that doesn't actually spell out their individual parts. The end result is what you hear on the recording.

I have presented the tune in the form of the lead sheet we used for the recording. The intro contains only the chord symbols and two voicings written in whole notes. These voicings are suggestive of the mood I wanted the tune to begin with. The arpeggiated voicings and the rhythm I played for the intro on the recording occurred in reaction to what Duduka and Hans played. Val and I then divided up the **AABA** form much as we did for "A Bit for Miss Fitt," i.e., violin took **A¹** and **B**; guitar played **A²** and **A³**. Val and I each soloed for one chorus. But at the end of my solo, the D.S. sent us to the bridge rather than **A¹**. I chose to do this for the sake of contrast and brevity.[29] Then during the final cadence of **A³** we took the coda, which is in essence a vamp ending. For the coda, I composed the specific guitar part in advance, but left the violin free to improvise over the changes inferred by what I played. Val did this with an eye toward bringing our story to an end, as we all listened and reacted to one another.

Let's begin with a harmonic analysis of the changes to "Stirrings Still." Notice how the tune seems to begin (both the Intro and the top of each **A** section) in what could be considered the key of E Major. But the cadences at the end of **A¹**, **A²**, and **A³** clearly establish the song's key as A Major. (Remember that f♯–11/A is the same as A6(2), just as a–♯5 is also the same as F∆/A.)

Example 199

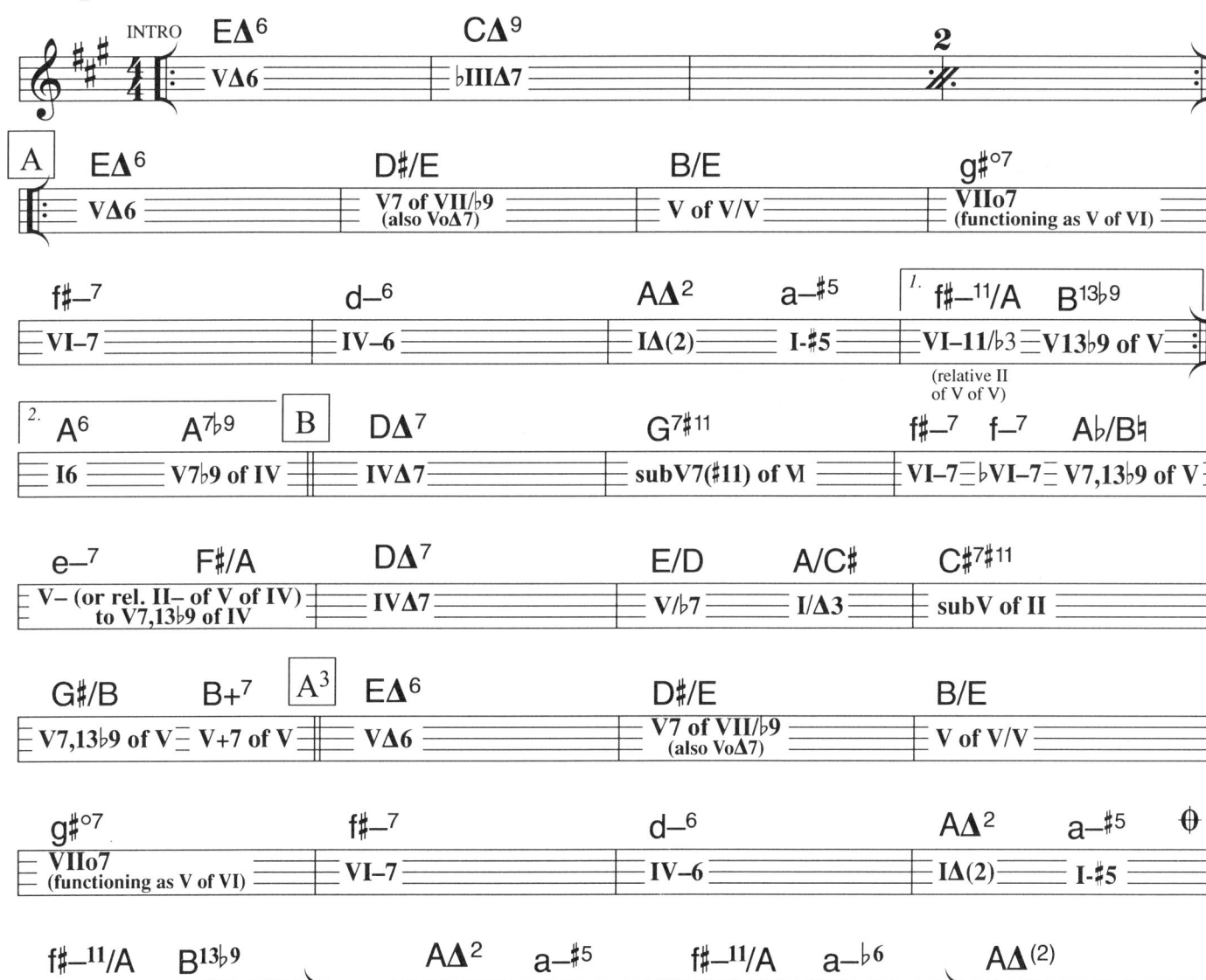

---

[29] I previously mentioned this type of exception to the strict adherence to the song form in the Introduction, p. 5, n. 1.

Now let's examine some actual voicings that I used for the chord changes of "Stirrings Still." This should help you get a handle on why I've represented the chords with the symbols I've chosen, as well as how to accommodate any necessary chord tone omissions (such as those previously discussed in the polytonal chords chapter, pp. 141–143) when voicing these chords.

Example 200

Now we'll check out the actual tune, which is presented in the lead sheet form we used for the recording. This is followed by a transcription of my improvised guitar solo that has the changes above and the harmonic analysis of each note below.

Stirrings Still

Solos on song form: then D.S. al Coda

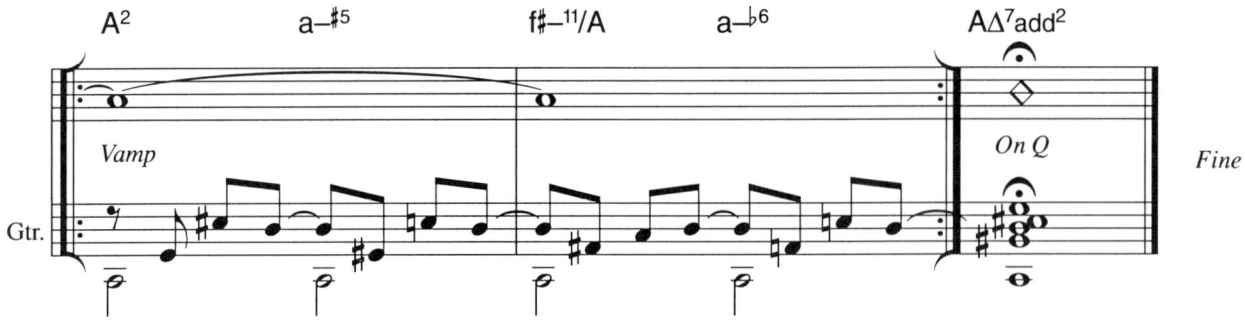

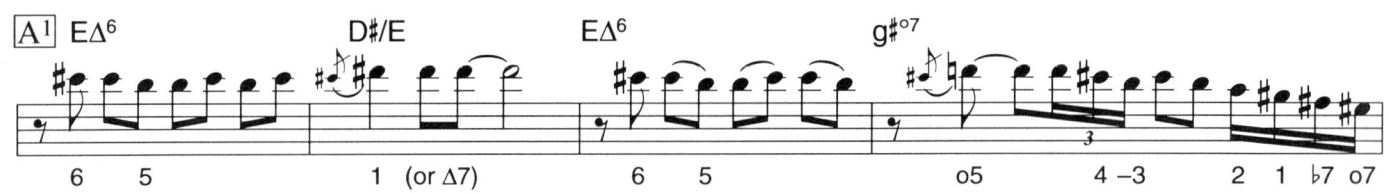

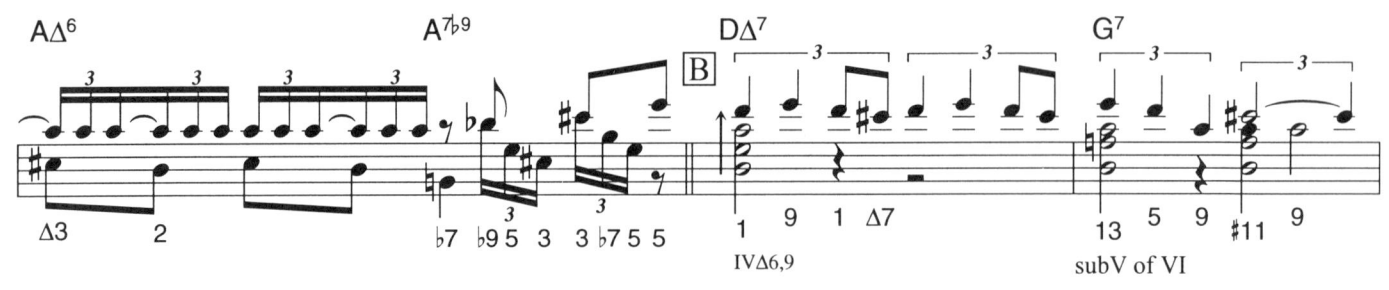

222

Letter **B** of my solo contains examples of several of the voicing techniques previously mentioned. The first chord of the first bar of **B** is voiced in fourths, and the second bar contains two drop 2 voicings. The third bar contains two arpeggiated versions of open root position −7 chords. The fourth bar begins with a voicing in fourths and is followed by two drop 2 voicings of altered dominant 7th chords whose roots are omitted (i.e., A713♭9 and A+7♯9). The fifth bar contains a drop 2 voicing of a DΔ7 whose Δ7 moves to Δ6 in the alto voice, and whose root has also been omitted. These omitted voices are the voices that would be dropped in the drop 2 voicings, and consequently may not be as readily recognizable to some of you.

* * * * *

223

There are so many facets of any composition, improvisation, or performance, that no single means of analysis is capable of conveying the totality of what is experientially obvious when one listens to music. Music unfolds in time as we listen to it. Consequently, we naturally hear and perceive the relationship between chords in accordance with their sequential presentation. For example, a CΔ7 chord followed by an f– chord tends to make the second chord sound like the subdominant minor chord. But if that same f– chord is then followed by a B♭7 chord, it is clear that the f– is also part of a secondary II V progression. This second interpretation doesn't negate the first; it merely adds another layer of harmonic information through a process of "harmonic reinterpretation" that is revealed as the music unfolds in time. Sometimes these aspects are more clearly perceived from a different vantage point, one which lets us check out the overall harmonic structure of a piece of music. This is kind of like the "overall" I IV V structure we find in the blues. But as our music has become more harmonically sophisticated, we often find that the relationships between chords and/or a song's various sections can't be adequately explained in relation to only one key. Even the last tune we covered, "Stirrings Still," showed some signs of straining the credibility of analyzing every chord in relation to one key, because both the intro and the top of each **A** section could have been analyzed as being in the key of E Major, rather than in relation to the A Major to which the song resolves, and the bridge could have been analyzed as if it were in the key of D Major.

There aren't any definitive rules for determining when an actual modulation between keys has or has not occurred. And since we can pass through many distant keys in the course of a piece of music, it can be difficult to ascertain when such harmonic motion through even remote keys is a modulation and when it is not. The best guideline I've found comes from my counterpoint teacher Paul Caputo, who likens the distinction between "modulation" and "passing through" to that of walking into a hallway with many interconnected rooms. If you merely "pass through" a room to get to another, then you haven't spent sufficient time there to have "done anything." Conversely, if you spend some time in a room, drink a cup of coffee, or read a book, then you've done something in that room that is akin to modulating. In other words, if the music stays in a new key for awhile, and/or subsequent chords are clearly related to the new key, then you've probably modulated to that new key. But if you hit upon a chord that is related to another key on your way to a chord related to the key you just left, or still another key, then it is unlikely that the chord you merely touched upon constitutes a modulation.

As a method of illustrating how modulation actually occurs, and to aid you in distinguishing it from merely passing through a chord from a distant key, I would like to draw your attention to another way to look at the overall harmonic shape or structure of a composition. This aspect is sometimes referred to as the "structural function" of harmony.

The next tune we will examine, "Bergamo" (track 14), provides us with an opportunity to analyze the form and harmonic structure from this different perspective, because while this tune is constructed in an **AABA** song form, the key relationships between the various sections of the form differ from those in any of the tunes we've addressed so far. As a composer I employed this structural harmonic difference for aesthetic reasons that are intended to mirror the physical structure of the northern Italian town for which the tune is named.

Bergamo is, in fact, two towns built on top of one another: Bergamo Alta, dating from before the twelfth century, and Bergamo Bassa, built during the early twentieth century. Like the town of Bergamo, my composition has a two-tiered design. The basic structure is a standard **AABA** song form, but with a twist: the first **A** section is in the key of CΔ, while the second **A** section is in the key of EΔ. This is followed by the bridge (**B**), which begins in the key of A♭Δ. By using a series of cadences that reinterpret various subdominant minor chords to give them dual functions (as the relative II–7 chords of the secondary dominant chords which they precede), the bridge passes through three keys (A♭Δ, BΔ, and DΔ) on its way back to the key of CΔ, where we began, for the last **A** section of the initial statement of the song.

However, there is an additional structure within the basic design of the **AABA** song form. This structure is based on the relationships between the various keys of the sections within the composition's form. Some of you may have noticed that the three basic keys that correspond to the sections of the song form outline an augmented triad: A^1 = CΔ, A^2 = EΔ, **B** = AbΔ, and A^3 = CΔ again. In addition, the bridge (**B**) passes through three tonalities that outline a diminished triad (AbΔ, BΔ, and DΔ). The intentional use of this dual structure was employed to mirror the dual level design of the town of Bergamo (i.e., the three Δ tonalities whose roots outline an augmented triad = Bergamo Alta, while the three tonalities whose roots outline a diminished triad = Bergamo Bassa). This is further alluded to by the fact that + triads are constructed solely of Δ3rds, and O triads are constructed solely of −3rds.

The song itself is preceded by an introductory vamp based on the relationship between the tonic chord of the piece (CΔ) and its subdominant minor (in this case both f−6 and Bb13 are used). This tonic Major and subdominant minor relationship occurs throughout the composition and also mirrors the dual level structure of the town of Bergamo. The introductory vamp is echoed and expanded upon in the coda that concludes the piece.

The improvisation is based on the chord changes and song form. I've placed the changes above each bar of the solo.

First let's look at an analysis of the harmonic structure of the song form. A^1 is in the key of C Major. A^2 is in the key of E Major. **B** is divided into three phrases: (1) the first four bars in the key of Ab Major, (2) the next two bars in the key of B Major, and (3) the last two bars of **B** divided between the key of D Major (Lydian) and the set up for the return to the Key of C Major in the last bar. A^3 is in the key of C Major. All of which gives us an overview of the key relationships between the different sections of the tune.

Example 201

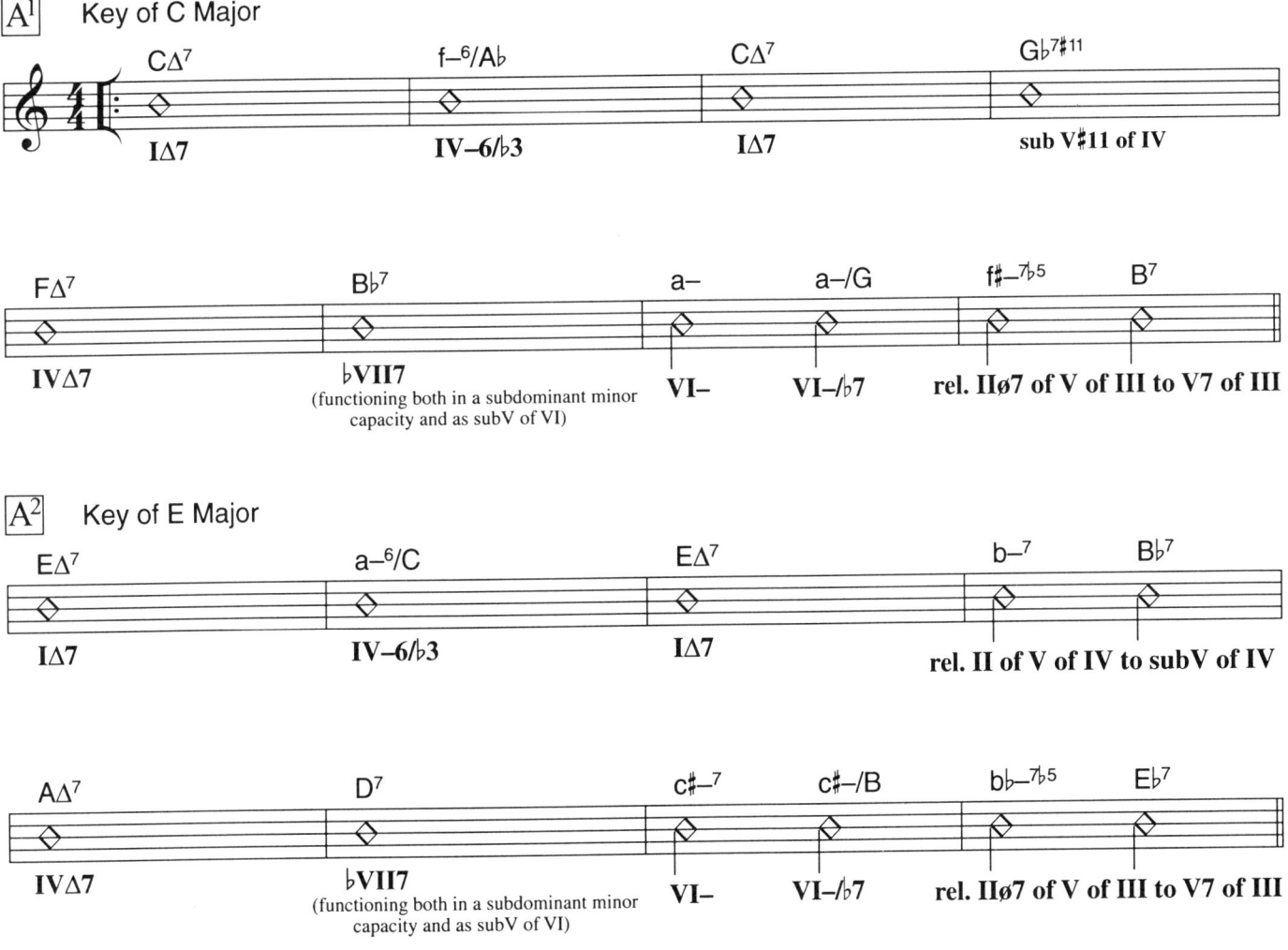

Even though the intro and coda are not intended to be improvised upon, they do illustrate the fundamental harmonic relationship upon which I based the tune "Bergamo," i.e., IΔ to IV–, and the coda passes through several distant tonalities on its way to the final cadence that concludes the piece. So let's examine these two sections, which function as adjuncts to the basic **AABA** song form.

Example 202

Now let's check out a solo guitar performance of "Bergamo" as recorded on track 14 of the accompanying CD.

Bergamo

❋ (see example 204 for D.S.)

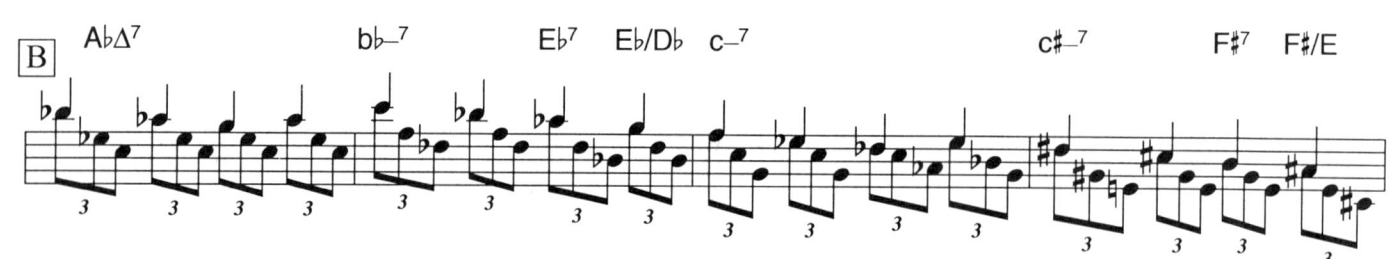

231

Vamp till cue

On cue

harmonics at 7th fret

Fine

The observant among you will recognize the approach used for letter **B** of my solo as having its foundation in some of the early exercises presented in this book (Chapter 1, exercises 6, 7, and 8; Chapter 2, exercises 14 and 15).

Because so many of the voicings in the head and solo of "Bergamo" are either drop 2 or drop 3 voicings, I will point out only those occurring during the head, and leave it to you to discover the ones in my solo.

Since the voice that is dropped, not the distance that voice is dropped, determines whether a voicing is drop 2 or drop 3, it is permissible to lower the dropped note by more than one octave, as I have done with the drop 2 voicings in bar 37. Such voicings are analogous to some of the open position voicings we previously discussed. But it would be misleading to call them drop 2 open or drop 3 open, because most drop 3 voicings are already open position voicings.

There are also times when an available tension replacing a chord tone can appear to alter the order of the notes in a voicing. Yet once we locate the position of the chord tone that an available tension has replaced, it becomes clear this is not the case. For example, in the drop 3 voicing of d–11 that begins bar 38, the 11th has replaced the 5th. Similarly, in the drop 2 voicing of ab–9 that begins bar 84 of the coda, the 9th has replaced the 5th.

Example 203

235

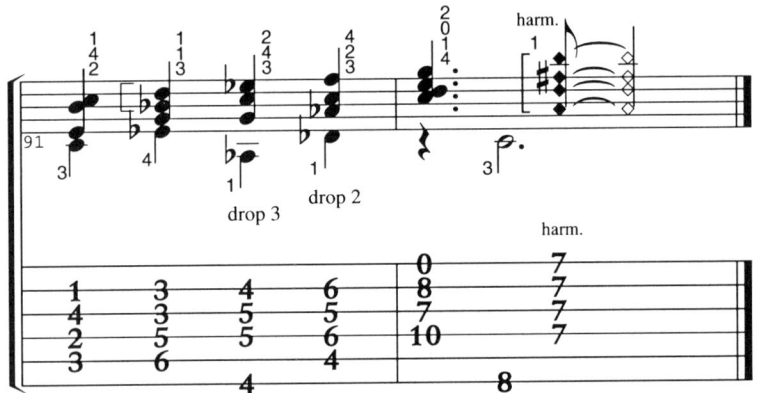

In my solo rendition of "Bergamo" I have availed myself of some of the interpretive liberties previously mentioned. For example, in the second bar of **A²** during the recap, I play the diatonic descending thirds in the bottom two voices as quarter note triplets instead of as written. The first time through the head I play it as written on pp. 228 and 233.

Example 204

Conclusion

There are many ways to acquire knowledge, and still many more ways to understand knowledge once it has been acquired. Music is essentially an aural phenomenon. Most of us love music for what it brings to us as an aural phenomenon. Yet all great music has an inner logic, which I've repeatedly compared to that of language. This metaphor, however, is employed only as a pedagogical device and should not be taken literally, for music communicates what words are insufficient to express. Only poetry comes close to using language in a manner that is suggestive of what great music expresses.

We all have different aptitudes, and at different stages of our lives these aptitudes vary greatly. For example, children raised in multilingual environments have little difficulty acquiring facility in the different languages to which they are exposed. Yet adults whose minds are fully developed often find learning a new language quite difficult. Part of the reason I've used language as a metaphor for acquiring new musical skills is that the process often resembles that of an adult learning a new language. The experience seems almost as alien to actually playing music, as diagramming a sentence does to speaking. This difference reveals something about how we learn, for the acquisition of knowledge is often very different from its implementation. This difference only seems to grow with age.

Most children speak for quite some time before they learn to read. Similarly, many musicians play music before they learn to read it. And some great jazz musicians never learned to read, Wes Montgomery and Django Reinhardt being prime examples. But they profoundly understood music in the terms in which all great musicians understand music, namely, the aspects of sound that are manifested in music through the interaction of its three prime elements: rhythm, melody, and harmony. The degree to which one understands the interaction among these three essential musical elements is largely the degree to which one understands music. Whether one can verbalize this understanding is of little importance when compared to the musical demonstration of this understanding.

This book focuses predominantly on harmony, and how melody interacts with and can be generated by harmony. The book's limited focus on rhythm is not indicative of rhythm's importance; rather it has more to do with keeping the book to a manageable size. Rhythm may in fact be the most important of music's three prime elements, so do not undervalue it, and do study it seriously!

I have designed this book to help unravel some of the mystery of how jazz musicians improvise. This is done by explaining some of the forms and the harmonic structures upon which jazz musicians often improvise and by offering guidance into how to employ an array of techniques that can lead to the freedom to play any note over any chord in any situation. All great jazz musicians have the facility and knowledge to play with this kind of freedom, whether they acquired these abilities through the methods I've presented or by other means. For my way is not the only way; it is merely the way I learned to understand what was going on in the music which I felt compelled to play. When I play music, I don't think about anything but the music, and I think in terms of sound, not theory. But there was a time when I did use the same methods I've presented here to help myself to decipher what was going on in music that I wanted to master. It is my sincere hope that this book can be helpful to those who seek to understand the music that so many of us love. Please remember that the music came before any attempts to explain it, and that the explanations are but one way to describe what the music manifests aurally. Whenever you are unclear, always refer to the music. Never forget that the music is the reason we do all the hard work, the studying, and the practicing. I also encourage you to search diligently for new music to investigate in a spirit of openness, because that will ensure you'll remain receptive to the unlimited possibilities that music presents. Despite the volume of words I've used in writing this book, it seems appropriate to conclude with this often cited quote of ambiguous origin: "writing about music is like dancing about architecture," to which I add: the music can speak for itself, though it can only be comprehended by those who not only listen but hear!

Glossary of Terms Used in Text

8VA — 8VA is a shorthand method of indicating that a note, line, portion of a line, or a voicing should be played one octave higher than written. Since the guitar is an instrument that sounds one octave lower than written, employing this symbol for higher pitches saves the use of ledger lines above the staff.

8VB — 8VB is a shorthand method of indicating that a note, line, portion of a line, or a voicing should be played one octave lower than written.

Cadence — A cadence is a progression of two or more chords used at the end of a composition, section, or phrase, which conveys a sense of either temporary or permanent repose. This concept applies to melodies as well as chords, and especially to the way the two interact with one another.

Chord — A chord is a group of four notes usually constructed of a triad plus another note which either doubles one of the notes of the triad (root, 3rd, or 5th) or adds a note a 3rd above the 5th, resulting in a 7th chord, so-called because the note added a 3rd above the 5th is a 7th above the root (either Δ7th, or –7th, or O7th). In jazz 6th chords are commonly found, but these can usually be interpreted as 1st inversions of other chords, e.g., C6 is the 1st inversion of a–, and a–6 is the 1st inversion of f#Ø7.

Counterpoint — Counterpoint is a technique so frequently used in polyphonic music that the two terms (counterpoint and polyphony) are virtually synonymous. The techniques of counterpoint are extensive and varied. They essentially deal with the handling of the various voices within a composition. Such music consists of two or more melodic lines sounding simultaneously, preferably with each line possessing a high degree of independence, which manifests itself in a variety of ways. For example, rhythmic independence can be achieved with staggered entrances or by altering the value of the notes for a voice (i.e., augmentation or diminution). This will often achieve rhythmic independence even where the intervallic shapes of the lines imitate one another, as is often the case.

Diatonic — Diatonic is a term which refers to melodies or chords whose construction is limited to the notes of one specific key as exemplified by the Major scale (or minor scale if in a diatonic minor tonality). For example, in the key of C, diatonic chords have no ♭s or ♯s, because C is the key of no ♭s or ♯s.

Improvisation — Improvisation is the art of spontaneous composition and is often associated with jazz music.

Interval — An interval is the distance between two or more notes. If the notes are sounded successively, they are a melodic interval; if sounded simultaneously, they are a harmonic interval. Intervals are essentially a unit of measurement in western music, the smallest of which is called a half step. There are twelve half steps to the octave. These twelve notes (available in different octaves depending on the range of the instrument or voice) comprise all of the available pitches (notes) of our musical system.

The names of the various intervals refer to the number of scale steps from lower to higher, as follows: c to c = prime (unison), c to d = 2nd, c to e = 3rd, c to f = 4th, c to g = 5th, c to a = 6th, c to b = 7th, and c to c = octave. These comprise the so-called simple intervals, because they do not exceed the range of an octave. (See glossary example 1.)

Glossary Example 1

Simple Intervals:

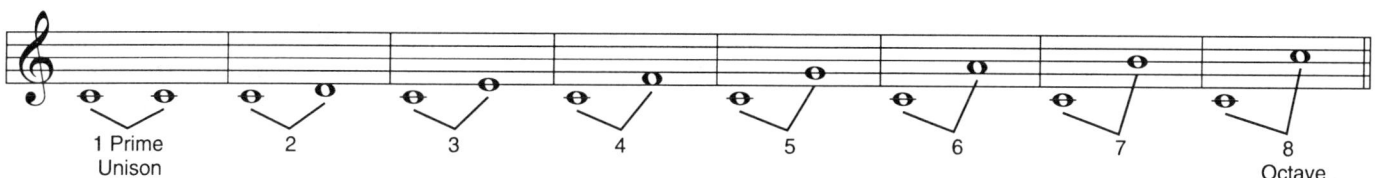

The intervals larger than an octave are called compound intervals. They are as follows: c to d = 9th, c to e = 10th, c to f = 11th, c to g = 12th, and c to a = 13th. It is rare to see an interval that exceeds a 13th. But to determine the name (number), merely take the simple interval and add 7. (Based on the 8 note scale, counting the spaces between notes, there are 7, i.e., 1 to 2 is 1, 2 to 3 is 2, etc.) (See glossary example 2.)

Glossary Example 2

Compound Intervals:

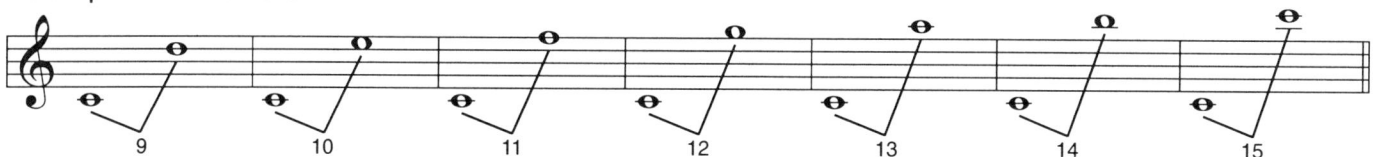

The basic names of the intervals (2nd, 3rd, 4th, etc.) are based on those that naturally occur in a Major scale. All of these intervals may be enharmonically altered by raising or lowering their pitch with the use of accidentals (♯ = sharp, ♭ = flat, ♮ = natural, × = double sharp, ♭♭ = double flat). (See glossary examples 3 and 4.)

Glossary Example 3

Enharmonically Altered Simple Intervals:

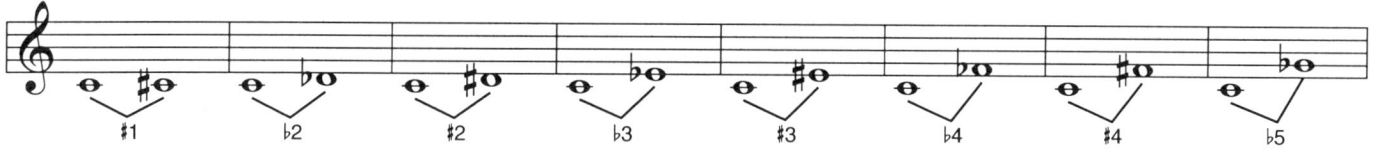

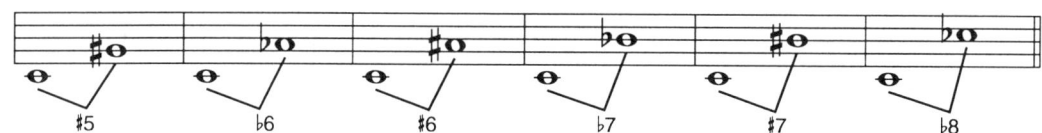

Glossary Example 4

Enharmonically Altered Compound Intervals:

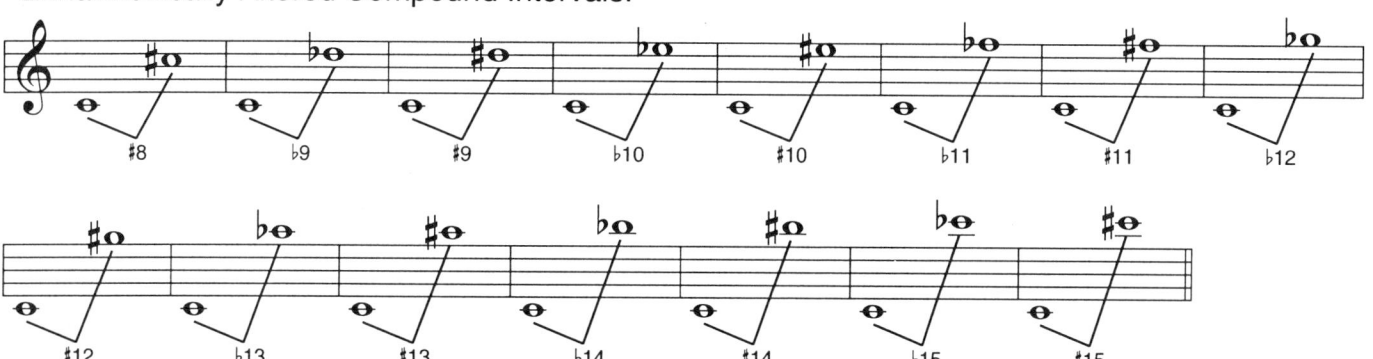

239

This process will alter the interval name as well as the pitch. For example, c to e is a Major 3rd, c to eb would be a minor 3rd.

When 4th or 5th intervals are expanded from what diatonically occurs in a Major scale, they become augmented intervals. For example, if the perfect 5th that exists between the root (C) and the 5th (G) of a C Major scale had the 5th raised by a half step (making it a G♯), the resulting interval could be designated as either an + (augmented) 5th or as a ♯5th. Conversely, when 4th or 5th intervals are contracted from what diatonically occurs in a Major scale, they become diminished intervals. For example, if the same perfect 5th between C and G were contracted by lowering the G to Gb, the resulting interval could be designated as either a O (diminished) 5th or a b5th.

Due to the placement of the two half steps which exist in our Major scale (between the 3rd and 4th degrees, and between the 7th and 8th degrees), certain enharmonically altered intervals rarely occur, such as b4, which is in effect a Major 3rd, or ♯7th, which is essentially an octave. (Do not confuse ♯7 with Δ7.)

It is important to remember that the intervallic structure of intervals is consistent regardless of key or starting note. For example, all Major 3rds are equidistant when measured from low to high (or vice versa). That is, c to e♮ is a Major 3rd, with a distance of 4 half steps between the c and the e♮, just as gb to bb is a Major 3rd, with a distance of 4 half steps between the gb and the bb.

There are times when the name of an interval (Δ7, for example) can also refer to the name of a type of chord, so be careful not to confuse these. The chord will usually have both a prefix, which is the chord's root designation, and a chord quality such as EbΔ7, where the Eb is the root designation, and the Δ7 is the chord quality. This is not the case with the name of an interval.

Inversion — Inversion is a term applied to different methods of exchanging or substituting higher or lower tones, parts, or voices. These methods may be applied to intervals, chords (and triads), and contrapuntal parts.

Mode — [This definition is excerpted from *Schirmer Pronouncing Pocket Manual of Music Terms,* 5th ed., ed. by Theodore Baker (New York: Schirmer Books, 1995), pp. 148–149.] A generic term applied to ancient Greek melodic progressions and to church scales established in the Middle Ages and codified in the system of Gregorian chant. The intervals of the Greek modes were counted downwards, and those of the medieval modes were counted upwards, so the intervallic contents were different between the Greek and the church systems. However, the church modes retained the Greek names of the modes. If played on the white keys of the piano, the church modes are: from *C* to *C,* Ionian; from *D* to *D,* Dorian; from *E* to *E,* Phrygian; from *F* to *F,* Lydian; from *G* to *G,* Mixolydian; from *A* to *A,* Aeolian; and from *B* to *B,* Locrian. The modes continued to underlie all western music through the 17th century, then gradually gave way to the common Major and minor keys.

Phrasing — Phrasing refers to the use of proper separation and articulation of the various divisions within a musical line or phrase. There are no hard and fast rules—one must be guided by one's own judgment. But some of the basic units to work with are: (1) the duration of each pitch (i.e., short or long); (2) the means of articulation of each pitch (strike, slur, slide, bend, hammer on, or pull off); (3) the dynamic level of each pitch (loud, soft, etc.); (4) the dynamic curve of the phrase as a whole (start loud and get quiet, or vice versa); (5) the rhythmic character of the phrase (lay back, or push forward). These are just some of the variables to consider.

Polyphonic (polyphony) — (From the Greek, meaning many voiced.) One of the three basic musical textures (the other two being monophonic and homophonic). Music is considered to be polyphonic if two or more voices (parts) have individual melodic significance. Contrapuntal music exemplifies this principle, especially as applied in the styles of Palestrina and J.S. Bach.

Swing — Swing is a metaphor commonly used to refer to the rhythmic feel and pulse of jazz music. Think of the motion of a swing, where each cycle involves: initial motion sufficient to move the swing towards its apex, and a deceleration as it approaches this apex, in preparation for the acceleration that returns the swing to its point of origin. Then the cycle repeats, just like one beat follows the next. If the cycles are equidistantly paced, they can be almost metronomically perfect, but within each cycle there is a great deal of room for fluctuation and movement. The great jazz composer and bass player Charles Mingus once described the beat within the swing feel as a large circle that gives ample room to accommodate variations in each player's phrasing, provided each player indeed lands within the circle of each beat.

Triad — A triad is a group of three notes, usually constructed of a root (which names the triad) plus a note a 3rd above the root, and a note a 5th above the root, which is also a 3rd above the 3rd. This configuration applies to root position. There are, of course, other possible inversions of the three notes of this arrangement.

Voice(s) — Voices are the individual parts of a composition or chord. This term comes from the tradition of choral composition, where each voice has an independent part, and the leading of the lines of each part creates the polyphonic effects in the music. From top to bottom the voices are: soprano, alto, tenor, and bass. This concept is often applied to the four notes of a chord and can greatly assist one in creating better voice leading, especially on chordal instruments like the guitar, piano, vibes, marimba, and accordion, or bandoneon.

Voice leading — The practice and art of treating each note of a chord as a separate voice. Generally from bottom to top they would be: bass, tenor, alto, and soprano. It is important to arrange these voices in such a way as to give independent logic to each voice while maintaining the overall harmonic integrity that they collectively produce.

Credits for Companion CD

All compositions written by Ken Hatfield. All compositions (except tracks 1, 8, and 9) are published by Arthur Circle Music. Both Ken Hatfield and Arthur Circle Music are affiliated with ASCAP. Tracks 1, 8, and 9 are published by Mel Bay Publications. Sound recordings of tracks 4, 6, 11, 12, 13, and 14 are the sole property of Arthur Circle Music and are being used by permission; they were recorded at Nola Studios, New York City. Sound recordings of tracks 1, 2, 3, 5, 7, 8, 9, and 10 are the property of Mel Bay Publications and were recorded at Park West Studios, Brooklyn, New York.

1. Blues Etude 1 — Ken Hatfield, guitar.

2. Pinky's Blues — Ken Hatfield, guitar; Hans Glawischnig, bass; Jeff Hirshfield, drums.

3. Pinky's Blues — Ken Hatfield, guitar.

4. Riff for Brother Jack — Ken Hatfield, guitar; Hans Glawischnig, bass; Duduka da Fonseca, drums. From the CD *Phoenix Rising* (ACM 9512).

5. Funkissimo — Ken Hatfield, guitar; Hans Glawischnig, bass; Jeff Hirshfield, drums.

6. El Otro — Ken Hatfield, guitar.

7. Moon over Astoria — Ken Hatfield, guitar; Hans Glawischnig, bass; Jeff Hirshfield, drums.

8. Prosodic Permutations — Ken Hatfield, guitar; Hans Glawischnig, bass; Jeff Hirshfield, drums.

9. Prosodic Permutations — Ken Hatfield, guitar; Hans Glawischnig, bass; Jeff Hirshfield, drums.

10. Necessary Appurtenances — Ken Hatfield, guitar; Hans Glawischnig, bass; Jeff Hirshfield, drums.

11. Yo Es — Ken Hatfield, guitar; Dom Salvador, piano; Hans Glawischnig, bass; Duduka da Fonseca, drums. From the CD *Phoenix Rising* (ACM 9512).

12. A Bit for Miss Fitt — Ken Hatfield, guitar; Valentin Gregor, violin; Hans Glawischnig, bass; Duduka da Fonseca, drums. From the CD *Dyad* (ACM 3482).

13. Stirrings Still — Ken Hatfield, guitar; Valentin Gregor, violin; Hans Glawischnig, bass; Duduka da Fonseca, drums. From the CD *Dyad* (ACM 3482).

14. Bergamo — Ken Hatfield, guitar.

About the Author

Guitarist and composer Ken Hatfield is internationally recognized as one of the leading proponents of jazz played on the acoustic classical guitar. Ken has performed as a solo artist and with his own ensemble at such prestigious venues as The JVC Jazz Festival, The Knitting Factory, The Classic American Guitar Show, The Smithsonian Institution, and the North Wales International Jazz Guitar Festival. In addition, he has performed and/or recorded with numerous jazz artists, including Charlie Byrd, Jack McDuff, Chico Hamilton, Jimmy McGriff, Maurice Hines, Charles Aznavour, Bob Cranshaw, Grady Tate, Harold Mabern, Marcus Miller, Kenny Kirkland, Dom Salvador, João Donato, Kenny Werner, Claudio Roditi, and many others.

A prolific and eclectic composer, Ken's experience includes commissions to write ballet scores for Judith Jamison, the Washington Ballet Company, and Maurice Béjart's Ballet of the Twentieth Century in Brussels, Belgium. He has also composed music for film and TV, including the score for Eugene Richards' award-winning documentary *but, the day came*. Ken's composition "Positive Influences," co-written with Bonnie Lee Sanders and Jules Ruggiero, was nominated for the MAC/ASCAP "Song of the Year" award in 2004. Arthur Circle Music has released four books of Ken's compositions, as well as five critically acclaimed CDs of his music, each of which features Hatfield playing the acoustic classical guitar in a jazz context. His CDs *Dyad* and *Phoenix Rising* established a firm presence on the national jazz radio charts, and his fifth release as a leader, *The Surrealist Table,* was chosen by *Jazziz* magazine as number 3 of the top 20 acoustic guitar albums as part of an illustrious group that spans the last quarter century (March 2004).

Ken studied with Norfolk, Virginia's guitar guru John Griggs before leaving his hometown to attend the Berklee College of Music, where he joined the faculty at the age of 19 after one year's attendance. He received a Bachelor of Arts degree from the State University of New York and studied counterpoint privately with Paul Caputo in New York City.

Acknowledgements

It is with the deepest gratitude that I thank Jeanette Sisk for her tireless work as typist and editor for the text of this book, and for the support and encouragement she generously provided me throughout the time it took to write it and correct its various drafts and proofs. Without her hard work this book would not exist. I also thank John Roberts for doing such a professional and meticulous job engraving the book, especially my handwritten examples and transcriptions. Thanks to Paul Caputo for his advice on explaining some of Schoenberg's concepts regarding vagrant chords. And a special thanks to John Griggs for always being there to answer practical questions about pedagogy, layout, and content. Thanks to John Buscarino for encouraging me to create the book I wanted to create. And last, but by no means least, I thank the folks at Mel Bay Publications, particularly Bill Bay and Corey Christiansen, for giving me the opportunity to write a book that is designed to be as comprehensive as this one is.

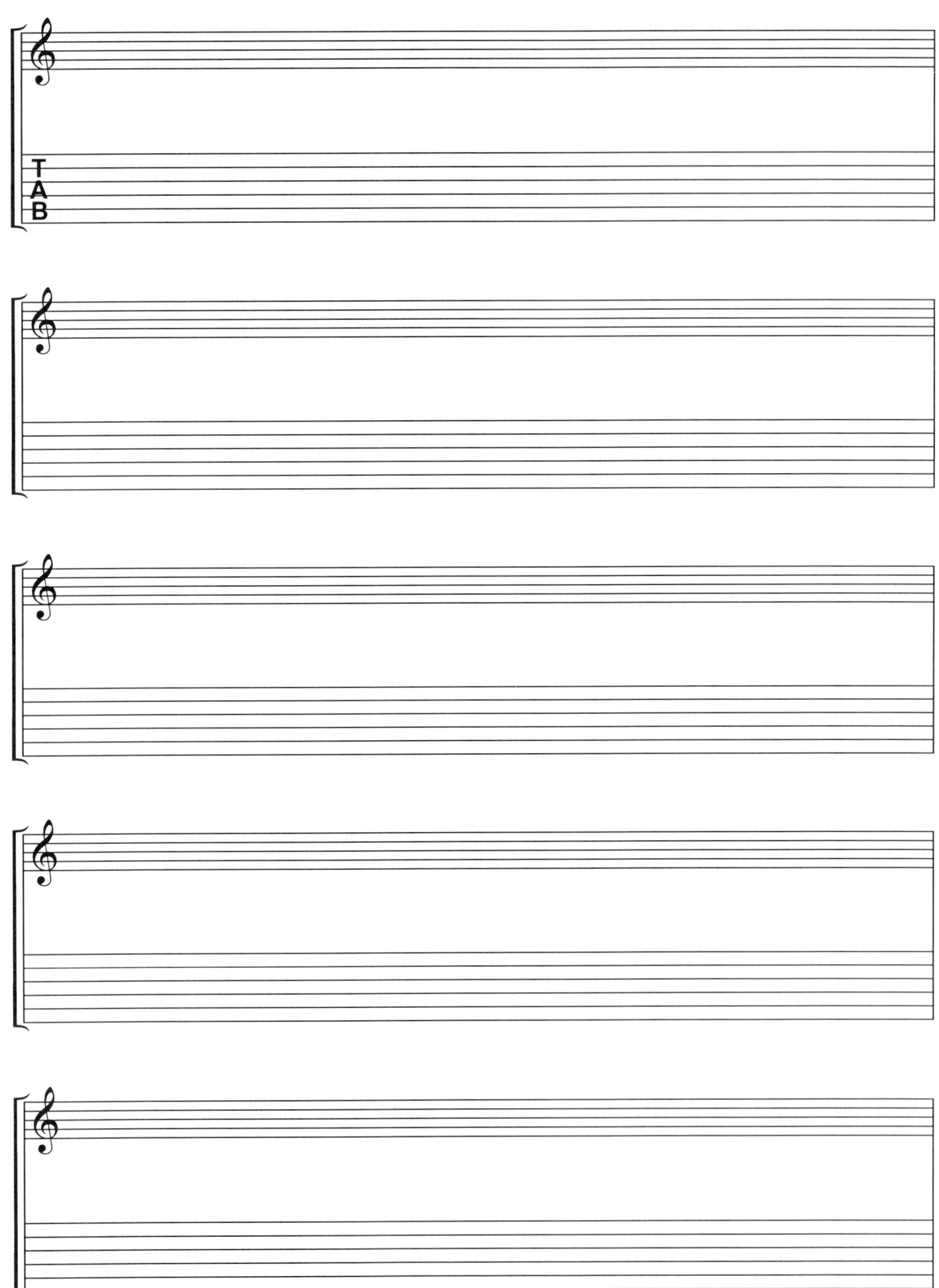

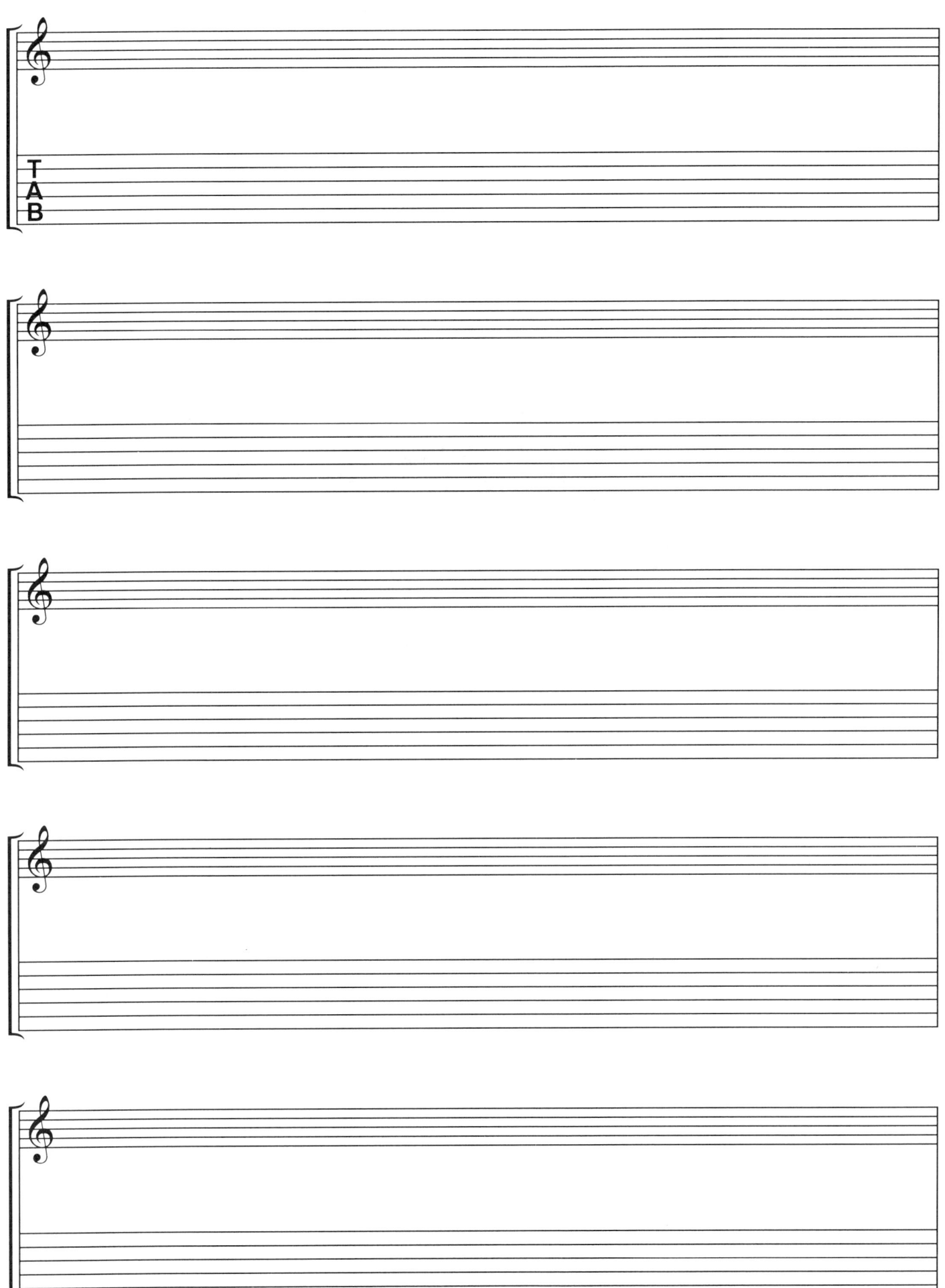